Vladimir Nabokov and the Art of Moral Acts

SRLT

Northwestern University Press
Studies in Russian Literature and Theory

Vladimir Nabokov and the Art of Moral Acts

Dana Dragunoiu

NORTHWESTERN UNIVERSITY PRESS / EVANSTON, ILLINOIS

Northwestern University Press
www.nupress.northwestern.edu

Printed in the United States of America

10 9 8 7 6 5 4 3 2 1

Library of Congress Cataloging-in-Publication Data

Names: Dragunoiu, Dana, author.
Title: Vladimir Nabokov and the art of moral acts / Dana Dragunoiu.
Other titles: Studies in Russian literature and theory.
Description: Evanston, Illinois : Northwestern University Press, 2021. | Series: Northwestern University Press Studies in Russian literature and theory | Includes bibliographical references and index.
Identifiers: LCCN 2021011353 | ISBN 9780810143999 (paperback) | ISBN 9780810144002 (cloth) | ISBN 9780810144019 (ebook)
Subjects: LCSH: Nabokov, Vladimir Vladimirovich, 1899–1977—Criticism and interpretation. | Free will and determinism in literature. | Ethics in literature.
Classification: LCC PS3527.A15 Z678 2021 | DDC 813/.54—dc23
LC record available at https://lccn.loc.gov/2021011353

To my family

Contents

Acknowledgments

I have received the help of many friends, colleagues, mentors, and family members in writing this book. Moreover, some of my friends solicited on my behalf the help of *their* friends, and these friends-of-friends shared with me their specialized knowledge unstintingly and without hesitation.

First, I owe a significant debt to the readers of my various chapters and, in certain cases, of the entire manuscript. My two anonymous reviewers at Northwestern University Press paid me the compliment of reading the manuscript the way I wished it to be read *and* of finding ways to improve it. The deeply mourned and much missed Gennady Barabtarlo commented upon, and was frequently irritated by, my claims in chapters 3 and 5. A number of his objections triggered insights and reformulations that I cherish to this day. Stephen Blackwell read, more than once, chapters 1 and 6, and responded each time with incisive and thoughtful commentary. The grace notes in these chapters are owed to him. Gerard de Vries assisted me in two important ways over half of a decade. First, his comments on chapters 5 and 6 sent me in many rewarding directions. Second, he placed at my disposal his vast collection of Nabokoviana when I was cut off from my university library during a glorious sabbatical spent writing in Aix-en-Provence and again, three years later, during the inglorious months of the COVID-19 pandemic. Chapter 5 also benefited from the analysis of Tatyana Gershkovich, whose productive comments led me to reconceptualize a number of my claims in this chapter. The final typescript was significantly improved by Leona Toker's close engagement with it. Her perceptive comments made me rethink a number of key claims and saved me from a number of overstatements. Stanislav Shvabrin answered, with a Russian gentleman's exquisite patience and a Russian scholar's erudition, questions pertaining not only to the poetry of Pushkin and Nabokov, but to all manner of tricky translations from Russian into English. Catherine Khordoc and Monica Manolescu guided me through the thickets of Proust's French and Chrétien's Old French. Max Nelson and Andrew Wallace oversaw my efforts at translation of passages from ancient Greek and Latin. The Kant scholars Gordon Davis and Joel Madore helped me untangle the knotty problems I encountered when applying Kant's ethics to Nabokov. Marion A. Schmid, Katharine Streip, and Pyra Wise answered—patiently and with consistent good humor—my many questions regarding Proust. My friend and colleague Siobhain Bly Calkin, medievalist extraordinaire, was a constant guide throughout this long journey. Among the many pleasures afforded by this book are my recollections of Professor Calkin's bemusement at the strange requests coming from the "Nabokov scholar" down the hall.

Second, I also owe considerable gratitude to friends and mentors who contributed to my work in ways both related and unrelated to the special areas of expertise drawn upon in the chapters that follow. The seed from which this book grew was planted at the Nabokov Upside Down Conference in Auckland, New Zealand, organized in 2012 by the doyen of Nabokov studies, Brian Boyd. Professor Boyd has nurtured the careers of many a Nabokovian, and he nurtured mine from the earliest steps I took into the field. He served as a trusted and tireless mentor from the moment he agreed to supervise my Nabokov dissertation twenty-five years ago at the instigation of his former dissertation supervisor, the late Patricia Brückmann. As an incoming PhD candidate in the Department of English at the University of Toronto, I had been invited to tea by Professor Brückmann at her home a few blocks from campus. Her home was full of beautiful and interesting objects, but what she wanted me to notice—to the exclusion of everything else—was the two-volume biography of Nabokov, written by her former student. The two thick volumes of Brian Boyd's biography were the only ornaments gracing the mantel of her fireplace.

I also owe thanks to the members of the Carleton English Research Working Group, who read my work in progress and encouraged me during the various phases of its writing. These are my friends and colleagues from the eighteenth and nineteenth floors of Dunton Tower: Franny Nudelman, Stuart Murray, Barbara Leckie, Jody Mason, Julie Murray, Grant Williams, Siobhain Bly Calkin, Micheline White, and Sarah Waiswisz. Over the years, I have also benefited from random acts of scholarly generosity by Suzanne Fraysse, Paul Keen, Katherina Kokinova, Marc Saurette, Péter Tamás, and Inge Wimmers.

The typescript became a book thanks to my editor at Northwestern, Trevor Perri, who shepherded it through the process of review, revision, and acceptance with his characteristic patience and grace. Simon Turner, my research assistant, spent many long hours helping me prepare the typescript for production. I would have been unable to complete this task during the pandemic without Simon's expert assistance. Three librarians at Carleton's Macodrum Library—Patricia (Patty) Paquette, Denize Tan, and Christine Taylor—worked their virtual magic so that I could check my quotes during the second wave of the COVID-19 pandemic. And finally, the typescript landed in the ever-so-capable hands of Anne Gendler, the book's project manager, whom I remembered fondly from the days when she guided my first book into print. I felt especially lucky when Ms. Gendler sent the typescript to Paul Mendelson, the same eagle-eyed copy editor of my first book.

My home institution also played an important role in making this book possible: thanks to a Carleton University Research Achievement Award, I had the time I needed to work through the moral philosophy of Kant and the logic of the duel of honor. During the fall term of 2020, I was awarded a FASS 2020 COVID-19 Research Assistantship. I wish to thank my faculty dean, Dr. Pauline Rankin, for the care and generosity she showed in establishing this funding initiative, which benefited students and faculty at a difficult time.

Finally, there is my family. My husband—Andrew—and my parents—Ana Maria and Graham—placed their trust in my book with unwavering confidence. They never let me forget that I was writing a book, or supposed to be writing one, or that it was time to clinch the writing of it. I am deeply grateful that their faith never wavered. When I began writing this book, my children—Harry and Sasha—were toddlers, interested in playing Poohsticks, making tents out of bedsheets, and watching *Masha and the Bear*. Today they are full-fledged teenagers, caught up in their own adolescent passions and concerns. When I addressed them in my first book, I expressed the hope that I would have the pleasure one day of reading their "books." Today, a decade later, I find myself wishing for something different: I hope they get to accomplish what is closest to their hearts and make our world a better one.

Note on Editions, Translations, and Transliteration

This book follows a modified Library of Congress transliteration system. To make the body of the main text more readable to a general audience, first and last names ending in *-ii* have been changed to *-y*, such as Anatoly or Belinsky rather than Anatolii or Belinskii. I have also, for the sake of readability, collapsed *-iia* endings to *-ia*. For the same reason, names beginning with *ia-* or *iu-*, such as Iurii and Iazykov, have been changed to Yury and Yazykov. Names are given in their standard English form when one exists. Bibliographic references, including the notes, follow the standard Library of Congress transliteration system. Unless otherwise noted, I am responsible for the translations offered in this text.

Translations from Chrétien's *Erec et Enide* and *Yvain* are mine. For quotations from *Perceval*, I have used William W. Kibler's translation (Chrétien de Troyes, *The Story of the Grail (Li Contes del Graal), or Perceval*, ed. Rupert T. Pickens [New York: Garland, 1990]). Quotations from the original texts are identified by verse number. They are drawn from the following Old French manuscripts collected by Michel Zink in Chrétien de Troyes, *Romans suivis des "Chansons," avec, en appendice, "Philomena"*: for *Erec et Enide*, BN fr. 1376; for *Le Chevalier de la charrette* (*Lancelot*), BN fr. 794; for *Le Chevalier au lion* (*Yvain*), BN fr. 1433; for *Le Conte du Graal* (*Perceval*), the Berne Manuscript 354.

For citations from *Aucassin et Nicolette*, I have used Roger Pensom's translation. Citations from the Old French are identified by chapter and verse number.

For quotations from *La Chanson de Roland*, I have used D. D. R. Owen's translation (*The Song of Roland: The Oxford Text* [London: Allen and Unwin, 1972]). Citations from the Old French are identified by chapter and verse number.

For quotations from *Sir Gawain and the Green Knight*, I cite the line number of the Middle English text and use James Winny's modern English translation.

With the exception of references to Kant's *Anthropology from a Pragmatic Point of View*, parenthetical references to Kant's work follow conventional practice by referring to volume and page numbers of the standard German edition of Kant's works, *Kant's Gesammelte Schriften*, edited by the Royal Prussian (later German) Academy of Sciences (Berlin: Georg Reimer, later Walter deGruyter & Co., 1900—).

Shakespeare's plays are cited by act, scene, and line numbers from the editions mentioned in the Bibliography.

Quotations from Nabokov's four-volume translation and commentary to Pushkin's *Eugene Onegin* are identified by volume and page numbers.

Russian-language citations from Tolstoy's *War and Peace* are taken from *Polnoe sobranie sochinenii* in ninety volumes published in Moscow by Gosudarstvennoe izdatel'stvo "Khudozhestvennaia literatura," 1935–58. These come after references to the English translation by Rosemary Edmonds in two volumes.

Unless otherwise noted, English-language citations of Proust's novel are given first and refer to the six-volume edition of *In Search of Lost Time* (*SLT*) translated by C. K. S. Moncrieff, T. Kilmartin, and A. Mayor, and revised by D. J. Enright (New York: Modern Library, 2003). French citations from Proust's *À la recherche du temps perdu* (*RTP*) refer to the second Pléiade edition published in four volumes under the direction of Jean-Yves Tadié (Paris: Gallimard, 1987–89). In-text references to these editions identify citations by volume and page number. References to the French text are further cross-referenced with the *Nouvelle Revue Française* edition (NRF) that Nabokov read before the publication in 1954 of the revised three-volume Pléiade edition edited by Pierre Clarac and André Ferré. The in-text references to the NRF volumes are identified by NRF's classification system as it appears on the flyleaf of its volumes:

Du coté de chez Swann	Tome I, 2 volumes
À l'ombre des jeunes filles en fleurs	Tome II, 3 volumes
Le Coté de Guermantes I	Tome III, 1 volume
Le Coté de Guermantes II, Sodome et Gomorrhe I	Tome IV, 1 volume
Sodome et Gomorrhe II	Tome V, 3 volumes

La Prisonnière	Tome VI, 2 volumes
Albertine disparue	Tome VII, 2 volumes
Le Temps retrouvé	Tome VIII, 2 volumes

References to the NRF editions come immediately *after* the references to the 1987–89 Pléiade edition and are identified by three numbers in the following sequence: tome, volume, page. Thus, the first reference to a citation from the NRF edition in the introduction is cited as follows: 8.2.38 (that is, Tome VIII, volume 2, page 38).

Abbreviations

A	Vladimir Nabokov, *Ada, or Ardor: A Family Chronicle* (1969), in *Vladimir Nabokov: Novels 1969–1974*, ed. Brian Boyd (New York: Library of America, 1996), 1–485.
"AG"	Vladimir Nabokov, "Abram Gannibal," in *Notes on Prosody and Abram Gannibal: From the Commentary to the Author's Translation of Pushkin's "Eugene Onegin"* (Princeton, NJ: Princeton University Press, 1964), 107–68.
Anth	Immanuel Kant, *Anthropology from a Pragmatic Point of View*, trans. Victor Lyle Dowdell, rev. and ed. Hans H. Rudnick (Carbondale: Southern Illinois University Press, 1978).
Besedy	Yury M. Lotman, *Besedy o russkoi kul'ture* (St. Petersburg: Iskusstvo, 1994).
"Bor'ba"	Sergey I. Hessen [Gessen], "Bor'ba utopii i avtonomii dobra v mirovozzrenii F. M. Dostoevskogo i Vl. Solov'eva" ["The Struggle between Utopia and the Autonomy of the Good in the Worldview of F. M. Dostoevskii and Vl. Soloviev"], in *Izbrannye sochineniia*, ed. Andrzej Walicki and N. Chistiakova (Moscow: ROSSPEN, 1999), 609–77.
BS	Vladimir Nabokov, *Bend Sinister* (1947), in *Vladimir Nabokov: Novels and Memoirs 1941–1951*, ed. Brian Boyd (New York: Library of America, 1996), 161–358.
C	Kwame Anthony Appiah, *Cosmopolitanism: Ethics in a World of Strangers* (New York: Norton, 2006).
Ch	*La Chanson de Roland*, trans. and ed. Léon Gautier, 5th ed. (Tours: Alfred Mame), 1875.
CPJ	Immanuel Kant, *Critique of the Power of Judgment* (1790), trans. Paul Guyer and Eric Matthews, ed. Paul Guyer (Cambridge: Cambridge University Press, 2000).
"CT"	Gordon Teskey, "'And Therefore as a Stranger Give It Welcome': Courtesy and Thinking," *Spenser Studies* 18 (2003): 343–59.
DBDV	Vladimir Nabokov and Edmund Wilson, *Dear Bunny, Dear Volodya: The Nabokov-Wilson Letters, 1940–1971*, rev. and ex-

panded edition, ed. Simon Karlinsky (Berkeley: University of California Press, 2001).

Def Vladimir Nabokov, *The Defense* (1930), trans. Michael Scammell in collaboration with the author (New York: Vintage, 1990).

Des Vladimir Nabokov, *Despair* (1936; revised 1965) (New York: Vintage, 1989).

"DiUZ" V. D. [Vladimir Dmitrievich] Nabokov, "Duel' i ugolovnyi zakon" ["The Duel and Criminal Law"], *Pravo* 50 (December 13, 1909): 2729–44; 51 (December 20, 1909): 2833–47.

DP *Duel' Pushkina s Dantesom-Gekkernom: Podlinnoe voenno-sudnoe delo 1837 Goda* [*Pushkin's Duel with d'Anthès-Heeckeren: The True Account of a Military-Legal Event 1837*] (Moscow: Belyi gorod, 2012).

Duel François Billacois, *The Duel: Its Rise and Fall in Early Modern France*, ed. and trans. Trista Selous (New Haven, CT: Yale University Press, 1990). Translation of *Le Duel*, 1986.

EO Aleksandr Pushkin, *Eugene Onegin: A Novel in Verse*, trans. Vladimir Nabokov, 4 vols., Bollingen Series 72 (New York: Bollingen, 1964).

Erec Chrétien de Troyes, *Erec et Enide*, in *Romans suivis des "Chansons," avec en appendice, "Philomena,"* ed. Michel Zink (Paris: Librairie Générale Française, 1994), 55–283.

Essai Paul Zumthor, *Essai de poétique médiévale* (Paris: Seuil, 1972).

FAR Ad Putter, *"Sir Gawain and the Green Knight" and French Arthurian Romance* (Oxford: Clarendon, 1995).

FQ Edmund Spenser, *The Faerie Queene*, ed. A. C. Hamilton, Hiroshi Yamashita, and Tshiyuki Suzuki (Harlow, UK: Longman, 2001).

Gift Vladimir Nabokov, *The Gift* (1963), trans. Michael Scammell with Vladimir Nabokov (New York: Vintage, 1991).

Gl Vladimir Nabokov, *Glory*, trans. Dmitri Nabokov with Vladimir Nabokov (New York: McGraw-Hill, 1971).

GMM Immanuel Kant, *Groundwork of The Metaphysics of Morals* (1785), in *Practical Philosophy*, ed. and trans. Mary J. Gregor (Cambridge: Cambridge University Press, 1996), 37–108.

H Frank Henderson Stewart, *Honor* (Chicago: University of Chicago Press, 1994).

HC Kwame Anthony Appiah, *The Honor Code: How Moral Revolutions Happen* (New York: Norton, 2010).

IA Bernth Lindfors, *Ira Aldridge: The Last Years, 1855–1867* (Rochester, NY: University of Rochester Press, 2015).

IB Vladimir Nabokov, *Invitation to a Beheading* (1959), trans. Dmitri Nabokov with Vladimir Nabokov (New York: Vintage, 1989).

L Vladimir Nabokov, *Lolita* (1955), in *Vladimir Nabokov: Novels 1955–1962*, ed. Brian Boyd (New York: Library of America, 1996), 1–298.

Lancelot Chrétien de Troyes, *Lancelot, ou Le chevalier de la charrette*, in *Romans suivis des "Chansons," avec en appendice, "Philomena,"* ed. Michel Zink (Paris: Librairie Générale Française, 1994), 495–704.

LE Immanuel Kant, *Lectures on Ethics*, ed. Peter Heath and J. B. Schneewind, trans. Peter Heath (Cambridge: Cambridge University Press, 1997).

LL Vladimir Nabokov, *Lectures on Literature*, ed. Fredson Bowers (San Diego, CA: Harvest, Harcourt, Bruccoli Clark, 1980).

LRL Vladimir Nabokov, *Lectures on Russian Literature*, ed. Fredson Bowers (San Diego, CA: Harvest, Harcourt, Bruccoli Clark, 1981).

LV Vladimir Nabokov, *Letters to Véra*, ed. and trans. Olga Voronina and Brian Boyd (New York: Alfred A. Knopf, 2015).

M Vladimir Nabokov, *Mary* (1970), trans. Michael Glenny with Vladimir Nabokov (New York: Vintage, 1989).

MM Immanuel Kant, *The Metaphysics of Morals* (1797), in *Practical Philosophy*, trans. and ed. Mary J. Gregor (Cambridge: Cambridge University Press, 1996), 363–603.

Must Stanley Cavell, *Must We Mean What We Say?* updated ed. (Cambridge: Cambridge University Press, 2002).

NB Vladimir Nabokov, *Nabokov's Butterflies: Unpublished and Uncollected Writings*, ed. Brian Boyd and Michael Pyle (Boston: Beacon, 2000).

NG Vladimir Nabokov, *Nikolai Gogol* (1944) (New York: New Directions, 1961).

NRF Marcel Proust, *À la recherche du temps perdu*, 8 vols., Éditions de la *Nouvelle Revue Française* (Paris: Gallimard, 1919–27).

NTI Siggy Frank, *Nabokov's Theatrical Imagination* (Cambridge: Cambridge University Press, 2012).

Othello William Shakespeare, *Othello*, ed. Edward Pechter (New York: W. W. Norton, 2017).

PAS Malcolm Bowie, *Proust Among the Stars* (New York: Columbia University Press, 2000).

Per Chrétien de Troyes, *Perceval*, in *Romans suivis des "Chansons," avec en appendice, "Philomena,"* ed. Michel Zink (Paris: Librairie Générale Française, 1994), 937–1211.

PF Vladimir Nabokov, *Pale Fire* (1962), in *Vladimir Nabokov: Novels 1955–1962*, ed. Brian Boyd (New York: Library of America, 1996), 437–667.

Pnin	Vladimir Nabokov, *Pnin* (1957), in *Vladimir Nabokov: Novels 1955–1962*, ed. Brian Boyd (New York: Library of America, 1996), 299–435.
PSS	Lev Tolstoy, *Polnoe sobranie sochinenii*, 90 vols. (Moscow: Gosudarstvennoe izdatel'stvo Khudozhestvennaia literatura, 1935–58).
PTB	Lev Tolstoy, "Perepiska L. N. Tolstogo s V. P. Botkinym," in vol. 4 of *Tolstoi: Pamiatniki tvorchestva i zhizni*, ed. V. I. Sreznevskii (Moscow: Kooperativnoe t-vo, 1923), 9–87.
RL	Alexander Pope, *The Rape of the Lock*, in *The Poems of Alexander Pope*, ed. John Butt (New Haven, CT: Yale University Press, 1963), 217–42.
RLSK	Vladimir Nabokov, *The Real Life of Sebastian Knight* (1941), in *Vladimir Nabokov: Novels and Memoirs 1941–1951*, ed. Brian Boyd (New York: Library of America, 1996), 1–160.
RTP	Marcel Proust, *À la recherche du temps perdu*, 4 vols., ed. Jean-Yves Tadié, Bibliothèque de la Pléiade (Paris: Gallimard, 1987–89).
RV	Irina Reyfman, *Ritualized Violence Russian Style: The Duel in Russian Culture and Literature* (Stanford, CA: Stanford University Press, 1999).
SGGK	*Sir Gawain and the Green Knight*, ed. Paul Battles (Peterborough, ON: Broadview, 2012).
SGGK	*Sir Gawain and the Green Knight*, ed. and trans. James Winny (Peterborough, ON: Broadview, 1992).
SL	Vladimir Nabokov, *Selected Letters, 1940–1977*, ed. Dmitri Nabokov and Matthew J. Bruccoli (San Diego, CA: Harcourt Brace Jovanovich, 1989).
SLT	Marcel Proust, *In Search of Lost Time*, 6 vols., trans. C. K. S. Moncrieff, Terence Kilmartin, and Andreas Mayor, rev. D. J. Enright (New York: Modern Library, 2003).
SM	Vladimir Nabokov, *Speak, Memory: An Autobiography Revisited* (1967), in *Vladimir Nabokov: Novels and Memoirs 1941–1951*, ed. Brian Boyd (New York: Library of America, 1996), 359–635.
SO	Vladimir Nabokov, *Strong Opinions* (London: Weidenfeld and Nicolson, 1974).
SVN	Vladimir Nabokov, *The Stories of Vladimir Nabokov* (New York: Vintage International, 1997).
VNAP	Thomas Karshan, *Vladimir Nabokov and the Art of Play* (Oxford: Oxford University Press, 2011).
VNAY	Brian Boyd, *Vladimir Nabokov: The American Years* (Princeton, NJ: Princeton University Press, 1991).
VNRY	Brian Boyd, *Vladimir Nabokov: The Russian Years* (Princeton, NJ: Princeton University Press, 1990).

WP	Leo Tolstoy, *War and Peace*, 2 vols., trans. Rosemary Edmonds (Harmondsworth, UK: Penguin, 1978).
Yvain	Chrétien de Troyes, *Yvain, ou Le chevalier au lion*, in *Romans suivis des "Chansons," avec en appendice, "Philomena,"* ed. Michel Zink (Paris: Librairie Générale Française, 1994), 705–936.
ZA	Leonid Grossman, *Zapiski d'Arshiaka* (1931) (Moscow: Khudozhestvennaia literatura, 1990).

Vladimir Nabokov and the Art of Moral Acts

Introduction

> Thus the moral worth of an action does not lie in the effect expected from it and so too does not lie in any principle of action that needs to borrow its motive from this expected effect. For, all these effects (agreeableness of one's condition, indeed even promotion of others' happiness) could have been also brought about by other causes, so that there would have been no need, for this, of the will of a rational being, in which, however, the highest and unconditional good alone can be found.
> —Immanuel Kant

PASCAL DENIED THE existence of free will when he asserted that "*La coutume est notre nature*,"[1] but custom had taught Vladimir Nabokov that his nature was free. As the son of a man who, having been born into great privilege, devoted his life's work to dismantling the structures which had sustained that privilege, Nabokov was suspicious of theories that treated human conduct as an extension of class interests. Later, as a father himself, Nabokov would regard his own son's fascination with toy cars and other movable objects as evidence for "the essentially human urge to reshape the earth." This urge, he insisted, is shared by every child "unless he is a born Marxist or a corpse and meekly waits for the environment to fashion *him*" (*SM* 621; emphasis in original).

Statements of this kind abound in Nabokov's writings from the beginning to the very end of his career. He saw himself as a self-fashioning subject whose personal freedom clashed not only with Marxist conceptions of human identity, but with all theories that understood the self to be externally determined. "There are two kinds of 'come what may,'" he writes in an early love letter to the woman who would become his wife, "involuntary and deliberate. Forgive me—but I live by the second one" (*LV* 8). Searching decades later for the signs of the forces that shaped his destiny, he declared that "neither in environment nor in heredity can I find the exact instrument that fashioned me, the anonymous roller that pressed upon my life a certain intricate watermark whose unique design becomes visible when the lamp of art is made to shine through life's foolscap" (*SM* 374). Philip Wild, one of the protagonists of the unfinished novel *The Original of Laura*, is caught up in an obsessive effort to reach the condition captured in the term Sophrosyne, which he defines as "a platonic term for ideal self-control stemming from man's rational core."[2]

This is a book about Nabokov's faith in freedom and the way in which his work expresses this faith through a constellation of problems that radiate from his conception of courtesy as the supreme testament of that freedom. The book argues that Nabokov's belief in the freedom of the will sits at the center of his thinking about ethics, and, by extension, that several striking (and sometimes counterintuitive) features of his moral philosophy are tied to this core belief. Studying these matters from the vantage point of courtesy makes visible Nabokov's attachment to anti-consequentialist moral paradigms and (what I will be referring to as) an ethics of inutility.

Accordingly, the book studies the ethical stakes of what might, at first glance, appear to be gestures and exchanges of limited moral significance: a pause to share a cold drink with family friends, a hand extended to receive a gentleman's kiss, a soccer ball discarded before it can cause awkwardness to a teenage boy who does not like sports. Scenes of this kind are charged ground for Nabokov for two interrelated reasons: first, because they provide him with an opportunity to resist deterministic narratives of human motivation and consequentialist ethical models; and second, because they enable him to make a case for the freedom of the will. These scenes stand as emblems of a moral vision that is, for Nabokov, every bit as demanding as it is in the writings of Immanuel Kant.

COURTESY AND KANT

Nabokov's insistence that courtesy bears witness to the will's freedom recalls Kant's courtesy to his physician as reported by Kant's friend, amanuensis, and the last of his three "official" biographers. E. A. C. Wasianski's recollection is repeated by Kant's subsequent biographers, but it is Erwin Panofsky's rendition of this event that aligns with Nabokov's understanding of courtesy most closely:

> Nine days before his death Immanuel Kant was visited by his physician. Old, ill and nearly blind, he rose from his chair and stood trembling with weakness and muttering unintelligible words. Finally his faithful companion realized that he would not sit down again until the visitor had taken a seat. This he

> did, and Kant then permitted himself to be helped to his chair and, after having regained some of his strength, said, "*Das Gefühl für Humanität hat mich noch nicht verlassen*"—"The sense of humanity has not yet left me." The two men were moved almost to tears. For, though the word *Humanität* had come, in the eighteenth century, to mean little more than politeness or civility, it had, for Kant, a much deeper significance, which the circumstances of the moment served to emphasize: man's proud and tragic consciousness of self-approved and self-imposed principles, contrasting with his utter subjection to illness, decay and all that is implied in the word "mortality."[3]

Kant's legendary gesture of courtesy serves as a heuristic for the four acts of courtesy in Nabokov's fiction that have inspired the writing of this book. In each of these cases, courtesy becomes a signifier of freedom understood as a quintessentially human capacity to replace the tyranny of nature with a freely chosen tyranny of duty.

As chapter 1 shows, my book singles out for attention four scenes in which images of courtesy are presented in near-identical terms from the early novel *The Defense* (*Zashchita Luzhina*, 1930) to the late *Ada, or Ardor: A Family Chronicle* (1969). Mrs. Luzhin, Helene Grinstein, Disa, and Lucette showcase moral excellence through heroic acts of courtesy that border on self-sacrifice. In each case, the courteous act is disinterested, has no utilitarian benefits, and is directed at unlikable or superfluous people. A fifth instance—alluded to parenthetically in *Pnin* (1957)—suggests that Mira Belochkin may have performed similar acts of courtesy before being killed at Buchenwald. The chapter argues that courtesy is a supreme virtue in Nabokov's ethics because it affirms Kant's claim that the capacity to do what is *right* (sometimes even in opposition to what appears to be consequentially *good*) is a testament of the will's freedom.[4] Unlike love and pity (the other two supreme values in Nabokov's moral universe), courtesy is subject not to the passions, but to moral obligation. In the case of courtesy, this moral obligation finds its most tangible expression in acts that treat the other with dignity and respect even when such acts collide with justified concerns about utility and interest.

Nabokov's understanding of courtesy as non-instrumental and divorced from considerations of utility is profoundly at odds with canonical conceptions of courtesy. In chapter 2, I trace the evolution of courtesy (as *courtoisie*) from both the chivalric texts of the French Middle Ages that Nabokov studied for his Modern and Medieval Languages tripos at Cambridge and the Renaissance texts that he references in his fiction, to its modern instantiations that Norbert Elias locates under the rubric *humanité*. These literary, historical, and theoretical contexts show—either by way of kinship or contrast—that Nabokov's conception of courtesy belongs to the same understanding of *Humanität* that Kant is said to have invoked in the presence of his physician. This understanding stands in sharp contrast to more conventional accounts of human behavior that see courtesy as an interested and utility-driven means of interpersonal exchange.

Nabokov's revisionist, counterintuitive conception of courtesy becomes especially vivid when we juxtapose the scene of the dying Kant with Adam Smith's figure of the "man on the rack" in *The Theory of Moral Sentiments*. According to Smith, stoicism in the face of suffering is no Kantian demonstration of the human capacity to rise above the vicissitudes of nature, but a means of soliciting the spectator's sympathy and approval. "Magnanimity amidst great distress appears always so divinely graceful," Smith writes, because we "wonder with surprise and astonishment at that strength of mind which is capable of so noble and generous an effort." The suffering individual is rewarded by the "applause and admiration which he is about to deserve by the heroic magnanimity of his behaviour."[5] Kant's gesture of courtesy to his physician and the four scenes of courtesy that anchor my book pit themselves against this transactional and self-interested account of human conduct.

Nabokov's Kantian understanding of moral value makes him see courtesy as a supererogatory act that signals the performer's capacity to ignore the kinds of calculation that, according to Smith, weigh the *effect* of one act over another and, by doing so, bury human agency under the detritus of utilitarian calculations of benefit. Kant's gesture of courtesy bespeaks *a humanity* defined—to invoke Panofsky's terms again—by "self-approved and self-imposed principles" that belie our "utter subjection" to illness, decay, and death. In the story about the dying Kant and in the four scenes of courtesy I single out from Nabokov's fiction, the human individual's heteronomous nature is made to yield to an autonomous will. This situates Nabokov's conception of selfhood at the antipodes of Smith's psychologically egoist view of the moral sentiments.

NABOKOV AND KANT

Nabokov was drawn to what Charles Taylor calls "the exciting kernel" of Kant's philosophy—namely, Kant's "radical notion of freedom."[6] Though the idea that an action must be voluntary to count as "moral" can be found at least as early as Aristotle, it is Kant who articulated the most compelling argument for the existence of a pure, moral will that makes voluntary acts possible. As the most influential proponent of human autonomy, Kant provides this book with a set of interpretive tools that make visible and intelligible aspects of Nabokov's ethics that would otherwise remain obscure or embedded in contradiction.

As the presiding spirit over Nabokov's ethics, Kant helps account for the "single continuum of beliefs" that, as Vladimir Alexandrov has argued, connects Nabokov's ethics, aesthetics, and metaphysics.[7] The coordination of beliefs drawn from these sister disciplines is a chief feature of Kant's philosophy. As Allen Wood reminds us, "the real significance of beauty and taste" for Kant "is chiefly a moral significance."[8] Kant's metaphysical conception of the self justifies this conflation by making possible both disinterested aesthetic appreciation and disinterested moral conduct.

In *Critique of the Power of Judgment*, Kant argues that "the beautiful is the symbol of the morally good" (*CPJ* 5:353) because the faculty that enables us to derive universally binding moral laws also enables us to make aesthetic judgments that we can also assume to be universally valid. The connection originates in a process of abstraction that insulates the mind from private concerns such as inclination, desire, and ambition: "*Taste* is the faculty for judging an object or a kind of representation through a satisfaction or dissatisfaction *without any interest*. The object of such a satisfaction is called *beautiful*" (*CPJ* 5:211; emphasis in original). Kant's claim that detachment is at once a moral and an aesthetic condition sets a precedent for Nabokov's insistence that good reading must combine "an artist's passion" with "a scientist's patience." Nabokov's argument also turns on the idea of detachment: "The enthusiastic artist alone is apt to be too subjective in his attitude toward a book, and so a scientific coolness of judgment will temper the intuitive heat" (*LL* 5). For both Kant and Nabokov, aesthetic impartiality derives from a moral commitment to that which is other.[9] Roger Scruton glosses this central premise of Kant's aesthetics in terms that are eminently suited to Nabokov: "Disinterested contemplation is a recognition that the object matters—matters so much that our interests have no bearing on our judgment."[10]

KANT IN LATE IMPERIAL RUSSIA

The Kantian claim that free will is the wedge that pries open the door for other metaphysical possibilities was a cornerstone of Russian idealist philosophy during the Russian Silver Age. As a self-proclaimed child of that Silver Age,[11] Nabokov shared the view articulated by Russia's idealist philosophers that free will is a miracle that paves the way for other miracles such as God and immortality.[12] As I have argued in *Vladimir Nabokov and the Poetics of Liberalism*, Nabokov's continuum of beliefs also extended to his politics. Kant's twofold claim that rational individuals are autonomous and endowed with the right to self-determination was mobilized by Russia's liberal-idealist philosophers and political activists as a powerful weapon in their struggle against tsarist autocracy. Nabokov's assertion that he was an "old-fashioned liberal" like his father, the distinguished statesman and "liberationist" V. D. (Vladimir Dmitrievich) Nabokov (1870–1922),[13] was an attempt to lay claim to a cluster of Kantian principles that structured his father's jurisprudence and political activism (*SO* 96; see also *SO* 113).

The Russian idealist philosophers whose writings constituted the philosophical background of the Russian Silver Age readily acknowledged their debt to Kant. Some were political activists who, together with V. D. Nabokov, played key roles in Russia's Union of Liberation and the Constitutional Democratic (Kadet) Party. These "liberationists" frequently identified Kant as the standard bearer of their struggles against tsarist autocracy. "There can be no sharper antithesis than that between Marx and Kant and idealist philosophy in general," wrote Peter (Pyotr) Struve (1870–1944), the leading theorist of the Union of Liberation and a prominent founding member of the Kadet Party.[14] Paul (Pavel) Novgorodtsev (1866–1924), another high-ranking liberationist and a close acquaintance of V. D. Nabokov, borrows Kant's definition of the human individual in a landmark document of the Russian Silver Age: "The person is the border between the kingdom of necessity and the kingdom of freedom, and it is in the moral calling of personhood that man first discovers his infinite tasks and his participation in the world of freedom."[15]

There are several routes by which Nabokov could have arrived at his knowledge of Kant. The strongest evidence comes from the extended research into nineteenth-century Russian intellectual history that he conducted for the fourth chapter of *The Gift* (*Dar*, 1937–38). In this chapter, the novel's protagonist, Fyodor Godunov-Cherdyntsev, writes a biography of the nineteenth-century Russian radical publicist Nikolay Chernyshevsky. As Fyodor notes in the biography, Kantian thought had penetrated deeply into Russian journalistic and philosophical writing by the time Chernyshevky and his confrères supplanted German idealism with "rational egoism" as the guiding ideology of the Russian intelligentsia (*Gift* 202).

But there were also earlier opportunities for Nabokov to become familiar with Kant. Russian translations of Kant's *Critique of Practical Reason* and *Critique of Pure Reason* appear as items 2198 and 2199 in the section titled "Religion, Philosophy, Psychology, Ethics" of his father's library catalog.[16] And though there is no proof that Nabokov read these particular volumes, scholars agree that he was intimately acquainted with his father's St. Petersburg library. Certainly, by the time he completed *Ada*, Nabokov could allude to Kant in a way that was contextually appropriate and thematically resonant.[17]

While it is most likely that Nabokov encountered Kant's first two critiques in his father's library, his encounter with Kant's third critique—*Critique of Judgment*—may have been mediated by Vladimir Solovyov, Russia's most respected and influential idealist philosopher. In his essay "Beauty in Nature," Solovyov defines beauty in Kantian terms. Moreover, the passage in question provides a significant precedent for Nabokov's own views:

> Formal beauty always shows itself as pure uselessness, whatever its material elements . . . And if [formal beauty] cannot be valued as a means for the satisfaction of one or another daily or physiological requirement, then this means it is valued as a goal in itself. In beauty—even with the most simple and primary of its manifestations—we meet up with something *absolute* that exists not for the sake of another but for its own sake, so that, by its very existence, it gladdens and satisfies our soul, which, resting on beauty, becomes tranquil and is liberated from life's strivings and labors.[18]

In conceptualizing courtesy as a proof of autonomy, Nabokov pitches his moral philosophy on the same nonutilitarian foundation that supports Kant's, Solovyov's, and his own aesthetics.

Kantian ideas also figured prominently in the work of at least one Russian intellectual of Nabokov's own generation. The Kantian philosopher Sergey Hessen (1887–1950) was the half-brother of George Hessen, Nabokov's best friend in the emigration. In his letters to Véra written from Prague between April 7 and April 11, 1932, Nabokov alludes to intending to visit Sergey Hessen (*LV* 173, 175). In my *Vladimir Nabokov and the Poetics of Liberalism*, I document Nabokov's engagement with Hessen's contributions to Russian émigré philosophy and the extent to which V. D. Nabokov's jurisprudence was influenced by the same Kantian intellectual traditions that inspired Hessen's work.[19]

COURTESY, INUTILITY, AND NATURAL MIMICRY

Kant's systematic assault on consequentialism and its most popular variant, utilitarianism, would have appealed to Nabokov's own passionate anti-utilitarianism. As the father of modern deontology, Kant argued that the moral worth of an act cannot be determined by "*the purpose* to be attained by it" but only by "the maxim in accordance with which it is decided upon" (*GMM* 4:399). Kant's insistence that outcome cannot serve as a benchmark for judging moral value has made him unpopular with many moral philosophers. Nabokov, however, would have been invigorated by the idea that utilitarian motivations strip actions of their moral worth. Like Kant, he associated moral excellence with a fidelity to formal principles of conduct motivated by duty. Though the actions he holds up for approval in his fiction may strike his readers as insufficient and ineffectual, these actions pay homage to a code of ethics that Nabokov associated with the refinements of his own upbringing and with his cherished view of personal identity as self-driven and self-fashioning.

As a testament to human autonomy, courtesy sits at the center of Nabokov's polemical anti-utilitarianism in matters of art, science, history, politics, and ethics. I argue that courtesy is a cardinal virtue in Nabokov's ethics because he understood it in the same terms as he understood art and natural mimicry—that is, as a refutation of deterministic accounts of human identity. By seeing courtesy as gratuitous, disinterested, and often dependent upon artful deception, Nabokov regarded it as proof of the human capacity to act in ways that are irreducible to deterministic accounts of behavior such as those postulated by Smith, Chernyshevsky, Darwin, Marx, and Freud. "We know the world to be good," he writes in "The Art of Literature and Commonsense," whenever we bear witness to our capacity to "wonder at trifles—no matter the imminent peril" (*LL* 374). Such examples of indifference to peril include "the hero who dashes into a burning house" and risks "squandering a precious five seconds to find and save, together with the child, its favorite toy," and a chimney sweep (depicted in a cartoon) "falling from the roof of a tall building and noticing on the way that a sign-board had one word spelled wrong, and wondering in his headlong flight why nobody had thought of correcting it" (*LL* 373). Nabokov insists that "these asides of the spirit" constitute "the highest forms of consciousness" and prove "the world to be good" (*LL* 374).

There are good reasons for agreeing with David Rampton when he observes that Nabokov prioritizes liberty above all else because, as an aristocrat, that is what he had known and felt necessary to defend.[20] Still, it remains important to note that Nabokov would have rejected and perhaps even felt wounded by the suggestion that his most cherished principles were refractions of class bias. Like Proust, he firmly believed that people's actions and beliefs are determined by the *intellectual* class to which they belong and that these classes of the intellect take no account of birth or social position (*SLT* 6.61; *RTP* 4.311; NRF 8.1.58). Proust's *ouvriers électriciens*, who possess far more learning and culture than *"les véritables illettrés"* of the Faubourg Saint-Germain (*RTP* 4.467; NRF 8.2.38), find their correlative in Nabokov's retired hot-dog stand operator who turns out to be the greatest poet of his generation (*L* 249).

FRA I MAESTRI DI COLOR CHE SANNO

As J. E. Rivers noted as early as 1977, Nabokov's work is "an achievement of literary synthesis." "To read a novel by Nabokov," he elaborates, "is to be exposed to a wide spectrum of allusions to and parodies of other authors, and occasionally to passages of explicit literary criticism."[21] Commentators have tended to agree with this assessment. Robert Alter has remarked that Nabokov's work is "sharply focused on a continuing critical recapitulation of a whole literary tradition,"[22] and John Burt Foster Jr. has observed that Nabokov's work is characterized by an "unusual skill in choosing details from writers in several traditions and synthesizing them to serve his special artistic purposes."[23]

My book's methodology is anchored in this insight. Chapters 3 through 6 show how Nabokov's lifelong interest in courtesy inflected his engagement with the writers he came to love best. Questions convening under the rubric of *courtoisie* in the medieval texts Nabokov studied at Cambridge provide a point of entry into scenes collected from his writings and some of the writers that Nabokov admired most intensely. As the book proceeds, it establishes constant points of reference to Pushkin, Shakespeare, Tolstoy, and Proust as part of an implied argument that Nabokov is in constant dialogue with these masters of his imagination, and that he returns again and again to problems and topics that he finds worked out in a relatively small collection of masterpieces.

Though Pushkin, Shakespeare, Tolstoy, and Proust are certainly not the only writers Nabokov loved or admired, these are the writers whom he read and reread throughout his life, and who thus became the most vocal interlocutors for his own fiction. By locating Nabokov's nodes of moral concern within the works of these four writers, my book situates Nabokov "*fra i maestri di color che sanno* [among the masters of those who know]" in a way that recalls Aristotle's pride of place in Dante's *La Divina Commedia* and Joyce's *Ulysses*, or Dante's own pride of place in Pound's *Cantos*. These comparative analyses are grounded in textual allusions even as they focus on the broader affinities and contrasts that make these *maestri* the constant companions of Nabokov's literary journey. Given that this journey begins with the chivalric literature that his mother read to him as a young boy and which Nabokov studied as an undergraduate at Cambridge, my book concerns itself with the medieval legacies that anchor Nabokov's conversations with the constant companions of his imagination.

THE ART OF MORAL ACTS

This book builds upon three decades of scholarship devoted to the figure that Michael Rodgers and Susan Elizabeth Sweeney call (in their introduction to *Nabokov and the Question of Morality*) "the moral Nabokov."[24] My book's understanding of the term "moral" is identical to theirs: that is, I use it to refer to ethical judgments about right and wrong behavior. The pioneering studies of Brian Boyd, Ellen Pifer, David Rampton, Richard Rorty,

Leona Toker, and Michael Wood have been extended by scholars such as Leland de la Durantaye, Michael Glynn, and Roy Groen. Eric Naiman's deliberately "perverse" (as he calls it) reading of Nabokov (a reading that rests on the claim that Nabokov's poetics is to be understood as an erotics) shows that "the moral Nabokov" has become an orthodoxy that no longer requires defense.[25] The following chapters, therefore, take for granted that Nabokov was, to quote Pifer, a writer who shows an "abiding interest in human beings, not only as artists and dreamers, but as ethical beings subject to moral law and sanction."[26]

Additionally, existing scholarship on Nabokov's ethics has consistently and conclusively challenged the false dichotomy between Nabokov the master stylist and Nabokov the humanist. In *Vladimir Nabokov: A Critical Study of the Novels*, Rampton articulates the flaws of this dichotomy with particular force.[27] Boyd, Pifer, Rampton, Rorty, Wood, de la Durantaye, and Paul D. Morris have each, in their own way, glossed Nabokov's maxim "style *is* matter" (*SL* 116; emphasis in original) as a claim that extends Nabokov's aesthetic commitments into the ethical domain. According to these arguments, Nabokov draws a series of analogies between the attentiveness to detail involved in the apprehension of beauty and the attentiveness to suffering that instigates a moral response.

The chapters that follow radicalize these claims by arguing that Nabokov's assertions about art's kinship to ethics are much more literal than previously acknowledged and that Nabokov measures moral worth by criteria that are generally identified with the aesthetic. As a virtue dependent on the *manner* of its expression, courtesy weds the ethical and the aesthetic in a way that obviates the analogy-based interpretations of existing scholarship in favor of a relationship grounded in identity. I depart from critical consensus on this subject by insisting that Nabokov's habit of conflating the moral with the aesthetic is no mere analogy, and that Nabokov's ethics is, startlingly, an aesthetics. His well-known dictum that "style *is* matter" loses the metaphorical and didactic dimensions that previous studies have ascribed to it and becomes as boldly direct as Nabokov's pithy phrase suggests. As an ideal that depends upon *how* an act is performed and not merely on *what* an act seeks to accomplish, courtesy makes it possible to say that this book's central subject is the *art* of moral acts.

CRUELTY AND RESPECT

My argument that Nabokov thought about ethics in Kantian terms sheds light on the long-standing debate about Nabokov's cruelty as a writer. The perception that Nabokov was cruel both in the fates he dealt his characters and in his elitist pronouncements of indifference toward the general reader have been summarized by de la Durantaye.[28] I argue in the following chapters that the cruelty (Martin Amis, Italo Calvino), sadism (Carl Proffer), and loathing (Joyce Carol Oates) readers have detected in his work[29] are consequences of his painful acknowledgment that lives *are* causally determined and that emotions which he considered to be involuntary (such as love and pity) cannot always be relied upon to do the work of ethics. As in Kant, however, this vision is balanced by the will's capacity to resist the pull of Darwinian competitiveness and Hobbesian brutality. Only decisions taken, and acts performed, by a moral will can break the grip of determinism and orient human conduct toward virtue. Nabokov's world is dark not because it has suffered a decline from a happier prelapsarian state, but because the moral will has not advanced it far enough from its original, savage condition. "Our hideous reversions to the wild state"—the memorable formula he invokes in his lectures on *Bleak House* (*LL* 87)—occur when the will slackens and the darkness is allowed to prevail.

Unlike Amis, Calvino, Proffer, and Oates, a number of Nabokov's readers have seen more light than darkness in his work. Foremost among such readers is Brian Boyd, the author of the magisterial two-volume biography of Nabokov and several monographs and essay collections on Nabokov's fiction. Boyd has consistently argued that Nabokov is a quintessentially generous writer who patterns his fiction in such a way as to enable his readers to experience the same thrill of discovery that Nabokov himself experienced when pursuing butterflies or contemplating the patterns that had shaped his life (*VNRY* 315). According to Boyd, Nabokov's work seeks to expose the suffering caused by cruelty, especially when such cruelty risks being occluded by the eloquence of silver-tongued narrators like *Lolita*'s Humbert Humbert or *Ada*'s Van Veen.

My book argues that the debate about Nabokov's cruelty or generosity as a writer is a consequence of his Kantian double vision. Nabokov's fictional worlds are battlegrounds between an autonomous will and heteronomous passions, and genuinely moral acts occur when the will triumphs over the passions by answering the call of duty. Such occurrences are rare, but they are all the more admirable for being so. Though Nabokov cherished and celebrated virtues such as love and pity (Tolstoy's and Dostoevsky's antidotes to the world's darkness), he also saw them as emotions that cannot be governed by the will and which, consequently, fall outside the precincts of the moral.

The claim that Nabokov portrays courteous acts as examples of moral excellence in no way suggests that Nabokov himself was a paragon of courteous conduct. (Writing in Nabokov's lifetime, Page Stegner observes that "for a man with such aristocratic and intellectual background, he demonstrates on occasion surprisingly bad manners.")[30] The assumption that Nabokov's moral philosophy might have a bearing on his personal conduct must confront two main objections. First, there is Nabokov's own protest against "Tom-peeping over the fence" of "the precious lives of great writers" (*LRL* 138). This particular objection has been raised by many a writer. In a letter to Edmond de Goncourt dated December 17, 1891, Oscar Wilde protests against the impulse to seek the writer in the work of art, or to assume "that to create Hamlet one must be a little melancholy, to imagine Lear, completely mad."[31] Lurking in these protests is the legitimate fear that literary criticism might devolve into literary gossip, or what Nabokov calls "the rustle of skirts and giggles in the corridors of time" (*LRL* 138).

The second objection against judging Nabokov's personal conduct against the moral ideals expressed in his fiction has to do with the disparity between theory and practice that animates both life and art. Medea's confession that she sees and approves the "better track" but follows "the worse" is a lament over the weakness of the will to direct action.[32] Indeed, it can be argued that moral ideals exist precisely because they are so hard to attain. Nietzsche argued that Kant "believed in morality, not because it is demonstrated in nature and history, but in spite of the fact that nature and history continually contradict it."[33] The same is true of Nabokov's insistence on the supreme value of courtesy in a world in which courtesy is frequently absent.

This disparity between facts and ideals is frequently underscored in the medieval and Renaissance writers Nabokov studied for his tripos and referenced in his work. As Morton W. Bloomfield notes, the heroes of the Arthurian corpus—Arthur, Gawain, Lancelot, and others—"were both worthy and ridiculous figures. They were to be taken seriously and admired and at the same time to be laughed at for their childishness."[34] It is telling in this context that Calidore, the Knight of Courtesy in *The Faerie Queene*, is absent from much of the book in which Spenser studies that virtue. Elizabeth Jane Bellamy's observation that Calidore might be "the most truant protagonist in epic literary history"[35] is fitting given the short distance between moral aspiration and disillusion.

MORAL ART AND DELIBERATE MORALIZING

A Kantian approach to Nabokov's ethics also sheds light on the perennial problem regarding the apparent contradiction between Nabokov's various statements about the relationship between art and morality. As many scholars have noted, Nabokov's claim to Edmund Wilson that *Lolita* (1955) is "a highly moral affair" (*DBDV* 331) sits oddly with his claim in his afterword to the novel that *Lolita* has "no moral in tow" (*L* 296). The distinction he draws in a letter from 1945 has also generated debate: "I never meant to deny the moral impact of art which is certainly inherent in every genuine work of art," he wrote to George Noyes on the subject of Gogol. "What I do deny and am prepared to fight to the last drop of my ink is the deliberate moralizing which to me kills every vestige of art in a work however skilfully written" (*SL* 56).

The cornerstone of Kant's moral philosophy is the idea that human persons are bearers of a special dignity that demands respect. Placing respect at the center of Nabokov's ethics makes it possible to square Nabokov's insistence that all genuine art contains a moral dimension with his equally insistent claim that "deliberate moralizing" is incompatible with art. The first claim acknowledges that what is covered by the rubric of the *moral* is not culturally or temporally contingent, but universally and unconditionally binding. At the same time, however, the existence of moral norms does not give writers the license to adopt a militant approach toward the moral. As the second claim suggests, art that engages in "deliberate moralizing" does not show a proper respect for the reader's own moral convictions and personal adventure in the act of reading. Seeing Nabokov's assertions about the moral nature of art through the lens of respect dissolves any contradictions that might lurk in, for example, observations such as Sweeney's when she notes that in spite of his obsessive probing of moral questions, Nabokov is always careful to leave such questions unanswered.[36]

Such respect for the reader's own convictions and investment in the reading act is a version of the "extreme courtesy" that James Merrill sees as the bond between art and manners in Proust's magnum opus:

> Manners for me are the touch of nature, an artifice in the very bloodstream. Someone who does not take them seriously is making a serious mistake. They are as vital as all appearances, and if they deceive us they do so by mutual consent. . . . Manners aren't merely descriptions of social behaviour. The real triumph of manners in Proust is the extreme courtesy toward the reader, the voice explaining at once formally and intimately. Though it can be heard, of course, as megalomania, there is something wonderful in the reasonableness, the long-windedness of that voice, in its desire to be understood, in its treatment of *every* phenomenon (whether the way someone pronounces a word, or the article of clothing worn, or the color of a flower) as having ultimate importance. Proust says to us in effect, "I will not patronize you by treating these delicate matters with less than total, patient, sparkling seriousness."[37]

As chapter 5 will show, *Pale Fire* bears the burden of Merrill's observation that courtesy is vital to human life, and that courtesy's deceptions are life-giving because they deceive by mutual consent. Chapter 6 argues that Nabokov ultimately recoiled from a key aspect of Proust's "extreme courtesy" when he was writing—in the years following the Holocaust—the darkest novels of his corpus: *Lolita* and *Pnin*. In the epilogue, I argue that courtesy recovers its innocence by the time Nabokov writes *Ada*, a work that draws a moral equivalence between the duties of the "artist" and those of the "gentleman" (*A* 393–94). As in the medieval conceptions of *courtoisie* that Nabokov studied at Cambridge, *Ada* shows that it is a *moral duty* to be courteous to those one does not love and an *art* to pretend delight in its performance.

Chapter One

Where Nature Ends and Art Begins: Courtesy, Love, Pity

In courtesy I'd have her chiefly learned;
Hearts are not had as a gift, but hearts are earned
By those that are not entirely beautiful.
—W. B. Yeats

NABOKOV'S FIRST NOVEL opens with an act of discourtesy. Lev Glebovich Ganin, the protagonist of *Mary* (*Mashen'ka*, 1926), finds himself stuck in an elevator in the company of a fellow émigré, Aleksey Ivanovich Alfyorov. Ganin's response to Alfyorov's inane but well-meaning efforts at conversation is decidedly rude: upon being released from the elevator's confinement, Ganin "gave Alfyorov a slight push and, having followed him out, relieved his feelings by noisily slamming the steel door behind him. Never before had he been so irritable" (*M* 4). Ganin is irritable because he finds it difficult to end an affair of three months' standing: "He was held back by a sense of honor and a sense of pity [*chuvstvo chesti i chuvstvo zhalosti*] which blunted the will of a man who at other times was capable of any kind of creative enterprise, any exertion, and who would set about a task eagerly and willingly, cheerfully intent on overcoming everything and winning all" (*M* 19; *Mashen'ka*, 58).

The circumstances that lead Ganin to act discourteously toward Alfyorov have been generated by a combination of honor and pity. Honor designates the self-esteem that comes with considering oneself worthy of respect. In Ganin's particular case—as a young man who no longer loves the woman to whom he has pledged himself as a lover—honor comes from the sense of feeling himself bound to a gentlemanly code of conduct. As Kwame Anthony Appiah observes, quoting Cardinal Newman's famous words, one of the most traditional ways of defining what it means to be a *gentleman* is to say that a gentleman is someone who never inflicts pain (*HC* 49). Since he expects the end of the affair to be painful for Lyudmila, it is natural for Ganin to feel pity for her and contempt for himself.

Ganin's treatment of Alfyorov constitutes a primal scene for a particular strain of inquiry into the status of honor and pity as supreme moral values. This will become a career-long project on Nabokov's part. In his third novel, *The Defense* (*Zashchita Luzhina*, 1930), for example, pity is cast as a cardinal virtue. Mrs. Luzhin, one of Nabokov's most compassionate heroines, is defined by her capacity

> to feel constantly an intolerable, tender pity [*nezhnuiu zhalost'*] for the creature whose life is helpless and unhappy; to feel across hundreds of miles that somewhere in Sicily a thin-legged little donkey with a shaggy belly is being brutally beaten. Whenever she did come across a creature that was being hurt, she experienced a kind of legendary eclipse—when inexplicable night comes down and ash flies and blood appears on the walls—and it seemed that if at once, at once, she did not help, did not cut short another's torture . . . , her heart would not stand it and she would die. Hence, she lived in perpetual, secret agitation, constantly anticipating a new delight or a new pity . . . (*Def* 105–6; *Zashchita Luzhina*, 367)

Pity leads her to marry the unworldly, lonely Luzhin (*Def* 190), and it can be argued that she loses him because of the discourtesy of an unnamed visitor who monopolizes her time at a most inopportune moment. Luzhin's suicide appears to be causally related to his wife's having been "taken advantage of" by an "importunate lady from Russia" when Luzhin urgently needs her (*Def* 215). Mrs. Luzhin responds to the Soviet lady's lack of civility with the kind of principled courtesy that will become the hallmark of Nabokov's English-language heroines:

> Mrs. Luzhin felt she was not paying enough attention to her husband's moods, something was slipping out of control, and yet she continued to listen politely to the newcomer's chatter and to translate her demands to shop assistants, and it was particularly unpleasant when a pair of shoes that had already been worn once turned out to be unsuitable, and she had to accompany her to the store while the purple-faced lady bawled out the firm in Russian and demanded the shoes be changed, and then she had to be soothed and her caustic expressions considerably toned down in the German version. (*Def* 216)

Mrs. Luzhin remains valiantly by the side of the awful lady from the Soviet Union for the same reason that Ganin feels himself obligated to act honorably toward Lyudmila (even though he betrays this sense of obligation when he breaks up with her). Ganin and Mrs. Luzhin feel themselves bound—respectively—by the demands of masculine and feminine codes of honor that collide with their personal interests.

Unlike Fyodor's discourtesy to Alfyorov, the discourtesy of the Soviet lady appears to have devastating consequences. In his English-language novels, Nabokov continued to explore the moral significance of courtesy by crafting increasingly complex scenarios in which both courtesy and discourtesy become entangled in tragedy. As Nabokov reimagines in his English fiction the selfless and refined courtesy Mrs. Luzhin extends to the unnamed Soviet lady, he consistently casts moral excellence as the heroic capacity to rise to the demands of courtesy precisely when courtesy is at its most vulnerable. In his first novel written in English, *The Real Life of Sebastian Knight* (1941), we witness a scene that will be replayed, with only slight variations, on two more occasions. The scene in question describes V.'s brief encounter with Helene Grinstein, the first of the four women V. tracks down in the hope of finding the last lover of his half-brother Sebastian. V.'s unannounced visit to Helene is untimely: Helene and her family are hosting a funeral reception for Helene's brother-in-law. After their brief interview, V. laments that Helene is not the woman whom he had been seeking:

> Somehow I felt sorry it had not been Helene Grinstein. Although of course she never *could* have been the woman who had made Sebastian so miserable. Girls of her type do not smash a man's life—they build it. There she had been steadily managing a house that was bursting with grief and had found it possible to attend to the fantastic affairs of a completely superfluous stranger. (*RLSK* 106)

Though Helene Grinstein's role in *The Real Life of Sebastian Knight* is minor, her capacity to rise to the challenge of courtesy during a time of acute emotional stress will become a touchstone moral response of more prominent Nabokovian heroines.

A strikingly similar scene is staged in *Pale Fire* (1962). Here, Kinbote recalls the pain that his invented alter ego, Charles Xavier, the former king of Zembla, caused his young wife Disa by his repeated infidelities. Tormented by remorse, Kinbote revisits Disa's sufferings in a series of harrowing dream visions:

> He would see her being accosted by a misty relative so distant as to be practically featureless. She would quickly hide what she held and extend her arched hand to be kissed. He knew she had just come across a telltale object . . . establishing beyond any doubt his unfaithfulness. Sweat beaded her pale, naked forehead—but she had to listen to the prattle of a chance visitor or direct the movements of a workman with a ladder . . . One might bear . . . the knowledge of her grief and pride but none could bear the sight of her automatic smile as she turned from the agony of the disclosure to the polite trivialities

> required of her. She would be canceling an illumination, or discussing hospital cots with the head nurse . . . and through the everyday plainness of the talk . . . , he, the groaning dreamer, perceived the disarray of her soul and was aware that an odious, undeserved, humiliating disaster had befallen her, and that only obligations of etiquette and her staunch kindness to a guiltless third party gave her the force to smile. (*PF* 590–91)

Disa is imagined as mastering her passions for the sake of courtesy at a moment when she could reasonably claim to be exempt from such a moral obligation.

Disa's fidelity to "obligations of etiquette" and her "staunch kindness" are reincarnated in Lucette, Van and Ada's half-sister in *Ada*. Lucette's frantic attempts to seduce Van nearly reach fruition when Ada's unexpected appearance in a film they are both watching on a transatlantic liner causes Van suddenly to abandon the theater. Though desperate to pursue him, Lucette is delayed by Robert and Rachel Robinson, "old bores of the family" (*A* 380), who take advantage of Van's abrupt departure to seat themselves next to her. Though she has staked her whole future on seducing Van, Lucette nonetheless bestows upon the Robinsons "her last, last, last free gift of staunch courtesy that was stronger than failure and death" (*A* 392).

Though these four episodes are unremarkable at first glance, they are records of Nabokov's preoccupation with the quiet heroism of upholding standards of civility even in the midst of personal crisis. The behaviors associated with courtesy are imagined as surviving even in the most harrowing circumstances: Mira Belochkin, Pnin's Jewish sweetheart murdered by the Nazis, is said to have adhered—against all odds—to the principles of courtesy as a prisoner in an extermination camp. Though the exact details of her murder remain obscure, the only detail that Pnin learns with certainty is that "being too weak to work (though still smiling, still able to help other Jewish women), she was selected to die and was cremated only a few days after her arrival in Buchenwald" (*Pnin* 395). Mira's courteous smile—encased in parentheses as if belonging to a moral dispensation that is irreconcilable with her grisly surroundings—is the historical precedent of the invented Disa's "automatic smile" to a guiltless third party and Lucette's free gift of courtesy to the Robinsons.

These scenes are connected, first, by the high emotional toll exacted by Mrs. Luzhin's, Helene's, Mira's, Disa's, and Lucette's respective acts of courtesy. Second, this courtesy is directed at (to quote V.) "completely superfluous stranger[s]." Though the Soviet lady and the Robinsons are not strangers to, respectively, Mrs. Luzhin and Lucette, they are distinctly and painfully superfluous to their concerns. Third, they are encountered at decisive moments in each novel where matters of life, death, and personal desire are in play. Taken together, these shared attributes may tempt us to dismiss these moments as morally irrelevant or perversely gratuitous. For what merit can there be in an ethics that is so costly yet consequentially so negligible? Are empathetic readers not expected to wish for Disa to abandon her "chance visitor" to his "prattle" and nurse her grief in the intimacy of her bedroom? What long-term benefit or consolation might the Robinsons derive from Lucette's sharing a cold drink with them in their cabin, a social occasion that turns out—most grimly because most literally—to be Lucette's "last free gift of staunch courtesy"? For this *does* turn out to be Lucette's final act of courtesy: shortly after departing from the Robinsons' cabin and being rejected by Van once more, Lucette commits suicide.

The scenes of courtesy culled from *Pale Fire* and *Ada* sit at the heart of the anatomy of courtesy that informs Nabokov's fiction. In the earlier *Pale Fire*, Disa's courteous conduct is defined as a "staunch kindness" that gets channeled through "obligations of etiquette." In *Ada*, Nabokov assigns a single nomenclatorial category to this blend of kindness and formal protocol: Van explains that it is Lucette's "staunch courtesy" that leads her to respond as she does to the Robinsons' ill-timed intrusion. This definition of courtesy as a synthesis of kindness and decorum is closely attuned to modern definitions of the word. The next chapter will show that this definition also captures core elements that Nabokov saw enveloped by the term. As a student of French medieval literature, Nabokov would have been intimately familiar with *courtoisie*'s broad range of signification informing the works that made up the reading list for his tripos.

As the chapter that follows will show, Nabokov's understanding of courtesy was as complex as it was in the medieval texts he studied at Cambridge, even if it departed from its medieval sources in significant ways. Nabokovian courtesy combines inner virtues with their external expression in self-approved rules of conduct. Thus, politeness alone does not qualify as courtesy for it lacks the companion virtues (pity, compassion, concern) that give courtesy its richness and vitality. At the same time, the inner virtues need the supporting role of decorum if they are to avoid causing injury through maladroit forms of expression. Nabokov knew this well: he recalls, for instance, how his "well-meaning" but "tactless" paternal grandmother always risked insulting the very people she wanted to help (*SM* 491).

Combining as it does inner virtue and outer expression, courtesy makes it possible to impose useful taxonomic distinctions in the chapters that follow. Thus, courtesy's reservoir of inner virtues differentiates it from the thin veneer of modes of behavior captured by terms such as etiquette, decorum, and politeness. By the same token, courtesy is not merely equivalent to the inner virtues, for these either remain silent in the absence of a technique of externalization or get expressed in ways that cause injury or insult. These taxonomic distinctions, however, are not meant to reduce or constrain courtesy's rich complexity. Courtesy, as understood by Nabokov and the medieval texts he studied at Cambridge, applies to situations that are as varied as life's predicaments. Nabokov's fiction highlights the urgency and immediacy of questions that convene under the broad rubric of courtesy: How does one break up with a lover whom one no longer loves? How does one reject someone without causing offense? Is honor more important than life? What are the limits of hospitality? What are the limits of courtesy? These are some of the questions that Nabokov's fiction obsessively dwells upon; by focusing on the range of scenarios that pose these questions, the chapters that follow show that courtesy is the linchpin in Nabokov's thinking about art and ethics.

These chapters will also show that Nabokovian courtesy is keyed into what might be called an "ethics of inutility." This connects Nabokov's moral vision to the deontological ethics of Kant[1] and distances it from the medieval texts he studied at Cambridge. Nabokov's desire to sever ethics from consequence-driven calculations leads him to think of courtesy as an art. I therefore agree with Page Stegner's early claim that Pnin's, and by extension Nabokov's, most important personal attribute is his "style," but I disagree with Stegner's companion claim that this style is placed into the service of an "escape from the impossible suffering and vulgarity in the world."[2] The following chapters challenge Stegner's overarching argument that "quality, style, beauty" serve as substitutes for "morality" in Nabokov's novels and that Nabokov's interest in "style" precludes an interest "in rights and wrongs."[3] I argue instead that Nabokov sees the style associated with courtesy, politeness, and related virtues not as a substitute for the moral but as its essence. As a moral impulse that has no recognizable utility but has discovered a graceful means of expression, Nabokovian courtesy is an art of the moral virtues.

The inutility of Nabokovian courtesy might seem at first glance to collide with his understanding of courtesy as an antidote to an emotion-driven life. Unlike Rousseau, Nabokov did not think of human emotions as reliably virtuous. Some of his most memorable characters lack kindness, pity, or humility. Love, the most obsessively studied emotion in his fiction, frequently finds expression in incest, pedophilia, rape, and murder. Nabokov's view of love has much in common with Proust's view of passion as an illness and love as a disease.[4] The capacity of Nabokovian courtesy to silence the voice of the passions is its most powerful link to Kantian moral philosophy and its most powerful proof of human autonomy. At the same time, courtesy's capacity to act in opposition to the passions underscores its performative nature and its complicity with deception. The moral imperative to mask the passions by graceful gestures of courtesy explains why Nabokovian courtesy is not just an *art*, but a *performance art* grounded in Nabokov's claim that all art is deception (*SO* 33; *LL* 5).

COURTESY AND DARWIN

As *Ada* cannily lets us discover for ourselves, it is Van's characteristic egoism that allows him to imagine that Lucette should have offered the Robinsons something like his own "humorous bad-sailor excuse" (*A* 392) instead of her selfless courtesy. To dwell on the kinds of questions asked by Van is to stake moral value exclusively in benefit, or, to use the word Nabokov favored in this context, *utility*. Casting himself as a high priest of the *inutile*, Nabokov seized upon what he saw as the gratuitous aspects of mimicry in nature as his most powerful refutation of Darwinian natural selection as an all-encompassing theory. According to Nabokov, nature's mimetic patterns showcase an artistry and sophistication that go well beyond an organism's need to deceive predators:

> "Natural selection," in the Darwinian sense, could not explain the miraculous coincidence of imitative aspect and imitative behavior, nor could one appeal to the theory of "the struggle for life" when a protective device was carried to a point of mimetic subtlety, exuberance, and luxury far in excess of a predator's power of appreciation. I discovered in nature the nonutilitarian delights that I sought in art. Both were a form of magic, both were a game of intricate enchantment and deception. (*SM* 465)

As a synthesis of dignified refinement, heroic struggle, and pure disinterestedness, Nabokovian courtesy serves the same purpose in his ethics as the heightened artistry of natural mimicry serves for his philosophy of science and aesthetics. Like mimicry in nature, courtesy allows him to celebrate a social phenomenon that both contributes to the Darwinian economy of survival and transcends it.

This duality informing Nabokov's understanding of courtesy has a precedent in book 6 of *The Faerie Queene*, generally known as the Legend of Courtesy. For Spenser, courtesy is the fairest flower in the virtues' "sacred noursery" because—paradoxically—it is at once the lowliest and loftiest of virtues:

> Amongst them all growes not a fayrer flowre,
> Then is the bloosme of comely courtesie,
> Which though it on a lowly stalke doe bowre,
> Yet brancheth forth in braue nobilitie,
> And spreds it selfe through all ciuilitie. (*FQ* 6.Proem.4.1–5)

As Gordon Teskey has argued, this dual nature of courtesy as both humble and exalted aligns Spenser's understanding of courtesy with the anthropological definition of "culture" as articulated, for instance, in Claude Lévi-Strauss's *The Raw and the Cooked* ("CT" 352). Like culture, courtesy is a flight and a release from the indignities associated with an embodied life. Like culture, too, it marks an effort at civilizing the self and the world. C. S. Lewis's definition of courtesy as a "supervenient perfection"[5] goes to the heart of Spenser's and Nabokov's conception of courtesy as a virtue that marks the final stage of the self's moral development. To quote Teskey again, "By courtesy the completed moral subject is given its finishing gloss" ("CT" 348). The fulfillment of this moral telos also marks the farthest distance that moral subjects have traveled from their biological origins. In short, courtesy dwells in the space where nature ends and art begins.

Courtesy's utilitarian dimension is made explicit in the great classic of courtesy literature, Castiglione's *The Book of the Courtier* (1528). Here, as elsewhere in Renaissance conduct books, courtesy is a social grace that promotes the aims of personal ambition. Nabokov's conception of courtesy, however, is more closely aligned with the conduct books of the medieval "*moralistes*," for whom personal ambition was not an acknowledged aspiration: Étienne de Fougères' *Le Livre des manières* (c. 1170), Robert de Blois' *L'Enseignement des princes* and *Le Chastoiement des dames* (c. 1250), and Philippe de Novare's *Les Quatre Ages de l'homme* (c. 1265). The medieval French courtly romances that Nabokov studied at Cambridge share a deep bond of kinship with these courtesy books. As Ad Putter observes, "From the very beginning, Arthurian romance gives advice similar to that found in courtesy books, and manifests in its detailed descriptions of feasts, meals, and polite conversation, a shared interest in etiquette" (*FAR* 64). Indeed, the "continual interplay" between these two genres makes it impossible to determine "whether romance influenced the courtesy book or vice versa" (*FAR* 65).

Like medieval romances and courtesy books, Nabokov portrays courtesy as an intrinsic good, that is, a set of behaviors that speaks for itself and serves nonutilitarian ends. To preserve its status as an intrinsic moral value, courtesy must operate not only in the absence of pity, kindness, or sympathy, but even in the presence of hatred or indifference. Like Kant's categorical imperative, courtesy must do its work regardless of inclination or desire. Lucette's parting words to the Robinsons—"I really needed that lovely cold drink" (*A* 394)—mask her indifference toward them relative to her total emotional investment in Van. Like the mimic butterfly's "game of intricate enchantment and deception," Lucette's polite words cast a spell on the Robinsons, an enchantment that is broken by the crushing news of her suicide a short time later. Though feeble and trite, Lucette's parting courtesy is not just a moral act, but an artistic one, too. It is at once beautiful and pointless, or, as Nabokov would have viewed it, beautiful *because* pointless.

As Ganin's discourtesy to Alfyorov or Van's discourtesy to the Robinsons attests, Nabokov knew how easily courtesy disintegrated in uncongenial contexts. Nabokov's fiction studies courtesy within networks of narrative complexity, and closely analyzes its triumphs and failures. The acts of courtesy performed by Mrs. Luzhin, Helene, Disa, and Lucette enact the ideal of supererogation that Toker finds throughout Nabokov's work. Lucette's going so far beyond what mere politeness requires during her encounter with the Robinsons (she does not simply address a few words to them, but accepts their invitation to have a drink in their cabin) is the kind of moral action that, to paraphrase Toker, Nabokov asks us to appreciate in others but recognizes that we may demand only of ourselves.[6]

COURTESY AND PITY

The fragility of courtesy in the face of forces beyond one's control provides an insight into an ethical distinction Nabokov draws between courtesy, on the one hand, and discourtesy and pity on the other. The acts of courtesy performed by Mrs. Luzhin, Helene, Disa, and Lucette underscore the selfless and disinterested nature of courtesy. By contrast, discourteous acts such as Ganin's conduct toward Alfyorov, the Soviet lady's monopolization of Mrs. Luzhin, and Van's bad-sailor excuse to the Robinsons remind us that discourtesy is always selfish and opportunistic. Courtesy calls for a principled refusal to expose one's indifference toward others which becomes most visible when one attends to social responsibilities in situations that make a real claim upon one's passions. To give oneself to others as Mira is imagined to have done with her fellow women prisoners at Buchenwald or Lucette does with the Robinsons is an image of refinement and freedom. Courtesy is a site of linkage between self and other, and Nabokov emphasizes its role in constituting the social world.

Though pity is a deeply cherished virtue in Nabokov's pantheon of values, it nonetheless has something important in common with discourtesy. In situations when pity is unwelcome (as it is, for instance, in the case of the Shades' pity for their daughter Hazel), pity becomes a species of discourtesy insofar as it chips away at the other's dignity. As an instinctive emotion rather than a laborious acquisition, pity—like love—is a passion and therefore cannot be held under the will's authority. By contrast, Nabokovian courtesy is grounded in an active will capable of honoring social obligations in the face of frustrations and appetites. Pity and discourtesy are, to invoke a Kantian vocabulary, heteronomous—that is, subject to laws external to the self-determining subject. Whereas we can will ourselves to act courteously, discourtesy—like love and pity—is a natural inclination.

This Kantian distinction helps untangle the curious relationship between courteous and discourteous acts in Nabokov's narratives of suicide, such as those in *The Defense*, *Ada*, and, most poignantly, *Pale Fire*. When confronted with Hazel, Hazel's blind date Pete Dean[7] behaves markedly unlike Mrs. Luzhin, Helene, Disa, and Lucette. Unlike Disa, Pete feels no obligation to participate in the "polite trivialities" expected of him. He does not feel that he "had to listen to the prattle" of an undesirable blind date. The motives behind Pete's clumsy excuse are painfully transparent when he

> Clutching his brow exclaimed that he had clean
> Forgotten an appointment with a chum
> Who'd land in jail if he, Pete, did not come. (*PF* lines 392–94)

Feeling redundant in the company of Jane Dean and her fiancé, Hazel boards a bus to return home, but makes a stop at a place known as Lochanhead and is believed to have committed suicide by drowning.

Pete's ungentlemanly conduct serves as a reminder that discourtesy can wound, sometimes irreparably. Nonetheless, the fact that Pete's discourtesy appears to be causally linked to Hazel's suicide need not mean that courtesy is a virtue *only* because it might help in averting disaster. Nabokov did not deny that mimicry conferred significant survival benefits, just as he did not deny that art serves a didactic function ("magic, story, lesson" is the formulation he used to describe the literature he admired to his students [*LL* 6]). Still, he strenuously denied that this is *all* that mimicry and courtesy do. The fact that discourtesy can lead to disastrous consequences is no proof that courtesy has moral value only because it can prevent such consequences or lead to good ones. By crafting an episode about a victim of discourtesy, Nabokov shows that courteous acts are always *potentially* life-giving, or, at the very least, always *potentially* wildly out of proportion to what they might appear to be. As Kant observed, however, this potential can be neither predicted nor calculated, and cannot therefore motivate moral acts. Like the aesthetic pleasures generated by art and mimicry, courtesy produces the kinds of goods and satisfactions that resist prediction or quantification.

Like Cincinnatus C.'s ontological makeup in *Invitation to a Beheading*, Pete's discourtesy to Hazel reminds us of the ineluctable opacity of others. Had Pete been aware of Hazel's acute emotional fragility, it is possible to suppose that he would have acted differently. Nabokov's intricate scenario highlights not only the impossibility of such knowledge, but also the role of courtesy as a moral hedge in a world in which the other is inescapably unknowable. As Mrs. Luzhin, Helene, Disa, and Lucette demonstrate, courtesy is a debt that we owe to others regardless of circumstances and consequences. The utilitarian principle that one should always act so as to produce the greatest aggregate happiness must fail not only because we cannot predict the consequences of our actions, but also because we do not know what happiness means for others.

Courtesy thus pays tribute to the unpredictability of the future and to the mystery of the other. Unlike pity, which must strain to divine the nature of the other's sufferings and desires for the sake of dispensing comfort and succor, courtesy can—and, indeed, must—do its work in the absence of such knowledge. The recipients of Mrs. Luzhin's, Helene's, Disa's, and Lucette's acts of courtesy must remain anonymous or superfluous in order to highlight courtesy's disinterestedness and agnosticism with regard to the other.

In his lectures on *Bleak House*, Nabokov describes pity as a marker of moral progress, a virtue (as he wrongly claims) unknown to the ancients, but intensely alive for writers like Dickens (*LL* 87). On other occasions, he underscores the heteronomous nature of pity when he identifies pity as an epiphenomenon of beauty. His gnomic definition of art as "beauty plus pity" highlights pity's dependence upon beauty: "Where there is beauty there is pity," he explains, "for the simple reason that beauty must die: beauty always dies, the manner dies with the matter, the world dies with the individual" (*LL* 251). The conception of pity as an emotional toll levied on the experience of beauty also hovers over the enigmatic couplet Humbert attributes to "an old poet": "The moral sense in mortals is the duty / We have to pay on mortal sense of beauty" (*L* 266). Such pronouncements are designed to celebrate Nabokov's own extraordinarily capacious understanding of beauty and his pity for its radical fragility. But they also suggest that pity is not subject to the authority of the will. Though grown into a full-fledged virtue from antiquity to the modern period (according to Nabokov), pity is not self-governing: in the absence of beauty or other pity-generating experiences, it is unclear what could summon our "moral sense" to duty. Humbert is frequently roused to pity by Dolly's fleeting beauty, yet this fact has no moral bearing on his relations with her. John Shade is harrowed by pity when he sees that his daughter has inherited none of his wife's beauty but only his own physical unattractiveness. Yet his pity proves—as Shade himself admits—to be demonic rather than life-giving. Pete Dean finds no beauty and feels no pity in the presence of Hazel. Giving in to his instinct to flee from the scene, Pete stands in need of a code of moral conduct capable of operating independently of his interests and emotions.

The scenario of Pete and Hazel's blind date shows that pity exists in a complex dialectic with courtesy. Pete's absence of pity toward Hazel is as hopelessly heteronomous as the pity-induced agitations that torment Mrs. Luzhin. The mark of Mrs. Luzhin's moral excellence lies less in the pity that she cannot help feeling than in her ability to channel that pity into behaviors associated with courtesy. In her courteous conduct toward the rude lady from Soviet Russia, Mrs. Luzhin showcases the capacity of courtesy to hide the passions that would interfere with its operation. By contrast, Pete's moral defeat lies in his failure to discipline his passions and act courteously. Unlike Mrs. Luzhin, who faithfully remains by the side of her annoying guest, Pete flees from the scene of the blind date because he lets his interests and emotions engulf his capacity to act in any other way.

Driven by pity to marry the physically unattractive Luzhin, Mrs. Luzhin enfolds her pity into delicate gestures of courtesy, such as teaching her husband how to kiss a lady's hands in an especially graceful way (*Def* 190, 252). At the same time, Hazel's physical unattractiveness underscores pity's helplessness in the absence of the refinements of courtesy. Given her acute self-consciousness, Hazel could have escaped the injury that she suffers on the blind date only if Pete had been able to perform an act of deception as complex as an intricate example of natural mimicry. An act of courtesy on Pete's part would have disarmed Hazel of her nagging self-doubt in the same way that it disarms the Robinsons' fluttery self-consciousness. Rather than dwelling on the possibility that Pete's courtesy might be fueled by repugnance or pity (or both), Hazel might have been made to forget her unattractiveness and made to marvel at the enchanting refinement of a young man's commitment to his social responsibilities. To paraphrase the final stanza of Yeats's prayer to his daughter, Pete might have succeeded in making Hazel *feel* beautiful through a performance of courtesy's "customs" and "ceremonies." Such a hypothetical courteous act on Pete's part might have been sufficiently powerful to protect Hazel from any suspicions that it was feigned. Like the duplicities of art and nature so often celebrated by Nabokov, the duplicities of courtesy strike us as beneficent by virtue of their gratuitous yearning to please and their power to put individuals at ease.

Nabokov depicts such an example of courteous deception when he describes his visit with a friend to his former Swiss governess, Cécile Miauton:

> As no conversation was possible because of Mademoiselle's deafness, my friend and I decided to bring her next day the appliance which we gathered she could not afford. She adjusted the clumsy thing improperly at first, but no sooner had she done so than she turned to me with a dazzled look of moist wonder and bliss in her eyes. She swore she could hear every word, every murmur of mine. She could not for, having my doubts, I had not spoken. (*SM* 457)

His description of his final glimpse of her—"the radiant deceit she had used in order to have me depart pleased with my own kindness" (*SM* 458)—is an image of courtesy that poignantly evokes the way courtesy must often employ deception in order to do its finest work.

Deceptions perpetrated in the name of disinterested courtesy involve a voluntary release from the heteronomy of the self. Such a claim is Kantian both in its understanding of disinterested moral actions as markers of freedom and also, as we shall see in chapter 5, in its illustration of Kant's qualifications of his famous prohibition against deception. Had Pete feigned interest in Hazel for the duration of the blind date instead of fleeing from the scene, he would have had to pretend that he did not find her repellent. An act of courtesy of this kind would double as an escape from one's heteronomous self and a demonstration of "that higher species of self-command" which the narrator of *Mansfield Park* identifies with the "principle of right" and "just consideration of others."[8]

Nabokov's desire to imagine courtesy as an ideally disinterested intrinsic good may account for the absence in his fiction of Machiavellian figures who deploy courtesy for mercenary ends. Though hyper-literate and hyper-cultured, Axel Rex, Humbert Humbert, Van Veen, and Demon Veen are successful with women not because they are courteous, but because they are unapologetic cads. Like their Russian predecessors (Onegin, Pechorin, Bazarov, and Dmitri Karamazov rush to mind), these Nabokovian villains are seductive not by virtue of an opportunistic courtesy, but in consequence of their scorn toward its precepts. Cordula's parting words to Van in the wake of an impromptu assignation serve as a case in point: "it was fun—even though you've been speaking to me not as you would to a lady friend but as you probably do to little whores" (*A* 366).

The hypothetical scenario in which Pete's courtesy might have temporarily distracted Hazel from her unattractiveness highlights pity's potentially corrosive effects in the absence of courtesy's refinements. Though Shade tells Kinbote that "pity is the password" (*PF* 601), he also tacitly recognizes its pernicious attributes when he invokes "the demons of our pity" to describe his and his wife's dominant emotional response to their daughter's unattractiveness (*PF* line 327). As Wood has argued, the phrase betrays Shade's guilty intuition "that pity is demonic, a destructive, unwelcome emotion."[9] According to Wood, Shade's assumption that Hazel committed suicide because of her sexual unattractiveness tacitly acknowledges the potentially degrading nature of pity. "It is a judgment on Shade and his wife," Wood argues, "that they find this flat little story so reasonable, and sufficient."[10]

PITY AND LOVE

As the target of her father's relentless pity, Hazel is never allowed to forget that she is unattractive. Though in hindsight Shade regrets his all-consuming pity, he must also know that pity's "demonic" nature is a consequence of its kinship to love. The view that love is a species of insanity is a common trope in the Western literary imagination. The aphorism ascribed to Prodicus, the sophist from Ceos active in the fifth century B.C.—"Desire doubled is love, love doubled becomes madness"[11]—has informed the Western canon from Euripides's *Hippolytus* to Proust's *In Search of Lost Time*. Yet the most intriguing analogue to Nabokov's view of love as a form of insanity can be found in the opening lines of Erasmus's *Ciceronianus, or A Dialogue on the Best Style of Speaking* (1528). Nosoponus, the target of the dialogue's satire, has been rendered ill by his slavish efforts to imitate Cicero's eloquent prose style. He explains that his relentless labor of ten years' standing has been dedicated to "the goddess which moves men's souls," whom the Greeks call "*πειθώ* [persuasion]." Bulephorus recognizes that there is an erotic subtext to this obsession with style, and he assures his ailing friend that he is intimately familiar with the condition that afflicts him: "I know what a powerful thing Love is and what it is to be *νυμθόληπτον*." The ancient Greek compound word that Bulephorus invokes—*nympholepton*—means "captive of a nymph."[12] This stitching together of the art of persuasion with imprisonment by nymphs anticipates Nabokov's most famous creation, the self-styled nympholept Humbert Humbert, who tries to captivate his readers with his eloquence.

Nabokov acknowledged that love—in all of its thorny complexity and variety—is a form of enslavement even as it irradiates the world with beauty and goodness. In his preface to *Bend Sinister*, he describes at length how the Soviets applied the "lever of love" to tie "a rebel to his wretched country by his own twisted heartstrings." Only Paduk's dim-wittedness and inexperience in such matters delays his realization that "by grabbing [Krug's] little child one would force him to do whatever one wished" (*BS* 164–65). Like pity, love erodes our autonomy by entangling us in the fate of another. Nabokov would have been familiar with such a conception of love from his earliest encounters with Russian literature. The "stylized Pushkin" (as Nabokov dubs *Eugene Onegin*'s narrator) suggests that freedom and creativity begin where love ends:

> Love passed, the Muse appeared,
> and the dark mind cleared up.
> Once free, I seek again the concord
> of magic sounds, feelings, and thoughts. (*EO* 1.124)

For Andrey Bolkonsky of *War and Peace*, the heteronomy of love reveals itself on the eve of his death when he discovers that human love can never be free because it is not an end in itself. Never gratuitous, never disinterested, human love is always striving "for something, to gain something or because of something" (*WP* 2:1090; *PSS* 11:387). Perhaps Nabokov had Bolkonsky's epiphany in mind when he has Van designate Lucette's final act of courtesy as a "*free* gift . . . stronger than failure and death" (*A* 392; emphasis added). Whereas we experience the promptings of love as irrevocable constraints on our freedom, courtesy—like Kant's famous claim that the beautiful has purposiveness without having an end goal (*CPJ* 5:220)—is born free and remains free to give.

Shade's suspicion that his pity for Hazel may have played a role in her demise might also be keyed into his awareness that pity is patronizing. When Eberthella H. refers to an old man "at the Exton railway station, who thought he was God and began redirecting the trains" as "a loony," Shade insists that the man is "a fellow poet." "Loony" "is the wrong word," he tells Eberthella. "One should not apply it to a person who deliberately peels off a drab and unhappy past and replaces it with a brilliant invention" (*PF* 610). Yet Shade's characteristically creative response to vilified and marginalized others is powerless against Hazel's troubles. Shade cannot treat his daughter's story with the same generous openness with which he treats the stories of others. "His picture of Hazel is quite clear and complete," Kinbote explains, "maybe a little too complete, architectonically, since the reader cannot help feeling that it has been expanded and elaborated to the detriment of certain other richer and rarer matters ousted by it" (*PF* 556). Though Kinbote is lamenting the fact that Hazel has usurped what he believes should have been his own central place in Shade's poem, the reader might nevertheless object to Shade's portrait of Hazel on the grounds that it is—as Kinbote intimates—narrowly reductive. Shade's imagination is hopelessly impoverished when it comes to articulating Hazel's story. His richly creative capacity to discern poetry in madness plunges into cliché when he tries to cope with his personal grief. His and Sybil's labored efforts at mutual consolation—"All little girls are plump," "That's the awkward age," "Less starch, more fruit! / She may not be a beauty, but she's cute" (*PF* lines 296, 300, 303–4)—inspire no confidence and bring no relief.

The complex relationship between pity and creativity is adumbrated in *The Gift* (the last novel Nabokov wrote in Russian) and *Bend Sinister* (the first novel he would write in the United States). One of Fyodor's unique gifts as a writer is the ability to experience

> a piercing pity—for the tin box in a waste patch, for the cigarette card from the series *National Costumes* trampled in the mud, for the poor, stray word repeated by the kindhearted, weak, loving creature who has just been scolded for nothing—for all the trash of life which by means of a momentary alchemic distillation—the "royal experiment"—is turned into something valuable and eternal. (*Gift* 164)

The "alchemic distillation" by which trash begets art has been described in similar terms by many writers: the final stanza of Yeats's "The Circus Animals' Desertion" is among the most famous examples. But this marvelous metamorphosis strikes us as beneficent only because, to use Fyodor's formulation, the pity that produces art is directed at categories of being (inanimate objects, young children) that lack autonomy. This explains why they stand in need of the remedial energies of pity. In his introduction to *Bend Sinister*, Nabokov explains that his own "pang of pity" for his "creature" leads him to dissolve the frame of his fiction by letting Krug know that "he is in good hands," and that "nothing on earth really matters, there is nothing to fear, and death is but a question of style" (*BS* 169). Whereas Fyodor's "royal experiments" remind us that art requires pity, Nabokov's compassionate gesture toward Krug suggests that the traditional subject of fiction—one *not* a "galley slave" but an autonomous agent in a world where actions matter—must come undone before pity can do its work. Like Dostoevsky's Grand Inquisitor who trades security for liberty or Woolf's militant benevolence that "offers help, but desires power,"[13] Krug's salvation comes at the cost of his autonomy.

COURTESY AND UTILITARIANISM

Nabokov's search for a disinterested moral good was animated by a loathing of all forms of determinism. The theories for which he expressed his greatest scorn—Chernyshevsky's rational egoism, Marx's historical materialism, Lenin's Soviet brand of Marxism—are all strictly utilitarian. Though it might seem perverse to submit Nabokov's reflections on courtesy to the yoke of a grand sociopolitical interpretation, doing so brings some important dimensions of his moral allegiances into focus. When Pete Dean takes one look at Hazel and uses the first pretext at hand to facilitate his departure, he could only have done so after making a quick and dirty calculation. Though no doubt unconscious, this calculation can only make sense if driven by a version of the utilitarian logic Nabokov identified as the engine of the Soviet regime's most egregious crimes. As he wrote to Edmund Wilson in a letter from 1940, "Another horrible paradox about Leninism is that these materialists found it possible to squander the lives of millions of real people for the sake of the hypothetical millions that would be happy some day" (*DBDV* 38). Pete is precisely such a flint-eyed utilitarian. In the confusion of his dashed hopes and disappointment, he must have figured that this particular blind date could have no future and that an infinitely better opportunity is lurking around the corner.

Pete and Hazel's ill-fated date urges us to regard the formalities of civilized life as unconditionally valuable. It asks that moral deliberation be freed from questions of pragmatic benefit. In a parallel universe, we might imagine Pete's hormone-soaked desire melting away at the sight of Hazel and disinterested courtesy taking its place. Though it is fruitless to speculate about the outcomes of such a hypothetical scenario (the blind date might have come to a routine, humdrum conclusion, or Hazel might have committed suicide in spite of the date's success), the morally relevant fact is that a courteous response on Pete's part would have absolved him of blame.

Pale Fire and *Ada*, the last two great novels of Nabokov's writing career, underline the importance of formal principles of conduct and the irrelevance of outcomes in moral deliberation. In *Pale Fire*, Pete and Hazel's date ends in tragedy because Hazel dies in the aftermath of a flagrant act of discourtesy. In *Ada*, Van and Lucette's date on a transatlantic liner ends with Lucette's suicide, this time in the wake of Lucette's sublime act of courtesy to the Robinsons. This delicate asymmetry suggests that Nabokov reflected deeply on the role of courtesy in our moral world. As a deontological principle of conduct capable of rising above utilitarian motivations, Nabokovian courtesy may be an artist's response to a political regime that consistently and unapologetically justified the imprisonment and extermination of "undesirables" with the utilitarian argument that the end justifies the means. Pete Dean's caddish response to Hazel adheres to the same logic, and the lesson we are invited to consider remains the same: Peter ought to have been courteous to Hazel not because, as so many fairy tales wistfully have it, she might be a beautiful princess held captive by an evil spell, but precisely because her identity should remain irrelevant. If nothing else, the courtesy that Mrs. Luzhin, Helene, Disa, and Lucette bestow upon their interlocutors casts these arbitrary and superfluous beneficiaries of their courtesy as unconditionally valuable.

Chapter Two

Courtoisie: Une Élégance Morale

> I think one of the very few "practical" actions
> I have ever been guilty of was to use part of
> that crystalline material to obtain an Honours
> degree.
> —Vladimir Nabokov

IN AN AUTOBIOGRAPHICAL poem titled "Youth" ("Iunost'") written in 1923 in Berlin, Nabokov envisions himself and other Russian émigrés as a band of knights in exile:

> My soul has not completed yet the scroll
> of epic wanderings through foreign lands.
> And at the crossroads witches are still
> singing in their seductive rags,
> —but swift's the horse and motionless the rider.
> Still there rises from a secret grotto
> an insane giant of despair, so he could
> hunch over and then hide away once more,
> abiding swiftly to the knight's command.
> Yes, knights . . . our path is simple, iron-clad,
> Alas, our feat is possibly futile,
> But gracious, and clear, and alive . . .[1]

Casting himself in the role of knight-errant, the speaker of these lines articulates a host of moral commitments that will inform Nabokov's ethics to the very end of his life. Though the alien landscapes through which the knight must travel are filled with dangers and temptations, the speaker is optimistic because he possesses a chief virtue of chivalry: self-mastery. This self-mastery is captured in the image of the "motionless horseman" (*vsadnik nedvizhim*[*yi*]) carried by a swiftly moving horse. His "repose," as Fitzgerald's Dick Diver might have called it, protects him from the seductive songs of witches and a giant's paralyzing despair. More important still, it enables him to embark upon a "*podvig*" (feat) that is "*bespoleznyi*" (inutile or futile).

As always in the case of Nabokov, the greater the inutility of an enterprise, the more binding ("*zheleznyi* [made of iron]") and beautiful ("*blagostnyi* [gracious]") it becomes.

D. Barton Johnson has noted that themes related to knightly honor and valor figure prominently in Nabokov's poetry from 1919 to the mid-1920s. Johnson attributes this to the death in combat during the Russian Civil War of Nabokov's cousin and playmate, Yury Rausch von Traubenberg.[2] The death of Nabokov's father a year before Nabokov wrote "Youth" gave the chivalric theme a new impetus. V. D. Nabokov, Nabokov's father, was one of the most distinguished and esteemed leaders of the liberal opposition against tsarist autocracy in late-imperial Russia and, after Lenin's seizure of power, against Soviet rule in the emigration. Nabokov's love and respect for his father are well-known aspects of his biography. The circumstances surrounding his father's death—at an émigré gathering during which V. D. Nabokov was shot as he fought to disarm the assassin who had fired upon a colleague—gave the tragic affair a chivalric inflection. In the mass of tributes, telegrams, and obituaries published in the aftermath of his murder, a number of words borrowed from the lexicon of chivalry were repeatedly used to describe the departed.[3]

By portraying his life's mission in chivalric terms, the young Nabokov was paying tribute to his soldier cousin and his own legendarily heroic father. But he was also breathing new life into the chivalric literature that had played an important role in his own personal biography during his childhood and during the time he spent as a student at Cambridge. As he recounts in *Speak, Memory: An Autobiography Revisited* (1966), his mother frequently read to him (in English) "tales about knights whose terrific but wonderfully aseptic wounds were bathed by damsels in grottoes" (425). He also recalls how his early sympathy for Arthurian chivalry made it impossible for him to understand the appeal of pacifism, and how Arthurian female characters—"Queen Guinevere, Isolda, a not quite merciless *belle dame*"—shaped his feminine ideal when he was eleven years of age (*SM* 377, 533).

During his time at Trinity College, Cambridge, between 1919 and 1922, Nabokov formally studied the chivalric literature of the French Middle Ages for his Modern and Medieval Languages tripos (*VNRY* 170). Months before penning "Youth," Nabokov had been distracted from his poetic labors by a mandatory reading list that included *La Chanson de Roland*, *Aucassin et Nicolette*, and two Arthurian romances—*Erec et Enide* and *Yvain*—by Chrétien de Troyes.[4] Nabokov's allusions in his own work to medieval and Renaissance chivalric texts confirm Boyd's claim that the experience of studying the literature of the French Middle Ages left Nabokov with a lifelong appreciation of it (*VNRY* 174). We might even say that Nabokov cherished this literature as deeply as Pnin cherishes his knowledge that Cinderella's iconic slipper was made not of glass (*verre*) but of fur (*vair*) (*Pnin* 411). Pnin's creator would have come to this knowledge from Chrétien (*Yvain* 1887; *Lancelot* 448, 508–9).

COURTESY AND CHIVALRY

In her study of French Arthurian poetry, E. H. Ruck defines chivalry as "the fusion of prowess—courage, strength and ability in combat—and *courtoisie*."[5] The lodestar of chivalric ethics, courtesy covered a much broader range of signification in the Middle Ages and the Renaissance than it does today. In his *Essai de poétique médiévale* (1972), Paul Zumthor notes that the term was tightly stitched into the idea of civilization: "The word *courtoisie* (*corteisie* in Old French) designates in the twelfth, thirteenth, and fourteenth centuries a specific fact of civilization [*un fait spécifique de civilisation*]." He traces its etymology to the adjective *courtois* (of the *court*) and the Latin *cohors* (a ruler's cohort). The fundamental meaning of *courtois* is, therefore, "that which concerns the court, fitting to the life of a court" (*Essai* 466).

The elaborate ceremonial rituals surrounding a knight's initiation into military service and the growing influence of women among the highest ranks of feudal societies gave *courtoisie* an important aesthetic dimension (*Essai* 467–68). Writing specifically about southern France, Zumthor notes that *courtoisie* was "less an ethics than an aesthetics" (468). *Courtoisie*'s aesthetic attributes were slower to assert themselves in the north of France because of that region's greater emphasis on chivalric action and a military code of ethics. But even in the north, *courtoisie*'s aesthetic elements were visible in values that might have been lifted straight out of Nabokov's early fiction: Zumthor refers to them as "the search for the rare and the strange, in that which pushes the imagination towards reverie or disinterested enterprise" (468).

Zumthor locates the specifically *moral* aspects of courtesy on a spectrum: at one pole, *courtoisie* directed itself toward the creation of "*formes belles*" (as these related to hierarchies of thought, sentiment, conduct, and taste), while at the other it concerned itself with the moral rectitude of particular actions (as defined by norms of conduct at a given court). This proto-Kantian privileging of a formalized code of moral conduct leads Zumthor to define *courtoisie* as "an art of living and a moral refinement [*un art de vivre et une élégance morale*]" (*Essai* 469). As a moral code concerned with the aesthetic, *courtoisie* encompassed both an internal and an external dimension: *corteisie* came to designate inner virtues such as modesty and self-mastery, while *mesure* came to signify their outer expression. A repertoire of ritualized gestures—the greeting, the bow, the kiss of peace, the permission to depart (*congé*) and the farewell—served as visible signs of the inner virtues.[6] The external expressions that convened under the rubric of *mesure*—"moderation of behavior, control over the passions, the spontaneous submission to a code which, in the twelfth century, requires more of an impulse of the heart than obedience to an etiquette" (469)—belong to the same grammar of values and gestures that Nabokov invokes when he describes his band of knights in "Youth." The motionless rider astride a swiftly moving horse and the giant made to return to his grotto by the knight's command are vivid images of the will's authority over the passions and its capacity to find an equilibrium between physical desires and spiritual aspirations. As an ethics and aesthetics of self-mastery, *courtoisie* served as the formal embodiment of that will.

The rising power of the urban bourgeoisie and the collapse of the petty knightly caste led to an erosion of the spiritual and moral dimensions of *courtoisie* (*Essai* 474–75). By the fifteenth century, only its aesthetic qualities survived. As Zumthor concludes, *courtoisie* continued to subsist in the highest circles of the nobility either as an urbane veneer or, nostalgically, as "a myth related to some glorious past that we pretend to revive" (475). Late medieval and Renaissance texts such as Malory's *Le Morte d'Arthur* and Spenser's *The Faerie Queene*, both of which render French Arthurian tales into English and are alluded to in Nabokov's fiction,[7] serve as eloquent expressions of this nostalgia. Looking back to medieval chivalry with the aim "to fashion a gentleman or noble person in vertuous and gentle discipline,"[8] *The Faerie Queene* portrays courtesy as a spiritual virtue that advances the interests of the state and partakes of the beautiful.

Nabokov's "Youth," written not long after his preparations for the tripos, pays homage to the medieval understanding of courtesy as a grammar of morals that weds the ethical to the aesthetic, the material to the spiritual. The poem's speaker predicts with confidence that his band of knights will have preserved throughout their errantry a "slow and fragrant" speech ("*blagoukhannoi medlennost'iu rechi*") and an "ancient simplicity in our / language, our clothes, and reserved movements [*nekoiu starinnoi prostotoi / rechei, odezhd i sderzhannykh dvizhenii*]."[9] As in medieval courtesy, such graces are the external signs of an inner moral fortitude: the knights are said to walk with a "relentless step [*strogoiu stopoi*]" and to accept "no defeat [*ne znaia porazhenii*]."[10] By combining moral discipline with gracious conduct, Nabokov's knights embody the meaning of medieval *courtoisie* as "*un art de vivre*" and "*une élégance morale*." Portraying his own exilic predicament in such terms, Nabokov is also replicating the nostalgia of Renaissance texts that return to the sites of medieval chivalry in search of a purer and more idealistic conception of *courtoisie*.

Chapter Two

COURTESY AND UTILITY

The most direct fictional descendant of "Youth's" band of knights is Martin Edelweiss, the protagonist of Nabokov's fifth novel, *Glory* (*Podvig*, 1932). The translation of the novel's Russian title into English gave Nabokov no end of trouble because *podvig* (the same word he employs to refer to his knights' quest in "Youth") has no English equivalent. Though he concedes that "exploit" comes closest to the meaning of the Russian term, he rejects its utilitarian connotations: "if you once perceive in 'exploit' the verb 'utilize,' gone is the *podvig*, the inutile deed of renown" (*Gl* xii). The *podvig* in question is Martin's decision to cross illegally into Soviet Russia for a mere twenty-four hours. His best friend, the sensible Englishman (and, given the novel's celebration of inutility, fittingly named) Darwin, is unable to see "the purpose" of Martin's mission. Darwin's efforts to see in it a narrative of utility—"Some plot against the good old Soviets? Want to see someone? Deliver a secret message, rig up something?"—signal the poverty of his imagination (*Gl* 199).

The "glory of high adventure and disinterested achievement" (*Gl* xiii) that drives Martin's mission and gives the novel its title openly invokes the chivalric plots Nabokov studied at Cambridge. This is not surprising given that Martin was raised—like his creator—on "the adventures of King Arthur's knights" (*Gl* 6). As scholars of Arthurian romances have frequently observed, a chivalric adventure's *pointlessness* was sometimes its very *point*. As Jean Frappier notes about the mysterious final adventure of *Erec et Enide* known as the "Joie de la Cort," Erec embarks upon it "driven by an act of pure will, by a chivalric amateurishness, and for the beauty of its name, Joy."[11] Its meaning, Frappier concludes, resides "precisely in its seeming superfluity."[12] Reto Bezzola, Sarah Kay, and Ad Putter have broadened the scope of Frappier's insight to argue that all of Erec's adventures seem pointless as they are occurring and become meaningful only after they have been recollected or related to others (*FAR* 170).[13] A deontologist of Nabokov's stripe might point out that such retrospective generation of meaning makes predictive utilitarian calculations unreliable.

Erich Auerbach's version of this argument offers a compelling reading of Martin's motivation for undertaking his journey. Auerbach would have recognized in Martin's aimless mission a chivalric search for "adventure, that is, perilous encounters by which he can prove his mettle."[14] Such adventures, Auerbach insists, served no political function or practical purpose; their only aim was the knight's self-actualization. Indeed, Auerbach treats chivalry as identical with *courtoisie* because he sees both as "directed toward a personal and absolute ideal—absolute both in reference to ideal realization and in reference to the absence of any earthly and practical purpose." Additionally, the virtues that generate this ideal are neither "a gift of nature" nor "acquired by birth," but must be learned through proper training and nurtured through a tireless exercise of the will.[15]

These arguments posit a significant distance between the chivalric search for adventure and utilitarian logic, yet Nabokov's conspicuous efforts to strip considerations of utility from Martin's mission suggest that he remained suspicious of the latent utilitarianism of medieval romance. His suspicions would have been justified, for even the most seemingly pointless adventures described in courtly romances occur within a larger regime of utility. Erec is shown to embark upon an adventure as "splendidly risky" ("*au risque splendide*") and seemingly pointless as Martin's when he undertakes the challenge known as the "Joie de la Cort,"[16] but the broader utility of his chivalric deed is never in question: Erec restores joy to Evrain's court and releases Maboagrain from the bad oath that holds him prisoner. All chivalric *aventure* had clear utility-driven aims and consequences: damsels are rescued from captivity; kingdoms are liberated from spells or tyrants; armies are saved by the self-sacrifice of a few intrepid warriors. What is more, the *glory* earned by such deeds was not disinterested. Knights embarked upon *aventure* in order to prove themselves worthy of the courts to which they wished to belong, and the fame they attained raised their status in the feudal hierarchies in which they dwelled.[17] Even though the meaning of Erec's adventures reveals itself only in hindsight, what is revealed is, to quote Kay, a retrospective "moral usefulness": Erec's adventures demonstrate that he has proven himself worthy of the coronation that marks the end of his errantry.[18]

The title of Nabokov's poem—"Youth"—signals an additional semantic and moral dimension of the implicit utility of medieval *courtoisie*. As Zumthor notes, the Occitan term *joven* (*jouvent* in French, from the Latin *juventus*) became attached to *courtoisie* and came to designate a quality that is central to Nabokov's ethics. To quote Zumthor's formulation, it signaled "a readiness without any forethought or calculation [*une disponibilité sans arrière-pensée ni calcul*], a natural propensity for giving and for love" (*Essai* 470). As T. A. Shippey notes, this "youthful" aspect of medieval courtesy and chivalric *aventure* might lead the modern reader to view it as "the ethic of an adolescent, or of a gambler."[19] Yet this ethic of "merriment and 'panache'"[20] had an important social and political meaning in the Middle Ages. The apparent pointlessness of so many chivalric adventures was "based on an awareness that stasis in realms or relationships can only be maintained by effort, action, reconquest. To hold anything, it has now and again to be risked." For Shippey, the "deliberate recklessness" and "seeming irresponsibility" of chivalric plots had a clear utilitarian function: it led to "an affirmation of the community of a court."[21]

Nabokov's effort to drain utility from the topos of the chivalric quest is one of the most significant features of his moral philosophy. But as in the case of the medieval romances he studied at Cambridge, such an effort is not to be misinterpreted as an indifference to suffering and injustice. Nabokov's fictional worlds are replete with what Susan Elizabeth Sweeney calls, on the subject of *Bend Sinister*, "unspeakable crimes, illegitimate sentences, specious punishments, and only the most tenuous sense of justice."[22] Additionally, as Zoran Kuzmanovich has noted, the worst of the crimes that drive his plots—kidnapping, rape, torture, and murder—are directed against children.[23] It is precisely Nabokov's recognition of the world's darkness and his refusal to place his characters into the service of dispelling that darkness that makes *Glory* such a puzzling and disquieting work.

Martin's suicidal "high deed" (*Gl* 204) begins to take shape during a conversation with a friend of the Zilanovs. The friend, Mrs. Gruzinov, explains to Martin that the Zilanovs' niece, Irina, suffers from a debilitating "mental deficiency" and that this irreversible condition is the consequence of having been sexually and psychologically traumatized during the Civil War. Irina's story hardens Martin's resolve to see his homeland again and thereby sets in motion a plot that is self-consciously modeled upon a chivalric quest. Even Soviet Russia takes on a name in Martin's imagination that seems more fitting for a medieval than a modern landscape: "The night of Zoorland seemed to him even darker, its wildwood deeper, and Martin already knew that nothing and nobody could prevent him from penetrating, as a free pilgrim, into those woods, where plump children are tortured in the dark, and a smell of burning and of putrefaction permeates the air" (*Gl* 150). But unlike the traditional chivalric quest, Martin's mission to prove his courage by penetrating into a landscape polluted by unspeakable crimes seems exclusively concerned with the ideal of self-mastery. He has no intention to rescue anyone, and the structure of the novel makes no attempt to suggest that he will.

In articulating the tension that unsettles our response to *Glory*, David Rampton notes that whatever victory is attained by Martin's high deed lies on the side of the tyrants: Martin's exploit simply adds his own life to the ledger of the dead, while Irina's blighted life remains unaltered. Yet, as Rampton observes further, the novel devotes much of its energy to preventing such a reading from coming into focus.[24] For Rampton, the gap between the high courage privileged by the novel and its nugatory benefits animates what he calls Nabokov's aesthetics of moral contradiction. Rampton does not dwell on the theoretical consequences of his observations, but his analysis makes visible Nabokov's effort to strip utility-driven calculations from the logic of moral deliberation. The contradiction noted by Rampton emerges only in a consequentialist moral reckoning wherein the moral merit of an action is judged by its consequences. For a deontologist like Kant, however, the expected futility of an action is morally irrelevant. Nabokov seems to go even farther than Kant by suggesting that the expected futility of Martin's exploit is the very ground of its virtue.

Though Martin is the most direct inheritor of the chivalric ideal Nabokov claims as his own in "Youth," residues of that ideal pervade Nabokov's fiction. Sebastian Knight's adoption of his British mother's family name signals not only his interest in chess (he signs his juvenilia with a black chess knight), but also his chivalric imagination. This second layer of signification is signaled by his response to his father's death in a duel fought on behalf of Sebastian's long-dead mother. The bitterness Sebastian felt toward his father after his father's remarriage turns into "ecstatic worship" when he learns "the reason of his father's fatal duel" (*RLSK* 13). While his half-brother V. can make no sense of their father's decision to risk his life in a duel for the reputation of a dead woman who abandoned him and their son, the duel fires Sebastian's imagination (*RLSK* 8–9).[25]

The chivalric ideal also survives in minor characters that cross the stage of Nabokov's fiction only to showcase their devotion to a chivalric code of ethics. Captain Belov, the scrupulously loyal friend of Sebastian and V.'s father, risks the severe legal repercussions that attach to participating in duels for the sake of serving as his friend's second. In the years following his friend's death, Belov risks his life to help his friend's family and is arrested and shot by Russian revolutionaries in the very act of rendering assistance (*RLSK* 8–9, 18–19). In *Bend Sinister*, the same principled loyalty and generosity are found in Krug's friend, the prosaic and colorless Maximov, who discerns no aesthetic reverberation in the word "loyalty," and yet worries about the misfortunes of his friends more than he worries about his own. The analogy that concludes Maximov's portrait is a vestige of the chivalric ethos: "had he been an old sea captain," the narrator explains, "he would have dutifully gone down with his ship rather than plump apologetically into the last lifeboat" (*BS* 237). Like their medieval forebears, Belov and Maximov take great risks to render assistance to others (*RLSK* 19; *BS* 247), and they do so without the expectation of recognition or reward.

FREEDOM AND UTOPIA

By severing utility from the chivalric ideal, Nabokov asserts the existence of something he cherished above all else: a radical conception of personal freedom. Like Kant, he located freedom in the human capacity to perform moral acts for their own sake rather than for the sake of a greater good. Nabokov understood consequentialism as a form of utopianism, and utopian thinking, in turn, as a form of tyranny incompatible with freedom. His views had an important precedent in an essay by a close acquaintance, the Kantian philosopher Sergey Hessen.

Hessen advanced this argument in an essay published in 1931 under the title "Bor'ba utopii i avtonomii dobra v mirovozzrenii F.M. Dostoevskogo i Vl. Solov'eva" ("The Struggle between Utopia and the Autonomy of the Good in the Worldviews of F.M. Dostoevsky and Vl. Soloviev"). The essay made its Russian debut in volumes 45 and 46 of *Sovremennye zapiski* (*Contemporary Annals*), which also carried installments of Nabokov's *Podvig*.[26] Hessen's two-part essay was highly regarded in the émigré circles in which he and Nabokov moved. Before its publication in *Sovremennye zapiski*, it had appeared in German in *Die Pädagogische Hochschule* and in French in *Le Monde Slave*. Its main argument has much in common with the ethics of *Glory*. The simultaneous publication of Hessen's essay and Nabokov's *Glory* between the same covers of Nabokov's favorite "thick journal" suggests that Nabokov's tendency to see consequentialism as a version of utopianism and, in turn, utopian conceptions of the good as threats to personal freedom, was part of an ideological stance shared by other Russian émigrés.

Hessen begins his essay with the claim that, in *The Brothers Karamazov*, Dostoevsky repudiates his utopian social idea of free theocracy. In Hessen's account, Dostoevsky triumphs over "the poison of utopia [*iad utopii*]" that infected him in his youth when he begins to recognize that utopia and personal freedom are incompatible ("Bor'ba" 621n1). As Hessen puts it, "the essence of any utopia lies in the abolition of human freedom" ("Bor'ba" 625). In *The Brothers Karamazov*, Hessen argues, Dostoevsky's "philosophy of the Good [*filosofiia Dobra*]" overcomes the utopianism of his earlier thinking, and human freedom becomes the cornerstone of his newly reconfigured worldview ("Bor'ba" 618–21).

Like many Russians living in exile, Hessen was consumed by the need to find an explanation for his country's postrevolutionary disasters. The essay's topicality is not explicitly stated, but the implication that utopianism had a hand in Russia's recent tragedy is transparently clear. Nabokov expressed his own conviction that utopianism was ultimately to blame for Russia's calamities in a letter to Edmund Wilson written nine years after the publication of Hessen's essay: "The paradox which explodes Marxism and other dreams of the Ideal State is that the first author is potentially the first tyrant of that state" (*DBDV* 36). In the same letter, Nabokov attempts to refute the very possibility of achieving an ideal state by arguing—in Kantian fashion—that consequences are intrinsically unpredictable: "Such is the artistic deceptiveness of nature's methods that the thing that eventually brings the most evil or the most benefit to most people is an unpredictable casual freak of a thing which could never have been suspected of developing into a general boon or blight. How glum Engels would have looked were he shown some modern factories" (*DBDV* 37).

Nabokov's desire to divorce chivalric ideals from utilitarian considerations is analogous to Hessen's desire to see in Dostoevsky's final novel a Kantian prioritization of personal autonomy over the common good. The moral good that survives Nabokov's and Hessen's critiques makes freedom an absolute value, or, to use Kantian terminology, an end in itself. To count as moral, an action must be irreducible to interest, inclination, or desire, and must be chosen for its own sake. The acts of courtesy showcased in Nabokov's fiction qualify as autonomous by virtue of their extreme inconvenience and glaring lack of benefits. It is worth noting that these emblematic acts of courtesy are typically associated with women in Nabokov's fiction. By contrast, male characters frequently exhibit moral excellence through behaviors that underscore the status of courtesy as a cardinal virtue of chivalry: they show sympathy for the underdog, conduct themselves gallantly in duels, and remain staunchly loyal to friends, wives, and lovers. These chivalrous actions serve as proof of their performers' personal freedom and as a marker of respect owed to those to whom these acts are directed.

Nabokov structures his fictions in such a way as to forestall the consequentialist argument that respect qualifies as a utilitarian good. Though the duel fought by V. and Sebastian's father gains Sebastian's affection and respect, its devastating consequences far outweigh these benefits. The acts of courtesy performed by Helene, Disa, and Lucette have trivial benefits relative to the emotional toll exacted by their performance. There is a glaring imbalance between the enormous effort required by their execution and the little good they attain. The acts of courtesy *Pnin*'s narrator or Pnin himself imagines Mira to have performed in the face of imminent death—distilled in the words "still smiling"—seem especially futile. While the elasticity of the utility principle makes it difficult to identify a value capable of eluding the ever-expanding net of consequentialist logic, it is nonetheless possible to say that Nabokov's ethical commitments are utilitarian in the narrowest possible sense. This minimalist usefulness might be compared to the way in which Kant's formula of the Kingdom of Ends can be said to be utilitarian—that is, as an ideal of *universal* dignity and respect.

COURTESY AND LOVE

The formal inventiveness of Nabokov's fictions has made it difficult to see the moral conservatism that structures his worldview. Only recently have scholars begun to acknowledge this.[27] For instance, Gennady Barabtarlo argues that the moral principles Nabokov espoused were not much different than the commandments spelled out in Deuteronomy and that his "old-fashioned high-principled morality" was not much different from that of Dante.[28] According to Barabtarlo, most of Nabokov's novels are studies in a self-absorbing passion that curtails moral judgment and responsiveness to another's pain: "Passion, if allowed to develop unchecked, leads to insanity, death, and perdition."[29] But in spite of seeing passion as the archenemy of moral conduct in Nabokov's fictional worlds, Barabtarlo exempts love from the category of the passions because of love's redemptive capacity to provide "a protective and beautifying coat of grace on drab reality and personal misery."[30]

The role that Barabtarlo assigns to love parallels the role that Shade assigns to pity when he tells Kinbote that "pity is the password" (*PF* 601). Yet neither love nor pity qualifies as a volitional moral act in Nabokov's work. Love and pity are involuntary passions in his moral worldview even if they connect to wider schemes of voluntary conduct such as marital fidelity or parental solicitude. In Nabokov's most autobiographical novel, *The Gift* (*Dar*, 1952), love and pity are portrayed as miraculous gifts. The gift of pity enables Fyodor to become an artist; the gift of love lies at the core of his relationship with Zina. The significance of the *unearned* beneficence of these gifts is signaled both in the novel's title and in Fyodor's ecstatic wonder that he should be their recipient (*Gift* 328). But the same mysterious gifts that enliven Fyodor's life manifest themselves in destructive ways elsewhere in Nabokov's fiction. Unlike Fyodor's literary creativity, Luzhin's chess-playing gift is a source of suffering. Humbert's love for Dolly and Shade's pity for Hazel injure as reliably as Albinus's lack of love for his family or Van's lack of pity for the victims of his vengeance.

In the literature that served as the foundation for Nabokov's studies at Cambridge, love played a key role in the chivalric ideal. Aldo Scaglione defines "the perfect knight" of courtly romance as one "who joins in his exemplary person the leading qualities of *arma*, *amor*, and *litterae*—the valor of the fighter, the refinement of the true lover, and the sophistication of the educated man of society."[31] Additionally, in the "all-important coupling of love and valor, *amor et militia*," the former characteristically served as the motivation for the latter.[32] At the same time, however, love was understood to belong to the order of the passions and, as a passion, was continually at risk of colliding with duty. In three works on Nabokov's reading list at Cambridge—*Erec et Enide*, *Yvain*, and *Aucassin et Nicolette*—romantic love is portrayed both as the most formidable enemy of chivalry and as its most reliable spur.

Love is central to chivalric romance because it puts other bonds to the test. In *Aucassin et Nicolette*, an anonymous medieval French *cantefable* (a story to be partly sung and partly told) that Nabokov both studied and admired (*VNRY* 174), Aucassin's love for Nicolette causes him to abscond from his responsibilities as the defender of his father's realm. The conceit that the lovesick Aucassin cannot fight for thinking of his beloved is a satirical reversal of the metaphor that Nabokov invokes as an idealized version of himself in "Youth." Though Nabokov's "motionless" rider is homesick rather than lovesick, he exhibits total control over his horse. By contrast, Aucassin "was thinking so intently about Nicolette that the reins fell from his hands and he completely forgot what it was he'd come to do! His horse, still feeling the sting of the spurs, carried him into the press of the battle and straight into the hands of the opposition."[33] Falling into enemy hands, Aucassin becomes doubly captive as a prisoner of love and a prisoner of war.

Love is represented as a similar threat to social duty in *Erec et Enide*: marriage has a disastrous effect on the chivalric career of Erec, the Knight of the Sparrowhawk, until his young wife, Enide, chastises him for dereliction of duty. The eponymous hero of *Yvain* avoids a similar charge of "*recreantise*" thanks to the intervention of Gawain, who reminds him of the shame suffered by knights who neglected their chivalric obligations for the pleasures of matrimony (*Yvain* 2484–88). Yvain is successfully reunited with his wife only after he has found a means of combining his love for her with a continued commitment to chivalric endeavor.

In Nabokov's fictional worlds, love similarly needs the restraining powers of the will to harmonize with duty. Romantic love in Nabokov's fiction is cruelly inconstant (Albinus, Sebastian) or tyrannically durable (Pnin, Van), a gift (Fyodor, Krug, Shade) or a curse (Pnin, Kinbote, Hugh). While Nabokov seems to embrace the conventional distinction between carnal and spiritual love in his earlier fictions, the distinction loses legitimacy by the time V. is made to quote from Sebastian's autobiographical novel *Lost Property*. As the writer of the letter tells the woman he has ceased to love, "It would be absurd of me to try and persuade you that you were the pure love, and that this other passion is but a comedy of the flesh. All is flesh and all is purity" (*RLSK* 88). His conclusion that "there is something essentially wrong about love" (*RLSK* 87) seems to emerge from the fact that love has stripped him of freedom and self-worth.

Nabokov's treatment of love in the four greatest achievements of his English-language fiction is far more disturbing than most readers of Nabokov are willing to concede. Such readers are especially—and for good reason—reluctant to agree with Humbert that he *loved* Dolly, given the cruelty and suffering he visited upon her. Lust or sexual obsession, they might say, are far more appropriate terms for Humbert's driving emotion toward her. In spite of its wide range of meanings, love implies a desire to protect rather than hurt and an inclination toward tenderness rather than cruelty. The suffering Humbert inflicts upon Dolly refutes his claim that he loved her during their period of cohabitation.

Nabokov, however, destabilizes taxonomic distinctions between different kinds of love by portraying love as resistant to schemas of categorization. His representations of erotic love run the gamut from the lyrically redemptive (as in the case of Fyodor with Zina) to the destructively narcissistic (as in the case of Humbert with Dolly or Van with Ada). Yet to draw the kinds of distinctions that might reserve the word "love" for Fyodor and Zina, but deny it to Humbert or Van, would be as unsatisfying as saying that Swann—given his obsessive jealousy—did not *truly* love Odette or that Tatyana—given her capacity to subordinate love to higher moral principles—did not *truly* love Onegin.

Nabokov's depiction of parental love is almost as troubling as his depictions of erotic love. Whereas Krug's love for his son makes him do whatever it takes to protect David, the love the Shades bear their daughter is not sufficiently transformative to make them empathize with her interest in the paranormal or to forget about her physical unattractiveness by focusing on her human essence. Yet, *Pale Fire* is not structured in such a way as to cast blame on the Shades; rather, their love is portrayed as a mystery that is as bewildering to them as to the reader. To conclude that the Shades did not love their daughter because their feelings toward her did not conform to a formulaic conception of parental love would be as misleading as concluding that Medea felt no love for her children when she murdered them or that Cholly Breedlove did not love Pecola when he raped her. (Toni Morrison's narrator insists that he did.)[34] Love's murky geometry—whether parental or erotic, or sometimes, harrowingly, both—is as ultimately confounding in Nabokov's novels as it is for Beckett's Molloy, who—in spite of having "toiled and moiled" at the act of sexual intercourse—still cannot be certain if what he experienced was "true love."[35]

The issue at hand is captured in the words "true" and "truly," and in our effort to establish such a comforting distinction. Nabokov's suggestion that love might be the right word for all of these extremes is disturbing, but it also underscores our desire to align love with the moral virtues. Far from ennobling Humbert by laying claim to "love" as a term that describes his emotions for Dolly, I am suggesting instead that Nabokov wants us to see the desperate and destructive elements that sometimes lurk within the term. The reflections on love that conclude Morrison's *The Bluest Eye* might serve as a fitting assessment of *Lolita*: "Love is never any better than the lover. Wicked people love wickedly, violent people love violently, weak people love weakly, stupid people love stupidly. . . . The loved one is shorn, neutralized, frozen in the glare of the lover's inward eye."[36] A century earlier, Anna Karenina anticipated these reflections on love when she observes that "there are as many kinds of love as there are hearts."[37] In reminding us that love is an unruly and amoral *passion* that is not—in itself—a moral virtue, Nabokov joins a long tradition of writers who similarly viewed love with both amazement and suspicion.

Love is as frequently unwelcome in Nabokov's fictional worlds as it is celebrated. Humbert's tyrannical love for Dolly serves as the most devastating example of such love. But even Pnin's humiliating love for Liza or Lucette's abject love for Van underscores love's double life as both blessing and affliction. Given its variety and murkiness, love needs the remedial powers of courtesy to suppress its propensity for cruelty and violence. As Zumthor observes, *courtoisie* played a central role in regulating the mechanisms by which romantic and conjugal love was perceived and practiced in the Middle Ages. In the south of France, love was understood as the nourishment and justification of *cortezia*. In the north, *courtoisie* dictated the rules of engagement between lovers. Grounded in generosity, discretion, and mutual fidelity, the art of courteous love included a complex repertoire of subtle exchanges of kindness and refined gestures of respect and affection (*Essai* 470–71). In a work from 1909 that Nabokov might have read while studying for his tripos, his compatriot Myrrha Borodine refers to Chrétien's conception of *amour courtois* as an "art of loving of such subtle a delicacy [*art d'aimer d'une délicatesse si subtile*]."[38] Henri Dupin agrees with Zumthor that courtesy was understood as a protocol of conduct for lovers: "Courtesy assumes and prescribes love and a certain manner of loving [*une certaine façon d'aimer*]."[39] The most important component of this courteous "manner of loving" was loyalty and fidelity: the lover had to show an unconditional "*loyauté et fidelité*" to love itself and to his "preferred and beloved lady."[40]

Courtesy is a supreme virtue in Nabokov's moral universe because it serves as a counterweight to the passions. Capable of operating not only in the absence of virtuous emotions but even in opposition to them, it serves a remedial role in a world characterized by a tragic asymmetry between inclination and doing what is right. Barabtarlo's hypothesis that Sebastian Knight is V.'s invention because his name is a near-anagram of "Knight Is Absent"[41] has both aesthetic and moral implications. "Knight is absent" might be the secret near-anagram embedded in Sebastian Knight's name because Sebastian's treatment of Clare betrays the chivalric code of conduct evoked by his adopted family name and his personal code of ethics. Sebastian forfeits the appellation of "knight" because he has failed to show loyalty and fidelity to the woman to whom he considers himself to be "sort of married" (*RLSK* 83). Within the lexicon of medieval ethics, he becomes a "*traître*" of "*l'amour courtois*" and chivalry itself.[42] Sebastian is a latter-day Yvain, whose betrayal of his vow to Laudine to return to her within a year's time transforms him from the "*amans verais*" and "*loiaus*" into "the disloyal, the deceitful, / The lying, the devious, / Who mocked and duped her" (*Yvain* 2605, 2719–21).

COURTESY AND PITY

Unlike love, pity was not considered to be an involuntary response in the literary works that constituted Nabokov's reading list at Cambridge or the Renaissance texts that nostalgically revisit those works. In her index of themes and motifs in twelfth-century French Arthurian poetry, Ruck locates pity under the rubric "courtesy to others."[43] In a similar vein, Dupin sees medieval "*pitié*" as the companion virtue of "*bonté*" (goodness) and sees both as key components of courtesy.[44] (What is more, Dupin reminds us that medieval texts frequently defined courtesy in terms that modern audiences identify with pity: namely, "the faculty of sympathy for the joy or sorrows of others.")[45] Though pity was conceived to be innate under ideal conditions, it had to be constructed through discipline, prayer, and practice when such ideal conditions were absent. Shade fears that there is something demonic about his pity for Hazel, but medieval and early modern writers were unequivocal in their view that pity was a virtuous and humanizing emotion. Pious Christians were expected to cultivate pity in order to overcome the promptings of original sin, and Arthur's knights were moved by pity to perform acts of courtesy or to embark upon perilous journeys to end the sufferings of others (*Erec* 1747–58; *Yvain* 3936–47, 4064–69, 4351–54).

Nabokov seems to agree with Shade and the medieval writers he read for his tripos about the vital importance of pity, but he also seems to suggest that there is something as "essentially wrong" about pity as Sebastian's narrator says there is about love (*RLSK* 87). Vladimir Vladimirovich's offer of employment to Pnin is rejected out of hand because Pnin's amour propre prevents him from accepting offers driven by pity. Wood's claim that Pnin's departure from Waindell is an "escape from pity" rings true.[46] Shade intuits—belatedly—that pity needs a screen to conceal its demonic dimension (*PF* line 327), and that he and Sybil ought to have shielded Hazel from their pity. Ada justifies her sexual infidelities by assuring Van that only her poor "feminine pity" made her become the mistress of Phillip Rack and Percy de Prey. She flatters Van by claiming that he is "above pity" because his "ego is richer and prouder than anything those two poor worms could imagine" (*A* 154).

By way of these examples, Nabokov highlights a key aspect of courtesy: namely, that courtesy is less an ecology of virtues than a technology for their proper expression. Unlike love and pity, courtesy cannot be felt but only performed. As John Erskine Hankins notes, "Courtesy becomes a virtue only in the exercise, for we can hardly think of a person as showing courtesy if he never sees or speaks to anyone else."[47] This leads Richard Chamberlain to suggest that courtesy is not technically a virtue but "a mode of behavior" or "a relational mode."[48] While courtesy can be productively identified as an act of kindness triggered by pity, not all expressions of pity are courteous. As the examples of Pnin and Hazel suggest, pity—unconcealed and unadorned by the habits of courtesy—is often unwelcome.

"To inferiors we owe," Kant is recorded by Herder as having said to his students, "not *favour* merely, but a courteous attitude; to superiors, not hatred, but courtesies; for *they are simply equals*. *All favour* is offensive" (*LE* 27:72; emphasis in original). These words give voice to a decidedly modern suspicion of pity. The idea that "*all favour* is offensive" indicts pity for its patronizing instincts, but such an indictment seems predicated upon an egalitarian ideal that trivializes the distance between high and low. The claim that pity humiliates would have struck thinkers and writers from antiquity to the Renaissance as specious. As a counterclaim to Kant's assertion that all "are simply equals," pity is morally imperative in a world in which inequality and its companion hardships are not only real but acknowledged to be so. These same thinkers and writers would have argued that pity was a means of conceptualizing, at the level of involuntary or constructed emotional responses, the possibility of human fellowship in rigidly stratified societies. This alone helps us to see the importance of the fact that the French word *pitié* emerges directly from the Latin *pietas*, which marks the possibility of connection across even greater hierarchical distinctions, in this case between the human and the divine.

Kant's anxiety that certain compassionate behaviors can demean and degrade hovers over most encounters between social unequals in Nabokov's work. When Sebastian retraces his steps on a Paris street because he has "cut a beggar," he seems less worried about the beggar's poverty (the act of giving him money is merely implied) than about the beggar's delicate ego (he reads "carefully" the handbill that the old man is distributing; *RLSK* 84). Sebastian's self-reproach ("Wait a minute, this won't do. I have cut a beggar . . .") suggests that he sees his offense as a failure against the standards of courtesy. Like the part of rhetoric we call "decorum," courtesy involves a host of interrelated judgments about what *will* or *will not do*. Just as courtly love involved a repertoire of amorous gestures, pity needs (to quote Dupin) "*une certaine façon*" of expression. Like Kant's admonition to his students about the debts of courtesy, Sebastian's reasons for retracing his steps because "this won't do" are not meant to suggest that pity is unimportant or less important than courtesy. Rather, as Herder's notes indicate, it is not *merely* favor that is owed to the less privileged. What is also owed is a commitment to an esteem-based dignity that, to quote Kant again, only "a courteous attitude" can provide.

COURTESY AND CLASS

As an ideal of knightly conduct elaborated from the imperative to distinguish mounted warriors (*chevaliers*) from foot soldiers, and nobles from commoners, *courtoisie* is inseparable from questions of class. Norbert Elias observes that courtesy developed in the Middle Ages as a reflection of aristocratic self-consciousness and efforts at self-legitimation.[49] Thus, in its most succinct definition, *courtoisie* is conduct that is proper to a court and, consequently, is often treated as a synonym of "courtliness." Nonetheless, its precise meaning was ceaselessly constructed and debated across the medieval texts that Nabokov read for his tripos. In its blend of compassion, generosity, humility, piety, gracefulness, and politeness, courtesy tended to be depicted as an act of kindness born of pity. Such acts involved succoring the afflicted, defending the weak, showing hospitality, and giving advice to those in need. Unlike charity, however, courtesy was intent upon preserving the dignity of both parties. Courteous acts had to be performed in ways that were not degrading. In *Yvain*, we see this element of courtesy when Arthur hastens to dismount from his horse as soon as he glimpses Laudine coming toward him to hold up his stirrup (*Yvain* 2372–77). By the same logic that makes Arthur unwilling to allow Laudine to lower herself before him, *dis*courteous behavior was related to inhospitality, insult, and slander.

Nabokov rejected social utopias because he believed them to be incompatible with freedom, yet he was sensitive to the suffering and hardship caused by social inequality. In his lecture "Russian Writers, Censors, and Readers," he depicts art as the offspring of the conflict between *what is* and *what ought to be*: "In the process of . . . defining the forces which struggled for the possession of the artist's soul," he notes, "I may, if I am lucky, tap the deep pathos that pertains to all authentic art because of the breach between its eternal values and the sufferings of a muddled world." This breach was particularly acute in Russia for "in the days of Pushkin or Gogol a large majority of the Russian nation was left out in the cold in a veil of slow snow beyond the amber-bright windows, and this was a tragic result of the fact that a most refined European culture had arrived too fast in a country famous for its misfortunes, famous for the misery of its numberless humble lives" (*LRL* 2).

As part of his effort to "tap," as he puts it, the "deep pathos" generated by the collision between the eternal values of art and the sufferings of a muddled world, Nabokov's definition of "authentic art" has something important in common with *courtoisie*, where the latter is understood as a mode of conduct that helps navigate a world entrenched in social hierarchies. As Zumthor notes, medieval *courtoisie* served as a circuit between two nodes of signification: whereas the *moral* node articulated individual qualities, the *social* node referred to the qualities obtaining in the collective. In both of these semantic orientations, moral status is connected to social status: *courtois* was understood as the antithesis of *vilain* (peasant, commoner) and *courtoisie* as the antithesis of *vilenie* (baseness, commonness, vileness). These dualities were caught in a dialectical tension, yielding paradoxical combinations such as "*un vilain courtois* [a courteous commoner]" (*Essai* 466). For Dupin, the pervasiveness of such combinations marked an implicit protest against class inequality and an appeal to divine justice to establish a hierarchy based exclusively on moral principles.[50] For Scaglione, the opposition *courtoisie/ vilenie* signals that *courtoisie* was understood to "perform a metaphysical function analogous to the theological one of divine grace." That is, *courtoisie* "acquired a transsocial value implying secular transcendence of social limitations: thus the poor or landless knights, even when nonnoble by feudal standards, could be redeemed and ennobled by courtesy alone."[51]

The term's aspirational migration from the social to the moral sphere is highlighted in *Aucassin et Nicolette*. Here, as elsewhere in the literature of the Middle Ages, courtesy designates a nobility of spirit: Nicolette, the story's female protagonist and a Saracen converted to Christianity, is a lady by nature rather than by birth, and the humble watchman who saves her is a gentleman of the spirit: "a worthy man, / valiant, polite and wise."[52] Revisiting the sites of medieval chivalry from the vantage point of the Renaissance, Spenser claims that courtesy can be found everywhere, from Calidore's courtly "gracious speach" (*FQ* 6.1.2.6) to the Salvage Man's "senselesse words" (*FQ* 6.4.11.8).

Nabokov learned about the role of courtesy in a stratified society from his parents. At the "court" that served as the training ground for his moral education, courtesy's egalitarian aspirations were often on display. In *Speak, Memory*, for instance, he recalls being invited with his father by the village schoolmaster for what turned out to be "a complex and lovingly planned meal" (*SM* 490). Like Spenser's Knight of Courtesy, who accepts without fussiness the hospitality of rustics (*FQ* 6.9.7), V. D. Nabokov's conduct in the schoolmaster's humble home is presented as a master class in the art of courtesy. As father and son sat down to enjoy the schoolmaster's meal, "the door flew open and Hristofor, a blue-nosed footman in a woman's woolen kerchief, ushered in sideways, with an idiotic smile, a huge luncheon basket packed with viands and wines that my tactless grandmother . . . had thought necessary to send us, in case the schoolmaster's fare proved insufficient. Before our host had time to feel hurt, my father sent the untouched hamper back, with a brief note that probably puzzled the well-meaning old lady as most of his actions puzzled her" (*SM* 491). This skillfully deployed act of courtesy impressed upon the young Nabokov the same moral lesson Kant tried to instill in his own students: that courtesy is a moral obligation "which has beauty because it springs from *equality*, and goes with self-esteem" (*LE* 27:72).

Yet Kant's formulation fails to account for the inverse relationship between social rank and moral concern that is also part of the dialectical tension between *courtoisie* and *vilenie*. Like other modern writers intensely preoccupied with courtesy, Nabokov was attuned to courtesy's efforts to diminish the pain associated with social inequality even as it served as a mechanism for entrenching such inequality. Marina Veen's "morbid fear of 'offending an inferior'" (*A* 59) implies that she has fully absorbed the basic rule of courtesy spelled out by Austen's Mr. Weston when he reminds his son, Frank, that he must treat Jane Fairfax with a *greater* attentiveness when she is residing with her impoverished relatives than "when she was the equal of everybody" in the home of the prosperous Campbells.[53]

Though Richard Rorty may be right when he states that Nabokov and Proust are writers preoccupied with individual perfectionism rather than human solidarity,[54] Rorty's claim becomes especially fruitful if this ideal of individual perfectionism is understood as ineluctably relational. In the medieval texts Nabokov studied at Cambridge, this was an axiomatic truth. As Shippey notes, a knight's setting out on *aventure* was a project of self-improvement whose ulterior motive was the "re-establishment of social bonds": the many trials that Erec must endure are tests of worthiness, and the poem ends with his coronation.[55] Such an ethics of perfectionism—at once personal and communitarian—turns on the same logic that moved Spenser to make Calidore, the Knight of Courtesy, set out alone on his quest. Calidore's solitariness is not to be understood as an indifference to the communal: as Richard Chamberlain and Teskey remind us, Spenserian courtesy is a longing for community and, as such, it shares important bonds of kinship with solidarity ("CT" 352–53).[56]

Yet Rorty's alignment of Nabokov with Proust is apt, for Proust, too, understood courtesy as a matter of providing the other—regardless of the other's social rank—with "the highest idea of himself" (*SLT* 3.587; *RTP* 2.721; NRF 4.2.109). By retracing his steps to read the handbill hawked by the beggar whom he had initially failed to acknowledge, Sebastian is conceding the beggar's right to self-regard and to the regard of others. This acknowledgment might be called a "street" version of the courtesy that Gawain shows throughout his long career as a paragon of courtesy. In *Erec et Enide*, he helps the maiden whose knight Erec has vanquished dismount from her horse and welcomes her to Arthur's court (*Erec* 1177–78). In *Sir Gawain and the Green Knight*, he shows the same high regard for the chatelaine when he interprets her flirtatious discourse in a way that reflects no discredit upon her.

Nabokov knew that courtesy was merely a palliative for living in what he called (perhaps channeling Stephen Blackpool) a "muddled world" (*LRL* 2). And when this awareness struck him with particular force, he too could view the refinements of courtesy with suspicion. In a story titled "The Circle" ("Krug," 1934), a satellite of *The Gift* and arguably Nabokov's most sensitive treatment of class, Innokenty Bychkov is the son of a fictional schoolmaster drawn in the image of the schoolmaster who serves lunch to the Nabokovs in *Speak, Memory*. Innokenty, a "stern plebeian," is "suffocated" by the "hatred" he feels for the wealthy and aristocratic Godunov-Cherdyntsevs, and no courtesy on their part can assuage the shame and scorn he feels in the face of his father's "grateful servility" (*SVN* 372). Nabokov indicts his gloomy protagonist for feeling "overkeenly the social side of things" (*SVN* 375), but he also admits that there is good reason for him to have felt this way. In spite of having extricated Innokenty's father from a "tacky political affair" that would have banished him "to the backwoods of the empire," and in spite of having invited him to participate in name-day celebrations and open-air amusements, Godunov-Cherdyntsev and his family did "not really" admit the young Innokenty "to the center of their existence" (*SVN* 372, 378). Never invited into the house, never included in an informal family meal, he experiences their courtesy as distance.

Unlike love, courtesy can only hang on the fringes of human intimacy. Like Woolf's Lily Briscoe, who realizes that the "usual tricks" of courtesy preclude the possibility of genuine human contact,[57] Innokenty feels marginalized and insulted because the Godunov-Cherdyntsevs offer him courtesy instead of love. When he meets Countess Godunov-Cherdyntsev many years later in Paris, she greets him with perfect courtesy: "'Of course I remember you, how could I not remember?' she said, gazing not at his face but over his shoulder as if somebody were standing behind him (she had a slight squint)." Yet this graceful greeting—claiming as it does that Innokenty is unforgettable—also suggests, by way of the Countess's squint—that it is not Innokenty himself who is imprinted on her memory. Rather, it is the lost life of aristocratic refinement and the people whom she has loved and lost that the Countess cannot forget. These losses plunge the Countess into the "momentary trance" from which she must recover before she can bring herself to invite Innokenty into her squalid Parisian flat (*SVN* 379). To Innokenty she speaks the language of courtesy, but the squinty gaze that glides past him speaks the language of lost love.

COURTESY, TIMELINESS, AND THE UTILITARIAN CALCULUS

Like the carnivalesque energies of fairy tales, courtesy's egalitarian instincts are as fugitive as the encounters in which they dwell. Bounded by narrow spatial and temporal horizons, courtesy bolsters claims such as those of Nancy Davis and Charles Taylor when they assert that deontological systems such as Kant's are disappointingly thin and morally uninspiring.[58] Unlike consequentialist models, which are always on the lookout for ways to increase the good, deontological models limit themselves to special obligations, restrictions, prohibitions, and—in Thomas Nagel's formulation—"the special claim of immediacy, which makes distress at a distance so different from distress in the same room."[59]

It is not surprising, then, that Kant should associate courtesy with "emergencies": "He who loves the Tartar, loves not his neighbor. Loving *all*, we love *none*, and our love is therefore less. In place of rendering assistance to everyone, there should be simple *courtesy*, which is (1) not hatred, and (2) a mere *calm* willingness to assist in emergencies, according to *our powers*" (*LE* 27:72; emphasis in original). Linking courtesy to emergencies, Kant reminds us that timing is a vital component of courtesy. As Spenser asserts, only the skilled know that it is important "*timely* to bestow" the duties associated with courtesy (*FQ* 6.2.1.9; emphasis added). Unlike utilitarian ethical models that aspire to a utopian horizon, courtesy seeks only a more purified version of itself at its outermost reaches. In its single-minded focus on the "now" or, as Kant might say, on emergencies, courtesy can be said to be an ethics of the pure present.

As a mode of conduct concerned primarily with the present, courtesy pays tribute to the deontological insistence that moral acts ought not to be based on consequences because we lack the capacity to foretell the future. This enables courtesy to preserve its innocence from the utilitarian calculations that were so repugnant to Nabokov and—as *raschët* (calculation)—to Russian writers as temperamentally different as Pushkin, Tolstoy, and Dostoevsky. Courtesy's compulsory spontaneity is highlighted during the luncheon hosted by the Vyra schoolmaster. The note Nabokov's father scribbles in response to his mother's tactless intrusion is "brief," and the offending hamper is sent away "before our host had time to feel hurt" (*SM* 491). The scene must unfold with lightning speed if it is to restore the hard-won pretense of equality between rich man and poor man in the schoolmaster's humble home.

Such a timely response is tragically lacking in Van's dealings with Lucette on the night of her death. Van believes that he has stumbled upon the perfect words for convincing his half-sister that she must find someone else to love, but the comforting thought that he will share them with her "on the morrow" turns out to be hopelessly belated (*A* 393). As a philosopher of time, Van will insist that the future is "sham" time (*A* 439), an insight born of the pain and guilt he suffers in the wake of Lucette's death. As Kant noted, the future's radical unpredictability serves as a powerful objection against utilitarian calculations. For Van, Lucette's suicide serves as a reminder that to put one's trust in consequentialism is to have the arrogance of thinking that one can foretell the future.

COURTESY AND JUSTICE

It is allegorically significant that Spenser's Calidore, the Knight of Courtesy, sets off on his quest at the point at which Artegall, the Knight of Justice, completes his journey.[60] In Nabokov, as in Spenser, the work of courtesy must begin where the work of justice ends. Courtesy must reach beyond the claims of justice because justice makes use of the same quantifying methods—the tallying of merit, the measurement of desert—that makes utilitarianism so objectionable in Nabokov's eyes. C. S. Lewis's definition of courtesy as an "unbought grace of life"[61] signals that courtesy can be neither bartered nor sold, but only freely given.

Courtesy's reach beyond the claims of justice is hinted at in *Pale Fire*. Though the novel's title alludes to Shakespeare's *Timon of Athens*, its mad annotator's *real* name—Botkin—alludes to a famous moment in *Hamlet*. Angered by Polonius's promise to receive the itinerant players according to the dictates of justice, Hamlet insists upon a different criterion of judgment: "God's *bodkin*, man, much better. Use every man after his desert, and who shall scape whipping? Use them after your own honor and dignity: the less they deserve, the more merit is in your bounty" (2.2.524–27; emphasis added). That Botkin's name lurks in Hamlet's expletive hints at the importance of courtesy to Kinbote's story. The residents of New Wye and the readers of *Pale Fire* owe Kinbote not the little that he might deserve, but the greatest bounty that they can offer.

Kinbote is little deserving of the Shades' compassion and courtesy: he spies on their grief, he secretly rents a house in the immediate vicinity of their holiday getaway, and he takes advantage of Shade's death to steal the manuscript of his poem. According to the standards of justice, Kinbote deserves significantly less than the Shades offer him, but according to the standard of courtesy invoked by Hamlet, Kinbote deserves much more than they manage to give. As the namesake of an oath ("God's bodkin" is a diminutive for "God's body"), Botkin-Kinbote plays the double role of divine dispensation and human curse.

PRIDE AND SELF-ESTEEM

Hamlet's injunction to Polonius to "use" the players "after your own honor and dignity" points to another crucial dimension of *courtoisie*: namely, its simultaneous commitment to a Christian humility and a pre-Christian self-regard. The latter is rooted in what Michel Foucault ascribes to Nicocles, a king of Cyprus whose understanding of the source of his moral obligations is decidedly pre-Christian. The subject of two discourses by Socrates, Nicocles understands his moral duties as an extension of his royal status: "Because I am the king, and because as somebody who commands others, who rules others, I have to show that I am able to rule myself."[62] Like Nicocles's insistence upon his rank and dignity as the ground of his moral obligations, courtesy's self-regard flows into a regard for others.

The chivalric literature of the Middle Ages and the Renaissance tends to refer to the positive self-regard of Nicocles as *self-esteem* and its negative counterpart as *pride* (*orgueil*). As arrogance or self-conceit, pride leads to tragedy, as it does in *La Chanson de Roland*, a work that Nabokov studied for his tripos. Roland's pride is at once the source of his greatness and his Achilles' heel: it saves Charlemagne's army, but does so in a Pyrrhic victory that could have been avoided. Significantly, Olivier rebukes Roland by referring to his pride as a form of *démesure*. He insists that Roland's stubborn pride is responsible for the disaster, "for prudent valour is not foolishness: / Caution [*mesure*] is better far than recklessness" (*Ch* 152.1724–25). In *The Faerie Queene*, the discourteous knight slain by Tristram is guilty of "proud disdaine" and "despiteous pryde" (*FQ* 6.2.11.6; 6.2.40.6), while Mirabella's "stubborne pride" leads Cupid to punish her for violating the laws of love (*FQ* 6.7.36.4).

Nabokov draws no such distinctions between pride and self-esteem. His use of the term "pride" suggests that he understood it as a version of medieval and Renaissance self-regard. In *Speak, Memory*, pride is given a positive valence when Nabokov describes how his father, as a young man, "exposed himself to the polar frost" in the hope of catching a "timely sickness" which would prevent his schoolmaster from discovering his unfinished homework (508). Nabokov clearly endorses the idea that "pneumonia" was preferable to "ridicule at the blackboard," for he emulates his father's conduct in a parallel episode during his own student days: in order "to avoid a recitation in class for which I was unprepared," his younger self deliberately slashed his leg with a razor. Though his father, "extremely strict in matters of conduct," could not praise such an action, his "first-hand knowledge of a boy's pride tempered the harshness of reproval and resulted in sudden forgiveness" (*SM* 523).

Whereas Mirabella's "stubborne pride" is punished in *The Faerie Queene*, Zina Mertz's "burning, watchful pride" in *The Gift* is valorized whenever it flares up in protest against her stepfather's antisemitic remarks (*Gift* 188). Kinbote tells us that "considerations of pride" ought to have stopped him from indulging in "an orgy of spying," but that "the itching desire" to see Shade at work ended up trumping such scruples (*PF* 496–97). Whereas Kinbote's pride is too weak to prevent him from doing what is wrong, Dolly's sense of pride is, like Roland's, self-destructive: "Pride alone," Humbert admits, made Dolly see their first sexual encounter to its conclusion (*L* 125).

Courtesy's dependence upon self-esteem explains why courtesy cannot operate from a position of shame and why medieval romances are replete with knights who must atone for their shameful conduct. Yvain experiences the lowest point of his fortunes when he is confronted with his own base conduct. Discovering himself unworthy of his wife's love, Yvain "hates nothing so much as himself, and does not know to whom to turn for comfort since he has caused his own death; but he would rather go mad than fail to take vengeance on himself for having deprived his life of all joy" (*Yvain* 2790–95). His subsequent madness and reversion to a savage state is a ritual suicide by which he cleanses himself of his shame (2804–26). By undergoing a ritual death and rebirth, Yvain recovers his self-esteem and, having done so, is able to place himself once again into the service of others.

COURTESY AND HOSPITALITY

As the knightly feudal warrior class gave way to the new absolute court aristocracy during the sixteenth and seventeenth centuries, *courtoisie* underwent several lexical and semantic transformations. First, it ceded ground to the ideal of good behavior captured by the term *civilité*; by the end of the eighteenth century, the term *politesse* (politeness) prevailed.[63] The long journey from *courtoisie* to *politesse* also involved a changing attitude to what it means to be part of a community. As "a welcoming openness to the strange," Teskey's definition of Renaissance courtesy explains why it was often synonymous with hospitality ("CT" 344). But the generosity and solicitude encompassed by courtesy-as-hospitality was lost in the transition from *courtoisie* to *politesse*. James Baldwin's encounter with the "impenetrable *politesse*" of the typical Parisian of the late 1940s underscores the loss of the community-building impulse Teskey identifies as courtesy's driving energy ("CT" 355).[64]

Yet Baldwin's account of his cold reception by the natives of Paris is no simple lament over the moral thinness of *politesse*. Indeed, for a gay African American fleeing from his racially segregated and homophobic homeland, it is precisely the "arrogant indifference on the part of the Parisian" to anything he might be or do that "makes so splendid the Paris air, to say nothing whatever of the exhilarating effect it has on the Paris scene."[65] Twentieth-century *politesse* lacks the warmhearted hospitality of *courtoisie*, but Baldwin welcomes it because it promotes a bracing cosmopolitan freedom. Put another way, Paris becomes for Baldwin a locus of courtesy where he is given the *space* to be himself. As such, this *space* can be understood as a Kantian respect for difference, or what we might call today "diversity."

Though Nabokov's sensibility was broadly cosmopolitan, his fictions do not celebrate the kind of polite *indifference to difference* that Baldwin encountered in Paris. Abandoned by Pete, Hazel insists on giving Jane Dean and her fiancé their space by departing from the scene. Hazel's refusal to be a third wheel is an act of courtesy, but Jane Dean and her fiancé's acceptance of Hazel's offer to leave is a callous act of discourtesy. This scenario underscores the difficulty of knowing when hospitality ought to be accepted and when it ought to be refused. As Nabokov knew intimately from the medieval writers he studied at Cambridge, courtesy must *fit* the person and the occasion.

HONOR AND HONESTY

Truth-telling was a cardinal virtue in the code of honor of knights and gentlemen. As Steven Shapin observes, truth occupied a formally central role in the moral order of late medieval and early modern gentlemanly society. If a man's truthfulness was thrown into doubt, he forfeited the trust mandated by cooperative enterprises.[66] This central role of truth is also embedded in the etymological link between *honesty* and *honor*. As Irina Reyfman notes in her cultural history of dueling in Russia, the Russian words for honor and honesty—*chest'* and *chestnost'*—enjoyed a much closer semantic kinship than they do in modern usage (*RV* 38). The logic that undergirds this kinship is easy to reconstruct: because it is dishonorable to tell lies, honesty becomes a marker of honor. Therefore, it is incumbent upon Spenser to have Calidore, the Knight of Courtesy, hate falsehoods and love "simple truth and stedfast honesty" (*FQ* 6.1.3.9). Maboagrain, the knight whom Erec fights and defeats in the "Joie de la Cort," cannot release himself from the bad oath he made in his youth because his sense of honor prevents him from fighting without doing his best. Throwing a match would be both dishonest and dishonorable, and therefore Maboagrain must wait patiently for an honest defeat (*Erec* 6082–6109). Gawain feels morally obligated to keep his promise to the Green Knight even though he is certain that such a commitment to *trewthe* (fidelity to his given word) is suicidal.

Yet in spite of this principled commitment to truth, courtesy frequently trades in deception. As Shippey notes, writers of medieval romances were far more aware than writers of our time that some virtues "depend on a certain deceit. Tact is one of these, politeness another; for while with friends one is naturally friendly, politeness is a deliberate (but not seriously deceptive) counterfeit extended to friends, enemies, or strangers alike."[67] Putter notes further that these courteous deceptions were especially relevant within the context of hospitality, where hosts were expected to express joy at receiving their guests: "Joy is part and parcel of the honour due to the guest" (*FAR* 73). The sense that courtesy must feign a sense of joy is on display in the iconic acts of courtesy performed by Mrs. Luzhin, Helene, Disa, and Lucette.

As an expectation of hospitality, joy was understood as "a quality that can be acted . . . to cover up an inner turmoil" (*FAR* 73). Gawain's relatives, for instance, do their best to simulate joy when they receive Yvain even as their grief overwhelms them (*Yvain* 3810–21). When Yvain asks for an explanation, his host reveals that the giant Harpin de la Montagne has threatened to kill his remaining four sons unless he hands him his daughter. This scene of hospitality compromised by grief at the prospect of losing a beloved daughter is inverted by Nabokov: John and Sibyl Shade find themselves in a position of having to show hospitality *after* having lost their daughter. They, too, must entertain invited guests and uninvited strangers by putting on a brave face in the midst of overwhelming personal grief. For them, as for Mrs. Luzhin, Helene, Disa, and Lucette, courtesy means to do what is expected of them regardless of circumstances.

Nabokov appreciated the deceptions of courtesy as keenly as he appreciated the deceptions of art and natural mimicry. The village schoolmaster's lovingly planned meal described in *Speak, Memory* included a dish that V. D. Nabokov disliked, but this fact does not obtrude on the afternoon's festivities thanks to "the beautifully simulated delight with which my father welcomed" the dish in question (*SM* 491). At their town home in St. Petersburg, a much more extravagant deception had been manufactured by Nabokov's parents for the sake of protecting the self-esteem of Elena Nabokov's former nurse. Born a serf, the former nurse was made to feel useful in her old age by being given the title of head housekeeper. As Nabokov recalls,

> Age had developed in her a pathological stinginess, especially in regard to sugar and preserves, so that by degrees, and with the sanction of my parents, other domestic arrangements, kept secret from her, had quietly come into force. Without knowing it (the knowledge would have broken her heart), she remained dangling as it were, from her own key ring, while my mother did her best to allay with soothing words the suspicions that now and then flitted across the old woman's weakening mind. Sole mistress of her moldy and remote little kingdom, which she thought was the real one (we would have starved had it been so), she was followed by the mocking glances of lackeys and maids as she steadily plodded through long corridors to store away half an apple or a couple of broken Petit-Beurre biscuits she had found on a plate. (*SM* 392)

The servants' mocking glances serve as a reminder of courtesy's aristocratic pedigree. Nabokov's account of these events leaves no doubt that his own parents would neither have permitted themselves nor, given their privileged position, felt the need for such derision.

Courtesy's compact with deception, however, also made it vulnerable to treachery. As Putter notes, the many hospitality episodes encountered in French romances "reflect on the dichotomy that can exist between polite gestures and underlying intentions" (*FAR* 83). Whereas joy often signified a host's good intentions, it sometimes masked a secret evil design. The friendly welcome Yvain receives at Pesme Aventure turns out to be a trap to inveigle him into the evil custom established by his treacherous host. As Putter notes, such scenes—carried over from the romances of Chrétien all the way to *Sir Gawain and the Green Knight*—remind us of the dangers of hospitality (*FAR* 95–96).

Courtesy's alignment with pretense accounts for the suspicion that courtesy generated during the Renaissance and thereafter. Sham courtesy was often denounced in courtesy books. Such condemnations were directed at insincere customs and ceremonies, and opportunistic calculations and false promises of service. Castiglione's *Il Cortegiano* depicts courtesy as a social refinement that can be confidently placed into the service of social advancement. In *The Faerie Queene*'s Legend of Courtesy, Spenser laments the devolution of "true curtesie" into "forgerie, / Fashion'd to please the eies" (6.Proem.5.1–4). By contrast, Nabokov insists on the innocence of courtesy by disentangling it from the promise of reward. The most that Mrs. Luzhin can expect by remaining by the side of the importunate lady from Soviet Russia is a return visit. Disa can only increase her emotional distress by participating in the polite trivialities expected of her. Van's account of the circumstances surrounding Lucette's sublime act of courtesy to the Robinsons suggests that he is haunted by the possibility that a less courteous Lucette might have lived.

Unlike Nabokov, modern writers often viewed courtesy's deceptions with suspicion. Courtesy is a useful tool for opportunists such as Austen's Mr. Willoughby and Mr. Elton, or mercenaries such as Henry James's Madame Merle and Gilbert Osmond. This aligns courtesy with its post-medieval conception as an instrument for careerism. Yet for writers such as Woolf and Proust, courtesy's deceptions are often associated, as they are in Nabokov, with premodern notions of chivalry. Proust's Narrator describes the Queen of Naples's exemplary courtesy toward Mme Verdurin as the natural outgrowth of her being "always ready to place herself chivalrously on the side of the weak." Noticing that Mme Verdurin is ignored by her own guests, the Queen of Naples decides "*to pretend* that for her, the Queen of Naples, the center of the evening, the focal point of attraction that had brought her there, was Mme Verdurin" (*SLT* 5.329; *RTP* 3.752; NRF 6.2.61; emphasis added). Minta Doyle feigns being more ignorant than she feels herself to be because she intuits that her ignorance rouses her host's sense of his own chivalry.[68]

These examples underscore courtesy's predilection for hyperbole. Minta must exaggerate her own ignorance in order to maximize Mr. Ramsay's chivalric self-image. The Queen of Naples's courtesy to Mme Verdurin involves making her feel like she is "the center of the evening." This "courteous hyperbole"—as Van refers to such examples (*A* 406)—risks being mistaken for the very feeling whose absence courtesy seeks to occlude. Chrétien insists that only "fools" misinterpret courtesy as love, but the scenario he describes in *Yvain* suggests that the category of this particular kind of fool is a broad one. The members of Arthur's retinue who mistake Laudine's exquisite courtesy for love (*Yvain* 2456–63) anticipate Mme Verdurin's error when she interprets the Queen of Naples's courtesy as something more than it is (*SLT*

5.431; *RTP* 3.824; NRF 6.2.158–59). No fool himself, Nabokov reported to his wife that he found it impossible "to grasp the truth through the exaggerated compliments" he received during his American lecture tours (*LV* 450).

COURTESY: "THE POETRY OF CONDUCT"

Van's justification for deceiving Lucette when she calls him on the telephone and asks to join him in his cabin turns on a puzzling distinction between general moral duties and the duties of artists and gentlemen. Having masturbated twice while Lucette was showing courtesy to the Robinsons, Van finds it easy to withstand the temptation of her offer and, to avoid a heartbreaking affair, tells her that he is not alone:

> No doubt he was morally right in using the first pretext at hand to keep her away from his bed; but he also knew, as a gentleman and an artist, that the lump of words he brought up was trite and cruel, and it was only because she could not accept him as being either, that she believed him. (*A* 393–94)

Van's confidence in the moral rightness of his lie is undercut by his recognition—"as a gentleman and an artist"—that he has betrayed his half-sister. The metaphor he invokes to justify the clumsy nature of his deception—"the lump of words he brought up"—makes the betrayal a matter of *form*. Like a badly digested meal, his words—"*Ya ne odin* (I'm not alone)"—are at once inartistic ("trite") and ungentlemanly ("cruel"). Van's lie to Lucette offends his artistic and gentlemanly sensibilities because it lacks two essential features of courtesy: artfulness and fitness.

The aesthetic qualities of courtesy are captured in Lewis's pithy summation of courtesy as "the poetry of conduct."[69] Courtesy's poetic dimension is inseparable from questions of *fitness* and, in rhetorical terms, *decorum*. Courtesy is not merely a matter of *fair* words, but *fit* words:[70] to be courteous, an action must fit the particularity of the occasion. Lucette's parting words to the Robinsons—"I really needed that lovely cold drink" (*A* 394)—are trite, but they are also quintessentially courteous because they fit the circumstances that prompt their utterance and use the locutions most familiar to their addressees. Van's guilt and shame are further exacerbated by Lucette's courteous response to his "trite and cruel" deception. Lucette's characteristic courtesy prevents her from attaching such adjectives to him (she refuses to think of him as being either "trite" or "cruel") and leads her to mistake his lie for truth: "it was only because she could not accept him as being either, that she believed him" (*A* 394).

Eric Naiman has argued that Nabokov's fiction "has a penchant for turning moral questions about life into procedural ones about reading," and therefore into substitutes for the questions that had obsessed Nabokov's Russian predecessors such as Dostoevsky, Tolstoy, and Chekhov.[71] But Naiman's insight becomes even more productive when reapplied to the ethical domain from which it springs. By privileging the same things that he insists upon with respect to reading, Nabokov understands practical ethics to be as procedural as the ethics of reading. Wood's claim that Nabokov's ethics of reading is "a question of scruple"[72] harmonizes with this view because Nabokov's practical ethics privileges the graceful gesture in the same way that his ethics of reading privileges the gratuitous detail.

This congruence between art and ethics accounts for the ceremonial actions performed by Nabokov's positive characters. The moral excellence of Joan Clements, Pnin's landlady and benefactress, is signaled by her manner of raising her hand "to exactly the right level for a Russian gentleman to kiss" (*Pnin* 408). Mrs. Luzhin's efforts to save her husband ultimately fail, but not before she teaches him such niceties as the proper way to kiss a lady's hands. The kisses that Luzhin bestows fastidiously upon his wife's hands before committing suicide ("*odnu ruku, potom druguiu, kak ona ego uchila* [one hand, then the other, as she had taught him]") are at once a heartrending farewell and a moving tribute to the beneficent role she has played in his life.[73] They are also, significantly, a latter-day version of the medieval *congé* and farewell, a knight's request for permission to depart and a ritualized leave-taking of the lady to whom he has pledged his troth.

Such delicate gestures of courtesy abound in Nabokov's fiction. Fyodor goes to the trouble of moving residences because he finds it impossible to protect himself from the "very kind, innocently intrusive bores who kept 'dropping in for a chat'" at the boarding house where he used to live (*Gift* 51). Pnin stealthily gets rid of the soccer ball he purchased for Victor after learning that Victor is indifferent to sports. Anticipating the epithet Zumthor applies to medieval *courtoisie*, Proust would have called Fyodor's and Pnin's fastidiousness "*une élégance morale*."[74] The great moral failures in Nabokov's fiction—Pete's glaringly false excuse for abandoning Hazel, Van's trite and cruel words to Lucette in the minutes that precede her suicide—sit at the antipodes of Fyodor's and Pnin's conduct.

THE DUEL AS CIVIL CONVERSATION

Within the lexicon of medieval courtesy, the conduct of Pete and Van would have qualified as "*vilain*." Nabokov's fictional "villains" (etymologically connected to medieval *vilainie*) are referred to as scoundrels, cads, and blackguards. These terms belong to the vocabulary of the modern European duel of honor, and it is no surprise that Nabokov should invoke it to pass judgment on his male characters. Anna Vladimirovna charges the narrator of "That in Aleppo Once . . ." with being "a bully and a cad" (*SVN* 562), and in his preface to *Despair*, Nabokov claims that both Hermann and Humbert are "neurotic scoundrels."[75] Demon is identified as a "cad" for having once told Marina that the birthmark on her hand "resembled a bedbug" (*A* 85). Vadim Vadimovich uses the same lexicon to express his contempt for Oleg Orlov's work as a spy for the Soviet Union—"What do you want, *merzavetz* (you scoundrel)?"[76]—and Krug uses the same term when he cries out to the men who are trying to pin down his child, "Leave him alone, *merzavtzy*!" (*BS* 327).

The counterpoint to the scoundrel and the cad is the *gallant* man, whose fearless conduct is guided by pure and unbending moral principles. Mayne Reid is "the gallant author" whose plots Nabokov and his cousin Yury enacted during the summers they spent together at Vyra (*SM* 533). Yury himself is killed in an attack on "a Red machine-gun nest" that Nabokov interprets as the fulfillment of "his lifelong thirst for intrepid conduct in battle, for that ultimate gallant gallop with drawn pistol or unsheathed sword" (*SM* 531). Anna Akhmatova's first husband, Nikolay Gumilev, is described as "the very gallant Russian poet" who retains his sangfroid throughout his arrest and execution by Lenin's secret police. Like Mira Belochkin, who is imagined to have gone to her death "still smiling" (*Pnin* 395), Gumilev "kept smiling" throughout his ordeal (*LL* 376–77). The men Nabokov admired are typically described as governed by a firm commitment to principle: his father "unswervingly" conformed to "his principles in private and public matters," and his tutor Lenski was "a very pure, very decent human being, whose private principles were as strict as his grammar" (*SM* 509, 506). Nabokov's portrait of Yury makes it clear that these moral principles are inseparable from the question of honor: "all emotions, all thoughts, were governed in Yury by one gift: a sense of honor equivalent, morally, to absolute pitch" (*SM* 531).

When reflecting upon his own conduct, Nabokov similarly applied standards of judgment associated with a gentlemanly honor code. Thus, shame predominates over guilt, as in an interview from 1965 in which Nabokov confesses to feeling "a kind of helpless shame" when reading "Mandelshtam's poems composed under the accursed rule" of the Soviets (*SO* 58). His fictional alter egos are similarly made to suffer the pangs of shame. Fyodor is enveloped in a "crimson mist of shame" as he imagines himself presenting his story about Yasha to Mme Chernyshevsky, and he feels "a kind of personal shame" for listening without protest to Zina's stepfather's antisemitic "rot" (*Gift* 41, 188).

Fyodor might also have felt shame when reading that Professor Anuchin found his biography of Chernyshevsky "repellent" in spite of its "swaggering erudition" (*Gift* 305, 306). Anuchin is described as "a man of shining moral purity and of great personal courage" whose legendary bravery aligns him with Gumilev and Fyodor's father. As the narrator explains, this was "the same Professor Anuchin who in 1922, not long before his deportation from Russia, when some revolvered leatherjackets had come to arrest him but became interested in his collection of ancient coins and were slow in taking him away, had calmly said, pointing to his watch: 'Gentlemen, history does not wait'" (*Gift* 305). Scenes such as this one are frequently coded as models of the highest masculine moral integrity in Nabokov's work. During his hypothetical reconstruction of his father's execution by the Reds, Fyodor imagines Godunov displaying the same sangfroid as Anuchin and Gumilev (*Gift* 137). Though Anuchin's negative review of Fyodor's biography of Chernyshevsky seems to be trumped by Koncheyev's claim that it is a "fabulously witty composition" (*Gift* 308), it is likely that Nabokov imagined his own father to have shared Anuchin's view of Fyodor's biography. Fyodor's irreverent approach to the life of a man who spent most of his adulthood as a political prisoner and exile might be rightly seen as a violation of the "principles of decency and personal honor deliberately passed from father to son" to which Nabokov laid claim in an interview from 1973 with Mati Laansoo.[77]

The grammar of shame that dominates Nabokov's moral reflections on the conduct of men is in keeping with his keen interest in the modern European duel of honor and the rites of courtesy associated with it. Courtesy was the trademark of gentlemanly conduct in the chivalric culture of honor that Nabokov identified as his special legacy in "Youth." As Dupin notes, though the virtues encompassed by medieval courtesy were valued for their own sake, it was also considered natural and legitimate for knights to worry about their reputations and good names.[78] In *La Chanson de Roland*, a poem that chronicles the Battle of Roncevaux Pass, Roland refuses to blow his horn to call for help because he is afraid that future poets will sing a "*mauvaise chanson* [*male cançun*]" about him and that he will lose "*ma gloire* [*mun los*]" in his homeland (*Ch* 83.1014; 87.1054).

The conception of honor that sits at the heart of the modern European duel is easy to reconstruct. As Julian Pitt-Rivers reminds us in his classic work of anthropology on the Mediterranean region, honor was understood as an extension of individual free will: "freedom of will is the first condition of honor" and, therefore, honor is incompatible with duress.[79] Men of honor treat others with respect and expect to be treated with respect in return. Courtesy designates the rituals associated with the demonstration of respect and those circumstances in which human relations are functioning as they ought. When the standards of courtesy are breached, insult occurs. Such insults had to be *resented* for the insulted party's honor to be preserved. As Shapin explains, this logic of obligatory resentment was a legacy of the Aristotelian idea that only a slavish nature would accept insult without protest.

The most common injuries that instigated combat included, to quote Shapin, "a physical attack on the integrity of one's body, an insult to a woman to whom one was attached, an imputation of disloyalty or cowardice."[80]

The modern European duel of honor emerged as a formal code of conduct for displaying resentment against such injuries and settling quarrels among gentlemen. Always risky and frequently fatal, the duel—like courtesy—was motivated by a desire to make respect the currency of civil discourse. The detailed handbooks identifying the appropriate means of expressing resentment and managing quarrels belonged to the same specialized category of literature dedicated to the education of gentlemen as did medieval and Renaissance courtesy books. As a result of the shared ambitions of courtesy texts and dueling manuals, their content often overlapped.[81]

This overlap has led Markku Peltonen to challenge the conventional view that the origins of the duel of honor lay in the medieval culture of knightly honor. Peltonen argues instead that the ideology of dueling emerged as an integral part of the theory of courtesy rooted in the Italian Renaissance.[82] But the dispute about the precise origins of the duel—in the chivalric rituals of single combat or in Renaissance conceptions of courtesy and civility—has little bearing on the accepted understanding of the duel of honor as a social practice allied with medieval and early modern conceptions of *courtoisie*. Shapin and Anna Bryson, for instance, see no contradiction in locating the origins of the modern duel of honor in Renaissance Italy while at the same time assuming an ideological continuity between the duel and its chivalric antecedents.[83] As a strategy for limiting and containing aggression in chivalric contexts, *courtoisie* is ideologically aligned with dueling. The question of provenance aside, historians agree that the modern European duel belonged to the repertoire of rules and rituals covered by the rubric of "civil conversation."[84]

As the next chapter will show, Nabokov was intimately familiar with the intricacies of the dueling code. Like his Russian literary forebears, he often wrote about duels in his fiction. Pushkin's last duel was a source of abiding and intense fascination to Nabokov, and he visited it again and again in his fiction and discursive writings. This fascination of a twentieth-century writer with the institution of dueling, and with Pushkin's mortal duel in particular, was no unthinking legacy of his patrician upbringing. As Reyfman observes, "In the Russian cultural imagination dueling apparently transcended the boundary of purely aristocratic experience and acquired the status of heroic behavior representative of national character." Pushkin's life and death, she notes further, played an oversized role in the Russian attribution of high moral value to the institution of dueling (*RV* 2–3).

Nabokov valued the duel's privileging of self-control, and he made some of his most admirable male characters exhibit the virtues associated with the dictates of the dueling code. He would have endorsed the claim that dueling was not a sanctioning of violence but a pragmatic mechanism for its containment, but he would have also insisted, as he did in regard to Darwinism, that dueling was irreducible to its utilitarian function as a deterrent of aggression. He would have noted, as Appiah does, that "to justify dueling because it deters discourtesy is to take a perspective from outside the world of honor" (*HC* 32).

Nabokov's intimate knowledge of the dueling code is frequently on display. In a letter to Wilson from 1949, he calls attention to the "dreadful mistake" that Wilson makes in *The Triple Thinkers* on the subject of Onegin's duel with Lensky (*DBDV* 245). Nabokov's observation that Wilson has used the corrupt phrase "called out" instead of the technically correct "called upon" indicates that Nabokov understood the duel as practitioners of the duel understood it—that is, as a civil conversation between social equals. This conversation had to be conducted according to the rules of courtesy: it is to Van's discredit that he is rude to Captain Tapper's seconds in spite of recollecting Demon's injunction "'*Ne grubit' sekundantam*' (never be rude to seconds)" (*A* 245). The flawless courtesy displayed by Captain Tapper and his seconds throughout the preliminary ceremonies and the duel itself not only reflects badly on Van, but reflects well on Nabokov when we notice that Captain Tapper and his seconds are gay (*A* 244–46, 249–50).

CHIVALRY AND GENDER

The chivalric cast of Nabokov's imagination gives his ethics a gendered inflection. When he contemplates Russian social history, the custom that repels him the most is wife-beating. When he sees a young peasant woman—Polenka—living on his family's country estate with "a bruise under her eye and a puffed-up lip," he immediately wonders if "her husband beat her on Saturdays" (*SM* 540). He portrays Pushkin's great-grandfather Abram Gannibal as a monster because he "differ[ed] in nothing from a . . . wife-flogging Russian of his day."[85] He can neither pass in silence nor dwell upon the "private torture chamber complete with pulleys, iron clamps, thumbkins, leathern whips, and so forth" that Gannibal rigged up for his first wife, Evdokya Dioper. One wonders if Dolly's death in "Gray Star, a settlement in the remote Northwest" might not be a dead echo of Dioper's being "packed away to a remote convent, where she died."[86]

Nabokov's band of knights in "Youth" would have balked at the idea that wife-beating was part of the Russian legacy that they were entrusted to preserve. Instead, they might have cited the parting instructions that Perceval's mother gives her son in Chrétien's *Perceval* (c. 1185) when she realizes that he will not be dissuaded from becoming a knight:

Should you encounter, near or far,
a lady in need of aid,
or a maiden in distress,
make yourself ready to aid
them, if they ask for your help,
for it is the most honorable thing to do.
He who fails to honor ladies
finds his own honor dead within.
Serve ladies and maidens
and you'll be honored everywhere. (*Per* lines 497–506; Kibler's translation lines 515–24)

It would be reductive to argue that Nabokov's moral imagination stopped at the boundaries of the chivalric literature that played such an important role in his youth. Additionally, it is important to remember that his early fiction frequently concerns itself with crimes such as premeditated murder. In his later fiction, however, Nabokov becomes less interested in glaringly criminal acts and trains his eye on crimes and moral failures that are more difficult to parse. These include Sebastian's treatment of Clare, Pnin's accusation that Vladimir Vladimirovich is a "dreadful inventor," Hazel's rejection by Pete Dean on their blind date, Lucette's getting tied up to a tree trunk in a game of knight-saves-damsel-in-distress. The literature Nabokov studied for his tripos at Cambridge suggests that these failures can be analyzed, at least in part, more fully and productively if viewed through the moral structures of chivalry even as these structures realign themselves as his career unfolds.

It is perhaps telling, then, to consider the ways in which Sebastian's decision to adopt his mother's chivalric family name—Knight—echoes some of the linguistic play with the referent "knight" in Chrétien's *Perceval.* Percival Q, the protagonist of Sebastian's novel *Success*, signals the importance of this chivalric text for Nabokov's novel. As a "commercial traveler" (*RLSK* 73), Sebastian's Percival is a latter-day version of the knight errant who gives Chrétien's romance its name.[87] Raised in the country by an overprotective mother, Perceval is enchanted when he sees a band of knights for the first time. Their sparkling armor leads him to believe that they are angels, but it is Perceval's nomenclatorial confusion concerning their identity that Nabokov seems to be alluding to when he has Sebastian abandon his Russian name in favor of the English name "Knight." When the knights' leader identifies himself as a knight to Perceval—"I am a knight [*Chevaliers sui*]"—Perceval mistakes the knight's identity for his name: "Fair sir, you who are called 'Knight' [*Biaus sire chiers, / Vos qui avez non chevaliers*]" (*Per* lines 169, 183–84; Kibler's translation lines 175, 189–90). In laying claim to his mother's family name, Sebastian similarly uses the common noun "knight" (representative of an individual's social standing) as a proper noun (representative of an individual's self-identity). But as Sebastian discovers, a chivalric name does not a knight make. His failure to treat Clare with respect is a betrayal of the cardinal law of the chivalric ethics that Perceval's mother imparts to her son on the eve of his departure and that Perceval will sometimes uphold but frequently betray. The gap between Sebastian's aspiration and his imperfection makes him a true inheritor of the chivalric traditions that he claims as his legacy and with which Nabokov was intimately familiar.

Sebastian's idealization of chivalry even as he fails to live up to its standards offers the most productive way of grappling with Nabokov's own complicated relationship with chivalry's alignment with courtesy. To say that Nabokov idealized courtesy is not identical to saying that he practiced courtesy more than other men of his rank, predicament, or generation. At the most, it might suggest that he chastised himself more severely than others for violating its rules. Nabokov made no bones about his own abject failures to live up to courtesy's demands: in *Speak, Memory*, he describes the "shame and self-disgust" that wracked his body in the wake of abandoning a grieving and destitute friend for the sake of collecting butterflies (467). Several chapters later, he confesses that he never forgave himself for his public attack on Boris Poplavsky's "unfledged verse." As he explains, Poplavsky "died young," and the "trivial faults" of his juvenilia in no way justified his own "ill-tempered review" (*SM* 607).

Other examples might be added to the list: his bullying conduct toward his gay brother, his irreverent biography of a national icon in *The Gift*, his extramarital affair with Irina Guadanini, and his notorious abuse of the translators of Russian and French texts. Far from discrediting courtesy as a cardinal virtue, such betrayals only burnish the values that convene under the rubric of courtesy as a moral ideal. Nabokov's self-loathing alter egos—"V" of "That in Aleppo Once . . . ," Vladimir Vladimirovich of *Pnin*, Vadim Vadimovich of *Look at the Harlequins!*—can be productively read as versions of Sebastian Knight. Though they are intimately familiar with the code of honor associated with knightly conduct and yearn to live up to its standards, they nonetheless stray from it in egregious ways.

Yet Sebastian's failure to act in accordance with the maxims of honor and courtesy that he embraces when he adopts his mother's name is no proof of the will's total helplessness in the face of such standards. Nabokov's heroically courteous female characters—Mrs. Luzhin, Helene, Disa, and Lucette—and his staunchly loyal and principled male characters—Belov, Maximov, Pnin—treat such maxims as implacable and inviolable obligations. In doing so, they demonstrate that the will is not only capable of determining action, but that the chivalric ideal of self-mastery is neither dead nor the exclusive prerogative of knights.

Chapter Three

The Duel of Honor: Nabokov, Pushkin, Kant

For fighting quarrels never are made for profit,
but for honor.
—*The Court of Civill Courtesie*

BEFORE LEAVING HIS study to fight his last duel, Pushkin prepared a package for Alexandra Osipovna Ishimova, a writer whom he had commissioned to translate some of Barry Cornwall's dramatic sketches for *The Contemporary* (*Sovremennik*). The accompanying letter, along with the package, was entrusted to Pushkin's servant for delivery to Ishimova's residence. It would turn out to be the last letter Pushkin would write:

> Dear Madame, Alexandra Osipovna,
>
> I regret extremely that it will be impossible for me to come at your invitation today. Meanwhile I have the honor to forward the Barry Cornwall. You will find at the end of the book some pieces marked with a pencil; translate them as you can—I assure you that your translating couldn't be better. Today I chanced to open your *History in Tales*, and I couldn't help becoming engrossed in them. That is how writing should be done!
>
> With the most profound respect and with complete devotion, I have the honor to be, dear Madame,
>
> Your most obedient servant,
>
> A. Pushkin[1]

By the time Pushkin's servant returned from his errand, Pushkin had already been brought back from the dueling site with a mortal wound.[2]

Pushkin's last letter shares something very important with the acts of courtesy performed by Mrs. Luzhin, Helene, Disa, and Lucette. The kinship is not accidental. Pushkin's letter to Ishimova and the quiet acts of courtesy that Nabokov holds up for approval in his fiction take for granted that courtesy is an inviolable moral duty. Furthermore, Nabokov understood that Pushkin's last letter belonged to the same grammar of moral principles as the duel that prompted its writing. In taking time to inform Ishimova that he will not be able to meet her, and then in taking even more time to encourage her literary ambitions, Pushkin demonstrated his commitment to a gentlemanly code of conduct in which personal honor finds its most visible expression as courtesy.

Like many of his compatriots, Nabokov was deeply fascinated with this iconic event in Russia's cultural history and referred to it on many occasions. In a talk delivered in Paris on the centenary of Pushkin's death, Nabokov offered his listeners (James Joyce among them) the following description of Pushkin's last duel: "Exactly one hundred years have elapsed since that twilight duel amid the snow, during which he was mortally wounded by a handsome lout who was courting his wife, one George d'Anthès, a young adventurer and total nonentity who later returned to France to survive Pushkin by half a century and die, an octogenarian and a senator with an untroubled conscience."[3]

Pushkin's biographers—Russian and non-Russian alike—agree with Nabokov that Georges d'Anthès was, indeed, "a handsome lout," "a young adventurer," and—relative to Pushkin—a "total nonentity." A French legitimist serving in Nicholas I's Cavalier Guards Regiment, d'Anthès openly flirted with Pushkin's wife and conducted himself ignobly throughout the prolonged drama that was enacted in the public's eye and ended in Pushkin's death. The contemptuous epithets that Nabokov uses to describe the man who killed Russia's greatest poet might suggest that Nabokov understood Pushkin's last duel as a tragic misallocation of values. Nabokov seems to be reproaching his best-loved poet for squandering his eminently worthier life in a senseless conflict with a man who ought to have been unworthy of his concern.

Yet in his annotations to his translation of Pushkin's *Eugene Onegin*, Nabokov warns his readers not to take a condescending attitude to the code of honor that compelled men of earlier generations to fight in duels. Though the warning in question refers specifically to Lensky's duel with Onegin, the argument is no less relevant to Pushkin's duel with d'Anthès. Nabokov's defense of dueling begins—significantly—with a condemnation of Soviet utilitarianism:

> In modern Russia, where little remains of the idea of honor—pure personal honor (I am not speaking of Stahanovets competition,[4] political touchiness, or nationalistic *gonor*)—readers, if not accepting passively the Lensky-Onegin duel in terms of some curious "feodal" legend or operatic libretto, are puzzled by its cause and baffled by its details. . . . Lensky's course of action, far from being a temperamental extravaganza, is the only logical course an honorable man could have taken in that set in those times. (*EO* 3.16)

Nabokov's reminder to his readers that Lensky—as a man of honor—could not permit himself to ignore Onegin's insult doubles as an affirmation of the reasons that led Pushkin to fight. To state the matter as clearly as possible, d'Anthès had repeatedly insulted him, and a duel was "the only logical course" of action that an honorable man like Pushkin could have taken.

In spite of knowing that such reasoning would sound anachronistic to a twentieth-century audience, Nabokov not only defends the institution of the duel on its own terms, but provides the ideological underpinnings that might justify his own sympathy for it. Pushkin's last duel, like his letter to Ishimova, belongs to the same order of "irrational and divine standards" that Nabokov celebrates as morally superior to those of "commonsense" (*LL* 373). In "The Art of Literature and Commonsense," he explains that these "irrational standards" involve gratuitous risks that most sensible people would find good reason to avoid: "I take my hat off to the hero who dashes into a burning house and saves his neighbor's child; but I shake his hand if he has risked squandering a precious five seconds to find and save, together with the child, its favorite toy" (*LL* 373). As a father himself, Nabokov must have known that this hypothetical child's parents would have preferred that no seconds be squandered on their child's favorite toy when the child's life was in danger. The poetic license Nabokov allows himself here signals his search for values that defy utilitarian accounts of human behavior. Honor, a virtue that dueling was meant to protect, provided him with precisely such a value.

The precious five seconds squandered in a life-and-death situation for the sake of a toy can serve as shorthand for the scenarios by which Nabokov illustrates moral excellence in his fiction. These perilous seconds help explain why the acts of courtesy performed by Mrs. Luzhin, Helene, Disa, and Lucette are the feminine counterparts of ritual acts of courtesy performed in duels by a select number of Nabokov's male characters. The dangerously squandered seconds also help distinguish between two ideological approaches to the modern duel of honor. As an instrument of preserving aristocratic privilege and self-policing, the duel of honor is an ideal subject for Marxist critiques such as those ventured by Victor Gordon Kiernan in his highly regarded monograph, *The Duel in European History*. For historians like Kiernan, the institution's absurdities and contradictions serve as exemplary Foucauldian articulations of power.

Nabokov, however, subscribed to the view expressed by historians like Billacois, who concludes his magisterial *The Duel: Its Rise and Fall in Early Modern France* with a reminder that the history of the duel cannot ignore the poetic elements of its subject: "No one will deny that, as a learned discipline, history must be rigorous and meticulously methodical. But (at least when, as here, it is dealing with institutions whose value is essentially symbolic) it loses too much if, in trying to be a science, it forgets to be poetry"

(*Duel* 242). Billacois' injunction to remember the poetic dimension of dueling also reminds us that Nabokov's thinking about ethics—illustrated as gestures of courtesy or a strict adherence to a ritualistic code of honor—is always at war with the all-consuming logic of utilitarianism.

V. D. NABOKOV AND THE DUEL OF HONOR

Pushkin's duel with d'Anthès holds a preeminent place in Russia's cultural memory. It also became the most powerful argument in favor of abandoning the duel as an instrument of settling conflicts of honor. Nabokov's father invoked this argument in a two-part article published in the St. Petersburg juridical weekly *Pravo* (*Law*, *Right[s]*). Russia's loss of Pushkin in a duel, he writes, renders "obscene" (*nepristoino*) any argument that would defend dueling as a genuine institution of honor ("DiUZ" 2737).

Nabokov made no secret of his intense love and admiration for his father. He unabashedly describes in his memoirs "the tender friendship underlying my respect for my father; the charm of our perfect accord; the Wimbledon matches we followed in the London papers; the chess problems we solved; the Pushkin iambics that rolled off his tongue so triumphantly whenever I mentioned some minor poet of the day" (*SM* 522–23). In an interview from 1973, he portrayed his own ethics as inseparable from those "principles of decency and personal honor deliberately passed from father to son."[5] But in spite of expressing moral outrage against other forms of ritualized violence such as bullfights and executions (*NB* 613; *SO* 18, 35), Nabokov does not seem to have sympathized with his father's argument that dueling was a barbaric and absurd social custom.

V. D. Nabokov begins his two-part essay "The Duel and Criminal Law" by attempting to refute the dueling institution's foundational principle that a duel can restore honor. He argues that apologists of the duel err when they assume, first, that "my honor can suffer from the actions of another," and, second, that "any heinous scoundrel can, by virtue of challenging someone to a duel, killing someone in a duel, or submitting to someone's fire in a duel, earn the stamp of nobility and unblemished honor" ("DiUZ" 2738). Duelists are not, he insists, motivated by higher ideals, but by the base desire for revenge (*chuvstvo mesti*; 2737). Having allowed themselves to become slaves to social convention, they show "timidity and cowardice [*robost' i trusost'*]" rather than courage (2740). Though a criminal lawyer himself, V. D. Nabokov argues that criminal law can neither eradicate nor even curb duels. The only solution, he argues, lies in the hands of self-respecting and honorable Russians who will sever the link between honor and dueling by refusing to fight in duels ("DiUZ" 2742).

The truth of V. D. Nabokov's observation was borne out. Appiah tells us that the duel died when the practice began to be viewed as ridiculous (*HC* 50–51). However, it was not V. D. Nabokov's own refusal to fight in duels that made the practice unfashionable. Indeed, shortly after publishing his eloquent condemnation of dueling, V. D. Nabokov was confronted with an insult to his honor that, in the words of his son, he "could not let pass" (*SM* 520). In a letter to the editor published in the ultraconservative *Novoe vremia* (*New Time*), N. V. Snessarev insinuated that V. D. Nabokov had married for money and was now a "kept man."[6] Nabokov's account of this moment in his father's life deserves to be quoted in full:

> Since the well-known rascality of the actual author of the article made him "non-duelable" (*neduelesposobnyi*, as the Russian dueling code had it), my father called out the somewhat less disreputable editor of the paper in which the article had appeared. A Russian duel was a much more serious affair than the conventional Parisian variety. It took the editor several days to make up his mind whether or not to accept the challenge. On the last of these days, a Monday, I went, as usual, to school. In consequence of my not reading the newspapers, I was absolutely ignorant of the whole thing. Sometime during the day I became aware that a magazine opened at a certain page was passing from hand to hand and causing titters. A well-timed swoop put me in possession of what proved to be the latest copy of a cheap weekly containing a lurid account of my father's challenge, with idiotic comments on the choice of weapons he had offered his foe. Sly digs were taken at his having reverted to a feudal custom that he had criticized in his own writings. (*SM* 520–21)

Nabokov's protracted agony in the wake of this revelation ended in tears of relief when, upon his return home, he discovered that "there would be no duel, that the challenge had been met by an apology, that all was right" (*SM* 524).

In recalling the dread he suffered in anticipation of the duel, Nabokov tallies up the enormous losses incurred by the practice of dueling in Russian history. He recalls not only the deaths of Russia's two greatest poets, Pushkin and Lermontov, but also the prominent families that had suffered "tragic deaths on the dueling ground in more or less recent years" (*SM* 522). He is repelled by the images that haunt him on the eve of his father's duel (*SM* 521), and Peter Shishkov, his fictional alter ego in the story that revisits the trauma he suffered on the eve of his father's anticipated duel, finds it "impossible, unbearable" to imagine his own father fighting in a duel (*SVN* 326). But unlike V. D. Nabokov, who invoked the commonsense argument that dueling only multiplies wrongs instead of redressing them ("DiUZ" 2740), Nabokov makes no gesture toward such a conclusion at the end of his long list of epitaphs.

As the anthropologist Frank Henderson Stewart has shown, ideas about honor have changed over time, but they have not significantly differed from one European country to another (*H* 149).[7] Furthermore, the idea that honor is more important than life has been expressed with consistent regularity both in European and Arabic contexts (*H* 145). In his essay on dueling, V. D. Nabokov refers to this key attribute of honor when he cites Vladimir Spasovich's defense of Evgeny Utin in the sensational trial that followed Utin's killing of Aleksandr Zhokhov in a duel in 1872: "the dueling ritual is a symbol of civilization that demonstrates that man can and must in certain cases sacrifice his greatest good—his life—for things that have no reason or meaning from *the materialistic point of view*: for his faith, his nation, his honor" (qtd. in "DiUZ" 2736; emphasis added).[8] V. D. Nabokov cites this argument in order to dismantle it, but his son was invigorated by the possibility that claims of honor could justify conduct that materialistic accounts of reality were unable to explain.

As E. H. Ruck reminds us, combat served as an ideal opportunity for a knight to demonstrate chivalrous behavior.[9] Nabokov sympathized with the institution of the duel not only because it preserved the last traces of a chivalric code of honor, but also because it seemed capable of refuting materialism and the ethical theory most closely associated with it: utilitarianism. Embedding mortal risk in highly ritualized conduct, the duel of honor occupies the same position in Nabokov's ethics that the heightened artistry of natural mimicry occupies in his philosophy of science and his aesthetics. In each, he found release from the grip of Darwinian compulsion and a challenge to live in freedom.

The claim made by Spasovich and others that honor is detached from materialistic considerations is obviously false. Honor's material rewards have always been considerable, and the loss of honor was (and still is, in spite of claims that the concept of honor has become obsolete)[10] often accompanied by expulsion from one's community. As an institution of honor, dueling was so deeply entrenched in certain groups that opting out—either by refusing to participate in a duel or by violating the rules of the dueling code—was tantamount to resigning one's membership from the group. Nabokov certainly knew that honor afforded significant rewards, yet this knowledge did not deter him from highlighting its nonutilitarian dimensions. Once again, his understanding of natural mimicry is useful here: while he liked to emphasize his conviction that mimicry could not be *fully* explained by a materialist-determinist account of biological evolution, he did not deny that mimicry conferred significant survival benefits. Replicating the relationship between the pragmatic and non-pragmatic he saw in natural mimicry, dueling allowed him to pay tribute to a practice that could be viewed as participating in the Darwinian economy of survival without being wholly reducible to it.

DISINTERESTEDNESS, AUTONOMY, AND HONOR

Nabokov's appeal to readers not to misunderstand Lensky's reasons for challenging Onegin concludes with an observation that demonstrates his intimate familiarity with a cardinal principle of dueling: "it is Onegin who behaves oddly (i.e., out of tune with the mentality given him by his maker in previous chapters)," Nabokov assures his readers, "when he not only accepts the challenge but fires first and shoots to kill. It should be remembered that a gentleman's honor was purified not so much by his own fire as by his coolly enduring that of his adversary" (*EO* 3.16–17). The idea that honor is restored by submitting to the adversary's fire (and *not* by shooting to kill) is fundamental to Nabokov's eagerness to describe dueling as disinterested and, because disinterested, autonomous.

The most notable record of this autonomy is the sangfroid (*khladnokrovie*) that the valiant duelist is expected to demonstrate throughout the dueling ritual. By mastering his passions (fear, anxiety, the desire for revenge), the brave duelist presents himself, to quote Billacois, as "magnificently autonomous" (*Duel* 216). The short stories that take dueling as their principal subject see Nabokov insisting on reading the duel as a study of autonomy. In "An Affair of Honor" (Nabokov's own approved translation of "Podlets," literally "The Scoundrel," 1927), the protagonist disgraces himself by absconding from a duel after having called out his wife's lover. The story's concluding lines depict the duel's symbolic urgency as antithetical to physical desire. Reflecting upon his cowardly behavior, Anton Petrovich seeks solace in a ham sandwich. Though he looks away in shame when the maid delivers it, he abandons himself to his appetite as soon as she departs: "he grabbed the sandwich with both hands, immediately soiled his fingers and chin with the hanging margin of fat, and, grunting greedily, began to munch" (*SVN* 221). This consuming hunger for animal flesh looks like Nabokov's representation of Anton Petrovich's surrender to a life without honor.

"Orache" ("Lebeda," 1932), the story inspired by the challenge issued by V. D. Nabokov to the editor of *Novoe vremia*, ends with a different outcome. V. D. Nabokov's fictional counterpart, G. D. Shishkov, submits to the fire of his opponent and then "discharged his pistol into the air" (*SVN* 327). Like V. D. Nabokov, the invented Shishkov is a Kadet member of the Duma who challenges a colleague to a duel when the latter casts aspersions on his honor (*SVN* 322, 324). In *Speak, Memory*, Nabokov describes his father as having been "extremely strict in matters of conduct" (523). It is clear that

"Orache" is an attempt to imagine how such strictness would have guided his actions in a duel.

The gallant conduct of G. D. Shishkov in his duel with Tumansky is the standard against which Nabokov measures the moral excellence of historical and literary duelists. In his lectures on Turgenev's *Fathers and Children*, he corrects Paul (Pavel) Kirsanov when the latter praises Bazarov for having acted nobly in their duel. "Actually," Nabokov tells his students, "Bazarov would have behaved still more nobly if he had coolly discharged his pistol in the air after enduring Uncle Pavel's fire" (*LRL* 90). Van, for all his faults, does behave nobly when, after having been wounded by Captain Tapper's fire, "with nice dignity discharged his pistol in the sun-hazy air" (*A* 249).

In his lectures on *Anna Karenina*, Nabokov gives an account of the logic behind his insistence that firing into the air after submitting to the adversary's fire was the acme of honorable behavior. "Vronsky shoots himself," Nabokov tells his students, "much for the same reason as that for which an insulted gentleman of his day would have challenged the insulter to a duel, *not to kill his man, but on the contrary to force him to fire at him*, the insulted one. Exposing himself to the other man's forced fire would have wiped away the insult" (*LRL* 174; emphasis added). Nabokov's summing up of what he calls "the basic idea of honor behind duels" is accurate (*LRL* 174). Writing about dueling in the American context, Kenneth Greenberg describes the rationale behind dueling in terms identical to those used by Nabokov: "Although some men dueled in order to kill a hated adversary, the vast majority dueled in order to demonstrate that they possessed the central virtue of men of honor: they did not fear death. The central purpose of a duel was not to kill, but to be threatened with death."[11] Though Nabokov concedes that "there have been cases when both men were out to kill each other," he nonetheless insists that a duel ought not to be motivated by a desire to kill, but rather by a moral imperative to show oneself willing to risk being killed (*LRL* 174). Billacois provides a more elaborate explanation of the duel's strange logic: "Life without honor is so devalued that it can be risked in a duel, which offers a simple way to reach an end that is infinitely superior to such life. The death to which one may put the other man in a duel is simply a secondary result of the essential re-establishment of honor." Quoting from a sixteenth-century treatise on honor by Giovanni Battista Possevino, Billacois explains why the institution of the duel approached the matter of death as being, in a sense, incidental: "Homicide is not the end of the duel, its end is the recovery of honor, and when homicide comes into it, it is by accident" (*Duel* 205).

Stewart's definition of honor as an entitlement to respect helps untangle this logical peculiarity of the dueling ethos. Stewart notes that this definition is uniquely suitable for explaining why insults are seen to violate honor: an insult is an offense against honor because it is an infringement of one's right to respect (*H* 21). Nabokov is correct, in theory, when he notes that the insulted party's challenge ought not to be driven by a desire for revenge, but rather by the desire to face mortal danger. By forcing his adversary to fire at him, the injured party demonstrates his courage and thus proves himself worthy of the respect denied him by the original insult. Whereas firing into the air *after* submitting to his adversary's fire would demonstrate mastery over his passions, shooting first and to kill (as Onegin does) proves that he is enslaved by his passions and is thus unworthy of respect. For Nabokov, as for apologists of the duel, the brave duelist's self-mastery serves as proof of his autonomy.

HONOR AND SUICIDE

To explain the logic that aligns honor with respect, Stewart invokes Kant's discussion of defamation as a violation of the respect implicit in the idea of honor (*H* 152). In *The Metaphysics of Morals*, Kant argues that duties of virtue arise from humanity's entitlement to respect: "Every human being has a legitimate claim to respect from his fellow human beings and is *in turn* bound to respect every other" (*MM* 6:462; emphasis in original). This universal right to respect is inseparable from the idea of honor: "defamation . . . is contrary to the respect owed to humanity as such. . . . The intentional *spreading* (*propalatio*) of something that detracts from another's honor . . . diminishes respect for humanity as such, so as finally to cast a shadow of worthlessness over our race itself" (*MM* 6:466).

But if the duty to respect oneself and others is straightforward enough, responding to instances of disrespect with a duel is wrong according to most religious and rational moral standards, including Kant's. At the most fundamental level, dueling risked—even invited—violating the basic moral imperative "Thou shalt not kill." Furthermore, both critics and defendants of the institution acknowledge that dueling is incapable of delivering justice and, as such, is an irrational method for settling disputes. The incompatibility of private warfare with peace and order is also generally acknowledged.

Dueling presents a limit case for Kant's ethics. Had he made the institution of dueling a subject of study, there can be little doubt that Kant—like V. D. Nabokov—would have condemned it. Nonetheless, dueling and Kantian ethics are founded upon the same understanding of honor as an entitlement to respect, and it is therefore possible to justify dueling by invoking Kantian moral reasoning. As I have already noted, this hangs on the traditional claim, advanced by Nabokov and others, that duels are fought not to kill an adversary but to restore honor by exposing oneself to mortal risk. By portraying the model duelist as one who fires into the air after having endured the fire of his opponent, Nabokov identifies the duel with the logic spelled out here by Appiah: "A gentleman's presence at a duel indicated willingness to die defending his honor and this established that he met one of the criteria for being honorable. Though risking your life might show you cared about honor, actually killing in defense of your honor showed only that you were a good, or, at the least, a lucky, shot" (*HC* 25).

Appiah's account of the logic of dueling makes it vulnerable to a Kantian critique from another angle. The duelist who establishes his own courage by compelling his adversary to fire first can be said to violate Kant's second formulation of the categorical imperative, which prohibits the treatment of others as means rather than ends. Yet this challenge can be overcome by the same argument Kant applies to sexual intercourse. Though he acknowledges that sexual intercourse violates the Formula of Humanity (because "in the sexual inclination, it is essential that one subject is presented to the other as object of enjoyment" [*LE* 27:637–38]), he nonetheless argues that the dignity of both partners can be preserved in monogamous matrimony:

> Now since one party is conceding possession of their substance to the other, each of them can only remain free if, in the bond of common sexual possession one of another, and in precisely the degree to which each possesses the other, the one who allows the other to have *dominium* over them at the same time subjects that other to their own possession, so that they each recoup themselves. The two of them mutually acquire each other; each becomes *dominus* of the other and in that case remains also self-possessing, and is free. (*LE* 27:638)

This structure of mutual surrender and recovery can be productively compared to a frequently invoked analogy for dueling: namely, the duel "as an extreme form of gift exchange."[12] Billacois' invocation of this analogy turns on the same logic as Kant's defense of monogamous sex: "In a duel the generous gentleman made his equal a gift which simultaneously required an equally invaluable gift in return. He did not subject his opponent, he did not abase him. He gave him recognition as a free agent, by using his own freedom in relation to him" (*Duel* 216).

But even if the duel's homicidal impulses are bracketed out, its reckless disregard for one's own life remains deeply troubling. Exposing oneself to mortal danger is a form of suicide, but the internal coherence of Kant's prohibition of suicide has provoked debate.[13] In Herder's notes on Kant's lectures, Kant justifies this prohibition in terms that anticipate the tripartite formulation of the categorical imperative. According to what was to become the Formula of Universal Law, suicide is wrong because the notion of duty cannot survive the death of the subject (*LE* 27:370). Suicide is wrong, too, because it is contrary to this early version of the Formula of Humanity: "That which a man can dispose over, must be a thing. . . . but man is no thing; so if, nevertheless, he disposes over his life, he sets upon himself the value of a beast" (*LE* 27:372–73). The rationale that will become associated with the Formula of the Kingdom of Ends is especially striking:

> Those who defend and teach the legitimacy of suicide inevitably do great harm in a republic. Suppose it were a general disposition that people cherished, that suicide was a right, and even a merit or honor; such people would be abhorrent to everyone. For he who so utterly fails to respect his life on principle can in no way be restrained from the most appalling vices; he fears no king and no torture. (*LE* 27:374–75)

Statements such as these suggest that Kant found it impossible to imagine a condition in which honor could be restored by suicide.

Kant's argument against suicide is at its most coherent when suicide is motivated by suffering. It is morally wrong, he asserts, to take one's life in order to avoid pain, for neither "the most excruciating pains and even irremediable bodily sufferings can give a man the authority to take his own life" (*LE* 27:628). Such a formulation harmonizes with Kant's rejection of inclination and desire as criteria for moral decision-making and aligns suicide with hedonism. But Kant would also have been able to dissociate suicide from hedonism by placing it under the rubric of self-respect. The duty of self-respect commands that the human individual "must preserve his honour, i.e., the *justum aestimum sui ipsius vel humanitatis in sui ipsius persona*, for humanity is an inviolably holy thing" (*LE* 27:602). Champions of the duel might reasonably invoke Kant's maxim to argue that although it is not necessary for people to live happily, it is necessary that they live honorably.

Kant admits that honor-driven suicides frequently derail the logic of the categorical imperative. What of cases such as those of Cato and Lucretia, he asks, in which a person commits suicide "from honorable motives" (*LE* 27:370)? These reflections lead him to consider the moral implications of dying on the field of battle. A soldier's death in battle, Kant argues, does not qualify as suicide because the dead soldier did not *choose* death. The critical distinction lies in intent: "There is a difference," Kant continues, "between the imprudence in which a wish to live is still present, and the intention to do away with oneself" (*LE* 27:372). In the context of war, the duty of self-preservation is superseded by values that also anchor the institution of the duel:

> He who runs away to save his life from the enemy, and leaves all his comrades in the lurch, is a coward; but if he defends himself and his fellows to the

> death, that is no suicide, but is held to be noble and gallant; since, in and for itself, life is in no way to be highly prized, and I should seek to preserve my life only insofar as I am worthy to live. A distinction has to be made between a suicide and one who has lost his life to fate. (*LE* 27:371)

Arguments such as these allow Kant to declare, as he does elsewhere, that "it is permitted to venture one's life against the danger of losing it" (*LE* 27:629).

Kant's distinction "between the imprudence in which a wish to live is still present" and "the intention to do away with oneself" can be cogently applied to defend the duel against the objection that fighting in a war is imposed rather than chosen. But as Nabokov reminds us, both in the context of Lensky's duel with Onegin and in his account of his father's anticipated duel with Suvorin, men of honor were every bit as devoted to the honor code as soldiers were devoted to the codes of military duty. According to this line of argument, a duelist may be guilty of imprudence, but his decision to fight in a duel need not contravene the perfect duty (to use Kant's terminology) to refrain from suicide. It bears noting in this context that a duelist risks death under conditions that are far more closely engineered than those of a soldier.

Just as Kant's soldier evades moral culpability by dying at the hand of fate, the dead duelist may evade the charge of suicide by invoking fate's unpredictability. As Billacois notes, fate played a critical role in the duel's symbolic economy. While a duelist showcased his autonomy by demonstrating his willingness to fight in a duel, fate was said to determine a duel's outcome: "This fight which was seen in terms of chance and luck escaped any relations of causality, any temporal sequence: it was said that in it Satan had 'given all the power to fate'" (*Duel* 239). Nabokov, accepting as he did that duels had a place in decent, high-minded societies, put much stock in the fact that Pushkin, like his own father, was a staunch believer in fate (*EO* 2.433; *Pnin* 345).[14]

HONOR VS. REPUTATION

In spite of stressing the importance of honorable conduct in both his lectures and formal writings, Kant seems to have been troubled by the conceptual slipperiness of honor. In the early lectures attended by Herder, he tried to address this by drawing a firm distinction between honor and self-esteem: unlike self-esteem, which "is rooted in morality," honor merely seeks "the good *opinion* of other people" (emphasis in original). Within this binary, honor becomes a synonym for *reputation*: "The pursuit of honor is more harmful to morality than any other passion; all others have something real about them, but this one is a phantom of the brain" (*LE* 27:44).

In *The Metaphysics of Morals*, Kant identifies this debased species of honor as *respectability* (6:464). And in *Anthropology from a Pragmatic Point of View*, he draws a distinction that is similar to the "bipartite" theory of honor that distinguishes inner honor (a personal quality) from outer honor (reputation) (*H* 18–19). Predictably, Kant asserts that inner honor is purer than the outer honor that a duel seeks to defend:

> Not allowing oneself to be intimidated by something that is sacred, by sarcastic derision even when it is more temptingly seasoned with taunts and trickery, but instead pursuing one's own course steadfastly, is a moral courage which many a person does not possess who otherwise excels as brave on the battlefield or in a duel. It takes a high degree of determination to do what duty demands, even at the danger of being ridiculed by others. It takes a high degree because love of honor is the constant companion of virtue; and he who can otherwise well withstand force seldom feels strong enough to endure ridicule if his claim to honor is sneeringly refused. (*Anth* 162–63)

Kant's meaning is clear: genuine moral courage lays aside self-conceit and abstains from responding with violence to injury and insult. Nonetheless, this inferior species of courage is not entirely negligible. If, as Kant states, "love of honor is the constant companion of virtue," it seems unrealistic (even for Kant) to expect virtuous people to disregard a "sneering refusal" to be treated with respect.

The most compelling evidence that the logic of Kant's writings on honor can accommodate dueling appears in Georg Ludwig Collins's notes on his lectures. No mere loophole, the argument provides a straightforward justification of the duel's moral legitimacy. "There are duties that are far higher than life," Kant begins, "that must often be performed by sacrificing life." Only "a worthless man," he continues, "values his life more than his person" (*LE* 27:375–76). By contrast, "the man of inner worth is not afraid of death, and would sooner die than be an object of contempt" (*LE* 27:376). The following set of injunctions, ending as it does with a question that is unambiguously rhetorical, suggests that outer honor mattered a great deal to Kant: "Humanity, in our person, is an object of the highest respect and never to be violated in us. In the cases where a man is liable to dishonor, he is duty bound to give up his life, rather than dishonor the humanity in his own person. For does he do honor to it, if it is to be dishonored by others?" The kinship between inner and outer honor is highlighted again a few sentences later: "At the moment when I can no longer live with honor, and become by such an action unworthy of life, I cannot live at all. It is therefore far better to die with honor and *reputation*" (emphasis added). "Moral life is at an end," Kant observes poignantly, "if it no longer accords with the dignity of humanity" (*LE* 27:377).

"TRUE HONOR"

The last line of argument that can be pressed into the service of a Kantian defense of the duel of honor is simultaneously the most explicit and the most troubling one. In his discussion of capital punishment in *The Metaphysics of Morals*, Kant confronts the possibility that the state cannot legitimately impose the death penalty on two types of homicides: a mother murdering her illegitimate child and a soldier killing another soldier in a duel. These cases are special, he explains, because they involve "true honor": "The feeling of honor leads to both, in one case the *honor of one's sex*, in the other *military honor*, and indeed true honor, which is incumbent as duty on each of these two classes of people" (emphasis in original). The exemption hinges on the law's inability to redress these particular violations of honor: "Legislation cannot remove the disgrace of an illegitimate birth any more than it can wipe away the stain of suspicion of cowardice from a subordinate officer who fails to respond to a humiliating affront with a force of his own rising above fear of death" (*MM* 6:336). The overwhelming force of social custom renders the law helpless in these cases. Just as a woman's sufferings would be exacerbated if she were to publicize her disgrace with a legal petition, an officer accused of cowardice would only demonstrate the truth of the accusation if he were to sue for libel. In Mika LaVaque-Manty's pithy summation of Kant's argument, "law should not punish where it cannot help."[15]

Kant's pairing of dueling and infanticide might appear sufficiently damning to serve as a conclusive indictment of dueling. But this is clearly not his intention. As often with Kant, the categorical imperative gains its supreme authority precisely by the exorbitant cost of its sacrifices. In this particular case, the example of the dishonored woman who kills her illegitimate child is not meant to trivialize human life or to suggest that honor is a spurious value. Instead, the unspeakable horror of infanticide is meant to elicit the ruthless tyranny of honor over affections and commitments that we would expect to trump all others. Capital punishment is inapplicable in these cases, Kant explains, because "the concept of honor . . . is here no illusion" (*MM* 6:336). Kant's writings on aesthetics are also relevant in this context: the honor-loving woman who kills her illegitimate child is analogous to the experience of the sublime insofar as it provokes us "to esteem" it "even contrary to our (sensible) interest" (*CPJ* 5:267).

THE DUEL AND DEONTOLOGY

Nabokov's most lyrical description of a duel is his speculative reconstruction of Pushkin's duel with the Decembrist Kondraty Ryleev in the spring of 1820 at Batovo, the country estate of Nabokov's paternal grandparents (*SM* 407;

EO 2.431–34).[16] Nabokov draws keen pleasure from imagining Pushkin stepping into the landscape where, as a boy, Nabokov himself used to fight his own "mock duels" with his cousin Yury (*EO* 2.433):

> I can feel upon my skin and in my nostrils the delicious country roughness of the northern spring day which greeted Pushkin and his two seconds as they got out of their coach and penetrated into the linden avenue beyond the Batovo platbands, still virginally black. I see so plainly the three young men . . . following their host and two persons unknown, into the park. At that date small crumpled violets showed through the carpet of the last year's dead leaves, and freshly emerged Orange-tips settled on the shivering dandelions. For one moment fate may have wavered between preventing a heroic rebel from heading to the gallows, and depriving Russia of *Eugene Onegin*; but then did neither. (*SM* 408)

This vision is so captivating that Nabokov forgets its conjectural nature by the time he pens his annotations to Lensky's duel with Onegin. Foreshadowing Kinbote's tactics, Nabokov lists Pushkin's apocryphal duel with Ryleev with two other duels that Pushkin is known to have fought before his duel with d'Anthès. The duel's speculative origins are revealed only to the reader willing to open a different volume of Nabokov's annotations to *Eugene Onegin* and obey the editorial injunction "see my n. to Four: XIX: 5" (*EO* 3.45).

Pushkin and Ryleev had much to lose by fighting in the duel imagined by Nabokov. Ryleev's losses, in particular, would have been immediately tangible: "He had just sent his wife," Nabokov tells us, "in her last month of pregnancy, to her estate near Voronezh, and was anxious to get the duel over—and, God willing, join her there" (*SM* 408). Pushkin's great works—*Eugene Onegin* foremost among them—were also in the future. But the specter of such losses elicited from Nabokov no comment, however subdued or laconic, about the absurdity of dueling.

No such condemnation flows from Nabokov's pen because the duel, with its code of ritual laws and its foundational assumption that honor is more valuable than life, provides him with an ethical model that claims to be able to rise above the consideration of interests. A duelist committed to the honor code rather than to honor's rewards embraces an ethics that is conspicuously at odds with utilitarian calculations. Appiah is especially eloquent on the duel's principled commitment to the logic of deontology, and his statements about dueling as an institution of honor can be viewed as an echo of Kant's famous claim that morality is born not of the search for happiness, but in the quest to become *worthy* of happiness:

> It's important to understand that while honor is an entitlement to respect—and shame comes when you lose that title—a person of honor cares first of

> all not about being respected but about being *worthy* of respect. Someone who just wants to be respected won't care whether he is really living up to the code; he will just want to be *thought* to be living up to it. He will be managing his reputation, not maintaining his honor. (*HC* 16; emphasis in original)

As Appiah notes further, "honor requires me to conform to the standard for its own sake, not merely for the sake of reputation and its rewards" (*HC* 18). Bending the duel toward other ends violates the deontological purity of its honor code (*HC* 44).

Yury Lotman and Billacois similarly underscore the duel's attachment to a deontological ethics. In contradistinction to military ethics, Lotman observes, where an officer's courage is measured by the extent to which it advances the aims of the state, the ethics of personal honor sees courage as "an end in itself [*samotsel'*]." For Lotman, the duel's origins in medieval chivalry highlight this nonutilitarian valuation of personal honor: "a knight's conduct is not measured by victory or defeat because its value is autotelic" (*Besedy* 165). Similarly tracing the duel of honor to chivalric ethics, Billacois identifies this type of honor as "a spiritual value," "an intrinsic, indivisible part of the man of honor." "In the land of chivalry," Billacois concludes, "honor has no sovereign other than free will" (*Duel* 207). Utilitarian considerations of benefits could play no part in an honorable man's decision to fight in a duel: "If the winning duellist survived the ordeal, he had no lasting reward: he had to hide, to go into exile, as though struck down with 'civil death,' and the honor he had so dearly won did not withstand the first subsequent challenge" (*Duel* 239–40).

Nabokov's understanding of the duel in deontological terms is enunciated most explicitly in *The Real Life of Sebastian Knight* (1941). The narrator, known throughout as V., fails to understand how his and Sebastian's father could throw away his own happiness and the happiness of his family for the sake of a senseless duel. Upon learning that his former wife's lover was alluding to his affair with the deceased woman many years after the fact, V.'s father challenges the lover to a duel. Fought in winter on "the bank of a frozen brook," the duel recalls Pushkin's duel with d'Anthès (*RLSK* 9). For V., his father's willingness to die in a duel of honor with "a fool and a cad" (*RLSK* 8) is unintelligible:

> It is hard for me to understand why a man of my father's worth should have risked his life to satisfy—what? Virginia's honor? His own desire for revenge? But just as Virginia's honor had been irredeemably forfeited by the very fact of her flight, so all ideas of vengeance ought to have long lost their bitter lust in the happy years of my father's second marriage. Or was it merely the naming of a name, the seeing of a face, the sudden grotesque sight of an individual stamp upon what had been a tame faceless ghost? And taken all in all

> was it, this echo of a distant past . . . , was it worth the ruin of our home and the grief of my mother? (*RLSK* 9)

Insofar as these questions are rhetorical, they serve as a powerful indictment of dueling. But this is more than a rhetorically driven argument against dueling, for V.'s concluding question is less straightforward than it might appear. Can a value such as honor be understood in terms of *worth*? Stewart's observation that "the more closely one looks at honor, the odder it seems" is relevant here (*H* 145). V.'s father was killed in a "beastly affair" that lasted a whole of "three minutes" (*RLSK* 9), yet Nabokov seems simultaneously to endorse V.'s moving condemnation of dueling and look beyond it. V.'s confusion, Nabokov suggests, arises from his failure to understand that a duel of honor can only be defended in terms that are hopelessly self-referential: honor is an absolute value that speaks for itself and serves its own ends. This seems to be the reason why Nabokov, unlike V., finds it impossible to criticize his own father for weighing personal honor (by challenging Suvorin to a duel; by trying to disarm Miliukov's assassins) more highly than his own life and his family's welfare.

The difficulty of defining honor in terms that are not merely circular is underscored in a recurring version of Lotman's memorable formulation of the dueling paradox: "The duel is a prejudice, but honor, which is forced to turn to it for help, is not a prejudice" (*Besedy* 169). V. D. Nabokov identifies this conundrum as a form of *credo, quia absurdum* (I believe because it is absurd) when he quotes from Eduard Kohlrausch's 1909 monograph on dueling: "I understand very well that dueling is an absurdity [*nelepost'*], but my feeling [*chuvstvo*] does not permit me to do away with this prejudice" (qtd. in "DiUZ" 2744). Like most Russian analysts of the duel, V. D. Nabokov invokes Bazarov's duel with Kirsanov as the quintessential illustration of this double bind:

> This is fine in theory, but when it comes to practice, even those who condemn dueling will fight in a duel. This was expressed by Bazarov in response to Kirsanov's challenge. He said: I believe that from the theoretical point of view this is nonsense, but practically speaking this is a different matter. In spite of being opposed to duels, he went to fight one. And this is not an isolated case. A vast number of people have fought in duels in spite of fighting most passionately against dueling. ("DiUZ" 2739)[17]

For V. D. Nabokov, this illustration of honor's tyranny serves as "the most difficult objection" to anti-dueling initiatives. Having dismantled in his essay the double bind's strange logic, V. D. Nabokov nonetheless succumbed to it himself two years later when he issued a challenge to Suvorin.

Like mimicry in nature, dueling enabled Nabokov to make a deductive move he found appealing: if, as Nabokov clearly believes, dueling transcends the logic of utilitarianism, fighting in a duel affords an honorable man the opportunity to perform his independence from utilitarian concerns. In Nabokov's pantheon of values, the duel becomes a last stand of human agency in a world that is increasingly understood as a complex interplay of physical forces and material interests. This yearning to see the duel as a performance of personal autonomy prevents Nabokov from dwelling on a feature of dueling that has troubled both its critics and exponents: its apparent capacity to rob its participants of their free will.

Recalling his former duels, Pushkin's protagonist in *The Prisoner of the Caucasus* (1822) portrays the duel as a cruel tyrant:

> A slave of honor, ruthless honor,
> he at close range had seen his end
> when in a duel he, firm and cold,
> would face the fateful lead.[18]

Nabokov quotes these lines apropos of Onegin's duel with Lensky, but he does not dwell on them (*EO* 3.51). Instead, he notes that the locution "slave of honor (*nevol'nik chesti*)" reappears in a famous poem that Lermontov wrote on the occasion of Pushkin's death. Like Nabokov, Lermontov sees Pushkin's death as a demonstration of agency: "He rose against the world's opinion / Alone, as before . . . and he's dead" ("On the Death of a Poet" ["Smert' poeta"], lines 7–8).[19]

Lotman, however, invokes Pushkin's locution ("*nevol'nik chesti*") to argue, as others have argued before him, that the duel's strong ritualistic nature "deprives its participants of individual freedom" (*Besedy* 174). Lotman's essay on dueling dwells on a question that has puzzled many readers of *Eugene Onegin*: why does Onegin shoot to kill, given his affection for Lensky and his acknowledgment that he has insulted him? For Lotman, the answer lies in the duel's annihilation of personal autonomy: once the logic of the duel begins to unfold, Onegin forfeits his agency and becomes "an automaton in the hands of the impersonal dueling ritual" (*Besedy* 175). Nabokov responds to the same question with perplexity. Onegin's behavior throughout the morning of the duel "has an uncanny dreamlike quality," Nabokov notes, and when Lensky is wounded "one almost expects Onegin to wake." "Onegin behaves as he never would have behaved in a normal state of moral awareness," Nabokov explains further. "Lensky, no doubt, has murderous intentions, but Onegin, a fearless and scornful marksman, would, if in his right mind, have certainly reserved his fire, and not even returned it but, if still alive, thrown it away, i.e., discharged his pistol into the air" (*EO* 3.40–41). Whereas Lotman exonerates Onegin by putting the blame on the tyranny of the dueling ritual, Nabokov chastises Onegin for not living up to the duel's code of ethics.

Nabokov was untroubled by claims, made by Lotman and others, that the duel's strong ritualistic nature deprives its participants of personal freedom because, like Kant, he perceived a crucial difference between the tyranny of nature and the tyranny of self-imposed duty. Subjecting oneself willingly to the logic of the dueling code is a servitude analogous to that showcased by the dying Kant who, trembling from weakness, did not permit himself to sit down until his physician had taken a seat first. For Kant, as for Nabokov, such voluntary servitude is—paradoxically—a marker of freedom, or to use Billacois' epithet for the brave duelist, a marker of being "magnificently autonomous."

THE DUEL AND THE DECEMBRISTS

Nabokov tried hard to preserve the deontological purity of the duel by severing it from utilitarian considerations, but he knew that other freedom-loving Russians had used it for political ends. Like his own father and most Russian liberationists, Nabokov revered the Decembrists. Named after their abortive uprising against Nicholas I on December 26 (O.S. December 14), 1825, the Russian army officers known collectively as "the Decembrists" recruited the duel in their struggle against tsarist autocracy. Nabokov's act of scholarly speculation in which he posits that Pushkin and Ryleev fought a duel at Batovo is tied up not only in a longing for a personal link to Pushkin, but also in a longing for a connection to Ryleev, a minor poet and famous Decembrist who was hanged along with four other rebels for his participation in the revolt. Ryleev stood to lose not only seeing his unborn child, Nabokov notes in his speculative reconstruction of Ryleev's duel with Pushkin, but he also stood to lose his hero's place in the annals of Russian history: "I can visualize the fearless lieutenant defying despotism on the bleak Senate Square," Nabokov tells us about Ryleev's leading role in the Decembrist revolt five years after the apocryphal duel in which fate wisely spared the lives of both Ryleev and Pushkin (*SM* 408).

In *Speak, Memory*, Nabokov tells us that his father was intimately familiar with the history of the Decembrists and felt deep sympathy toward their cause (409). By dint of his own voracious reading habits and his father's keen interest in Decembrist history, Nabokov would have known from an early age that the Decembrists embraced dueling as a form of political protest (*RV* 84; *Besedy* 166–67).[20] In Reyfman's account, the Decembrists' authority derived in part "from their reputation as the most devoted exponents of the honor code in Russia and thus the most ardent duelists. They projected the kind of resoluteness that guarded not only their own private space but also, decades later, the private space of others" (*RV* 134). The duelists' contempt for utilitarian considerations was yoked to the service of a covert liberationist agenda: their passion for "unnecessary risk was not just a way to demonstrate their bravery and experience the thrill of danger; it proved that they were free human beings, and that the choice of whether to live or die was, if not completely theirs (the role of chance—or Providence—was as essential in dueling as it was in gambling), then certainly not the state's" (*RV* 80). As Reyfman notes further, the heroic image of the duel rose even higher as a result of the severe punishments imposed on the Decembrists after their defeat (*RV* 84).

Given that the modern European duel of honor began life as a weapon in the struggle for personal rights and liberty, it is not surprising that the Decembrists should turn it to ideological ends. One of its main sources was the institution of "judicial combat" in which members of the military ruling class could settle legal disputes by fighting in single combat. Unlike modern duels, these "judicious duels" were legally sanctioned: they could only take place if they were "granted the field" by a feudal lord (*HC* 26–27). Modern dueling emerged when, to quote Reyfman's elegant formulation, the duel "evolved from public combats sanctioned by the king to private encounters in defiance of the king" (*RV* 43). As a private and illegal act of aristocratic privilege and self-policing, the modern European duel was, from its earliest beginnings, in conflict with state authority. Montesquieu's memorable words in *The Spirit of the Laws* explain why monarchs sought to suppress the practice: "Honor is in no way the principle of despotic states. . . . honor has its own laws and rules, which it cannot compromise; it is determined by its own caprice and cannot accept the caprice of another."[21]

In Russia, dueling was closely aligned with the earliest stirrings of liberal thought. Alexander Herzen, identified by Nabokov as "a famous liberal" and "the talented author" of one of "my father's favorite books" (*SM* 385), traced the institution of the modern duel to medieval chivalry. Published in 1848 in *The Contemporary* under the title "Some Notes on the Historical Development of Honor," Herzen's essay is a paean to the principle of personal inviolability: "*Man has learned to respect himself from the knight*. . . . The proud demand for the recognition of chivalric rights was the soil from which grew the consciousness of rights and dignity of man generally."[22] Writing under censorship, Herzen intimates that Russia's love affair with dueling in the 1830s and 1840s was fueled by the absence of institutional protections of personal rights and liberties.

Reyfman amplifies the story told by Herzen by noting that the duel became popular in eighteenth-century Russia when the nobility began to absorb Western ideas of personal autonomy and physical inviolability. By adopting the duel as a means of settling disputes, Russia's noble class sought to demonstrate its independence from state authority and its right to protect itself from the indignity of corporal punishment (*RV* 109). The duel's cardinal principle that all honorable gentlemen possess an equal and indivisible amount of honor made this possible. To quote Reyfman, "While [the duel's] capacity to instill civility among peers is most obvious, the duel also effectively prevented physical assaults of superiors against their subordinates. The duel rejected the superior's patriarchal right to punish, insisting on the essential equality of all noblemen" (*RV* 127).

THE POETICS OF MASTERY AND SELF-CONTROL

In the aftermath of Pushkin's duel with d'Anthès, the latter's second, Viscount Olivier d'Archiac, ended a letter he wrote to Pushkin's friend Prince Peter Viazemsky with a common formula of courtesy: "During this entire affair, the calm, the sangfroid, the dignity of the two parties were perfectly maintained" (*DP* 111). Yet when asked by Viazemsky to confirm the veracity of d'Archiac's account of the duel, Pushkin's second, Lieutenant-Colonel Konstantin Danzas, found it imperative to provide what he considered to be a crucial emendation.

Danzas protested against d'Archiac's pointed insinuation that Pushkin's shot had been fired against dueling regulations and with the forbearance of d'Anthès. According to d'Archiac, Pushkin had no right to ask for a replacement for his snow-filled pistol, but d'Archiac desisted from raising an objection when silently prompted by d'Anthès to permit Pushkin's request (*DP* 110). For Danzas, this claim was at once deeply "offensive" (*oskorbitel'nym*) to Pushkin's memory and a flagrant misrepresentation of the facts (*DP* 112). Pushkin's right to fire was never in question, Danzas insisted, and no secret signs were exchanged between d'Anthès and his second. No such objection was ever raised, Danzas elaborated, because the duel's written conditions stipulated that each principal had the right to a shot. What is more, Danzas continued, the substitution of the pistols was made expressly for the sake of d'Anthès: a shot delivered from a snow-plugged barrel would be substantially more powerful, and therefore more likely to cause fatal injury. Danzas's concluding words on the matter highlight the extent to which duels were seen as battles of will. In such battles, moral victories were regarded as falling to the duelist who had asserted most conclusively his mastery and self-control: "I accord full recognition to the valiant spirit [*bodrost' dukha*] that M. d'Anthès displayed during the duel; but I deny emphatically that he willingly subjected himself to a danger that he could have avoided. After he had fired his shot, it was not up to him to evade the fire of his adversary" (*DP* 113).[23]

In his Paris retelling of Pushkin's duel with d'Anthès, Nabokov wages his own war of words on Pushkin's behalf in terms that parallel those employed by Danzas and d'Archiac. Nabokov imagines Pushkin, already mortally wounded, winning a moral victory over his opponent by forcing him to admit spiritual defeat. Pushkin has fallen into the snow after being wounded by d'Anthès, yet Nabokov portrays him as gaining a spiritual ascendancy over his opponent: "there he is with a bullet in his belly, sitting crosswise in the snow and aiming at d'Anthès for a long, long time—so long that the other can stand it no longer, and slowly shields his heart with his forearm."[24] When Nabokov spoke these words in 1937, his scholarly standards were not as strict as they became during his work on the *Onegin* project. In the Paris lecture, he admits that his retelling of the final moments of Pushkin's duel is a species of "fictionized biography," and he acknowledges that this flight of fancy is a result of the love he feels for Pushkin's work. In his annotations to *Eugene Onegin*, however, scholarly integrity prevents him from indulging in such wistful longings, and he provides his readers with an account that conforms to the biographical record (*EO* 3.50).

Nabokov's assertion to his Paris audience that the wounded Pushkin aimed at d'Anthès for such an unendurably long time that the latter was forced to "slowly shiel[d] his heart with his forearm" inverts the sequence of events provided by Leonid Grossman in a "fictionized biography" from 1931 titled *Zapiski d'Arshiaka* (*The Memoirs of d'Archiac*). Purportedly an account of Pushkin's last duel from the perspective of d'Archiac, Grossman's fictional memoir claims that Pushkin "aimed for a long time [*tselilsia dovol'no dolgo*]" and that his aiming struck d'Archiac as indefinitely long ("*Pauza pokazalas' mne beskonechnoi*"; ZA 289). But Grossman notes further, as Danzas also noted in his letter to Viazemsky, that d'Anthès had already assumed the customary defensive posture of a duelist awaiting a shot (half-turned to the left, with his right arm covering his breast to minimize the target area) as soon as Pushkin announced that he was still strong enough to fire (ZA 288; *DP* 113). As others have noted before and after Grossman, d'Anthès assumed this classic defensive position long before Pushkin raised his pistol (ZA 288–89).

In spite of its acknowledged fictional dimension, Grossman's account is more faithful to the historical record and dueling conventions than Nabokov's account to his audience in Paris. Nabokov deliberately distorts Grossman's account in order to grant his beloved Pushkin a moral victory over his opponent.[25] Nabokov allows himself even greater poetic license than Grossman does when he ventriloquizes d'Archiac in his fictional memoir. First, Grossman's account does not seek to discredit d'Anthès as Nabokov does when he suggests that d'Anthès acted in a cowardly way by shielding himself during Pushkin's prolonged aiming. Second, Grossman's "*tselilsia dovol'no dolgo* [aimed for a long time]" is significantly less emphatic about the duration of Pushkin's aiming than Nabokov's "for a long, long time." Additionally, the "*beskonechnaia* [endless]" "*pauza* [pause]" ostensibly noted by Grossman's fictionalized d'Archiac is ascribed to him as a subjective perception ("*pokazalas' mne*" [seemed to me]) rather than an objective fact.

Grossman may have underscored the subjective nature of this "*pauza*" because he had found no record of it when completing his research for his fictional memoir and therefore was implicitly acknowledging its status as a poetic fabrication. For no such claim is made about Pushkin's aiming at d'Anthès in primary records concerning the duel. Neither d'Archiac nor Danzas—in their brief accounts to Viazemsky in the duel's aftermath—reported that Pushkin took a long time to fire his shot (*DP* 110, 112–13). Even in the closely detailed account given by Danzas to Ammosov twenty-five years later, no such suggestion exists.[26] The accounts of the duel written by Pushkin's closest friends immediately after his death also fail to mention that Pushkin's aim was long enough to be worthy of mentioning.[27] It is therefore not surprising that subsequent biographers make no mention of it in their respective accounts of the duel.[28]

While it is possible to imagine that Nabokov mistook Grossman's claim about Pushkin's long aiming as a matter of historical record, it is impossible to imagine that Nabokov could have viewed his own distortion of Grossman's account as anything other than a matter of artistic license. (He admits as much when he identifies his lecture as an example of "fictionized biography.") To repeat, Grossman makes clear that d'Anthès assumed a defensive stance long before Pushkin began aiming at him. Additionally, Nabokov must have known that his own reversal of this sequence of events would be viewed with suspicion by anyone familiar with dueling conventions or with iconic works of Russian literature. As an avid reader of Tolstoy from an early age, he must have recalled, for instance, Pierre's duel with Dolokhov in *War and Peace*. An inexperienced duelist, Pierre awaits Dolokhov's shot with "his broad chest directly exposed [*priamo svoeiu shirokoiu grud'iu stoial pered Dolokhovym*]." Horrified by his helpless vulnerability, both seconds cry out to him to cover himself with his pistol (*WP* 1.369; *PSS* 10:27).[29] Nabokov's 1937 description of Pushkin's last duel is a poetic fabrication calculated to grant Pushkin a moral triumph over his opponent: Nabokov wants Pushkin to humiliate d'Anthès by way of his superior mastery and self-control.

When Nabokov delivered his Pushkin lecture in Paris, he was already attached to the idea that such gestures of autonomy are the most reliable markers of masculine virtue. In *The Gift* he bestows a cheerful sangfroid upon Godunov, Fyodor's father. Fyodor cannot ascertain how his father perished, but he naturally suspects the Reds:

> Did they shoot him in the ladies' room of some godforsaken station (broken looking glass, tattered plush), or did they lead him out into some kitchen garden one dark night and wait for the moon to peep out? How did he wait with

> them in the dark? With a smile of disdain? And if a whitish moth had hovered among the shadowy burdocks he would, even at that moment, I *know*, have followed it with that same glance of encouragement with which, on occasion, after evening tea, smoking his pipe in our Leshino garden, he used to greet the pink hawks sampling our lilacs. (*Gift* 137)

Describing his father as a man of "even temper, self-control, strong will-power," Fyodor is certain "that had he caught me out in physical cowardice he would have laid a curse on me" (*Gift* 114).

Many years later in the lecture "The Art of Literature and Commonsense," Nabokov would portray the death of the Russian poet (and ardent duelist) Nikolay Gumilev in similar terms:

> One of the main reasons why the very gallant Russian poet Gumilev was put to death by Lenin's ruffians thirty odd years ago was that during the whole ordeal, in the prosecutor's dim office, in the torture house, in the winding corridors that led to the truck, in the truck that took him to the place of execution, and at that place itself, full of the shuffling feet of the clumsy and gloomy shooting squad, the poet kept smiling. (*LL* 376–77)

"Orache," the story that reimagines the agonies suffered by Nabokov's younger self in anticipation of his father's duel, doubles as a story of a young boy's education in the difficult art of self-control (*SVN* 324, 327).

PUSHKIN'S SCALES

Like Pushkin, Nabokov was convinced of his own high place in Russian literature. And also like Pushkin, he was willing to risk his life in duels. According to Boyd, he came close to being involved in four separate duels between the ages of 23 and 29. Three of these instances were sparked by attacks directed at his writing (*VNRY* 203, 287, 350). The fourth reveals a hazy disintegration of the honor code and portrays Nabokov as having strayed far from the cardinal principles of dueling.

The incident in question involved a Romanian violinist, Kosta Spiresco (Spirescu), whose violence was believed to have driven his wife to suicide. When a Russian émigré restaurant hired Spiresco in defiance of public outrage, Nabokov decided to take a stand. Boyd's version of the story is insightful:

> On the night of January 18, 1927, he and his friend Mikhail Kaminka visited the restaurant with their wives, and drew straws to be first to hit the "hirsute,

> ape-like" Spiresco.[30] Nabokov won, slapped him on the cheek and then, according to the newspaper report, "graphically demonstrated upon him the techniques of English boxing." Kaminka pitched in against the rest of the orchestra, who took Spiresco's side. At the police station where the three principals were taken, Spiresco refused to press charges, hinting instead that he would call them out to a duel. He declined however to take the addresses they proffered, and Nabokov and Kaminka waited at home in vain the next two or three days for Spiresco's promised seconds. (*VNRY* 271–72)

Notwithstanding the elements borrowed from the dueling ritual (the classic slap on the face, the wait for the insulted gentleman's seconds) and notwithstanding, too, that the breaking of rules in actual duels was the norm rather than the exception (*RV* 9–10), this incident is a parody of a duel. A brawl rather than a duel, it casts Nabokov as a hotheaded pugilist ready to use his superior strength and martial skills against a man in disgrace. V. D. Nabokov's refusal to call out Snessarev on the grounds that he was non-duelable seems to have been lost upon his son during this act of vigilante justice against a man so pointedly his social inferior. The racially tinged language Nabokov uses to describe Spiresco is also a far cry from the scrupulous, frequently hyperbolic courtesy that duelists were expected to employ in their interactions with each other.

The paternal legacy that shadows Nabokov's attack on Spiresco casts a negative light on the event in an additional way. Nabokov's companion, Michael (Mikhail) Kaminka, was the son of August (Avgust) Kaminka, a long-time friend and political associate who had risen with V. D. Nabokov at Berlin's Philharmonia Hall five years earlier to disarm the assassin who opened fire on the former leader of the Kadet Party, Paul (Pavel) Miliukov.[31] Though August Kaminka survived his act of heroism, V. D. Nabokov was instantly killed. Bound by the ties of their own friendship and burdened by the legacies bequeathed to them by their fathers, Nabokov and Michael Kaminka saw themselves as engaged in more than an attack on a social pariah. When Spiresco's seconds failed to appear, it must have become painfully evident that they were chasing ghosts.

Nabokov's quixotic efforts to keep dueling alive risk inviting the kind of bemused perplexity he ascribes to readers of Onegin's duel with Lensky. Though two poems from the 1920s and 1930s suggest that he had accepted the duel's demise, they also suggest that he continued to cherish its ideals even in the course of violating them. Nabokov wrote his 1931 poem "An Unfinished Draft" ("Neokonchennyi chernovik") shortly after friends convinced him that the man who had publicly panned his fiction was non-duelable (*SO* 39; *VNRY* 350). The poem concludes with a cartel of defiance. Scurrilous reviewers, Nabokov warns,

cower before me in dismay
because I'm wicked, cold, and gay,
[because I serve no one]
because honor and life I weigh
on Pushkin's scales and dare prefer
honor. . . .[32]

Pushkin also reappears as the proper measure in matters of life, honor, and artistic merit in "Youth," written only a year after V. D. Nabokov's death. Here, dueling is invoked as one of several distinctly Pushkinian, enchantingly nonutilitarian props of Russian culture that have become obsolete in the Soviet Union:

Hast [*uzhel'*] my homeland grown weary
of cloaks and roses, Delias, duels,
and the sacred leaf fall at Boldino?[33]

If these markers of authentic, pre-Soviet Russian culture (dueling, Boldino) are quintessentially Pushkinian,[34] the ethics intimated here are quintessentially Nabokovian. As in Kant, freedom proves itself most persuasively when working under the constraints of duty. Kantian, too, is the refusal to abandon one's hopes and obligations in the face of probable failure. For Nabokov, as for Kant, an action's moral status is independent of its consequences, and it is especially appealing for Nabokov that such an action becomes virtuous and heroic precisely at the moment when considerations of utility are ignored.

Chapter Four

Hospitality and the Cosmopolitan Ideal: Nabokov, Pushkin, Shakespeare

> Far from Arthur's court, the knight errant is a stranger; his unusual dress shows that he does not seek to be taken for any common traveler, but it displays, on the contrary, his intention to be taken for a combatant. And for all those who meet him on the road or at their door, even if he does not have hostile intentions hidden under his helmet, the knight errant—unknown—is a stranger whose weapons represent, first, a menace, and, second, an opportunity, with the possibility of assistance to the weak or honourable competition for the strong. Is he good or is he wicked?
>
> —Marie-Luce Chênerie

THE GIFT (*DAR*, 1952), the last novel Nabokov was to complete in Russian, conjures up a beguiling alternate reality about Pushkin. An invented biographer, A. N. Suhoshchokov, plays a prank on Fyodor's grandfather, Kirill Yliich Godunov-Cherdyntsev, when the latter returns to Russia after a long sojourn abroad. Having been reassured that Pushkin is still alive and publishing on a regular basis, Kirill Yliich is made to believe that the elderly man watching *Othello* in the adjacent box is Pushkin. The fantasy fails, however, to hold the attention of Kirill Yliich, who is soon diverted by more mundane concerns. Instead, it is Suhoshchokov himself who falls under the spell of his own deception:

> It seems funny now to recall what a strange mood came upon me then: the prank, as happens from time to time, rebounded, and this frivolously summoned ghost did not want to disappear: I was quite incapable of tearing myself away from the neighboring box; I looked at those harsh wrinkles, that broad nose, those large ears . . . shivers ran down my back, and not all of

> Othello's jealousy was able to drag me away. What if this is indeed Pushkin, I mused, Pushkin at sixty, Pushkin spared two decades ago by the bullet of the fatal coxcomb, Pushkin in the rich autumn of his genius. . . . The act finished; applause thundered. Gray-haired Pushkin stood up abruptly, and still smiling, with a bright sparkle in his youthful eyes, quickly left his box. (*Gift* 101)

This complex fantasy hinges, in part, on the longevity of Shakespeare's productive life relative to Pushkin's: had Shakespeare died at the same age as Pushkin, *Othello* and *King Lear* (two of "the three greatest plays ever written" according to Nabokov) would not have existed (*LRL* 106). By imagining Pushkin watching *Othello* in "the rich autumn of his genius," Nabokov attempts to will out of existence Pushkin's early death at the age of thirty-seven. It is also significant that this fantasy should come to life during a performance of *Othello, The Moor of Venice*, for Pushkin was the great-grandson of Abram Petrovich Gannibal, the so-called Moor of Peter the Great.

Born in modern-day Cameroon, Pushkin's maternal great-grandfather had been kidnapped as a young boy, sold into slavery, and presented as a gift to the Russian emperor. Peter the Great liked the boy, took him into his home, served as godfather at his baptism, and brought him along on his military campaigns. Later, Peter paid for his European education (he studied fortification, sapping, and mining at a military school). Upon his return to Russia, Gannibal enjoyed a distinguished military career under both Peter and Peter's daughter, the Empress Elizabeth. By the time of his death, he had attained the rank of general, had served as military commander of Reval, and had been appointed to oversee military engineering throughout Russia. Gannibal's name bears the traces of his sensational biography: Peter gave him his patronymic (Petrovich, son of Peter), and Gannibal himself chose his own surname after the great Carthaginian general Hannibal.[1] (According to Russian custom, the Latin *h* is rendered as a Russian gamma.) In his biography of Pushkin, T. J. Binyon sums up Gannibal's achievements in this way: "That a black slave, without relations, wealth or property, should have risen to this position is in the highest degree extraordinary: so remarkable, indeed, as to argue a character far beyond the common, one that was more than justified in appropriating the name and reputation of the great Carthaginian."[2]

In his own carefully researched notes on the origins and life of Gannibal, Nabokov eschews such encomiums. Instead, he laments the scantiness of reliable information, corrects the glamorized accounts of existing documents (including Pushkin's),[3] and gleefully strips Gannibal's story of its orientalist accretions. Nabokov insists that Gannibal's many vices were not exotic imports from his native Africa:

> Although Abram Gannibal used to refer to himself, in humble letters to grandees, as "a poor Negro," and although Pushkin saw him as a Negro with

> "African passions" and an independent brilliant personality, actually Pyotr Petrovich Petrov, alias Abram Gannibal, was a sour, groveling, crotchety, timid, ambitious, and cruel person; a good military engineer, perhaps, but humanistically a nonentity; differing in nothing from a typical career-minded, superficially educated, coarse, wife-flogging Russian of his day, in a brutal and dull world of political intrigue, favoritism, Germanic regimentation, old-fashioned Russian misery, and fat-breasted empresses on despicable thrones. ("AG" 158)

Still, Nabokov is at pains to emphasize that his portrait of Gannibal is woefully incomplete ("AG" 108). He goes on to explain that the "taxonomic problem" posed by Gannibal's mysterious racial origins will probably always remain unsettled and that his African home is veiled in mists even thicker than those surrounding Shakespeare's grandfather's farm at Snitterfield ("AG" 158, 160).

Yet the strict evidentiary rules that Nabokov adheres to in his account of the historical Gannibal give way to vertiginous speculation when he allows his imagination to roam freely over the possibility that Coleridge's Abyssinian maid singing of Mount Abora in "Kubla Khan" might have been Pushkin's great-great-grandmother and, further, that Pushkin's great-great-grandfather might have been a son of Dr. Johnson's Rasselas. He justifies these dizzying conjectures with the following conclusion: "There is nothing in the annals of Russian Pushkinology to restrain one from the elaboration of such fancies" ("AG" 161).

PUSHKIN, ALDRIDGE, OTHELLO

The nature of the fantasy that Nabokov weaves into the fictitious scene in which an aged Pushkin watches a performance of *Othello* goes far beyond the fantasy that Pushkin might have lived into old age. A secondary layer of signification in this beguiling thought experiment turns on the idea that Pushkin might have lived to see a production in which Othello was played not by a white actor in blackface, but, as Suhoshchokov recounts in his description of the production, by "the famous black tragedian Aldridge" (*Gift* 100).

Pushkin would have been fifty-eight years old when Aldridge performed the role of Othello thirteen times in November and December 1858 in St. Petersburg (*IA* 112). The reviews of these performances were consistently rapturous.[4] The Russian critics found only one reason to complain (*IA* 113): namely, Aldridge's decision to intersperse his English lines with German words for the sake of making the play more accessible to non-English-speaking audiences.[5] Yet this decision played only a small part in the general strangeness that pervaded these celebrated performances. Aldridge's supporting cast was a German-speaking Czech theater group that delivered Shakespeare's lines in German (*IA* 99). As the St. Petersburg correspondent for the Brussels paper *Le Nord* observed, many audience members "expected tears of laughter rather than tears of emotion, when they learned that Iago and Desdemona would reply to [Othello] in German."[6] Other commentators noted that only a very small percentage of the Russian audiences that flocked to see Aldridge understood either English or German.

Yet these multiple linguistic barriers were overcome by the curiosity aroused by the prospect of seeing a black actor on stage. As I. I. Panaev described the scene in the journal founded by Pushkin more than twenty years earlier, "The majority of inhabitants . . . were amazed and asked 'What is this?' Curiosity was rife. A *black* tragic actor! That is new and original! Although we don't know a word of English, certainly we cannot miss seeing a *black* tragedian! Besides, seeing an English Othello with a German Desdemona should be very strange and amusing."[7]

The elderly Pushkin of Nabokov's fantasy must also have found Aldridge's performance "strange and amusing." He is envisioned in this fabricated scene "taking a most eccentric delight in the acting of the African: his thick lips twitched, his nostrils were dilated, and at certain bits he even jumped up and down in his seat and banged with delight on the parapet, his rings flashing" (*Gift* 100–101). Pushkin's disorderly conduct appears to depend on precisely the sort of racially inflected cliché that Nabokov had taken such pains to avoid in his notes on Gannibal. Suhoshchokov's invented Pushkin conducts himself at the theater as Russian contemporaries might have expected his African great-grandfather to act had he been brought to the theater as a young boy after having been presented as a gift to the emperor.

One way to interpret Pushkin's riotous response to Aldridge's impersonation of Othello is to see it as an act of recognition: Pushkin experiences such an intense delight in the performance and departs from the theater smiling because he recognizes his own predicament in that of Othello. His excitement is generated by his recognition of their shared marital troubles and African blood. The fact that Othello is being played by an "African Tragedian" (to invoke the epithet used by Aldridge to refer to himself) bolsters this interpretation based on racial and domestic affinities. Perhaps Pushkin might even recognize in Othello's stirring eloquence his own poetic gift. In the context of this narrative of self-recognition, Pushkin's "eccentric delight in the acting of the African" expresses his relief at escaping Othello's fate so many years ago when his wife, Natalia, was caught up in a flirtation with a soldier for hire. But to see Pushkin merely identifying with Othello is to dissolve the very terms that, according to Nabokov, make art and life a moral project. It is to believe that there is no meaningful difference between oneself and others, or between "types" and singular personalities. To focus exclusively on the similarities between Othello and Pushkin replicates the errors of Nabokov's "medieval traveler who brings back from the East the faunal fantasies influenced by the domestic bestiary he possessed all along rather than by the results of direct zoological exploration" (*SM* 397).

Such an error is common in Nabokov's fiction. Hermann Karlovich, the narrator of *Despair*, justifies his murder of a vagrant by arguing that the vagrant is his perfect double. (Hermann needs Felix to resemble him in order to collect his own life insurance.) Hermann's claim, however, about Felix's ideal resemblance to himself is repeatedly thrown into doubt. This claim is ultimately seen as a reflection of Hermann's narcissism, his opportunism, and his pathological indifference to the lives of others. (His failure to notice that his wife is having an affair under his very nose risks tipping the novel into farce.) The feckless artist Ardalion, Lydia's lover, anticipates the failure of Hermann's crime by rejecting the very premise that inspires it. Hermann has proposed that people's faces can be broken down into "zoological types": "There are people with the features of apes; there is also the rat type, the swine type" (*Des* 40–41). Ardalion insists that "every face is unique" (*Des* 40), and he elaborates upon this claim in racial and aesthetic terms: "You'll say next that all Chinamen are alike. You forget, my good man, that what the artist perceives is, primarily, the *difference* between things. It is the vulgar who note their resemblance." When pressed further by Hermann, Ardalion concedes that resemblance matters, but only "when buying a second candlestick" (*Des* 41).

Ardalion's claim that artists focus not on sameness but on difference brings into focus the trap Nabokov sets in his invented encounter between Othello and Pushkin. Just as he traps us into condoning Humbert's violence against Dolly through cunning rhetorical effects, here Nabokov tempts us to see Pushkin and Othello as virtual doubles, or, to use the analogy invoked by Ardalion, as a pair of matching candlesticks. But seeing the trap as a trap is to discover a deeply rewarding interpretation of Pushkin's imagined encounter with Othello. This artistically richer interpretation anchors the scene in an act of *mis*recognition: Pushkin's unrestrained enthusiasm for the play and the "bright sparkle in his youthful eyes" have nothing to do with his African heritage or his marital troubles, or even his poetic gift. Underwritten by imagination rather than by narrow boundaries of shared origins or experience, the enthusiasm and sparkle are fueled by what Kwame Anthony Appiah claims to be instrumental for both the reading process and the cosmopolitan ideal: an "imaginative engagement" with the other (*C* 85). According to this reading, Pushkin draws eccentric delight in the play and leaves the theater smiling simply because he has witnessed a great work of art. His racially and psychologically unencumbered appreciation of *Othello* is, to borrow Gordon Teskey's formulation, a species of courtesy not because

Pushkin sees in Othello a projection of his own self, but because he sees Othello as a stranger.

"AS A STRANGER GIVE IT WELCOME"

Taking his cue from Hamlet's injunction to Horatio to treat the ghost hospitably ("And therefore as a stranger give it welcome"), Teskey defines courtesy as a regard for the ineluctable otherness of others ("CT" 344). Hospitality resides, Teskey elaborates, in the narrowing distance between host and guest: "The most ancient forms of courtesy, as we see in Homer, allow the stranger to remain strange—that is, to some extent hidden—even as the stranger is welcomed" ("CT" 345). This narrowing, but never quite vanishing, distance between host and stranger conjures up an ethic of hospitality that is programmatically at odds with the colonizing impulse to possess the other through knowledge: "Courtesy invites a partial disclosure and opens itself in turn to attention from the other, showing a welcoming openness to the strange. Courtesy does not seize the object or dive into its center: it moves into nearness with the otherness of the stranger" ("CT" 344).

For scholars of the Middle Ages and anthropologists of hospitality, such moving "into nearness" with the stranger is part and parcel of the ambivalence that makes hospitality at once obligatory and dangerous. As Julian Pitt-Rivers states, "The law of hospitality is founded upon ambivalence. It imposes order through an appeal to the sacred, makes the unknown knowable, and replaces conflict by reciprocal honour. It does not eliminate the conflict altogether but places it in abeyance and prohibits its expression."[8] In his recent study of French Arthurian romance, Ad Putter pays tribute to Dupin's insight that hospitality shown to strangers was a key component of medieval courtesy (*FAR* 51).[9] But as Pitt-Rivers, Putter, and Marie-Luce Chênerie observe, the Latin root of "hospitality" is *hospes*, which means both "guest" and "host." *Hospes*, however, also derives (through *hosti-pes*) from the word *hostis* (hostile stranger, enemy).[10] In Putter's summation, this network of etymological links serves as a reminder of "the age-old uncertainties and the dramatic potential inherent in the guest-host relationship. The host can always be hostile" (*FAR* 84). The complex protocols elaborated for the regulation of encounters between hosts and guests are an acknowledgment of the underlying danger of "situations in which strangers take hospitality from strangers" (*FAR* 52). For Chênerie, the ambivalence at the heart of hospitality extends to the figure of the knight errant and chivalry itself: "The ambiguity of errantry coincides precisely with that of chivalry insofar as the insignia and means of aristocratic power are more capable than others of being used for the good as for the bad."[11]

Teskey's definition of courtesy as hospitality directed at strangers informs my own desire to see Pushkin's unruly responsiveness to Aldridge's impersonation of Othello as an act of courtesy grounded in a series of failed recognitions that, in characteristic Nabokovian fashion, are keyed into aesthetic and ethical preoccupations. Eric Naiman's observation that "the word 'strange' is often coded in Nabokov's fiction as a marker of art"[12] is of a piece with Ardalion's insistence that art is anchored in difference. If the imaginary Pushkin's conduct during Aldridge's performance is triggered by his appreciation of the strangeness of the play rather than by his recognition of his own predicament in that of Othello, then Pushkin can be said to share Hamlet's regard for the otherness of others. His refusal to appropriate for himself parts of Othello's story might qualify as the kind of courtesy-as-hospitality that Teskey uncovers in Hamlet's injunction to Horatio. It might also be possible to say that this is why Hermann's stridently self-proclaimed status as artist fails to convince: Nabokov's imagined Pushkin earns his credentials as Russia's gold standard in matters of art and ethics by his responsiveness to difference. By contrast, Hermann's inclination to see "all Chinamen" as being "alike" (to quote Ardalion) is revealed to be both inartistic and immoral.

In "Nabokov's Fugitive Sense," Stephen Blackwell argues that Nabokov's multiple experiments in biographical writing—both historical and fictional—are variations on a single epistemological theme. Fyodor's failed biography of his father, Nabokov's Paris lecture on Pushkin, and V.'s efforts to capture Sebastian's "real life" showcase the futility of projects that seek to fix others into authoritative identities or historically accurate personal narratives.[13] Blackwell sees *Lolita* and *Pnin* as Nabokov's most mature expressions of the conviction that the lives of others remain beyond the reach of knowledge.[14] Building on Blackwell's insight, it is possible to say that the only *complete* biography in Nabokov's oeuvre—namely, Fyodor's biography of Chernyshevsky—attains this completeness at the cost of courtesy; that is, it does so by treating its subject discourteously.

Blackwell draws the title of his essay from a passage culled from Nabokov's scientific notes in which he observes that the taxonomic concept of species can only be useful in a "fugitive sense."[15] Because of constant scientific advances and inescapable individual bias, the notion of species can only be a "phase of evolutional structure" rather than a stable scientific fact.[16] According to Blackwell, Nabokov's "law of fugitive sense" informs not only his approach to scientific categories such as species, but also his various narrators' failed attempts "to capture and fix a simulacrum of static truth."[17] While the most complex expression of Nabokov's experiments in epistemic instability is incontestably *Pale Fire*, the 1943 story "That in Aleppo Once . . ." anticipates in significant ways *Pale Fire*'s dizzying hermeneutic conundrums. Victor Strandberg has identified this story as one of "the master magician's most puzzling excursions into his perverse playground of indeterminate meanings."[18] Fittingly, the story invites us to reflect upon the limits of knowledge through the lens of *Othello*.

"THAT IN ALEPPO ONCE . . ."

As former slaves who rose to high military rank in the service of white masters, Pushkin's maternal great-grandfather and Othello share a deep connection. But Nabokov also sees links between Othello and Pushkin. "That in Aleppo Once . . ." takes its title from Othello's last lines before he commits suicide. Priscilla Meyer grounds the story's parallel between Othello and Pushkin in a cluster of resemblances between Shakespeare's Venetian Moor and Russia's greatest poet. Like Othello, Meyer writes, Pushkin "suspected his wife Natalie of infidelity and perished in a duel over insinuations about it."[19] Meyer's summation of the connection is supported by the story's narrator who, as a poet himself, "finds pleasure in imitating the destiny of a unique genius (down to the jealousy, down to the filth, down to the stab of seeing her almond-shaped eyes turn to her blond Cassio behind her peacock-feathered fan) even if one cannot imitate his verse" (*SVN* 557). As Meyer notes, the "blond Cassio" imagined here stands in for d'Anthès, the blond-haired Frenchman who courted Natalia Pushkin and mortally wounded Pushkin in the duel provoked by that courtship.[20]

Plots about jealousy and infidelity are natural staging grounds for confrontations with the limits of knowledge. Given the recurrence of jealousy, unfaithfulness, and adultery as major preoccupations in Nabokov's work, it is unsurprising that allusions to *Othello*—"perhaps the most compelling study of jealousy ever written," according to David Rampton[21]—appear in *Laughter in the Dark*, *The Tragedy of Mr. Morn*, *The Gift*, *Transparent Things*, and *Pnin*. As Siggy Frank has shown, however, *Othello*'s presence in "That in Aleppo Once . . ." moves beyond the merely allusive to become "an integrated structural device" that determines the meaning and outcome of the narrative (*NTI* 172).

"That in Aleppo Once . . ." takes the form of a letter written by an unnamed narrator to a novelist, "V.," in the hope that V. might "clarify things for me through the prism of your art" (*SVN* 564). V. claims to have published his friend's letter without any editorial intervention, with the exception of having given the story a title that the story's narrator explicitly asked him not to use. The story ends with a request that has already been betrayed even before the story begins: "It may all end in *Aleppo* if I am not careful," the narrator concludes. "Spare me, V.: you would load your dice with an unbearable implication if you took that for a title" (*SVN* 564). As several scholars have noted, V.'s decision to go against his friend's express wish and use Othello's famous suicide speech as a source for the story's title is a kind of literary execution: the Shakespearean title suggests that the narrator commits suicide shortly after penning his letter.[22]

Suicide is only one parallel among many that link the narrator's life to that of Othello for, as Frank notes, the narrative is "pervaded by a constant sense of confusion and incoherence" that replicates *Othello*'s atmosphere (*NTI* 173). She notes further that both Othello and the story's narrator suffer from an obsessive jealousy that locks them within irrational, nightmarish worlds (*NTI* 173). Additionally, the Shakespearean title implies not only that the narrator kills himself, but that he may also have killed his wife (just as Othello kills Desdemona) and their dog (just as Othello once killed the Turk whom he describes as a "circumcised dog") (*NTI* 174–75). With respect to the title, Frank uncovers another major correspondence between the two texts: both Othello and the story's narrator attempt to exercise control over their lives' narratives by making an appeal to others (*NTI* 175). By writing to V., the story's narrator is making a plea to be remembered in a way analogous to Othello's request that Lodovico give a truthful account of "these unlucky deeds" (*Othello* 5.2.345–47).

These multiple correspondences are made visible by the story's title and the narrator's plaintive injunction at the very end of his narrative to avoid reading his story against the backdrop of Othello's destiny. The narrator himself resists such correspondences because, to quote Othello's self-description in the same speech in which he recalls his life at Aleppo, he is "perplexed in the extreme" (5.2.351). This extreme perplexity undermines, in advance, the interpretive stability generated by the cluster of analogies with *Othello*. (Analogies, by definition, seek to reduce perplexity.) Instead of generating interpretive confidence, these particular analogies breed doubt: both the narrator's and Othello's stories showcase the inscrutability of truth and the opacity of others. Ironically, the doubt that connects them also throws into doubt the connective threads that might give support to a stable interpretation.

"Although I can produce documentary proofs of matrimony," the narrator writes to V., "I am positive now that my wife never existed" (*SVN* 556). Like Othello's Desdemona and Pushkin's Natalia, the narrator's unnamed wife is much younger than her husband, but her youth is the only uncontested detail about her. Perhaps a capricious adulteress, perhaps a tormented wife, perhaps a pathological liar, she remains "a phantom" (*SVN* 557). After she confesses to having "stayed for several nights in Montpellier with a brute of a man," the narrator submits her to a series of interrogations that echo Othello's fruitless obsession to learn Desdemona's thoughts:

> I spent that night and many others getting it out of her bit by bit, but not getting it all. I was under the strange delusion that first I must find out every detail, reconstruct every minute, and only then decide whether I could bear it. But the limit of desired knowledge was unattainable, nor could I ever foretell the approximate point after which I might imagine myself satiated, because of course the denominator of every fraction of knowledge was potentially as infinite as the number of intervals between the fractions themselves. (*SVN* 560)

The narrator seems right to surmise that his increasingly frantic efforts to learn the truth were as futile as Achilles's efforts to overtake the tortoise in Zeno's famous paradox.

Puzzling over his predicament, the narrator begins to believe that his wife might have been as hungry for knowledge about him as he was for knowledge about her: "If she has remained a phantom to me, I may have been one to her: I suppose she had been solely attracted by the obscurity of my poetry; then tore a hole through its veil and saw a stranger's unlovable face" (*SVN* 557). In Iago's hands, the argument that we cannot love a stranger is mercilessly pursued to a fatal conclusion. As Iago tells Othello, Desdemona's rejection of "many proposèd matches / Of her own clime, complexion and degree" points to her depravity: "a will most rank, / Foul disproportions, thoughts unnatural" (*Othello* 3.3.231–35). Iago also insinuates that Desdemona will experience, if she has not already, the same kind of repugnance and regret ascribed by the narrator of Nabokov's story to his own wife: "Her will, recoiling to her better judgment, / May fall to match you with her country forms, / And happily repent" (*Othello* 3.3.239–41).

The aporia we are being asked to confront here is that the strangeness of strangers is at once attractive and repellent; the quiddity of the stranger (Othello's exotic identity, Nabokov's narrator's obscure poetry) is at once repugnant and seductive, menacing and captivating. Brabantio, Desdemona's father, welcomes Othello into his home ("Her father loved me, oft invited me, / Still questioned me the story of my life" [1.3.127–28]) because he is as enchanted by Othello's stories as his daughter. But believing that his hospitality has been betrayed, Brabantio dies of "pure grief" over his daughter's marriage to Othello (5.2.211). Putter's and Chênerie's reminders that the word "hospitality" encompasses both hostility and welcome are useful here: hospitality, unlike love and its magnetic pull, is a virtue that must be cultivated with great effort precisely because the strangeness of strangers both threatens and captivates. Understood as hospitality to strangers, courtesy is a virtue that teaches us how to live with strangers in the presence of uncertainty and peril.

OTHELLO AND THE PROBLEM OF OTHER MINDS

Othello's story tips into tragedy because he cannot accommodate himself to a world in which both the self and the other remain strange. Iago succeeds in bringing Othello under his thumb, first, by exploiting Othello's insecurities as an outsider, and, second, by making him feel threatened by the strangeness of Desdemona. Iago's first strategy hinges on his own epistemic privilege as a Venetian "insider" when he assures Othello that, as a stranger, he is unfamiliar with the perfidy of Venetian wives: "I know our country disposition well: / In Venice they do let God see the pranks / They dare not show their husbands" (3.3.203–5). Additionally, Iago insists that only "a will most rank" could be attracted to someone who differs so radically from "her own clime, complexion and degree." He predicts that it is only a matter of time before Desdemona will recoil from her "thoughts unnatural" and will begin experiencing the more natural attraction of "her country forms" (3.3.232–39).

The second strategy by which Iago succeeds in destroying Othello is by staging for him what is referred to in philosophical discourse as the problem of privacy, or "the problem of other minds." The long, painful exchange during which Iago infects Othello with suspicion turns on convincing Othello, first, that Iago knows something he will not reveal ("By heaven, thou echo'st me / As if there were some monster in thy thought / Too hideous to be shown" [3.3.109–11]), and, second, that this monstrous thought will always remain unknowable to Othello:

> OTHELLO: By heaven, I'll know thy thoughts!
> IAGO: You cannot, if my heart were in your hand,
> Nor shall not, whilst 'tis in my custody. (3.3.164–66)

Iago's goal, of course, is to reveal his own thoughts to Othello while at the same time convincing him—by way of analogy—that Desdemona's thoughts are permanently beyond his ken.

Iago's success turns on his ability to make Othello hunger for something unattainable: that is, full knowledge of a wife who is cut off from him not only by ineluctable existential separateness, but also by race, gender, and culture. Othello's insatiable desire to know Desdemona—to tear the veil from what remains "hidden"—manifests itself first in an act that weds imperialist violence to an iconic act of discourtesy: he strikes her (4.1.234). Lodovico's response to this irruption of violence further alienates Othello from Venetian life: "My lord, this would not be believed in Venice, / Though I should swear I saw't" (4.1.236–37).

But while Othello must perish because he cannot assuage his hunger to seize the other in the fullness of knowledge, the hunger for coming into proximity with the strange conjures into being captivating visions of journeys to exotic destinations and romantic encounters between strangers. This is the vision that hovers over the four-sided encounter that brings together Othello, Gannibal, Aldridge, and Pushkin in the fabricated scene in *The Gift*: Pushkin's very existence, like the presence of an African American tragedian in a Russia in the grip of serfdom, is a testament to the possibility that unions such as Othello and Desdemona's may turn out to be creative rather than destructive. This is precisely the fruitful scenario invoked by Nabokov in his afterword to *Lolita* when he chastises the American publishing industry for its inability to countenance a novel about "a Negro-White marriage which is a complete and glorious success resulting in lots of children and grandchildren."[23]

What Nabokov does not mention, but must surely have known, is that such a plot would have been comic rather than tragic. Desdemona's consumption of Othello's exotic tales sets in motion a plot that, under a different generic dispensation, could have tipped into comedy as effortlessly as *Much Ado About Nothing* (there, too, suspicion demands "ocular proof" of marital infidelity, but with happy consequences). Desdemona's fascination with the strange and the far away is the same fascination studied by Monica Manolescu in her book *Jeux de mondes: L'Ailleurs chez Vladimir Nabokov*. This preoccupation with "geographies of elsewhere"—to use Manolescu's lyrical phrase—inspires Fyodor's decision to write the biography of his father. Fittingly, it is a line from Pushkin's *Journey to Arzrum*—"The frontier held something mysterious for me; to travel had been my favorite dream since childhood"—that sets in motion this particular literary project (*Gift* 94–95). The historical figures depicted as Fyodor's father's spiritual kinsmen—Pushkin, Marco Polo, Russia's explorer-scientists such as Nicholas (Nikolay) Przhevalsky, Peter (Pyotr) Kozlov, and Gregory (Grigory) Grum-Grzhimaylo—are internally connected by a longing for encounters with the strange.

CURIOSITY AND MONSTROSITY

Mary McCarthy intuited rightly that Nabokov's "tenderness for human eccentricity, for the freak, the 'deviate'" was coextensive with his scientific interests—"the naturalist's taste for the curious," as she calls it.[24] Godunov, the most distinguished of Nabokov's fictional scientists, passes on his love of travel to distant lands to his son:

> Then, when I fell under the spell of butterflies, something unfolded in my soul and I relived all my father's journeys, as if I myself had made them: in my dreams I saw the winding road, the caravan, the many-hued mountains, and

> envied my father madly, agonizingly, to the point of tears—hot and violent tears that would suddenly gush out of me at table as we discussed his letters from the road or even at the simple mention of a far, far place. (*Gift* 106–7)

As such romantic descriptions suggest, Nabokov shared Fyodor's longing for the distant and exotic. In a letter to Véra from 1926, he describes a window display that weds his fascination with chivalry to the allure of faraway places: "an ancient little book, opened on the first page—a journey of some Spaniard to Brazil in 1553. The drawing is charming: the author in knight's armor—chain-mail, cuirass, helmet—all fit and proper—he is riding a llama, and behind him there are natives, palm-trees, a snake around a tree-trunk" (*LV* 59). When asked in 1966 about his most cherished occupations, Nabokov noted that the "pleasures and rewards of literary inspiration are nothing beside the rapture of discovering a new organ under the microscope or an undescribed species on a mountainside in Iran or Peru." Had there been no revolution in Russia, he added, he might have dedicated his life not to novels but to travels in search of unknown butterflies (*SO* 100).

But Nabokov also knew that travel and scientific exploration risked a version of the epistemic imperialism that drives Othello to destroy himself and Desdemona. The words from *The Journey to Arzrum* that inspire Fyodor's biographical project cast the boundary between self and other in "mystery," and Godunov himself seems to reside in a mist akin to the colored air that encircles him when he enters the base of a rainbow at Ordos (*Gift* 77). Fyodor declares his biographical project a failure because he finds himself incapable of capturing the essence of his father's personality. Like Othello, who kills Desdemona because he cannot know her thoughts, Fyodor "kills" the biography because he feels himself incapable of solving the mystery at the core of his father's life: "And now I continually ask myself what did he use to think about in the solitary night: I try fervently in the darkness to divine the current of his thoughts, and I have much less success with this than my mental visits to places which I have never seen" (*Gift* 119).

Alexander Dolinin has argued that Fyodor's decision not to complete his father's biography is justified, in retrospect, by his published biography of Chernyshevsky. But Fyodor's *Life of Chernyshevsky* proves that a *complete* biography written by "a real artist" treats its subject not with courtesy but with contempt (it does not "extol" as Dolinin puts it, but "defames").[25] Galya Diment makes a similar observation when she notes that in spite of its sensitive treatment of some aspects of Chernyshevsky's life and its acknowledgment of Chernyshevsky's heroism, Fyodor's biography is an unfair lampoon. As Diment notes further, the biography was so deeply offensive to Nabokov's compatriots that even the characteristically tolerant editors of *Sovremennye zapiski* decided to suppress it.[26]

Conceptualizing courtesy, as Teskey does, as "a welcoming openness to the strange" ("CT" 344) makes it possible to see Fyodor's abortive biography of his father as diametrically opposed to the impulse that drives Othello to murder Desdemona. Like Hamlet in his encounter with his father's ghost, Fyodor allows his father to remain a stranger in a narrative that doubles as an act of welcome. It is thus possible to see Fyodor's incomplete biography as a gesture of courtesy that moves into nearness with the stranger while allowing the stranger to remain hidden. Othello's murderous desire to strip bare Desdemona's thoughts is replaced by a reverential wonder toward the unknown:

> In and around my father . . . there was something difficult to convey in words, a haze, a mystery, an enigmatic reserve which made itself felt sometimes more, sometimes less. It was as if this genuine, very genuine man possessed an aura of something still unknown but which was perhaps the most genuine of all. . . . . It sometimes seems to me nowadays that—who knows—he might go off on his journeys not so much to seek something as to flee something, and that on returning, he would realize that it was still with him, inside him, unriddable, inexhaustible. I cannot track down a name for his secret, but I only know that that was the source of that special—neither glad nor morose, having indeed no connection with the outward appearance of human emotions—solitude to which neither my mother nor all the entomologists of the world had any admittance. (*Gift* 114–15)

The courtesy Fyodor extends to his father by declaring his biography a failure replicates Hamlet's hospitality toward his own father's ghost. Hamlet justifies his injunction to Horatio to give the ghost a stranger's welcome by reminding him that "there are more things in heaven and earth, Horatio, / Than are dreamt of in your philosophy" (1.5.174–75). By acknowledging but refusing to penetrate the mystery of his father's life, Fyodor is endorsing Hamlet's claim that courtesy is morally imperative in a world filled with marvels.

Fyodor's epistemological humility in the face of his father's life also flows from his recognition that curiosity can be tyrannical. In his imaginative reconstruction of his father's journeys, Fyodor recalls "the tyrant Shiusin, who used to cut open pregnant women out of curiosity and who, one cold morning, seeing some porters fording a stream, ordered their legs to be amputated at the shin in order to inspect the condition of the marrow in their bones" (*Gift* 122). The Kirghiz fairy tale that Godunov liked to tell Fyodor ascribes such horrors to the insatiable nature of human curiosity; the fable's lesson is encapsulated in the old Kirghiz woman's words that "a human eye . . . wants to encompass everything in the world" (*Gift* 133–34). Nabokov will transmit Shiusin's monstrous curiosity to Humbert, another monster whose insatiable desire for knowledge expresses itself as an image of violent penetration: "My only grudge against nature was that I could not turn my Lolita inside out and apply voracious lips to her young matrix, her unknown heart, her nacreous liver, the seagrapes of her lungs, her comely twin kidneys" (*L* 154). In his afterword to *Lolita*, Nabokov declares that curiosity is a crucial ingredient in the production of "aesthetic bliss," but these examples confirm that he also knew that curiosity could be a catalyst for violence and horror.

XENIA AND COSMOPOLITANISM

The Kirghiz tale and the story of Shiusin emphasize the destructive effects of curiosity, but curiosity can also serve as a prelude to hospitality. This is what happens in the case of Brabantio, who opens his home to Othello in order to hear his exotic tales, and in the case of Hamlet, who welcomes the ghost as a gesture of faith in the mysteries of the universe. In its adjectival form, "curiosity" signals a desire to know the unknown: to say that something or someone is "curious" is an acknowledgment of being confronted with the strange (a "curious occurrence"), but it might also mean that someone is hungry for knowledge (a "curious neighbor"). To say that someone is "incurious" is to suggest an indifference to strangeness: the typical Parisian, according to Baldwin, exhibits none of the "faintest personal interest, or curiosity, concerning the life, or habits, of any stranger" and therefore "keeps the traveler at an unmistakable arm's length."[27]

Nabokov's account of his own émigré years in Europe redirects Baldwin's words about the incuriosity of Parisians from hosts to guests. The passage dwells less on the lack of hospitality of the German and French hosts than on the Russians' arrogance in believing that their foreign hosts were unworthy of their attention:

> As I look back at those years of exile, I see myself, and thousands of other Russians, leading an odd but by no means unpleasant existence, in material indigence and intellectual luxury, among perfectly unimportant strangers, spectral Germans and Frenchmen in whose more or less illusory cities we, émigrés, happened to dwell. These aborigines were to the mind's eye as flat and transparent as figures cut out of cellophane, and although we used their gadgets, applauded their clowns, picked their roadside plums and apples, no real communication, of the rich human sort so widespread in our own midst, existed between us and them. It seemed at times that we ignored them the way an arrogant or very stupid invader ignores a formless and faceless mass of natives; but occasionally, quite often in fact, the spectral world through which we serenely paraded our sores and our arts would produce a kind of awful convulsion and show us who was the discarnate captive and who the true lord. (*SM* 594–95)

Nabokov identifies here the incuriosity of the Russians toward their foreign hosts as identical to the incuriosity that nurtures the colonist's violence and brutality toward an invaded subject.

What is implicitly absent in the scenarios described by Baldwin and Nabokov is captured in what the ancient Greeks called *xenia*. "Guest-friendship" in its literal translation, *xenia* was a mutually reciprocal code of conduct that regulated the behavior of hosts and guests. The plots that emerge from violations of *xenia* stretch from Paris's abduction of Helen to the defilement of Odysseus's home by Penelope's suitors, and include Gawain's betrayal of the exchange-of-winnings game at the Green Knight's castle, Othello's marriage to Desdemona without Brabantio's knowledge, and d'Anthès's public flirtation with Natalia Pushkin. Though these examples suggest that honoring the principles of *xenia* ought to be sufficiently straightforward as to require no elaboration, the plots that they give rise to suggest that *xenia*'s covenants are difficult to uphold. Like Aldridge's efforts to bridge the distance between Shakespeare's English and his Russian audiences by inserting German words into his speech, the laws of *xenia* seek a universal language where none exists and prescribe a universal set of behaviors that are often unintelligible.

Xenia's search for a working equilibrium between universalism and particularity aligns it with the cosmopolitan ideal. Theorists of cosmopolitanism often assert that cosmopolitanism is best understood, to quote Appiah, as a "challenge" rather than a "solution" (*C* xv). Coined by the Cynics in the fourth century B.C., the very term "cosmopolitan" (etymologically "citizen of the cosmos") is predicated on a contradiction. In Appiah's formulation, the cosmopolitan ideal theorized in Greek antiquity resided in the irreconcilable aspirations of belonging to one's polis (a city-state that commanded a subject's loyalty) and the universe (a world of strangers that lacks a shared identity capable of holding the subject to an imposed discipline) (*C* xiv). An individual committed to the cosmopolitan ideal seeks to assuage the imperialist's desire for unconstrained mobility without laying claim to the imperialist's universalizing authority. No melting pot, the cosmopolitan ideal is the challenge to preserve tribal quiddities in the absence of the very borders that generated those quiddities in the first place.

As an "ethics for strangers" (in Appiah's formulation), cosmopolitanism is a species of hospitality, or *courtoisie*, directed at strangers. Taking diversity for granted, courtesy and cosmopolitanism privilege respect above all other virtues. As Appiah puts it, "A tenable cosmopolitanism tempers a respect for difference with a respect for actual human beings" (*C* 113). Universal respect for human dignity is one of the twin aims of Kant's foundational cosmopolitan text "Toward Perpetual Peace." (Its second aim is the containment of global conflicts.) In Martha Nussbaum's account of the intellectual continuities that connect Stoic cosmopolitanism with Kant's modern iteration, the ideal of universal respect fosters and defends local affiliations because they are understood to promote human flourishing.[28]

Nabokov's cosmopolitan inclinations are a well-known feature of his biography. The most admired figures in his life—Pushkin, his own father—had established reputations as cultural cosmopolitans in spite of their fervent patriotism. Nicholas Nabokov, Nabokov's cousin and future composer and cultural diplomat, recalls V. D. Nabokov in this way: "Uncle Vladimir had in his bearing, his manner of speech, and his whole appearance something distinctly aristocratic, and, like many liberal Russian gentlemen of his time, he was worldly, ironic, a bit haughty, and cosmopolitan" (qtd. in *VNRY* 185). This cultural cosmopolitanism, however, did not interfere with his patriotism. Nabokov recalls how during the Russo-Japanese War, he had to snatch an entire *bombe* of lemon sherbet at a seaside café in Abbazia because his father, upon noticing two Japanese officers sitting at a table nearby, insisted upon his family's immediate departure (*SM* 375). His father's "patriotic dismay" at discovering that his sons could read and write English but not Russian led him to arrange for daily lessons with the village schoolmaster (*SM* 376). This effort to ensure that his sons were literate in Russian was nonetheless tempered by a cosmopolitan respect for the diversity found within the borders of a violent and brutal imperialist state. As Nabokov recounts, his father's choice of tutors was guided by "the ingenious idea of engaging each time a representative of another class or race, so as to expose us to all the winds that swept over the Russian Empire" (*SM* 490). The Tenishev School was similarly selected for its "policy of nondiscrimination in matters of rank, race and creed" (*SM* 517).

Pushkin's ardent patriotism was especially conspicuous in his responses to the nationalism of his friend, the Polish poet Adam Mickiewicz.[29] But as in the case of V. D. Nabokov, Pushkin's patriotic feelings did not obtrude on his cosmopolitan approach to cultural matters or on his posthumous reputation. As Caryl Emerson writes, "Pushkin came to represent a style of creativity so cosmopolitan that a Russian man (or woman) of letters was presumed to be at home, linguistically and culturally, anywhere in Europe."[30] On his own behalf, Nabokov expresses his contempt for "regional" literature (*SM* 496) and Slavophilism, which he called "one of the most tedious creeds ever thought of" (*EO* 2.236). He recalls with nostalgia his "cosmopolitan childhood" and with lasting dismay a fellow Cantabrigian who "wriggl[ed] out of a proposed tennis double upon learning that his partner was to be a Hindu" (*SM* 562, 592). During the period of his European expatriation, he describes himself as "a lanky cosmopolitan expatriate in flannel bags and beret" (*SM* 466).

Rachel Trousdale assigns Nabokov a role similar to that played by Pushkin in relation to his literary descendants. For Trousdale, Nabokov is a "vital starting point" for a generation of postcolonial, exiled and diasporic writers who see in his works models for "alternatives to national identity."[31] Writers like Salman Rushdie and Zadie Smith, Trousdale contends, have turned to Nabokov's work "both because his work draws explicitly on so many national cultures, and because it rejects the notion of geographically defined national identity. Nabokov's fictional worlds both emphasize the importance of physical geography—the misty mountains of Zembla, the woods of Ardis—and render geography meaningless."[32]

J. E. Rivers anticipates Trousdale's conclusions when he observes that Nabokov's literary references display "a cavalier disregard for barriers of language and national frontier."[33] His most likable characters inherit this trait, displaying a quiet cosmopolitan panache that readers are clearly meant to appreciate. Pnin has "Americanized" himself by shedding many of his European habits (*Pnin* 301). His American hostess at The Pines, Susan Cook, summons her husband's friends to tea in a rudimentary but confident Russian: "Timofey, Rozochka! *Tshay*!" (*Pnin* 392). The "smart, relaxed Joan Clements, who had been all over the world," is said to know "how to raise [her hand] to exactly the right level for a Russian gentleman to kiss" (*Pnin* 408, 410).

The *most* cosmopolitan among Nabokov's fictional cosmopolitans remains Fyodor's father. A passionate explorer of foreign lands and a scientist with a network of international contacts, Godunov is home everywhere and nowhere. As a maximally committed cosmopolitan, he is decidedly unpatriotic; his conspicuous idleness during the First World War leads "one jaunty newspaper" to deride him for being "more concerned with Asian bugs than with the glory of Russian arms" (*Gift* 128). Fyodor imagines with pleasure

> how Russian public opinion would have wrung its little hands had it learned that at the height of the war Godunov-Cherdyntsev had traveled to Geneva to meet a fat, bald, extraordinarily jovial German professor . . . , that they had come together there in a small room in a modest hotel for a scientific consultation, and that having discussed what was necessary (the subject was a work of many volumes, stubbornly continuing publication in Stuttgart with long-standing cooperation of foreign specialists on separate groups of butterflies) they peacefully parted—each in his own direction. (*Gift* 129)

In spite of recalling the sharp misery of his own grief, Fyodor does not reproach his father for departing on an expedition (his last, as fate would have it) in the midst of war. Others, however, did: "The fact that at the most alarming time, when Russia's borders were crumbling and her inner flesh was being eaten away, Konstantin Kirillovich suddenly planned to abandon his family for two years for the sake of a scientific expedition into a remote country, struck most people as a wild caprice, a monstrous frivolity" (*Gift* 131).

Godunov's cosmopolitan lack of patriotism and his willingness to abandon his family during wartime for the sake of scientific exploration suggest that he has attained the highest of the three spiritual states described by the twelfth-century theologian Hugh of St. Victor: "The man who finds his homeland sweet is still a tender beginner; he to whom every soil is as his native one is already strong; but he is perfect to whom the entire world is as a foreign land." Reflecting upon this passage in his 1952 essay "The Philology of World Literature," Erich Auerbach reorients Hugh's aphorism in a way that can also serve as a gloss for Godunov's special brand of secular cosmopolitanism: "Hugh's intended audience consisted of those individuals whose goal it was to free themselves from their love of this world. But it is also a good path to follow for anyone who desires to secure a proper love *for* the world."[34]

XENIA AND XENOPHOBIA

Though Fyodor portrays his father as a cosmopolitan par excellence, he does not show how a cosmopolitan respect for others might express itself. Unlike most of his contemporaries, Godunov is sensitive to the colonizing impulse of scientific nomenclatorial practices and is angered rather than flattered when a mountain ridge is named after him: "To ascertain and preserve the ancient native name of a pass," Fyodor reports him as having written, "is always both more scientific and more noble than to saddle it with the name of a good acquaintance" (*Gift* 113).

But if Godunov respects local traditions and eschews the imperialist's instinct for appropriation, respect for people or "guest-friendliness" is not in his repertoire of virtues. "He was entirely uninterested in ethnography," Fyodor reports, "and in camp he practiced shooting, which served as an excellent precaution against any importuning" (*Gift* 113). His dislike of "Chinese roadhouses" (118) and unwillingness "to sacrifice even one hour's collecting" for the sake of visiting the holy city of Lhasa (which he dismisses as "one more filthy little town" [113]) is a testament not only to Nabokov's anti-didactic literary temperament, but also to a nagging suspicion that the cosmopolitan ideal might always be eluding our grasp.

While Godunov preserves what might be called his cosmopolitan innocence by deliberately avoiding encounters with strangers, Fyodor violates the dictates of *xenia* during a bus ride in Berlin. Fyodor's venomous response to a stranger whom he takes for a German departs so completely from the principles of *xenia* that it lapses into *xenophobia.* Fyodor knows better, yet this knowledge proves helpless against the rage that he experiences when a man, in settling down in a seat in front of him,

> bumped him with his knee and with the corner of a fat briefcase with a leather handle, and this trivial thing turned his irritation into a kind of pure fury, so that, staring fixedly at the sitter, reading his features, he instantly concentrated on him all his sinful hatred (for this poor, pitiful, expiring nation) and knew precisely why he hated him: for that low forehead, for those pale eyes; for *Vollmilch* and *Extrastark*, implying the lawful existence of the diluted and the artificial; for the Punchinello-like system of gestures (threatening children not as we do—with an upright finger, a standing reminder of Divine Judgment—but with a horizontal digit imitating a waving stick); for a love of fences, rows, mediocrity; for the cult of the office; for the fact that if you listen to his inner voice (or to any conversation on the street) you will inevitably hear figures, money; for the lavatory humor and crude laughter; for the fatness of the backsides of both sexes, even if the rest of the subject is not fat; for the lack of fastidiousness; for the visibility of cleanliness—the gleam of saucepan bottoms in the kitchen and the barbaric filth of the bathrooms; for the weakness for dirty little tricks, for taking pains with dirty tricks, for the abominable object stuck carefully on the railings of the public gardens; for someone else's live cat, pierced through with wire as revenge on a neighbor, and the wire cleverly twisted at one end; for cruelty in everything, self-satisfied, taken for granted; for the unexpected, rapturous helpfulness with which five passersby help you to pick up some dropped farthings; for . . . Thus he threaded the points of his biased indictment, looking at the man who sat opposite him—until the latter took a copy of Vasiliev's newspaper from his pocket and coughed unconcernedly with a Russian intonation. (*Gift* 81–82)

To abridge this impassioned—one might even say hysterical—diatribe is to diminish the magnitude of the challenge facing those cosmopolitans—Fyodor among them—for whom such xenophobia is at once shameful and overwhelming. Fyodor is chastened and delighted by the lesson he is made to learn by way of this encounter: "How clever, how gracefully sly and how essentially good life is! Now he made out in the newspaper reader's features such a compatriotic softness—in the corners of the eyes, large nostrils, a Russian-cut mustache—that it became at once both funny and incomprehensible how anyone could have been deceived" (82).

The lesson that Fyodor takes away from this episode is clearly meant to reinforce something that his "reason knew" already, but that his passions made him disregard: namely, that native Germans "could also include genuine, completely human individuals with unselfish passions, pure sorrows" (*Gift* 80). Yet this cleverly staged lesson in tolerance—hinging, as it does, on the discovery that the loathsome German turns out to be a likable Russian—shares an affinity with Captain Ramballe's comic insistence in *War and Peace* that Pierre Bezukhov must be a Frenchman because he performed a heroic deed and Frenchmen alone are capable of heroic deeds (*WP* 2:1071; *PSS* 11:365). Ramballe's good-natured unwillingness to countenance the possibility that Pierre is Russian or that the act of saving his life could be anything less than "an heroic action [*velikoe delo*]" is of a piece with Fyodor's sense that some Germans might be nice if they were to look and act like Russians.

Fyodor also knows that xenophobia is incompatible with an artistic sensibility: "The Russian conviction that the German is in small numbers vulgar and in large numbers—unbearably vulgar was, he knew, a conviction unworthy of an artist" (*Gift* 81). Yet for all his artist's knowledge and instinct, Fyodor gets caught in the trap that Pushkin evades during the fabricated scene that makes him witness Aldridge's impersonation of Othello. Fyodor's savage diatribe against Germans aligns him, ironically, not with Pushkin but with Hermann, the murderer who reduces the quiddity of individuals to "zoological types."

The lesson that Fyodor learns in the aftermath of his encounter with the alleged German is a tempting heuristic for Nabokov's act of vigilante justice against Spiresco. Fyodor's outburst of silent hatred toward the man on the bus erupts into real violence in Nabokov's attack on Spiresco and the race-inflected language—"hirsute, ape-like [*volosatyi, obez'ianopodobnyi*]"—he uses to describe him.[35] Yet the next day's vigil, during which Nabokov and Kaminka await Spiresco's seconds, suggests that they had somehow revised their image of Spiresco. Like the loathed German who turns out to be a likable Russian, Spiresco undergoes a metamorphosis: from social pariah who can be cudgeled in public with impunity, he becomes a social equal with whom Nabokov deigns to fight in a duel.

THE POETICS OF DISTORTION

The famous speech from which V. culls the title for "That in Aleppo Once . . ." draws a series of complex distinctions between national, racial, and religious identities:

> Set you down this;
> And say besides that in Aleppo once,
> Where a malignant and a turbanned Turk
> Beat a Venetian and traduced the state,
> I took by th' throat the circumcisèd dog,
> And smote him—thus! (*Othello* 5.2.356–61)

Like Venice, Aleppo was an exotic outpost for trade between East and West in the Renaissance. In Othello's famous speech, Aleppo is not a place of peaceful cosmopolitan commerce, but the staging ground for violence between a Christian Venetian and a Muslim Turk. The lines testify to the triumph of white imperialist discourse as Othello, a former African slave, identifies himself with the cause of his white employers. He locates himself squarely on the side of Christian Venetians who must defend their faith and civilization through violence. Yet at the same time, these famous last words testify to the slippery nature of racial, national, and religious affiliations. As Othello delivers these lines he stabs himself and thus casts himself in the role of the malignant Turk who elicited his violent fury in Aleppo. These lines identify Othello as both insider and outsider within the society that he serves: he is at once "turbanned Turk" and Venetian, a traducer of Christian states and its loyal defender.

The network of correspondences that connects the narrator of "That in Aleppo Once . . ." to Othello is, as Frank has argued, the story's most important structuring device. Nabokov wants us to notice these correspondences and place them in the service of interpretation. But he also seems to want us to treat them with suspicion. Like the implications of the ominous final telephone call in his short story "Signs and Symbols," the regime of correspondences invites resistance. (Strandberg's claim that it is "unlikely that Nabokov's narrator . . . measures up to the self-punishing grandeur of Othello's last gesture" is an example of such resistance.)[36] Since the correspondences are generated, as Frank has noted, by V.'s decision to cull his title from Othello's suicide speech (for in its absence, the story would remain "indeterminate and elusive"), it is the title that provokes the greatest suspicion and resistance (*NTI* 176).

By choosing a title that the story's narrator rejects in advance, V. has betrayed his friend's wishes. Like Kinbote's abduction of Shade's manuscript, the betrayal can be understood as an act of theft, an act of discourtesy, and an example of editorial bad faith. All three descriptors signal V.'s lack of respect toward a narrator who does not want the particulars of his own experience to be dissolved in the story of another. As in the case of Kinbote's annotations to Shade's poem, the choice of title is more revealing about V. than about the narrator. Like the narrator of *Pnin*, V. hates happy endings and is condescending toward his subject (*Pnin* 314). The narrator's hope that V. might "clarify things for me through the prism of your art" (*SVN* 564) is fulfilled, but not in the way that he had hoped. As a determining force in the narrator's destiny, the Shakespearean title *clarifies* in the way that a photograph becomes blank through overexposure. The story loses both meaning and originality by having been presented to the public as an *overclarified* version of *Othello*.

Nabokov's own artistic inclinations run counter to those of V. Instead of searching for meaning in correspondences, Nabokov favored the comic inversion: most closely relevant here is the reappearance, in *Pnin*, of Shakespeare's white, aristocratic Desdemona as an "old colored charwoman" who "gossiped daily" with God (*Pnin* 325). There are others, too: in Dostoevsky's *Crime and Punishment*, Luzhin is a crass materialist obsessed with the advantages that money can buy; in Nabokov's *The Defense*, Luzhin is a chess grand master who cannot survive in the world of material objects and interests. Similarly straying from the source of one's origins, the tender-hearted and pure-souled Pierre—known as "M'sieur Pierre [*Ms'e Pier*]" in society before he becomes Count Bezukhov (*WP* 1:22; *PSS* 9:25)—reappears in *Invitation to a Beheading* as Cincinnatus's tormentor and executioner. Nabokov's best-known inversion is the parodic transformation of *Anna Karenina*'s famous opening lines in the opening lines of *Ada*: "All happy families are more or less dissimilar, all unhappy ones are more or less alike."

The regime of correspondences that structures "That in Aleppo Once . . ." is the same kind of trap that invites us to see Pushkin identifying with Othello on the basis of their shared racial affiliations, marital troubles, and poetic gifts. It is tempting to see the call to resist such identifications as part of Nabokov's rejection of the concept of species as a fixed category and his frequently parodic engagement with his literary predecessors. We might say that race becomes, in Nabokov's hands, a legitimate concept only in a *fugitive* or *parodic* sense.[37] It functions, that is, as a temporal marker—a "phase of evolutional structure" as Nabokov calls it—where similarity becomes difference as soon as the taxonomic or literary framework is altered.

KNOWING AND ACKNOWLEDGING

The false correspondences in "That in Aleppo Once . . ." and the fabricated scene in which Pushkin watches *Othello* are inseparable from the problem of other minds. In Stanley Cavell's enunciation of the problem, the epistemological doubt surrounding privacy as it developed in Western philosophy under the influence of Descartes is a distortion of the pain we feel in consequence of our separateness from the world and others. According to Cavell, skepticism about the possibility of knowing other minds is an evasion of our limited capacity to exercise moral agency. Drawing inspiration from the famous opening words of Kant's *Critique of Pure Reason*, Cavell concludes that our ethical "powerlessness presents itself as ignorance—a metaphysical finitude as an intellectual lack" (*Must* 263).[38] Like Cavell, Nabokov shared Kant's great insight that human reason is burdened by questions that it can neither answer nor ignore. This paradox lurks within Nabokov's description to George Feifer in an interview from 1976 of what surprised him most about life: "the marvel of consciousness—that sudden window swinging open on a sunlit landscape amidst the night of non-being; the mind's helpless inability to cope with its own essence and sense."[39]

Cavell illustrates his claim by way of a theatrical metaphor that is especially relevant to V.'s betrayal of the narrator's wishes in "That in Aleppo Once . . ." and the fictional encounter between Pushkin and Othello that Nabokov stages in *The Gift*. According to Cavell, the conditions of theater spectatorship serve as a close analogy of the existential predicament enunciated by Kant (*Must* 333). By being expected to remain silent, hidden, and passive, members of the audience are confronted with their radical separateness from the actors onstage. This epistemological revelation is accompanied by the ethical revelation that we are "helpless before the acting and the suffering of others" (*Must* 338). According to Cavell, tragedy seeks to help us bear the burden of that fact.

The cornerstone of Cavell's contributions to philosophy is an ethics of acknowledgment that aims to serve as an antidote to the problem of other minds. Cavell replaces the insistence on knowledge as the primary mover of moral action with a form of sympathy that can operate in the absence of such knowledge. In Cavell's hands, the classic epistemological quest for knowledge-as-certainty (as expressed, for instance, in assertions such as "I know you are in pain") is abandoned in favor of a response that acknowledges the other's experience without the guarantee of knowledge (expressed by Cavell as "I acknowledge that you are in pain even if I cannot know it"). Patchen Markell's elaboration of Cavell's distinction is especially useful here: "What matters in our relation to another, Cavell suggests, is not knowing something special about him, or knowing him (his pain, pleasure, humanity, character, or very being) in a way that could evade doubt once and for all. What matters, instead, is *what we do* in the presence of the other, how we respond to or act in the light of what we *do* know."[40]

The question of how we acknowledge others and how others acknowledge us animates Cavell's writings on ethics and the ethics of courtesy itself. By returning to the theatrical metaphor he invokes to illustrate the problem of other minds, Cavell is able to distinguish between morally appropriate and inappropriate forms of acknowledgment. As David Macarthur observes, Cavell invokes the term *theatricality* "to signal an unnaturalness or distortion in our relations with one another. To *theatricalize* another is to treat them as if they were an actor on a stage performing for a self that . . . is unresponsive or indifferent or cold or callous towards the other."[41] Theatricalizing the other is a species of solipsism insofar as it involves treating the other as "a fictitious creature, a figment of my imagination" (*Must* 337). V.'s choice of title for the narrator's elusive story involves precisely the kind of reduction of the other described by Cavell. In betraying the narrator's request to avoid the suggested title from *Othello*, V. denies the narrator's genuine otherness by yoking his story to the story of another.

Within the terms bequeathed to us by Cavell, Pushkin's riotously demonstrative response to Aldridge playing Othello models the right kind of acknowledgment or courtesy. His expansive, uninhibited gestures of appreciation are keyed into the kind of expressive sympathy Cavell calls "acknowledgment." Teskey helps us see that this kind of acknowledgment also goes by the name of "courtesy": Pushkin's response is a form of courtesy because it "moves into the presence of the unknown as if the unknown were not an object but rather another subject, a stranger." Teskey's conception of courtesy as a method of *thinking* about the other that resists what he calls the traditional "metaphorics of grasping" similarly turns on a key Kantian distinction between objects and subjects, means and ends ("CT" 344). But to qualify as a form of Cavellian acknowledgment or Teskeyan courtesy, Pushkin's response cannot be animated by the epistemological certainties that might obtain from a sense of shared identities and affiliations. As Teskey might say, Pushkin must *think* about Othello not as an object of knowledge to be seized and appropriated, but as "an encounter with the strange as a stranger" ("CT" 344). By way of his extroverted responsiveness, Pushkin is also meeting Cavell's fundamental requirement for acknowledgment: that is, he is *doing* something and visibly *revealing* something in response to what is happening on stage (*Must* 257).

Cavell's understanding of acknowledgment as a *demonstrated* act of sympathy and goodwill is the shortest route to seeing his conception of acknowledgment as a form of courtesy. Unlike inner virtues such as love and pity, courtesy is an external mode of conduct that relies entirely on its performance. Additionally, Cavell's conception of acknowledgment demands—as courtesy does, too—that others be taken at their word. Whereas knowledge depends on factuality and veracity, courtesy and acknowledgment accept, in the name of respect, the other's word as true and meaningful (even if conspicuously false or unintelligible). Aldridge's acclaimed performances in St. Petersburg serve as images of such courteous acknowledgment. The applause was consistently rapturous in spite of the fact that most members of Aldridge's Russian audiences could understand neither Shakespeare's English nor Aldridge's German insertions into Shakespeare's text.

Fyodor's abortive biography of his father is also a form of acknowledgment that—to quote Cavell—"goes beyond knowledge . . . not, so to speak, in the order of knowledge, but in its requirement that I *do* something or reveal something on the basis of that knowledge" (*Must* 257). The incomplete biography of Godunov resides in a liminal space where reported facts rub up against an unresolved and perhaps unresolvable mystery. In *The Real Life of Sebastian Knight*, V.'s triumphalist conclusion that "I am Sebastian, or Sebastian is I" is no overcoming of Fyodor's epistemological dilemma. V.'s conclusion is best understood as a boast provoked by a host of failures—the failure to reach the dying Sebastian in time to hear his closely guarded secret; the failure of learning something meaningful about Sebastian from his last mistress; the failure to uncover his "real life." The "overly insistent, self-ironic ring" that Blackwell detects in V.'s reportage belies V.'s claim to have transcended the self's existential isolation.[42]

The precedents for V.'s bold conclusion—Elizabeth I's apocryphal remark "I am Richard II"; Flaubert's apocryphal "I am Madame Bovary"; Catherine Earnshaw's "I am Heathcliff"—suggest that such declarations might be making a claim about an extreme form of sympathy which, by virtue of its intensity, is capable of transcending our private solitudes. Yet such a reading would be naively optimistic. Like V.'s claim about becoming Sebastian, these precedents *redraw* rather than *erase* the boundaries between the self and the other. In her elaboration of her claim that she *is* Heathcliff, Catherine explains that their spiritual union does not dissolve the fact that the world which lies beyond them remains resolutely and painfully alien: "If all else perished, and *he* remained," she tells Nelly Dean, "I should still continue to be; and if all else remained, and he were annihilated, the universe would turn to a mighty stranger."[43]

Acknowledgment, like courtesy, makes it possible to exercise moral agency from a position of epistemic doubt. As a skeptic, Nabokov conceded that the individual mind is hopelessly isolated from its surroundings. But as a cosmopolitan, he was also curious about what was concealed behind that isolation. Like the Aleppo recalled by Othello and the Venice where he marries Desdemona, these spaces are hubs of commerce and migration. As Jeremy Waldron has eloquently put it, the human condition is intrinsically cosmopolitan even if we might wish to deny it:

> Humans are curious and adventurous animals: they travel, they migrate, they trade, they fight, and they plunder. And they report back what they have found out about the ways in which others live (and trade and fight etc.). They bring back tales of exotic customs as well as the exotic goods they have purchased or stolen. One result of this is that custom, practice, language, and social and military organization seldom stay local. . . . For human cultures, it is the rule, not the exception, that ideas and ways of doing things are propagated and transmitted, noticed and adapted. No doubt—from a purist's point of view—they are violated and distorted in the process; but my point is that there is nothing normative about the purist's point of view.[44]

Like Waldron, Nabokov did not romanticize the means by which people interact with one another. In his biographical sketch of Gannibal, he reminds his readers that Gannibal was used as a trapping of imperial swagger at Peter's court: "a blackamoor in attendance was a symbol of supreme luxury and grandeur, and the tsar must have awaited his 1706 New Year gift from his envoy with as much eagerness as he did shipments of lilies and lilacs" ("AG" 148).

But he also draws keen pleasure from the discovery that Gannibal did not need to go so far as to adopt the name of the great Carthaginian conqueror to assert his African heritage. "Officially," Nabokov explains, "the name of Peter I's godchild had become Pyotr Petrovich Petrov (Christian name, patronymic, and surname), but he had grown used in Turkey to the name of Ibrahim and was allowed to call himself by its Russian counterpart, Avraam or Abram." In his next observation, Nabokov notes that what Gannibal perceived to be alien to his personal heritage—the name Pyotr—was, as a result of the cross-currents of migration, already stitched into his African identity. "Actually," Nabokov writes, Gannibal "should not have boggled at bearing his godfather's name: after all, it had been a Petrus Aethiops (Pasfa Sayon Malbazo) who published in Rome, about 1549, after thirteen years of labor, the New Testament in the language of Abyssinian liturgy (that is, Geez, the ancient Ethiopic, which was later replaced by Amharic)" ("AG" 152).

Significantly, Nabokov is not claiming a link grounded in identity between Abram Gannibal and Petrus Aethiops. Rather, he draws satisfaction from the romantic circulation of a name—a kind of paradoxical nomadic stability—across languages, texts, and routes of transcontinental migration. The name of Petrus Aethiops, one of the three Ethiopian monks to arrive in Rome in the sixteenth century bearing Ethiopic biblical manuscripts, signals both proximity and distance between Gannibal's African homeland and the Russian court where he selected a name for himself.

In the section describing his tutor Lensky's poetic but underappreciated Magic Lantern Projections, Nabokov recalls that one such performance was entitled "Africa—the Land of Marvels" (*SM* 502). This land of marvels stirred young Nabokov's imagination as Petrus Aethiops stirred the imagination of Nabokov's older self, and both had the same effect on him as the English word "childhood" when he was clambering over wet rocks at Abbazia as a young boy: "the English word 'childhood,' which sounds mysterious and new, and becomes stranger and stranger as it gets mixed up in my small, overstocked, hectic mind, with Robin Hood and Little Red Riding Hood, and the brown hoods of old hunchbacked fairies" (*SM* 374). The scene of the fictive Pushkin watching the real Aldridge impersonate Shakespeare's Othello on a Russian stage suggests a similar commingling of the strange with the familiar. Nabokov imagines here an aged but still youthful Pushkin responding with enthusiastic signs of welcome toward scenes and words that might have struck another as familiar, but which strike Pushkin's overstocked but inexhaustibly curious mind as stranger and stranger.

Chapter Five

The Art of Lying: Nabokov, Tolstoy, Botkin

> What exactly is poetry if not insight into the most secretive essence of *things*? i.e., of reality. Carlyle says somewhere: "the heart of nature is everywhere music; if you can only reach it." In any profound outlook, there has to be the poetic.
> —Vasily Botkin

> *Emma*: And how did you think Miss Fairfax looking?
> *Frank*: Ill, very ill—that is, if a young lady can ever be allowed to look ill. But the expression is hardly admissible, Mrs. Weston, is it? Ladies can never look ill.
> —Jane Austen, *Emma*

BY THE WINTER of 1858, when Fyodor's grandfather is made to believe that Pushkin is the man sitting in the neighboring box watching Aldridge play Othello (*Gift* 100), Pushkin's star was on the wane. His poetry was held in disdain and the journal that he had founded in 1836, *The Contemporary* (*Sovremennik*), had been taken over by the radical publicist Nikolay Chernyshevsky, the subject of the fourth chapter of Nabokov's *The Gift*.

Chernyshevsky's ascent to power at *The Contemporary* and his efforts to subordinate Russian art to sociopolitical concerns did not go unchallenged. Among Pushkin's most eloquent and principled defenders was Vasily Petrovich Botkin (1811–1869), a prominent intellectual and a valued friend of Nekrasov, Turgenev, and Tolstoy. More than half of the pages that make up Fyodor's biography of Chernyshevsky are devoted to the aesthetic wars that roiled *The Contemporary* between 1853 and 1862. It is fitting, then, that the memoirist Suhoshchokov should become captivated by a fantasy in which Pushkin was not only still alive in 1858 when Aldridge assumed the role of Othello in St. Petersburg, but—presumably—still editing *The Contemporary*. The fantasy becomes all the more poignant because 1858 was the year in which Pushkin's defenders were decisively routed and *The Contemporary*, with Chernyshevsky at the helm, became a political journal that was militantly opposed to its founder's artistic legacy.

In Fyodor's biography of Chernyshevsky, Botkin is mentioned alongside Tolstoy, Turgenev, Grigorovich, and Druzhinin as one of Chernyshevsky's jeering "mockers" (*Gift* 249–50). Fyodor provides detailed accounts of these men's repeated attacks on Chernyshevsky both in private (in letters and amateur theatricals) and in the press. These accounts suggest that Nabokov must have been aware of Botkin's efforts to refute Chernyshevsky's utilitarian criticism on two major occasions.[1] The first of these involved Botkin's translation of a number of passages from Thomas Carlyle's *Heroes and Hero Worship* published in *The Contemporary* in October 1855, January 1856, and February 1856.[2] A second effort involved the publication in January 1857 (also in *The Contemporary*) of an article titled "The Poems of A. A. Fet" in which Botkin offered a riposte to Chernyshevsky's materialist aesthetic by defending the autonomy of art and the artist.[3]

Nabokov would have disagreed with Botkin's repeated claim in his essay on Fet that "sincerity and truthfulness" are the key elements of poetry,[4] but he would have enthusiastically endorsed Botkin's companion claim that art is "a means for uncovering the poetry that is contained in the very basis of life" and that life's prosaic elements become "incomparably more poetic" when subjected to scrutiny.[5] Botkin's comparison of lyric poetry to the stained-glass windows of Gothic cathedrals might have served as one of Nabokov's favorite tropes for the artist's capacity to coax a drab reality into producing magnificent visions. "If one looks at them from the outside," Botkin writes, "how dark and dim they appear! But go inside and these previously dim, dark sketches shine forth in sharp, flowing, bright tones; they pour into the furthermost vaults of the edifice their quiet rainbow light that sparkles on the surging forms plunged in the mystical twilight."[6]

Gerard de Vries has argued that Vasily Petrovich Botkin stands behind Kinbote's mask. Identified in the novel's index as an "American scholar of Russian descent" (*PF* 659), Botkin serves—in de Vries's account—as a veiled tribute to Pushkin. De Vries sees Botkin's presence in the American university town of New Wye as a testament to Vasily Botkin's prophetic claim that Pushkin's art would survive the attacks leveled against it by Russia's radical critics. According to this view, Pushkin becomes a sort of contraband that Nabokov has Botkin smuggle into his adoptive homeland.[7]

It is usual to look for the earliest stirrings of *Pale Fire* in Nabokov's unfinished novel *Solus Rex*, but Kinbote's real name—Botkin—also establishes a vital connection between *Pale Fire* and *The Gift*. The historical Botkin (mentioned in *The Gift*) and the invented Botkin (mentioned in *Pale Fire*) are deceptively minor figures in the texts in which they appear. Nonetheless, they play key roles in defending an artistic philosophy that Nabokov identified with Pushkin.

Pale Fire's links to *The Gift* also connect it to *Invitation to a Beheading*, a novel whose first draft Nabokov wrote during a short break from his Russian magnum opus. While drafting Fyodor's biography of Chernyshevsky, Nabokov recalls interrupting his work to write the first draft of *Invitation to a Beheading* in "one fortnight of wonderful excitement and sustained inspiration" (*SO* 68).[8] Scholars have come to recognize that *Invitation to a Beheading* was somehow occasioned by Nabokov's work on the Chernyshevsky chapter in *The Gift*, and Brian Boyd and Alexander Dolinin have argued that the central plot of a prisoner awaiting execution in *Invitation to a Beheading* has its origins in Chernyshevsky's unhappy life.[9]

One might speculate further that the "beings akin to him" that await Cincinnatus at the very conclusion of *Invitation to a Beheading* include not only revered figures like Pushkin, but also Pushkin's loyal defenders who had faced off with Chernyshevsky during the aesthetic wars of the 1850s and '60s. Nabokov's immersion in these wars would have familiarized him not only with Botkin's staunch defense of Pushkin, but also with his defense of Tolstoy against the same utilitarian critics who held Pushkin in disdain. The allusions in *Invitation to a Beheading* to Tolstoy's *War and Peace* suggest that Nabokov may have regarded both novels as escape hatches from the prison house of writing Chernyshevsky's biography.

Irina Paperno's work on *The Gift* provides the most direct link between *War and Peace* and *Invitation to a Beheading*. Paperno argues that Fyodor's literary experiments in *The Gift* were influenced by the theoretical principles of Russian formalism.[10] More specifically, she speculates that Nabokov's most immediate source of information for these formalist principles was Viktor Shklovsky's *Substance and Style in Lev Tolstoy's "War and Peace"* (*Material i stil' v romane L'va Tolstogo "Voina i mir,"* 1928). According to Paperno, the devices singled out for attention by Shklovsky in his study of *War and Peace* are the same devices that Nabokov uses in *The Gift*.[11] Reading *War and Peace* in conjunction with Shklovsky's book would have provided Nabokov with a similar kind of antidote as the writing of *Invitation to a Beheading*, for both works collide with Chernyshevsky's view that art ought to be placed into the service of social objectives.

SINCERITY AND TRUTHFULNESS

Botkin's claim that art must always be truthful and sincere was a principle he shared with Tolstoy. At the end of "Sevastopol in May," one of the wartime sketches Tolstoy sent to *The Contemporary* while serving in the Crimean War,[12] his narrator makes the following claim: "The hero of my tale, whom

I love with all the strength of my soul, whom I have tried to set forth in all his beauty, and who has always been, is, and always will be most beautiful, is—the truth [*pravda*]."[13] In *War and Peace*, Tolstoy's protagonists come into contact with this special kind of truth during heightened moments of being, such as the epiphanies Andrey Bolkonsky experiences on the battlefield at Austerlitz ("all is vanity [*pustoe*], all is delusion [*obman*] except these infinite heavens" [*WP* 1.326; *PSS* 9:344]) or when he gazes at the gnarled old oak on his way to Otradnoe ("the same stupid, meaningless tale . . . the same old delusion [*obman*]!" [*WP* 1.492; *PSS* 10:154]). These epiphanies portray truth as a barely remembered state of grace and life on earth as a long dalliance with deception, a catchall term in Tolstoy's fictional universe for the constellation of moral failings—vanity, ambition, hypocrisy—that make up our fallen nature.

This existential deception finds its social correlative in the *lie*. As in Kant, for whom lying "most *trenchantly* separates human society, of which truth is the bond" (*LE* 27:59), lying is a straying from the moral path in Tolstoy's universe. Pierre Bezukhov is made to confront the disastrous consequences of lying to himself and others in the aftermath of his duel with Dolokhov: "Folly . . . folly! Death . . . Lies [*lozh'*] . . ." are the words he mutters to himself as he absorbs the fact that he has shot (and perhaps even killed) his wife's lover (*WP* 1.369; *PSS* 10:27). Reflecting upon these events a few hours later, Pierre traces the origins of the duel to the lie he told Hélène the night he became engaged to her:

> "But how was I to blame?" he asked. *Because you married her without loving her; because you deceived both yourself and her.* And vividly he recalled that moment after supper at Prince Vasily's, when he spoke those words he had found so difficult to utter: "*Je vous aime*—I love you." "It all started from that! I felt at the time"—he reflected—"I felt at the time that it was wrong, that I had no right to do it. And so it has turned out." (*WP* 1.370–71; *PSS* 10:28)

Pierre is not alone in suffering the consequences of lying to oneself and others. Natasha is nearly destroyed by Anatole Kuragin's lies, and the Rostovs are bankrupted by Count Rostov's failure to face the truth about his messy finances. Lying is always wrong, and telling the truth is always the right thing to do in Tolstoy's fictions. As Kant might say, "the love of truth" is "the basis of all virtue" in Tolstoy's fictional landscapes (*LE* 27:60).

In spite of valuing art's deceptions, Nabokov insists upon a strict commitment to truth in his rigorously literal translation of *Eugene Onegin*:

> In transposing *Eugene Onegin* from Pushkin's Russian into my English I have sacrificed to completeness of meaning every formal element save the iam-

> bic rhythm: its retention assisted rather than hindered fidelity . . . to my ideal of literalism I sacrificed everything (elegance, euphony, clarity, good taste, modern usage, and even grammar) that the dainty mimic prizes higher than truth. (*EO* 1.x)

Yet this inflexible faithfulness to the literal "truth" grades into a very complex fantasy in *Pale Fire*. It is as though Nabokov had intuited that "the ideal" to which he aspired might be every bit as affected as Cordelia's pronouncement, in the name of truth, that she loves Lear neither more nor less than her "bond" requires.

As numerous scholars have noted, the principles that guided Nabokov's work on *Onegin* are turned on their head in *Pale Fire*, but not as straightforward comedy or as a condemnation of editorial bad faith.[14] René Alladaye calls *Pale Fire* a "contrapuntal parody" of Nabokov's annotated translation of *Onegin*;[15] Robert Alter sees it as a "philosophic novel" whose primary concern is how each individual mind filters and re-creates reality;[16] John Haegert calls it an exercise in "the art of misreading";[17] Maurice Couturier argues that *Pale Fire* "stages the liberating struggle which each reader must fight in order to create his own text."[18] These claims call attention to the strangeness of a work in which theft and madness are reimagined as artistic and moral virtues.

Pale Fire is surely the most intricate and deceptive of Nabokov's deceptive fictions.[19] Its riddles continue to spark debate and occasion monographs. Yet what has gone unnoticed is the extent to which Nabokov makes deception a matter of moral concern. *Pale Fire* is not only a formally deceptive text, but one that endows deception with a complex moral purpose. Reading Nabokov alongside *War and Peace* makes visible the reasons why he frequently casts a particular kind of deception as a key ingredient of courtesy. That Nabokov should spar with Tolstoy about the moral value of deception makes sense given that Tolstoy was the novelist whom Nabokov came to admire above all others.[20]

THE SOUL IMMORTAL: PIERRE BEZUKHOV AND PIERRE DELALANDE

Though Nabokov's most sustained engagement with *War and Peace* is *Pale Fire*, his first extended engagement with Tolstoy's longest novel is *Invitation to a Beheading*. The three-thousand-page biography of a 600-year-old oak, titled *Quercus*, which Cincinnatus reads with desultory interest during his incarceration, recalls the ancient, enormous oak (*WP* 492; *PSS* 10.154) that presides over Andrey Bolkonsky's spiritual rebirth in the aftermath of his disillusionment at Austerlitz:

> Employing the gradual development of the tree (growing lone and mighty at the edge of a canyon at whose bottom the waters never ceased to din), the author unfolded all the historic events—or shadows of events—of which the oak could have been a witness; now it was a dialogue between two warriors dismounted from their steeds . . . so as to rest under the cool ceil of its noble foliage; now highwaymen stopping by and the song of a wild-haired fugitive damsel; now, beneath the storm's blue zigzag, the hasty passage of a lord escaping from royal wrath; now, upon a spread cloak a corpse, still quivering with the throb of the leafy shadows; now a brief drama in the life of some villagers. (*IB* 122–23)

Quercus parodies novels that share the "girth" of *War and Peace*: its "scientific descriptions of the oak itself, from the viewpoints of dendrology, ornithology, coleopterology, mythology," recall *Moby-Dick*'s scientific disquisitions on whales and whaling; its "paragraph a page and a half long in which all the words began with 'p'" (*IB* 123) recalls the stylistic quirks of Joyce's *Work in Progress* (*Finnegans Wake* after 1939). But the novel's chief conceit—that the gaze of an oak can provide a more truthful historical narrative than fallible historians—parodies Tolstoy's central claim in *War and Peace* that history is the accumulation of a multitude of impersonal events that lie beyond the ken of human observation and narrative.

The melancholy reflections that flit across Cincinnatus's mind as he reads *Quercus* ("what matters to me all this, distant, deceitful and dead—I, who am preparing to die?" [*IB* 123]) echo Andrey's thoughts as he drives past the gnarled old oak: "Others—the young—may be caught anew by this delusion [*etot obman*], but we know what life is—our life is finished!" (*WP* 1.492; *PSS* 10:154). These curious echoes are strengthened a paragraph later when Rodion the jailer enters Cincinnatus's cell bearing "what he called frühstück" (*IB* 124). For readers of *War and Peace*, the arrival of Cincinnatus's breakfast will recall the onset of Liza's labor—announced by what she misdiagnoses as indigestion produced by "this morning's *fruschtique* (as Foka the cook calls breakfast)" (*le fruschtique* [*comme dit Foka—povar*] *de ce matin*). Deducing the true cause of Liza's suffering, Maria summons the midwife (*WP* 1.378; *PSS* 10:36). As if in sympathy with Liza, Cincinnatus expects heartburn from Rodion's "frühstück" (*IB* 124) and is surprised a few pages later by the arrival of his mother—a midwife (130).

These echoes signal an important link between the two novels. Everything that happens to Cincinnatus—his fear of death, his hope for escape, his suffering because he does not know when he will die—strains toward the epiphany that has already been foreshadowed in the novel's epigraph: "*Comme un fou se croit Dieu, nous nous croyons mortels*" ("As a madman believes himself to be God, we believe ourselves to be mortal"). The author of this gnomic epigraph is identified by his surname only—Delalande—and the work from which the epigraph is culled is his *Discours sur les ombres*. Delalande also makes an appearance in *The Gift*: we learn there that his given name is Pierre. In his prefatory remarks to *Invitation*'s English translation, Nabokov reveals that he has been playing a game with his readers when he attributes the epigraph to "Pierre Delalande, whom I invented" (*IB* 6).

There are good reasons for Pierre Delalande to share the given name of Pierre Bezukhov, the protagonist of *War and Peace*. Delalande's words contend that we are mistaken to think of ourselves as mortal; mortality is a kind of human folly, a derangement of perception. This insight echoes an epiphany experienced by Pierre Bezukhov during his imprisonment by the French:

> "Ha-ha-ha!" laughed Pierre. And he said aloud to himself: "The soldier did not let me pass. They took me and shut me up. They keep me prisoner. What 'me'? Me? Me—my immortal soul! Ha-ha-ha! Ha-ha-ha! . . ." he laughed with the tears starting to his eyes. . . . High overhead in the luminous sky hung the full moon. Forests and fields beyond the confines of the camp, unseen before, now stretched visible in the distance. And still farther beyond those forests and fields the bright, quivering, limitless distance lured the eye into its depths. Pierre glanced up at the sky and the stars twinkling remote and far-away. "And all that is mine, all that is in me, and all that is *me*," thought Pierre. "And they took all that and shut it up in a shed barricaded with planks!" He smiled and went to lie down and sleep beside his companions. (*WP* 2:1207; *PSS* 12:105–6)

Cincinnatus experiences something very similar, but his revelation develops in two parts. The light show in the Tamara Gardens, presented to him as a treat during his incarceration, recalls the backdrop of Pierre's revelation: "The lights covered an ever-increasing area: now they stretched out along a distant valley, now they were on the other side of it, in the form of an elongated brooch, now they already studded the first slopes; once there they passed on from hill to hill, nestling in the most secret folds, groping their way to the summits, crossing over them!" (*IB* 189). And though Cincinnatus feels intimations of his soul's freedom and immortality throughout his imprisonment, it is only on the execution block that these intimations blossom into full-blown certainty: "with a clarity he had never experienced before—at first almost painful, so suddenly did it come, but then suffusing him with joy, he reflected: why am I here? Why am I lying like this? And, having asked himself these simple questions, he answered them by getting up and looking around" (*IB* 222). Whereas Pierre's revelation concludes with his return to sleep "beside his companions [*poshel ukladyvat'sia spat' k svoim tovarishcham*]," *Invitation* ends with Cincinnatus making his way "in that direction where, to judge by the voices, stood beings akin to him" (*IB* 223).

Kinbote's predicament echoes that of Cincinnatus. They are both misfits who cope with their solitude by dreaming of escape into worlds that are more congenial to them. The scenes Kinbote imagines of his royal alter ego's incarceration in his Zemblan castle specifically recall Cincinnatus's incarceration. While anticipating execution, (Nabokov's fictional) Cincinnatus and (Kinbote's fictional) Charles Xavier are tormented by sounds of digging in the walls of their respective prisons. In the case of Charles, it is "the noise of rapping and ripping" of the castle walls by "the two Soviet professionals" who (in their search for the Zemblan crown jewels) threaten to uncover the secret passage by which Charles hopes to make his escape (*PF* 529–30). In the case of Cincinnatus, it is the noise made by M'sieur Pierre, who rigs up a scheme to entertain his victim by making him believe that rescue is imminent. The fake rescue is a key component of M'sieur Pierre's perverse understanding of courtesy: his various gestures of courtesy are a horror inflicted upon Cincinnatus that he barely survives. The suggestive asymmetry illustrated here—the Soviet tunnel as a false *threat* to the King's escape and M'sieur Pierre's tunnel as a false *promise* of escape—is part of a network of asymmetries stitched into Nabokov's insight that the deceptions of courtesy must have art on their side to perform the work of ethics.

Though imagined as a courteous performance to entertain Cincinnatus, M'sieur Pierre's tunnel is a grotesque deception that leads to crushing disappointment. The deception is devastating because, like Pete's lie on his blind date with Hazel, it merely reaffirms a well-known truth: in the case of Hazel, it confirms her physical unattractiveness; in the case of Cincinnatus, it confirms that he is in prison and has no friends who might risk their lives for his freedom. By contrast, "the noise of rapping and ripping" in Zembla's castle walls is a deception that a homesick, lonely, and mentally ill Kinbote would welcome as an enticing diversion. This kind of benevolent deception is a courtesy that Kinbote extends to himself.

Kinbote's fabricated Zembla, so lovingly detailed and vividly imagined, is no less mendacious than Cincinnatus's drab world. The dystopia that holds Cincinnatus captive is a degraded version of our world, or, as Vasily Botkin might have said, is like the stained-glass windows of a Gothic cathedral when viewed from the *outside*. By contrast, Kinbote's resplendent invention is at once a release from the prison bars of his own psychic anguish and a romantic foil to Shade's provincial New Wye. In short, Zembla is the marvelous effect of seeing stained-glass windows from *inside* a Gothic cathedral.

The delicate asymmetry between Cincinnatus's world and Kinbote's Zembla draws a meaningful distinction between two kinds of deception. Both of these are related to courtesy. Whereas discourteous deceptions are morally wrong because they degrade and imprison, courteous deceptions are morally admirable because they uplift and liberate. In characteristic

Nabokovian fashion, the distinction is grounded both in intent and artfulness. Alter is right when he observes that the "vividness" of Kinbote's Zembla lends it "a kind of authority" that "does not allow us to dismiss it as 'mere' fiction."[21] For Nabokov, *artistic* deceptions transcend the Kantian prohibition against lying, or, what is the same for Kant, treating the other as a thing. Deceptions of this kind address the other as a spiritual being who is at once immortal (as Delalande reminds us) and attuned to the unique attractions of the aesthetic. In doing so, such deceptions identify themselves as courtesies, for it is courtesy that, to quote Proust's Narrator, aims to present individuals with "the highest idea" of themselves (*SLT* 3.587; *RTP* 2.721; NRF 4.2.109). By contrast, M'sieur Pierre's self-styled "rare combination of outward sociability and inward delicacy" (*IB* 85) reimagines such courtesy as farce.

THE DECEPTION OF ART AND THE ART OF DECEPTION

Cincinnatus's soul-saving revelation coincides with a disintegration of his universe. Coming apart before his very eyes, this world is exposed as a poorly constructed artifact. Its miseries, in turn, are shown to be the consequences of its lack of what Shade might have called "richly rhymed life" (*PF* line 970). Cincinnatus's foul world is reminiscent of the operatic performance that marks the beginning of Natasha's fall from grace in *War and Peace*. The seeds of Natasha's moral corruption at the hands of the Kuragins are planted in a setting that is every bit as artificial and poorly constructed as the world that imprisons Cincinnatus. Both Natasha and Cincinnatus intuit the inauthenticity of their surroundings even as they become engulfed by them. Listening to the sounds of digging in the prison walls, Cincinnatus blames himself for believing "in them so much that I infect them with truth" (*IB* 138). The operatic performance initially strikes Natasha as "so grotesquely artificial and unnatural that she felt alternately ashamed and amused at the actors." But this setting of "painted cardboard and oddly dressed men and women" softens the virtuous, innocent Natasha and she begins to experience "a state of intoxication" that makes her ripe for corruption (*WP* 1:663; *PSS* 10:326–27).

The artificial operatic performance that sets the stage for Natasha's loss of innocence and the dingy world that cannot accommodate the sensitive, gentle Cincinnatus serve as synecdoches for their creators' clashing artistic sensibilities. During moments of emotional distress, Tolstoy tended to view art with suspicion. In the immediate aftermath of his brother's death by consumption, for instance, he declared in a letter to Fet that "art is a lie, and I can no longer love a beautiful lie."[22] While in "About What Is Called

Art" ("O tom, chto nazyvaiut iskusstvom," *PSS* 30:253), an unfinished essay from 1896, Tolstoy concedes that art partially compensates for the injustices of nature (by allowing a man without legs to experience the pleasures of dancing, the northerner to feel the heat of the south, the cold egoist to discover the pleasures of love and pity), in his completed essay on art, *What Is Art?* (*Chto takoe iskusstvo?* 1898), he regards art with suspicion because it deceives.[23] The operatic performance that corrupts Natasha is a distillation of the corrupting forces of culture. Its moral failures belong to the same order as "the evil and falsehood of life [*zlo i lozh' zhizni*]" that torment Pierre and make him yearn for "the possibility of goodness and truth [*vozmozhnost' dobra i pravdy*]" (*WP* 1:635; *PSS* 10:298).

This conceptual congruence between evil and deception has a distinguished philosophical pedigree. We see it in Plato's claim that poets should be banished from the ideal republic because they trade in deception. Descartes concluded that material substance must exist because God cannot be a deceiver. Locke asserted that "all the artificial and figurative application of words eloquence hath invented" are "for nothing else but to insinuate wrong *ideas*, move the passions, and thereby mislead the judgment, and so indeed are perfect cheat."[24] Kant claimed that the duty of truth-telling is "a sacred command of reason prescribing unconditionally, one not to be restricted by any conveniences."[25]

Yet Nabokov's effort to find moral value in deception is not without precedent. We see it in Hamlet's injunction to Gertrude when he instructs her to *fake* fidelity if she cannot feel its pull: "Assume a virtue if you have it not" (3.4.162). We see it in Ibsen's censure of Gregers's radiant, destructive truth and his celebration of the "life-lies" that Relling dispenses to the wounded and ungifted.[26] Wilde's remarks in his essay "The Decay of Lying" are especially relevant to courtesy's compact with deception: "the aim of the liar is simply to charm, to delight, to give pleasure. He is the very basis of civilized society, and without him a dinner-party, even at the mansions of the great, is as dull as a lecture at the Royal Society."[27] And we even see it in Kant, whose ideas about lying were not always as inflexible as they became by the time he wrote *The Metaphysics of Morals* and "On a Supposed Right to Lie from Philanthropy." In Herder's notes to the lectures he delivered twelve or thirteen years before these works were written, Kant expresses a more relaxed view of the truth-telling imperative: "Certain untruths are not called lies, because the latter are *strictly untruths* that are contrary to *duty*." He adds that "*untruth*, to the great *advantage of another*, still has something *sublime* in it, that is near allied to virtue" (*LE* 27:61).[28]

Nabokov agrees with Tolstoy that art *is* deception even as he disagrees with him about the consequences of this particular insight: "All art is deception" (*LL* 146); "art at its greatest is fantastically deceitful and complex" (*SO*

33); "every great writer is a great deceiver, but so is that arch-cheat Nature. Nature always deceives" (*LL* 5). Literature was born, Nabokov liked to tell his students, "not the day when a boy crying wolf, wolf came running out of the Neanderthal valley with a big gray wolf at his heels: literature was born on the day when a boy came crying wolf, wolf and there was no wolf behind him" (*LL* 5). It is revealing that Nabokov turns this cautionary tale about the dangers of deception into a parable of art's origins. The story's first tellers would have certainly seen the boy's deceptions as a reckless disregard for the security of the tribe. For the instinctively anti-utilitarian Nabokov, however, it is precisely this gratuitous recklessness that engenders art and separates the boy from his "baboon-like parents, great sticklers for the truth" (*SO* 11).

In *What Is Art?* Tolstoy anticipates Nabokov's use of "The Boy Who Cried Wolf" fable, but—as Eric Naiman has observed—with a different end in view: whereas Nabokov focuses on the boy's *inventiveness*, Tolstoy's boy engages in an artistic act when he succeeds in replicating *truthfully* and *sincerely* the feelings he experienced when he encountered or imagined encountering a wolf.[29] For Tolstoy, art is born when the boy *infects* his audience with his own fear:

> A boy having experienced, let us say, fear on encountering a wolf, relates that encounter, and in order to evoke in others the feeling he has experienced, describes himself, his condition before the encounter, the surroundings, the wood, his own lightheartedness, and then the wolf's appearance, its movements, the distance between himself and the wolf, and so forth. All this, if only the boy when telling the story again experiences the feelings he had lived through, and infects the hearers [*zarazhaet slushatelei*] and compels them to feel what he had experienced—is art. Even if the boy had not seen a wolf but had frequently been afraid of one, and if wishing to evoke in others the fear he had felt, he invented an encounter with a wolf [*pridumal vstrechu s volkom*] and recounted it so as to make his hearers share the feelings he experienced when he feared the wolf, that also would be art. (*What Is Art?* 58; *PSS* 30:64–65)

Tolstoy's concession that not only experience but imagination, too, can serve as a catalyst for art appears to bring his analogy within shouting distance of Nabokov's inversion of Aesop's fable. But, in fact, the artistic sensibilities described here are miles apart from those described by Nabokov. For Tolstoy, art is born of *feelings*, and whether experienced or imagined, these feelings are ineluctably genuine and, because genuine, aesthetically valuable. By contrast, Nabokov's only concern is the deception that the boy perpetrates against his fellow villagers; what the boy *feels* and *experiences* beyond the desire to deceive is beside the point.[30]

THE BODY ELOQUENT: MARIA AND HAZEL

In spite of his enduring "esteem" for *Invitation to a Beheading* (*SO* 92), Nabokov seems to have recoiled from its triumphalist claim that the powers of the spirit can overcome material reality. In the novels he wrote after *Invitation*, his vision darkens as the autonomy and eloquence of the spirit are trumped by the miseries of the flesh. The body of David Krug is mutilated; the body of Dolly Haze is violated; the body of Hazel Shade is found to be so unattractive as to make life a burden. In all these cases, the body speaks the language of pain and the spirit is helpless in the face of that pain.

The body, which is intensely expressive in both Tolstoy and Nabokov, traps us in unhappy marriages or destructive obsessions. Pierre is doomed the moment he is stirred by the sensuality of Hélène's body: "He was conscious of the warmth of her body, of the smell of perfume, and heard the slight creak of her corset as she breathed" (*WP* 1:237; *PSS* 9:251–52). But the same eloquence of the flesh can light up a life. We see the body's life-giving energies when Andrey dances with Natasha for the first time: "But he had no sooner put his arm round that slender supple quivering figure, and felt her stirring so close to him and smiling up into his face, than her charm mounted to his head like wine, and he felt himself revived and rejuvenated when they stopped to get breath and he released her and stood watching the other couples" (*WP* 1:541; *PSS* 10:204).

When bodies are eloquent in the wrong way, we see the most powerful evidence that Nabokov's moral vision—unlike Tolstoy's—yearns for a rule-based, Kantian moral framework that can hold out the possibility of acting in ways that contradict natural impulses. The unattractive body which can never hope to seduce a suitor is a central preoccupation in both *War and Peace* and *Pale Fire*. Andrey's sister, Maria, and Shade's daughter, Hazel, confront us with the possibility that Kant acknowledged to his students: that some lies can perform the work of ethics by way of art. It is tempting to think that Nabokov had Maria in mind when he invented Hazel: both young women are said to be homely and lonely, both are attuned to life's spiritual dimensions, both grow up within the orbit of their fathers' lives, and both are said to nurture a secret desire for romantic love (*WP* 1:254; *PSS* 9:270; *PF* line 383). But whereas Maria finds love and happiness at the end of her journey, Hazel ends her life by suicide.

The parallels between Maria and Hazel also extend to their fathers. Both Nikolay Bolkonsky and John Shade love their daughters, and the knowledge that their daughters are physically unattractive makes them suffer. As a man of the world, Prince Bolkonsky intuits (correctly) that Anatole Kuragin finds Maria "*diablement laide* [devilishly ugly]" even as he pretends to flirt with her (*PSS* 9:276).[31] Shade suffers far worse when he recalls the clumsy lie that Pete Dean utters when he is introduced to Hazel. Both Anatole and Pete conduct themselves like cads during these abortive romantic encounters, but Pete's lie is given a radically different inflection than Anatole's. Tolstoy respects Prince Bolkonsky for such sharp-sightedness even as he acknowledges how painful it is for Maria to listen to her father's warnings that Anatole is only interested in her dowry and in Mlle Bourienne, her *mademoiselle de compagnie* (*WP* 1.263, 1.265; *PSS* 9:279, 9:281). But in the scenario that Nabokov stages in *Pale Fire*, it is Shade who is pitied for seeing his daughter with the same ruthless objectivity as Prince Bolkonsky sees Maria.

Unlike Natasha, Maria escapes from being ensnared in Anatole's ignoble schemes because she stumbles upon the truth: she accidentally witnesses Anatole embracing Mlle Bourienne in the winter garden (*WP* 1:266; *PSS* 9:282). Maria needs such an accidental encounter because Anatole is such a skilled deceiver that even those who see the truth are helpless against his deceptions: Maria refuses to believe her father when he tells her that Anatole is only interested in Mlle Bourienne (*WP* 1:265; *PSS* 9:282), and Natasha disbelieves Sonya when Sonya warns her about Anatole's dishonest intentions (*WP* 1.684–85; *PSS* 10:348). Hazel, however, receives no such gift from her maker. She, too, has an encounter with an ignoble suitor but, unlike Maria's encounter with Anatole, Hazel's blind date with Pete ends in disaster. Pete's feeble lie is no match for Anatole's expert lying, yet Pete seems to have far greater power to determine the outcome of events than Tolstoy is willing to grant to Anatole.

The episode of the blind date and—according to Shade—its causal role in Hazel's suicide have bred scholarly suspicion. David Rampton refers to the blind date as "a gag" because it seems capriciously trivial in comparison to the tragedy that follows.[32] Shoshana Knapp calls the suicide "a grossly disproportionate response to a passing slight" and Eric S. Petrie is certain that Nabokov intended his readers to distrust such a "comic-book formula."[33] Pete's discourtesy and Hazel's suicide *appear to be* causally related for two reasons. The first has to do with the tyranny of consequentialist thinking: we tend to read tragic events as consequences of moral decision-making. The second reason has to do with the Shades' fixation on their daughter's physical unattractiveness; as Michael Wood notes, they cannot shake off the feeling "that she is a genetic and cultural disaster."[34] The explanation that she kills herself because she cannot bear "this last confirmation of her ugliness" only seems plausible because it accords with the Shades' expectations.[35] By reducing Hazel's complex inner life to the "small mad hope" that someone might find her sexually desirable (*PF* line 383), Shade sets up Hazel for failure. Unable to see past his daughter's physical undesirability, Shade replicates in advance (and over and over again) Pete's discourtesy toward her.

The final reason Nabokov would have wanted to discourage readers from seeing a causal link between Pete's lie and Hazel's suicide can be illuminated by Kant. As Christine Korsgaard has aptly observed, Kantians consider it "inconsistent with respect for others to regard their actions as simply a *consequence* of what *you* do."[36] To see Hazel's suicide as a direct consequence of Pete's lie is another version of the insult that Pete directs at her; that is, it is to say that Hazel has no agency of her own and must be treated as an object of moral concern by those who have the power to determine her fate. Readers of *Pale Fire* must not replicate Pete's discourtesy toward Hazel by transferring her agency to Pete and thus denying her the dignity to which she is rightfully entitled. In short, a *Kantian* and *courteous* reading of Hazel's plot must place the responsibility for Hazel's suicide not on Pete but on Hazel herself.

BEAUTY AS THE ALCHEMY OF LOVE

Pierre's prolonged marital sufferings are generated by his failure to see the truth about Hélène before being manipulated into marrying her. Maria is spared the suffering that would have come from marrying Anatole by discovering the truth about him before she can make an error as tragic as Pierre's. But even more generously, Maria is given the gift of grace and beauty precisely at the moment that is most propitious for Nikolay Rostov to fall in love with her. When they meet at Voronezh, Maria is transfigured: her characteristic physical awkwardness gives way to "a movement full of dignity and grace" and she speaks "in a voice in which for the first time new deep, womanly notes vibrated" (*WP* 2:1125; *PSS* 12:23). The transformation is so unexpected that the narrator feels compelled to provide an explanation:

> Just as when a light is lit inside a carved and painted lantern, suddenly revealing in unexpected, breath-taking beauty of detail the fine, intricate tracery of its panels, which till then had *seemed* coarse, dark and meaningless [*kazavshaiasia prezhde gruboiu, temnoiu i bessmyslennoiu*] so was Princess Maria's face suddenly transfigured. For the first time all the pure, spiritual, inward travail in which she had lived till then came out into the open. All her inner searchings of spirit, her sufferings, her striving after goodness, her resignation, her love and self-sacrifice—all this now shone forth in those radiant eyes, in her sweet smile, in every feature of her tender face. (*WP* 2:1126; *PSS* 12:23–24; emphasis added)

Rostov falls in love with her because this transformation makes him discover in Maria "an altogether rare and unusual being [*sovsem osobennoe i neobyknovennoe sushchestvo*]" (*WP* 2:1126; *PSS* 12:24). A similar transformation is granted to Pierre after the weeks he spends as a prisoner of war. The narrator reports that he "no longer *seemed* stout [*On ne* kazalsia *uzhe tolst*]" (*WP* 2:1194; *PSS* 12:92; emphasis added); and Natasha finds that "he has *somehow* grown so fair and smooth and fresh-looking—as though he had just come out of a bath [*On sdelalsia* kakoi-to *chistyi, gladkii, svezhii; tochno iz bani*]" (*WP* 2:1326; *PSS* 12:223; emphasis added). Tolstoy's language ("seemed [*kazavshaiasia, kazalsia*]," "somehow [*kakoi-to*]") indicates that it is not Maria and Pierre who have changed, but Rostov and Natasha who now see them through the lens of love. Botkin would have said that love grants Rostov and Natasha the gift of seeing Maria and Pierre *poetically*, or, as his beloved Carlyle might have said, of experiencing them as "music."

But no such vision is granted to those who love Hazel. Shade loves his daughter deeply and is proud of her eccentric intelligence. Nonetheless, his love yields no vision akin to Rostov's altered perception of Maria or Natasha's altered perception of Pierre. Unlike Tolstoy's language, which suggests that Maria's and Pierre's transformations are altered states of perception, Shade's language puts the onus of transformation on Hazel herself. As Shade ruefully observes, "the dingy cygnet never turned / Into a wood duck" (*PF* lines 318–19). The rare occasions when Hazel transcends her unattractiveness are not consequences of parental bias, but a matter of fortuitous circumstance: her mother's furs "made / Her almost fetching; and the mirrors smiled, / The lights were merciful, the shadows mild" (lines 360–62).

When love fails to serve as an antidote to life's cruelties, Tolstoy's characteristic response is to call for loving "more" (*bol'she*) and loving "better" (*luchshe*) (*WP* 2:1092; *PSS* 11:388). But this Tolstoyan injunction is no help if love is understood to be a passion that exists beyond the will's authority. Tolstoy himself appears to have conceded this in *Anna Karenina*. For all her knowledge that she *ought* to love her daughter Annie, Anna feels no love for her, and Vronsky's love of Anna is no match for his love of freedom and life in society. Anna's sacrifice of Karenin and her beloved son for Vronsky, and Natasha's betrayal of Andrey with Anatole, shows that abandoning oneself to one's passions can often lead to self-destruction and the destruction of innocent others.

Yet Natasha's and Anna's moral failings are engineered differently from those staged in Nabokov's fictions. Natasha's betrayal of her promise to Andrey is a necessary development in a plot that will culminate in her marriage to Pierre. While it is more difficult to ascertain what teleological end might obtain from Anna's tragedy beyond hints that emerge from the novel's biblical epigraph ("Vengeance is mine; I will repay"), Tolstoy provides much kinder choices to his protagonists than Nabokov does. Both Natasha and Anna could have found rich sustenance in the loves they had already been granted (an absent but beloved fiancé in the case of Natasha, a beloved son in the case of Anna) before they succumb to Anatole's and Vronsky's courtships.

Nabokov's representations of love in the four masterpieces of his English-language fiction offer starker dilemmas. Humbert's pedophilia, Kinbote's homosexuality in a homophobic America, Pnin's love for the callous Liza Bogolepov, and Van's incestuous love for Ada belong to another register of desire than Anna's adultery with Vronsky or Natasha's abortive elopement with Anatole. Whereas, as Nabokov notes in his lectures on *Anna Karenina*, Tolstoy's scenarios demand that physical desire be subordinated to spiritual love (*LRL* 146–47), the plots of *Lolita*, *Pale Fire*, *Pnin*, and *Ada* confirm Proust's sense that only someone who is *not* in love can imagine "that one chooses the person one loves after endless deliberation" (*SLT* 4.128; *RTP* 3.94; NRF 5.2.92).

To act in accordance with what Nabokov calls in his lectures on *Anna Karenina* "the eternal demands of morality" (*LRL* 147), Humbert, Pnin, Kinbote, and Van ought to have renounced altogether the kind of love that held them captive. For these fictional characters, there is no satisfying alternative to their illicit, futile, or destructive love. In Nabokov's mature fiction, love is an emotion that cannot be trained into being what it is not already or moved from one taxonomic category to another. It is as impossible to imagine the Shades loving Kinbote or Pete loving Hazel as it is impossible to imagine Humbert loving Charlotte, Charles loving Disa, or Van loving Lucette. Like Swann's helpless love for Odette, these plots turn on the futility of holding love to a moral standard or to an imposed discipline.

Shade's love for his daughter seems so anemic and so unlike traditional conceptions of love that some readers might wonder if it is love at all. Fyodor's love for his mother is transforming even after "the beauty of which he had been so proud had faded." It takes no time at all for his vision to readjust itself and recognize, after a three years' absence, "everything that he had loved: the pure outline of her face, narrowing down to the chin, the changeful play of those green, brown, yellow, entrancing eyes under their velvet brows" (*Gift* 86). Clarissa Dalloway, another fictional parent of a fictional child who inherits none of her mother's beauty, shows a "mixture of amusement and pride" in the fact that her daughter "play[s] hockey." Instead, Shade's vision comes uncomfortably close to that of Peter Walsh, who, childless and emotionally unencumbered, sees Clarissa's daughter as "a silent stolid creature" with "nothing of her mother in her."[37] Van's awareness of love's distortive optics and memory's bias for "*otsebyatina* ['what one contributes oneself']" make him realize that he—as someone who loved and continues to love Ada—will never know if Ada had been "really beautiful" or "at least what they call attractive" (*A* 441, 159).

COURTESY AS ARTFUL CONDUCT

Pierre's moral excellence is inseparable from his instinctive love of truth and his loathing for deception. In the circles of St. Petersburg high society, this makes him a boor. His first appearance in the novel is marked by a double act of discourtesy: first, "he had left a lady before she had finished speaking," and second, "he detained another who was wishing to get away from him" (*WP* 1:10; *PSS* 9:12). In Tolstoy's world, such discourtesies are—counterintuitively—signs of a character's moral probity. Referred to by Anna Pavlovna as "*ma tante*," the old lady whom Pierre walks away from is described in terms that anticipate how V. and the Robinsons appeared to Helene Grinstein and Lucette when they bestowed their courtesy upon them: she is someone whom no one "knew or wanted to know or was interested in [*nikomu neinteresnoi i nenuzhnoi*]" (*WP* 1:8; *PSS* 9:10). The guests who perform the "ceremony of greeting" her interpret the fulfillment of this "tiresome duty" as license to ignore her for the rest of the evening (*WP* 1:8; *PSS* 9:10). Pierre's failure to participate in this empty ritual marks him as a virtuous innocent in a hypocritical, callous society. Like Anna's unwillingness to conceal her illicit love for Vronsky for the sake of her reputation, Pierre's unwillingness to feign his feelings is the moral standard against which the actions of others are judged and found wanting.

Pierre is the novel's moral center because, as Andrey tells Natasha before his ill-fated departure for Europe, "he has a heart of gold" (*WP* 1:567; *PSS* 10:230). Andrey's praise is keyed into Pierre's inability to dissemble: "My dear fellow," Andrey tells him after Anna Pavlovna's soirée, "one can't everywhere and at all times say all one thinks" (*WP* 1:26; *PSS* 9:30). Pierre is unable to heed this advice, yet his characteristic kindness enables him to smooth over the pain he causes by his maladroit truth-telling. The offense he causes one of Maria's pilgrims when he insists that her beloved miracle-working icon is "a trick" (*obman*) causes no lasting harm. There is such "sincerity" (*iskrennost'*) in his contrition that both the pilgrim, Pelageyushka, and Maria, her benefactress, quickly forgive his indiscretion (*WP* 1:459–60; *PSS* 10:121–22).

These small discourtesies have no bearing on Pierre's moral integrity because Pierre's feelings and instincts are always trustworthy. This can be traced to Tolstoy's debt to Rousseau: like Rousseau, he believes in the intrinsic goodness of human nature, or what Donna Tussing Orwin calls his belief "that the natural life was moral."[38] The most virtuous characters of *War and Peace*—Platon Karataev, Maria, Pierre—are always guided by their moral intuitions, and those who temporarily stray from the path of virtue—Andrey, Natasha, Nikolay—do so because they become corrupted by the false values of society. Pierre's marriage to Hélène is a perfect example of such straying.

Still, Tolstoy concedes that feelings are not always trustworthy moral guides. Maria suffers from the knowledge that her love for her own children is more intense than her love for her orphaned nephew (*WP* 2:1392; *PSS* 12:288–89). Nikolay Rostov knows that he must conceal the fact that he was not fond of Nikolenka (*WP* 2:1392; *PSS* 12:289) and that he loves his daughter Natasha more than he loves his other children (*WP* 1:1368; *PSS* 12:265). But in spite of acknowledging the necessity of concealing feelings that collide with what is right, Tolstoy identifies moral excellence with acts of truth-telling. Rostov responds to Maria's fear that he cannot love her because she is plain and disfigured by pregnancy with a logico-causal inversion that Shade might have envied: "Not dear for being pretty," he assures her, "but pretty for being dear [*Ne po khoroshu mil, a po milu khorosh*]" (*WP* 2:1368; *PSS* 12:264).[39] The frankness of the first half of this graceful formulation risks injury because it acknowledges that Maria is not conventionally pretty. The second half, however, compensates for this potentially hurtful truth by endowing Maria with a different kind of beauty. Maria, who had struck Anatole as being "*diablement laide*," becomes a *jolie laide* in her husband's affections.

But why is Shade, a devoted family man and poet of distinction, insensitive to the beauty-producing effects of love? Reading Shade's relationship with Hazel through the lens of Nikolay Rostov's tender words to his wife uncovers an enduring mystery at the heart of Shade's relationship with Hazel. Shade's love for his daughter, however tender and intense, is nonetheless hopelessly inert next to Nikolay's love for Maria. Unlike Nikolay, whose love turns plainness into beauty, Shade—in spite of his aching love and pity—sees his daughter in the same light that Pete sees Hazel or Anatole sees Maria. Indeed, Shade sees Hazel in a way that is strikingly similar to the way in which Anna notices Karenin's ears for the first time upon her return from Moscow.[40] Tellingly, the unattractiveness of Karenin's ears is code for Anna's discovery that she no longer loves her husband. The pathos of Shade's personal tragedy resides in his too-ready understanding of Pete's flight from Hazel's side. A more conventional kind of love would have rendered him incapable of understanding why Pete found Hazel so decisively unattractive. Whereas Nikolay becomes a poet when he speaks his personal truth to Maria, Shade becomes less of one when he laments—however eloquently and compassionately—his daughter's homeliness.

Beginning with Shoshana Knapp in 1987, a number of scholars have argued that Nabokov wants his readers to see beyond Shade's sanctioned portrayal of Hazel.[41] These readings share the sense that Hazel's portrayal in Shade's poem is untrustworthy and serves as another example of the "reader entrapment" that Leona Toker identified in *Lolita*. We might say that the trap here is the trap of discourtesy, for to accept Shade's portrait of Hazel at face value is also to accept Pete's impression of Hazel (even if it is not to sanction his conduct). Shade's portrait and Pete's escape from the blind date are fundamentally analogous insofar as they present Hazel not with "the highest idea" of herself, but with something significantly less.

SHADE AND POPE

Pale Fire's indebtedness to Pope, Swift, and other Augustan luminaries underscores the disturbing congruence between Shade's portrait of his daughter and the image of Hazel that made Pete flee from the scene of the double date. As Jay Arnold Levine noted as early as 1966, *Pale Fire* is "a new *Dunciad*, with elements of *A Tale of a Tub* and the *Memoirs of Martinus Scriblerus*."[42] Thomas Karshan, D. L. Macdonald, de Vries, and Lisa Zunshine have built on Levine's insight by tracing the various ways in which *Pale Fire*'s composite structure pays tribute to what Zunshine calls the "sophisticated mockeries" of Pope and Swift.[43] These studies also reveal the indebtedness of Shade's poem to Pope's mock-heroic epic *The Rape of the Lock* and the extent to which Hazel's story rewrites this text.

It is fitting that Shade's "Pale Fire" should be, as Levine calls it, a "Popean poem"[44] given that Shade is a Pope scholar. It is also fitting that Hazel's tragedy should be keyed into Pope's satire on feminine beauty, given that her parents believe that she lacked beauty and committed suicide as a result. Pope's Belinda is in many crucial aspects Hazel's foil: burdened with an excess of sexual appeal, Belinda is subjected to a mock sexual violation when the Baron surreptitiously steals a lock of her hair. Distressed by the loss, Belinda laments her condition in terms that readers of *Pale Fire* will find oddly familiar: she wishes that she had "un-admir'd remain'd / In some lone Isle, or distant *Northern* Land"; she regrets having been induced to roam with "youthful Lords" instead of remaining safely at home; she draws no consolation from the knowledge that she is not "the first mistaken Maid, / By Love of *Courts* to num'rous Ills betrayed" (*RL* 4.151–60; emphasis in original).

Belinda's lament over her misguided love of court life and her companion wish that she had never laid eyes on "Hampton-Court," where the "rape" of the lock occurs (*RL* 4.150), serve as suggestive intertexts for the Shades' decision to send Hazel "to a château in France" in compensation for her lack of a "white-scarfed beau" (*PF* lines 333–36). As de Vries has noted, Shade's "white-scarfed beau" is a direct descendant of the "white-glov'd Beaux" who pays court to Belinda (*RL* 5.13). Hazel's return from the French château—"in tears, with new defeats" (*PF* line 337)—suggests that Nabokov is satirizing the Shades' social vanity in significantly darker hues than those used by Pope when he has Clarissa warn Belinda that the "Glories" of beauty are fleeting and that "Merit" alone "wins the Soul" (*RL* 5.15; 5.34).

But Belinda is deaf to Clarissa's words. She attacks the offending Baron with an ornamental hairpin—"a deadly *Bodkin*" (*RL* 5.88)—and demands the restoration of her lock. Shade's rationalization of Hazel's suicide as a consequence of Pete's scorn implies that Hazel also experienced violent emotions after being subjected to Pete's ungentlemanly conduct. But as Zunshine points out, Pope's work sets out to ridicule the irrationality of equating the loss of a lock of hair with the loss of sexual innocence and the violent impulses that might follow from such a loss.[45] The web of allusions to *The Rape of the Lock* suggests that Shade's inference that Pete's conduct provoked Hazel's suicide is as far-fetched as the mock-heroic conceits that animate Pope's satire.

Pale Fire's debt to Pope poses a series of questions that have a bearing on Hazel's suicide. Why does Nabokov make Shade a Pope scholar when both he and Shade scorned Pope's age? As Zunshine reminds us, Nabokov declared "the Age of Reason" hopelessly "pedestrian" and the "most inartistic of centuries" (*EO* 3.505, 506). Zunshine is perplexed by Shade's decision to dedicate his scholarly career to a writer whom he seems to find vulgar. Squeezed in among lines describing the Shades' vigil on the night of Hazel's blind date, the quoted line from Pope's *An Essay on Man*—"See the blind beggar dance, the cripple sing"—is declared by Shade to have "the vulgar ring / Of its preposterous age" (*PF* lines 419–21). In a rejected draft, he calls Pope's age "heartless" (*PF* 584). Whereas Zunshine reads Shade's negative attitude toward Pope as a reflection of the prevailing view toward him in 1940s America, D. L. Macdonald speculates that Nabokov may have intended Shade's readers to hold this judgment against him.[46]

In a more recent analysis of *Pale Fire*'s complex relationship with Pope, Karshan argues that Shade is offended by Pope's dancing beggar because he misreads it "as a mockery of the weak and ill-favoured, and therefore feels in it a cruel response to people such as Hazel" (*VNAP* 221). Pope's argument, however, is that self-love protects us from reason's sharp-eyed judgment: whereas reason acts as a "sharp accuser,"[47] self-love becomes the sponsor of happiness by erecting hedges against reason's cruel truths. For Karshan, Shade's misreading of Pope's lines is connected to his misreading of Hazel's predicament. Just as Shade is unable to concede that a blind beggar may be moved to dance, he fails to countenance the possibility that Hazel's unattractiveness may be something other than a curse: "Since Shade tends to conceive of beauty as an aspect of nature and an endorsement of something or someone's place in 'life'—the life of society—he fostered in his daughter the impression that because she was unattractive she was unnecessary" (*VNAP* 222). Karshan's conclusion is especially critical of Shade: "If Shade had been more of a satirist, had made any effort to stand outside the myth that a rich world of fantasy is open only to those whose beauty has bought them access, Hazel might not have killed herself" (*VNAP* 222). The "central irony"

Karshan detects in the literary games played by *Pale Fire* is "that happiness requires a level of self-deceit that can also be regarded as madness" (*VNAP* 199). Shade purchases the studied tranquility that pervades his poem at the cost of downplaying his and Sybil's complicity in the social mores that played a role in Hazel's suicide.

De Vries also views the Shades with suspicion. Whereas Pope's treatment of beauty is satirical, de Vries notes, the Shades ardently wish on Hazel's behalf the very values that are discredited in Belinda's world.[48] Shade calls Pope's age "heartless," but, as de Vries observes, it is Pope's beautiful Belinda rather than Hazel who is advised that other things are more important to a girl's happiness than beauty. De Vries is as puzzled as Knapp, Petrie, and Wood by the Shades' obsession with Hazel's looks. These scholars argue that Hazel must have suffered deeply from her parents' inability to see beyond her physical unattractiveness.[49]

SHADE AND MRS. Z.

In the aftermath of his visits to Mrs. Z. and Jim Coates, Shade begins the final canto of his poem with a series of bold resolutions; the first of these is—significantly—the resolution to "spy on beauty as none has / Spied on it yet" (*PF* lines 835–36). However, as Kinbote notes, "the sun does not rise" on this "preparatory burst of would-be inspiration" (629), and Shade's promise to spy on beauty generates nothing more exciting than a bathetic description of the quotidian routines that prop up his creative process. For Karshan, this is a moment when Nabokov aligns Shade most closely with Pope's mock-heroic speakers and their "astonishingly trivial" concerns (*VNAP* 213).

There is poetic justice in Shade's failure to spy on beauty for, in spite of Hazel's death, Shade has not learned to keep his eye and heart engaged in the kind of activity that might have helped him discover (to quote Vasily Botkin) the poetry that dwells at the core of reality. His immediate response to meeting Mrs. Z.—"I was trapped" (*PF* line 772), he recalls—and his hasty departure from her home are identical to Pete's response to Hazel. Just as Pete aborts the blind date, Shade aborts his mission to ask Mrs. Z. about her mystical vision. Shade justifies his discourteous departure by invoking reasons that are at once ungentlemanly and inartistic: he resents having to eat the fruitcake that Mrs. Z. foists upon him, is irritated by her attempts to flatter him, secretly agrees with her when she calls herself "dense," and desists from asking her the question that he wanted most fervently to ask because he's afraid that she might use the question as an inroad for intimacy (lines 773–97).

Mrs. Z. is a key component of the moral and aesthetic problematic of

Pale Fire. This deceptively superfluous figure makes her first appearance in *Speak, Memory* in a thought experiment that anticipates Nabokov's invention of Shade:

> I wonder, however, whether there is really much to be said for more anesthetic destinies, for, let us say, a smooth, safe, small-town continuity of time, with its primitive absence of perspective, when, at fifty, one is still dwelling in the clapboard house of one's childhood, so that every time one cleans the attic one comes across the same pile of old brown schoolbooks, still together among later accumulations of dead objects, and where, on summery Sunday mornings, one's wife stops on the sidewalk to endure for a minute or two that terrible, garrulous, dyed, church-bound McGee woman, who, way back in 1915, used to be pretty, naughty Margaret Ann of the mint-flavored mouth and nimble fingers. (*SM* 572–73)

Though the obligations of courtesy are as onerous here as they are for Sybil when she must "endure" Kinbote's company or for Shade when he refuses to endure Mrs. Z.'s effusive chatter, Mrs. McGee leaps into artistic life by being seen through that very perspective which Nabokov claims to be "anesthetic" and "primitive." In a Flaubertian move by which the tedium of quotidian life is transformed into high art, Nabokov endows Mrs. McGee with a first name and an unforgettably racy youth. Shade, however, fears pollution by coming into contact with the garrulous Mrs. Z., just as Pete fears to be seen with an unattractive date. Neither one can imagine a richer life lurking behind the unattractive exterior.

READING COURTEOUSLY: HAZEL AS DISA

It is possible to argue that the courtesy that Pete and Shade withhold from Hazel is smuggled into *Pale Fire* through the back door. When asked by a BBC interviewer in 1962 about his aim in writing *Lolita*, Nabokov insisted that he wrote it for reasons that apply to all of his books: "I've no general ideas to exploit, I just like composing riddles with elegant solutions" (*SO* 16). Among the existing solutions to the riddles of *Pale Fire*, two interpretations see Hazel's fate in an especially poetic light. In Boyd's metaphysical reading, Hazel gets a fairy-tale version of her father's newfound belief in the immortality of the soul. Boyd sees Hazel appropriating for herself, from beyond the grave, the kinds of transformations that Tolstoy bestows upon Maria, that Kinbote lays claim for himself by way of Zembla, and that Botkin applied to poetry generally in his essay on Fet.[50]

Boyd's revised theory is compelling not only because it fits into the pattern of so much of Nabokov's fiction, but also because it grants Hazel the beauty which her parents have so achingly yearned for on her behalf; that is, Hazel is transfigured into the resplendently beautiful Disa. Boyd's theory is analogous to the magic lantern invoked by the narrator of *War and Peace* to describe Maria's transfiguration: Disa is Hazel lit up from the inside, or, to return to the metaphor used by Vasily Botkin, she is like a stained-glass window seen from a cathedral's interior. This reading also casts Shade in the role played by other Nabokovian protagonists (the narrator of "The Vane Sisters" and Sineusov of "Ultima Thule" come to mind) who cannot decode messages from the otherworld embedded in the trivia of their daily existence.

René Alladaye advances a narratological reading of *Pale Fire*'s authorial enigmas in which Hazel merely pretends to die and reveals herself as the author of the novel.[51] Alladaye's theory turns on the idea (borrowed from chess) of "promotion": like a pawn that gets promoted to any piece (usually a queen) that the player chooses upon reaching the final rank of the chessboard, Hazel reaches the final rank and becomes the "queen"—that is, the author—of the book. As Alladaye concludes, "the reason why Hazel resembles Kinbote is simply that she *is* Kinbote, or rather *impersonates* him."[52]

Boyd's and Alladaye's theories can be thought of as gestures of courtesy that elevate Hazel to a position that she has been otherwise denied. According to Boyd, Hazel survives in the afterlife where she reimagines herself as King Charles Xavier's Queen Disa, whose "pale-skin, dark-hair beauty" (*PF* 587) stands in sharp contrast with Hazel's homeliness. Though still unhappy and unrequited in love, Hazel-as-Disa no longer resembles the unattractive Shade; rather, she resembles the beautiful Sybil (*PF* 587). Shade's recollections of Hazel (her smiles that resembled "a sign of *pain*"; the *moaning* sounds she would emit while sitting on her bed [*PF* lines 350–55; emphasis added]) become sublimated in Disa's aristocratic title: she is the Duchess of *Payn* and *Mone* (*PF* 562, 660).

Yet Disa's beauty is no consolation in the doubly fictional world in which she dwells. Her royal husband, the homosexual Charles of Zembla, recoils from her physical charms like Pete recoils from Hazel. In Disa's case, being beautiful but unloved leads to the same kind of desolation experienced by Hazel. Disa's life refutes Shade's assumption that beauty is a key ingredient for happiness.[53] This lesson brings it into close proximity with *The Rape of the Lock.*

But in spite of the shared misery of Disa's and Hazel's lives, Kinbote does not imagine Disa ending her life by suicide. Instead, he imagines her continuing to live with grace and dignity at her villa on Cap Turc. This resilience seems related to the fact that her life is shot through with art. Her misfortunes cease being *mere* misfortunes and become part of the same "*glorious* misfortunes" that keep Kinbote alive (*PF* 486; emphasis added). As shorthand for art's and courtesy's contributions to civilized life, the radiant adjective is analogous to Swann's gallant habit of lending "an artistic dignity [*une dignité artistique*]" (*SLT* 5.516; *RTP* 3.885; NRF 6.2.246) to the people he encounters by comparing them to works of art.

But there is no one in New Wye to endow Hazel with the kind of artistic glamour that Lang is likely to have endowed upon Sybil when he made her portrait (*PF* line 682) or with the kind of "special beauty" that Mikhaylov captures in his portrait of Anna Karenina.[54] What is more, Hazel's unredeemed fate on what Van might have called "this pellet of muck" (*A* 398) seems to be the norm in the world of *Pale Fire*. By the time the curtain drops, the stage is littered with the corpses of Shade, Hazel, and the young man—Jack Grey—who shoots Shade and commits suicide while awaiting trial. These deaths, like Kinbote's isolation and Hazel's depressive state, depict a world that is far darker and far more merciless than the "intensely, brilliantly cruel" world discerned by Wood in the scenes of aristocratic life depicted in *War and Peace*.[55]

Yet, as in *Agamemnon*, *Hamlet*, and tragedy generally, neither the high body count nor the prevailing darkness dominates the experience of reading *Pale Fire*. As in *Lolita*, what strikes the reader most forcefully is its combination of beauty, comedy, and romance. And as in *Lolita*, too, this is achieved by the narrative's ability to draw our attention away from troubling moral questions that would interfere with our aesthetic enjoyment. Still, *Pale Fire*'s pleasures are inflected differently from those of *Lolita*. Whereas Humbert's heightened lyricism and humor point to the complicity between art and cruelty, Kinbote's narcissistic commentary suggests that art can serve as an antidote to cruelty.

The world of *Pale Fire* needs art and its life-sustaining deceptions because its reality suffers from the "cheapness" lamented by Woolf.[56] We might say as Alter does that *Pale Fire* insists upon the idea that art—as delusion—"is strictly necessary to make life livable."[57] Only the delusions of art, and emphatically not the facts of reality, can provide someone like Kinbote with a reason to live and someone like Shade with a reason to write. If Hazel does commit suicide, as Shade believes her to have done, we might say that she does so because her life is aesthetically unredeemed. Shade's conclusion that "I understand / Existence, or at least a minute part / Of my existence, only through my art" (*PF* lines 970–73) doubles as a lament that his "art" could make no sense of his daughter. As Barbara Wyllie observes, Hazel's presence in Shade's poem suggests "that this was a child who figured in his life as an awkward, confusing disruption."[58] It is one of the novel's central ironies that Hazel gets a "richly rhymed life" (*PF* line 970)—replete with poltergeists and messages from the beyond—in a madman's commentary rather than in her father's poem.

THE LIE INELOQUENT: HAZEL AND KINBOTE

Kinbote is right to observe that "Hazel Shade resembled me in certain respects" (*PF* 577): they are both lonely and misunderstood; they both yearn for the kind of adjustment in perception experienced by Nikolay and Natasha when they fall in love with Maria and Pierre, respectively. Kinbote's claim to kinship with Hazel is prompted by an uncanny occurrence that takes place when Kinbote reads about Hazel's love of anagrams: "She twisted words: pot, top, / Spider, redips. And 'powder' was 'red wop'" (*PF* lines 347–48). These verses have a discombobulating effect upon Kinbote not only because he, too, loves anagrams, but because he considers the spider/redips anagram to be specifically his own: "One of the examples her father gives is odd. I am quite sure it was I who one day, when we were discussing 'mirror words,' observed (and I recall the poet's expression of stupefaction) that 'spider' in reverse is 'redips,' and 'T.S. Eliot,' 'toilest'" (577).

Shade's stupefaction is caused by the sense of déjà vu that he must have experienced upon hearing Kinbote use Hazel's anagram. But readers of Kinbote's annotations are also made to experience the frisson of déjà vu because they, too, have already encountered this particular anagram in Kinbote's extended comment to line 181, in which he describes his encounter with Sybil the morning after Shade's birthday party. Significantly, this is a party to which Kinbote was not invited. Sybil, intuiting Kinbote's disappointment, gives an excuse that comes uncomfortably close to Pete's lie to Hazel: "We did not ask you," Sybil tells Kinbote, "because we knew how tedious you find such affairs" (*PF* 554).

Like Pete's lie to Hazel, Sybil's lie to Kinbote is both transparently false and crushingly predictable. Having anticipated precisely such an excuse, Kinbote uses it as an opportunity to present Sybil with a book. The words he utters while offering it to her—"Please, dip or redip, spider, into this book" (*PF* 554)—serve as the anchor for what will become a network of associations that connect Hazel to Kinbote, and Sybil herself to what Kinbote calls "impossibly rude hostesses" and "even ruder guests" (554). The book in question is

> the third and last volume of the *Bibliothèque de la Pléiade* edition, Paris, 1954, of Proust's work, wherein I had marked certain passages on pages 269–271. Mme de Mortemart, having decided that Mme. de Valcourt would *not* be among the "elected" at her soirée, intended to send her a note on the next day saying "Dear Edith, I miss you, last night I did not expect you too much (Edith would wonder: how could she at all, since she did not invite me?) because I know you are not overfond of this sort of parties which, if anything, bore you." (*PF* 554–55)

Sybil's lie is especially hurtful to Kinbote because he finds nothing "tedious" about "such affairs." The "bitter wait" by the telephone the day of Shade's birthday elicits no invitation, and Kinbote spends the evening spying on the festivities next door (*PF* 552).

Readers no doubt sympathize with the Shades for not inviting a madman to Shade's birthday festivities. Indeed, to invite someone like Kinbote to a party might qualify as a grave discourtesy to the other guests. Like Gawain's relatives who must mask their grief with a pretense of joy when receiving Yvain, the Shades suppress their own grief in their interactions with Kinbote. As Boyd observes, Shade approaches Kinbote with "gentle forbearance" (*VNAY* 433), and his "kindness and sensitivity" contrast sharply with Kinbote's "crazy selfishness" (*VNAY* 435). Still, the emotional charge of the novel seems to demand an even greater courtesy than the Shades grant Kinbote. To paraphrase Emma Woodhouse's lament over the duties of civility, the Shades are always doing more than they wish but less than they ought.[59]

Intriguingly, Kinbote's Proustian offering to Sybil was replicated by Nabokov himself during an interview with J. E. Rivers in Montreux on August 11, 1973. In preparation for the interview, Rivers wrote Nabokov that he would like to talk to him about Proust. As Rivers tells the story,

> When Nabokov, accompanied by his wife, came down to meet me, he was carrying a copy of *Pale Fire* into which he had placed a white index card to mark a certain passage. When the conversation turned to Proust, he said: "Perhaps you have read this little book of mine, *Pale Fire*." He went on to say that the passage he had marked gave the best summary he knew of his current opinion of Proust and *À la recherche*. I opened the book to the page Nabokov had indicated; it described the revenge Charles Kinbote takes on Sybil Shade for not inviting him to John Shade's birthday party.[60]

Kinbote's ostensible aim in drawing Sybil's attention to Mme de Mortemart's exclusion of Mme de Valcourt from her soirée is to revisit his and the Shades' agreed-upon view of Proust's novel as a "ghoulish fairy tale" that was "totally unconnected with any possible people in any historical France." But the bitterness of his own exclusion from Shade's party leads Kinbote to revise his former view. Now he wants Sybil to agree with him that "we were wrong in denying our little *beau ténébreux* the capacity of evoking 'human interest': it is there, it is there—maybe a rather eighteenth-centuryish, or even seventeenth-centuryish, brand, but it is there" (*PF* 554). What Kinbote seems to want from Sybil is an acknowledgment that the actions of "impossibly rude hostesses" (554) have an impact beyond fiction in the realm of lived experience. As Rivers sums it up, Kinbote wants her to "read the story of her own hypocrisy."[61]

But Kinbote is also (knowingly or not) alluding to himself when he refers to Proust's "even ruder guests." As de la Durantaye notes, Kinbote is, indeed, "beyond the pale" in his "overstepping the boundaries of neighborly friendliness, overstepping the bounds of tact and tastefulness in nearly everything he does, overstepping the boundaries of editorial and even juridical propriety in absconding with Shade's text, and finally overstepping the bounds of a critic and editor" in his notes to Shade's poem.[62] Still, it is doubtful that Nabokov wants us to conclude that he is beyond the pale of courtesy. The Shades try to hide their lack of courtesy to Kinbote by lying (Sybil) and by granting an additional stroll the following day (Shade) (*PF* 559). But in spite of these compensations, the rejection consumes Kinbote and sends him into a frenzy of annotations as he admonishes his readers to absorb the magnitude of the "bad hurt" he has suffered: "see, frequently see, note to line 181" (*PF* 559).

The Shades' complicated relationship with Kinbote refutes Kant's understanding of courtesy as a "simple" virtue whose obligations are substantially less demanding than those of love:

> He who loves the Tartar, loves not his neighbor. Loving *all*, we love *none*, and our love is therefore less. In place of rendering assistance to everyone, there should be simple *courtesy*, which is 1) not hatred, and 2) a mere *calm* willingness to assist in emergencies, according to *our powers*. Out of *rectitude* (but not *ardent desire*) there may be sacrifice; to that I am not obligated, though I am to courtesy, which has beauty because it springs from *equality*, and goes with self-esteem. (*LE* 27:72)

Nabokov agrees with Kant's view that courtesy may help where love cannot, but he sees courtesy as making far greater moral demands than Kant would have us believe. For Nabokov, courtesy is never "simple" because (1) it involves significantly more than an absence of hatred; (2) the emergencies that demand it are not rare but ubiquitous; and (3) the measure of "our powers" is impossible to quantify or predict. To be consistently and unfailingly courteous to someone as narcissistic and unpleasant as Kinbote is to respond to emergencies and make sacrifices that go far beyond the standards of courtesy spelled out by Kant. The duties Nabokov associates with courtesy are as outsized and unattainable as the intimacy that Kinbote yearns for in his dealings with Shade, or that Tolstoy requires of love when he has his positive characters strain toward loving "more" and loving "better."

Yet this *is* the standard against which the novel measures its failures of courtesy. If we are to trust Kinbote's account of the haunted-barn episode, the Shades failed to pretend interest in Hazel's fascination with the occult (Sybil's mocking remarks cause Hazel to dissolve into tears; *PF* 576).

These failures to pretend—that Hazel's spiritualism might be worth their interest, that Hazel might be physically attractive, that Kinbote is not merely insane—account for the deep pathos of *Pale Fire*. Kinbote's oversized egotism and shameless intrusion upon the Shades' private life erode whatever sympathy a reader might feel for him, but Nabokov still wants readers to feel the sting of the "brutal anonymous note" that tries to inform Kinbote that he suffers from bad breath (*PF* 505). While there is *truth* in the epithets Sybil uses to describe him to others (she calls him "an elephantine tick; a king-sized botfly; a macaco worm; the monstrous parasite of a genius" [561]), such truths are hard to square with Hamlet's injunction to Polonius to treat the itinerant players to a richer hospitality than they might deserve (*Hamlet* 2.2.524–28). Similarly, we feel hurt on Kinbote's behalf when the Zemblan stories he confides to Shade come back to him "via the Common Room" with "obscene accretions" (*PF* 508).

If, in aesthetic terms, Hazel would benefit from the transformative deceptions of art, in ethical and psychological terms she would benefit from the daily deceptions of courtesy. To keep despair at bay, she needs someone to ascribe to her, as Chrétien ascribes to all of his heroines, a stereotyped beauty that meets the expectations of "*le goût courtois* [courteous taste]" of medieval romance.[63] She also needs the kinds of things Kinbote invents for himself: loyal supporters, sensitive friends, and "amusing, very amusing" lovers (*PF* 541). She needs the hocus-pocus make-believe that the Wizard of Oz performs on Lion, Tin Man, and Scarecrow to make them believe that they possess—respectively—courage, heart, and brains. She needs to pretend for herself, or have someone pretend on her behalf, that she is one of Mme de Mortemart's "elect," or that she will—eventually, if not quite yet—be found to be what Nikolay discovers Maria to be: that is, "an altogether rare and unusual being" (*WP* 2:1126; *PSS* 12:24).

THE LIE ELOQUENT: HAZEL AND DISA

In spite of the fact that Pete and Disa occupy two separate ontological planes, the parallel events that link Shade's New Wye to Kinbote's Zembla make it possible to see them as each other's foils. It is no accident, then, that Kinbote tells the story of Disa in the immediate aftermath of Shade's account of Pete's cruel response to Hazel on their blind date. The two lines of verse that prompt Kinbote to embed Disa's story within the context of the night of the blind date make reference (fittingly again) to the seaside city of Nice, where Hazel was conceived (*PF* lines 433–34). This is an annotation to which Kinbote enjoins us to return repeatedly and with good reason: this is the place where Hazel, during her embryonic existence, was the bearer of the hope nursed by all parents, namely that their children be born (to quote a Popean epithet dear to Shade) "supremely blest" (*PF* 579). Within Kinbote's Zemblan narrative, this is the place where Hazel (as Disa) still dwells supremely blessed by the powers of imagination.

The story of Disa, triggered by Shade's recollection of Hazel's conception on the French Riviera, exhibits the high-voltage prose style that Nabokov's readers will recognize from Pnin's reflections upon Mira's death at Buchenwald and Humbert's regret over Dolly's stolen childhood. It is a style that, on the one hand, is anxious to communicate heightened moral significance and, on the other, is worried that the moral significance could be upstaged by its own showy locutions. The most electrifying lines of this entry describe a devastating act of truth-telling in which Charles, Kinbote's stand-in in Zembla and Disa's homosexual husband, confesses that "he did not love her." The episode is so painful that it becomes permanently etched in Charles's mind:

> Upon hearing him out, she sank down on the lawn in an impossible posture, examining a grass culm and frowning, he had taken his words back at once; but the shock had fatally starred the mirror, and thenceforth in his dreams her image was infected with the memory of that confession as with some disease or the secret aftereffects of a surgical operation too intimate to be mentioned. (*PF* 590)

Charles's confession to Disa that "he did not love her" recalls—in reverse—Pierre's lie to Hélène when he tells her "*Je vous aime*." Charles takes his words back at once because this confession works upon Disa like a toxin. That a truth should have such a lethal effect serves as a reminder that Pete's lie is morally wrong not because it is a lie, but rather because it exposes a painful truth.

The delicate asymmetries that link these scenarios illustrate important differences between Nabokov's and Tolstoy's views on art and ethics. The famous conclusion to Keats's "Ode on a Grecian Urn"—"Beauty is truth, truth beauty"—aims to suggest an ideal congruence between these two clauses, but there is a sense in which Nabokov and Tolstoy help us see how they might stand as meaningful alternatives: in *Pale Fire*, "beauty is truth"; in Tolstoy, "truth is beauty." Whereas Pierre's doom lies in his failure to tell Hélène and himself the truth, Charles's decision to tell the truth blights Disa's life and Pete becomes complicit in Hazel's premature death by not telling the *right kind of lie*.

Knowing that he cannot take back his words, Charles's "dreaming self" makes "extraordinary amends" for his devastating act of truth-telling. These amends turn on the capacity of dreams to do what the historical Botkin claimed on behalf of poetry generally: his dreams, Kinbote reports, "transformed the drab prose of his feelings for her into strong and strange poetry"

(*PF* 589). In these recurring dreams, Disa becomes—as Lucette does, too, in Van's family chronicle—memorialized in a grand act of courtesy:

> He knew she had just come across a telltale object—a riding boot in his bed—establishing beyond any doubt his unfaithfulness. Sweat beaded her pale, naked forehead—but she had to listen to the prattle of a chance visitor or direct the movements of a workman with a ladder. . . . One might bear . . . the knowledge of her grief and pride but none could bear the sight of her automatic smile as she turned from the agony of the disclosure to the polite trivialities required of her. She would be canceling an illumination, or discussing hospital cots with the head nurse, or merely ordering breakfast for two in the sea cave—and through the everyday plainness of the talk, through the play of the charming gestures with which she always accompanied certain ready-made phrases, he, the groaning dreamer, perceived the disarray of her soul and was aware that an odious, undeserved, humiliating disaster had befallen her, and that only obligations of etiquette and her staunch kindness to a guiltless third party gave her the force to smile. (*PF* 590–91)

Disa's forced smile ("replaced—as soon as the visitor left—by that impossible little frown the dreamer could never forget") recalls the smile summoned by Hazel to console Jane Dean and her fiancé during the awkward aftermath of Pete's departure: "and with a smile / She said she'd be *de trop*, she'd much prefer / Just going home" (*PF* lines 398–400).

Like Pete Dean, Jane Dean and her fiancé do not feel the "obligations of etiquette" as keenly as Hazel and Disa do. Instead of pretending that Hazel is not *de trop*, they escort her to the bus stop and leave her there (lines 400–401). This coldhearted, discourteous response is the norm in the world of *Pale Fire*; to act courteously, as Hazel and Disa do, is a heroic virtue in Nabokov's world reserved only for those who have, as Shade says about Hazel, "strange force / Of character" (lines 344–45). It seems at once morally and aesthetically fitting that Van and Charles try to atone for the love they could not feel for the women who loved them by images of courtesy that unlike love—can be willed into being and is free to give.

V. BOTKIN AND VASILY BOTKIN

In his lectures, Nabokov allows himself to indulge in a fantasy that commits Tolstoy exclusively to the side of the beautiful as the good:

> What one would like to do, would be to kick the glorified soapbox from under his sandalled feet and then lock him up in a stone house on a desert island with gallons of ink and reams of paper—far away from the things, ethical and

> pedagogical, that diverted his attention from observing the way the dark hair curled above Anna's white neck. (*LRL* 140)

It is possible to imagine Kinbote as the product of this particular fantasy. Mary McCarthy was the first to conclude that Kinbote is the nom de plume of "a harmless refugee pedant named Botkin who teaches in the Russian department and who fancies himself to be the exiled king of Zembla."[64] D. Barton Johnson radicalizes McCarthy's observation when he notes that "V. Botkin is the source from which all else flows."[65] In a similar vein, Wood writes that "Botkin is the static in Kinbote's story, the buzz and the hum of repression, the self Kinbote has buried."[66] Botkin, like his invented aliases, is cut from the same cloth that Tolstoy loved so deeply but sought so hard to repress. In creating Botkin and his two alter egos, Nabokov resurrects the historical Botkin, who shared his conviction that Tolstoy ought to have paid exclusive attention to such aesthetic matters as the dark curls above Anna's neck.

It is artistically fitting that Botkin should share the name of the man who not only defended Pushkin from Chernyshevsky, but also tried to persuade Tolstoy to pay no attention to Chernyshevsky and his confrères. Like Nabokov's invented Botkin, Vasily Botkin worshipped poetry, loathed revolutionary extremism, and was notoriously paranoid about his personal safety.[67] By the end of his life, his egoism, paranoia, and epicureanism had reached such outlandish proportions that even his closest friends came to view him with repugnance. Like his fictional namesake, he died lonely and forgotten.[68]

Yet at the height of Botkin's influence, Tolstoy counted himself among his closest friends and greatest admirers. Orwin justifies Tolstoy's deep attraction to Botkin by invoking Tolstoy's own sensual nature, and by proposing that Botkin's philosophical hedonism provided Tolstoy with a unique opportunity to regard his sensuality as a good rather than an evil.[69] The twenty-five letters that make up the six-year correspondence between Tolstoy and Botkin register a degree of intimacy and mutual affection that leads V. I. Sreznevsky to speculate that only a portion of the correspondence has survived.[70] In Botkin's last letter to Tolstoy, he complains of his failing eyesight in tones that anticipate Kinbote's frequent complaints about his migraines. At the same time, he draws consolation from "my old faith and my old gods," and assures Tolstoy that "we pray to the same gods even though your faith sometimes slackens" (*PTB* 84–85).

The cardinal principles of this shared faith are spelled out in a long letter from Botkin to Tolstoy (dated December 4, 1857), and in Tolstoy's response to this letter (dated January 4, 1858). Both letters lament the radical critics' indifference to the kind of "pure art" that transcends the topical. In his own letter, Tolstoy tries to convince Botkin to become the editor of a new periodical whose singular aim would be "artistic pleasure [*khudozhestvennoe naslazhdenie*]." "The journal will prove nothing and know nothing," he continues, "its only criterion will be cultured taste. It will not tend in this or that direction and it will not concern itself with the needs of the public" (*PTB* 57).

Tolstoy's journal was not to be, and—as Botkin was wont to remind him—Tolstoy's own faith in the gods of "artistic pleasure" frequently wavered. In spite of being a firm believer in his protégé's enormous literary gifts, Botkin did not hesitate to tell him, in a letter dated May 6, 1859, that *Family Happiness* suffers from a "disgusting Puritanism [*protivnyi puritanizm*]" and "smells like an old noble-born, boarding-school maiden [*pakhnet staroi institutkoi*]" (*PTB* 71). Botkin's resurrection in the pages of *Pale Fire* pays homage to Tolstoy's early literary career when, under Botkin's influence, Tolstoy scorned the soapbox and championed the same values that anchored Pushkin's and Nabokov's own creeds.

But perhaps the most eloquent link between the historical Botkin and Nabokov's invented Botkin comes to light when we consider the vast discrepancy between the persona that rises before our eyes in Botkin's correspondence with Tolstoy, and the Botkin bequeathed to us by those unfamiliar with Nabokov's Russia and his Russian compatriots. The same Botkin whose letters the young Tolstoy eagerly awaited ("Your letters are extremely useful to me," he writes Botkin as part of his lament that some of Botkin's letters to him had not reached him [*PTB* 53]) struck non-Russians as a buffoon. As the Russian translator of Thomas Carlyle's *On Heroes, Hero-Worship, and the Heroic in History*, Botkin felt it incumbent to visit Carlyle at his home in England.[71] With Carlyle absent, the task of receiving Botkin fell to his wife, Jane, who describes their encounter to her husband in a letter dated July 11, 1858, as follows:

> Botkin (what a name!), your Russian translator, has called. . . . He burst into the room with wild expressions of his "admiration for Mr. Carlyle." I begged him to be seated, and he declared "Mr. Carlyle was the man for Russia." I tried again and again to "enchain" a rational conversation, but nothing could I get out of him but rhapsodies about you in the frightfullest English that I ever heard out of a human head! It is to be hoped that (as he told me) he reads English much better than he speaks it, else he must have produced an inconceivable translation of "Hero-Worship." Such as it is, anyhow, "a large deputation of the Students of St. Petersburg" waited on him (Botkin), to thank him in the strongest terms for having translated for them "Hero Worship," and made known to them Carlyle. And even the young Russian ladies now read "Hero Worship," and "unnerstants it thor—lie." He was all in a perspiration when he went away, and so was I!

> I should like to have asked him some questions; for example, how he came to know of your Works (he had told me he had had to send to England for them "at extreem cost"), but it would have been like asking a cascade! The best that I could do for him I did. I gave him a photograph of you, and put him up to carrying it in the top of his hat![72]

It is unsurprising that this meeting ended with both interlocutors breaking into a sweat. What they achieved was no mean thing given the chasm between their native languages, national habits, and modes of discourse. In spite of being frustrated by Botkin's broken English, Jane Carlyle nonetheless understands that Botkin's hyperbolic claims about her husband's reception in Russia are not to be taken literally: the Russia that awaits Carlyle as a savior, the "large deputation" of Carlyle-worshipping students, the young Russian ladies who understand his work "thoroughly" are the exaggerated locutions of courtesy. In turn, Botkin gallantly pretends total submission to Jane Carlyle's charm as both woman and hostess when he agrees to carry her husband's photograph in his hat.

This scene of screwball comedy, where Botkin and Jane Carlyle speak at cross-purposes and part ways in a cloud of effusive affability, is the shadow standard against which the failures in courtesy are measured in *Pale Fire*. Jane Carlyle's attempt to enchain the over-enthusiastic Botkin to a rational conversation belongs to the same order of solicitude as Joan Clements's efforts to keep a despairing Pnin chained to his seat so that she can comfort him with cartoons whose humor eludes him. These images of courtesy have little in common with Sybil's valiant attempts to protect herself and her husband from Kinbote's unwelcome intrusions. Though Jane Carlyle does not *see* Botkin poetically—that is, she does not take him for "an altogether rare and unusual being"—she *pretends* that he is by treating him with courtesy. This highlights the ways in which poetry and courtesy often amount to the same thing.

Cut off from his homeland and tormented by migraines and mental illness, Kinbote-Botkin makes as clownish an impression on his American acquaintances as the historical Botkin made on Jane Carlyle. Both Botkins remind us, to quote Gordon Teskey, that courtesy is a virtue "reserved chiefly, though by no means exclusively, for strangers" ("CT" 355). As a novel about various forms of alienation—from the norms associated with feminine beauty (Hazel), from homeland (Botkin), from community (Jack Grey)—*Pale Fire* identifies courtesy as an art and celebrates art and courtesy's life-giving deceptions. Structured around a series of collisions between truth and make-believe, it pits its faith in a world willing to overlook the truth and nurture illusion.

Just as Humbert tries to entrap his readers into agreeing with him that

Dolly was an irresistibly seductive nymphet, Shade's poem traps its readers into accepting his claim that Hazel was physically unattractive. Yet courteous readers might *refuse* to see Hazel as ugly, and suspect, instead, that there might be something in Hazel that Shade overlooks and that might have made her (to quote the maxim invoked by Rostov) "not dear for being pretty, but pretty for being dear." To experience such a transformative act of vision, the reader must approach the world not like Shade, but like Kinbote, who, as Alter notes, *reads* Appalachia, waxwing, crystal land, but *sees* Zembla, revolution, stalking assassin.[73]

Kinbote is not a nice person, yet his distorted vision of the world is significantly unlike the distortions of reality produced by Nabokov's murderers and sexual predators. As a "fugitive from pain" (as Toker refers to Pnin, but might also have referred to Kinbote) and "a mad version of a Nabokovian artist" (as Alter does call him), Kinbote seeks to overcome the "granite and gravity" (*PF* 540) of his life through an act of levitation that lifts him into the lighter sphere of art's deceptions.[74] By contrast, Nabokov's villains—one thinks of Hermann and Humbert—labor under the reverse logic when they translate poetic possibilities (doppelgängers, nymphets) into the "granite and gravity" of literal truths (rape, murder). Kinbote's special brand of misreading is ultimately a gesture of courtesy and a declaration of love. His unreliable vision does what love is said to attain without effort and what courtesy attains with a great deal of it: namely, it makes the ugly beautiful. That this conclusion should cast both love and courtesy as versions of insanity is not something that Nabokov would have resisted. For good or ill, love is always a kind of madness in his fiction, and courtesy—with its haughty repudiation of prudence and self-interest—is a madness that, in its artful mimicry of love, touches the sublime.

Chapter Six

The End of Courtesy, the End of Art: Nabokov and Proust

> And the third occasion was when Gilberte said to me: "If you like, we might after all go out one afternoon and then we can go to Guermantes, taking the road by Méséglise, which is the nicest way," a sentence which upset all the ideas of my childhood by informing me that the two "ways" were not as irreconcilable as I had supposed.
> —Marcel Proust

ART'S CAPACITY TO find beauty where none seems to exist aligns it with courtesy. Shade, who fails to find physical beauty in his daughter, is the antithesis of Swann, the quintessentially courteous principal character of the first volume of Proust's *À la recherche du temps perdu*, who finds beauty in others by noting their resemblance to figures depicted in works of art. The first instance in which Marcel, Proust's narrator,[1] describes this particular habit of Swann involves a kitchen-maid at Combray, "a poor sickly creature [*une pauvre créature maladive*]" whose illicit pregnancy "swelled and stoutened every part of her, even including her face and her squarish, elongated cheeks" (*SLT* 1:110–11; *RTP* 1:79–80; NRF 1.1.113). Whereas for readers of *Pale Fire* the unfortunate kitchen-maid might recall Shade's descriptions of Hazel, for Swann she bears a striking resemblance to Giotto's Charity in the Arena Chapel at Padua (*SLT* 1:110–11; *RTP* 1:80; NRF 1.1.113–14).[2]

This habit of finding the poetic within the quotidian is only one of Swann's many graceful refinements. Swann's "reserve and discretion" are so well-honed that Marcel's middle-class relatives never suspect that he enjoys a brilliant social position in the most exclusive aristocratic circles of the Faubourg Saint-Germain.[3] Yet Swann's refinement does not always protect him from the callous conduct of others. Marcel's great-aunt, for instance, allows herself to treat him "with scant ceremony" (*SLT* 1:22; *RTP* 1:18; NRF 1.1.30) and the Duchess of Guermantes, an intimate friend, refuses to the end of Swann's life to be introduced to his daughter.

The courtesy that makes Swann at once so attractive and vulnerable plays a role in the theory of art that undergirds the *Search*. As the young Marcel discovers through his meditations on the twin steeples of Martinville, the principal obligation of art is preservation. The artist's calling is that of "a memorialist [*un mémorialiste*]," for artistic acts of commemoration are the only guarantees of survival into the future (*SLT* 1:259; *RTP* 1:181; NRF 1.1.247). This epiphany serves as the finale to "Combray" and is restated, in more grandiloquent terms, at the conclusion of *Le Temps retrouvé* when Marcel sums up the "essence" of the work we have presumably been reading as the "re-creation" (*la recréation*) of his life through "the memory of impressions [*la mémoire d'impressions*]" (*SLT* 6:525; *RTP* 4:621; NRF 8.2.258). In a twist on the Cartesian axiom, remembering ratifies being. James Merrill might have said that this is part and parcel of Proust's "extreme courtesy": Marcel's treatment of every detail with nothing "less than total, patient, sparkling seriousness"[4] is a courtesy that enables memory to certify existence.

Humbert Humbert, the narrator and protagonist of *Lolita, or the Confession of a White Widowed Male*, and Vladimir Vladimirovich, the narrator of *Pnin*, share Proust's conviction that art ought to serve memory. Vladimir Vladimirovich, entomologist and "prominent Anglo-Russian writer" (*Pnin* 389, 397), writes *Pnin* not only to chronicle the comic misadventures of his eponymous hero, but also to memorialize what Pnin makes every effort to forget: the young woman to whom Pnin was briefly engaged in Russia and who perished in a Nazi concentration camp. Humbert claims ascendancy over Dolly's other abductor, Clare Quilty, by insisting that his memoir will make Dolly "live in the minds of later generations." By locating Dolly among the "aurochs and angels" preserved in "durable pigments," Humbert is making a Proustian claim that his memoir guarantees Dolly a "refuge" and "immortality" in art (*L* 291).

As we shall see later, Humbert shares Swann's habit of seeing resemblances between people and works of art. He also inherits Swann's capacity to woo the world with his wit, eloquence, and specialized artistic knowledge. But unlike Swann, Humbert uses his gifts for evil ends: his wit and eloquence are put to the service of justifying rape and child abuse. Like Swann's habit of seeing people as art, Humbert's memoir underscores the functional equivalence between art and courtesy. For the artfulness of *Lolita* works like courtesy—namely, it puts readers at ease in awkward situations, or, to use the terms invoked by Humbert, it uses cunning rhetorical devices to mask criminal events: "You can always count on a murderer for a fancy prose style," Humbert states on the first page of his memoir. Humbert's transformation of a repugnant crime into a beautiful story is a sinister version of Kinbote's sublimation of his drab reality into the resplendent Zembla and Swann's insistence that the sickly kitchen-maid resembles Giotto's Charity. Readers who respond to the aesthetic pleasures afforded by Humbert's narrative share something important with Mrs. Luzhin, whose courtesy makes her remain by the side of the awful lady from Soviet Russia while the latter unleashes verbal abuse upon a German saleslady. Though Humbert's lush style is the antithesis of the Soviet lady's crude vituperations, it compels his readers to continue reading and, by doing so, to replicate Mrs. Luzhin's courtesy when she continues to remain by the side of her repellent guest.

Unlike Nabokov's fictions in which art and courtesy are portrayed as supreme civilizational achievements, in *Pnin* and *Lolita* they signal vulnerability and complicity in the world's darkness. This separates them from *Bend Sinister* (arguably the *darkest* of Nabokov's novels) and *Pale Fire*, written before and after—respectively—*Lolita* and *Pnin*. Although Krug is one of Nabokov's most discourteous characters, *Bend Sinister* and *Pale Fire* portray art as it is depicted elsewhere in Nabokov's fiction: namely, as a refuge from life's cruelties and an antidote to tyranny and injustice. In *Lolita* and *Pnin*, however, art itself loses its innocence and becomes an accessory to darkness. Instead of being portrayed as civilizational achievements, art and courtesy become sophisticated tools of obfuscation and brutality.

In *Lolita*, courtesy's artful non-utilitarianism is inscribed in Dolly's "absolutely top-notch tennis," but instead of being celebrated as a radiantly human capacity to ignore the claims of self-interest, it becomes another marker of Dolly's failure to determine her own ends. Though enchantingly artistic, her "perfect form" is ultimately "sterile" because it confers no advantage against her adversaries. Her "politeness" on the court (as her coach, Electra Gold, dubs it) turns out to be a liability, and "permit[s] a second-rate but determined player, no matter how uncouth and incompetent, to poke and cut his way to victory" (*L* 217–19). Dolly's politeness on the tennis court is ethically analogous to Mira Belochkin's imagined conduct during her final days at Buchenwald. Pnin learns from a Washington investigator that Mira would have been selected to die shortly after arriving at Buchenwald because she was deemed unfit for work. The invincible smile ascribed to her ("though still smiling, still able to help other Jewish women") seems like a hopeless mechanism of self-defense on the part of Pnin or Vladimir Vladimirovich (*Pnin* 395). Mira's surviving smile is an image of courtesy stranded in a doomed world that has been evacuated of all vestiges of humanity.

Pnin and *Lolita* depict a loss of faith in the moral dimension of art and courtesy because they were composed at a time when it was difficult to wrest beauty and meaning from a world that was so deeply abhorrent. As a frequently quoted letter to his sister from June 1946 attests, Nabokov experienced the opening of the Nazi extermination camps as trauma: "Much as one might want to hide in one's little ivory tower, there are things that torment too deeply, e.g., the German vilenesses, the burning of children in ovens,—children as funny and as strongly loved as our children."[5] Written in the years following the Holocaust,[6] *Lolita* and *Pnin* express a deep sense of suspicion toward art and courtesy for the very reasons that made art and courtesy so deontologically valuable in less harrowing times. Dolly's tennis style is strikingly graceful, but it yields no "utilitarian results" (*L* 217). Whatever solace Pnin or the narrator might have drawn from the image of Mira going to her death "still smiling," this solace can only serve as a palliative given that Mira was "cremated only a few days after her arrival in Buchenwald" (*Pnin* 395).

Mira's cremation at Buchenwald is *Pnin*'s "figure in the carpet." For the novel titled *Pnin* begins *and* ends with descriptions of a journey to "Cremona," an American town that recalls the musical traditions associated with the world's earliest famous luthiers, such as Antonio Stradivari and Giuseppe Guarneri. Yet by the time that Pnin takes the wrong train to Cremona, the town's "mellow Italian name" (*Pnin* 302) evokes less the nonutilitarian pleasures associated with fine musical instruments than the *crem*atoria built by the Nazis as hyper-utilitarian instruments of genocide.[7] It is in Cremona, as he waits to be called to the lectern to deliver his lecture, that Pnin experiences a vision of Mira and other loved ones murdered by the Nazis and the Bolsheviks. "Murdered, forgotten, unrevenged, incorrupt, immortal," these ghosts sit among the members of the "Cremona Women's Club" as synecdoches of Pnin's later claim that "the history of man is the history of pain!" (*Pnin* 316, 419).[8]

Lolita engineers a scenario in which readers are invited to feel at home reading descriptions of rape and child abuse, or—what is the same—encouraged to extend their readerly courtesy to a rapist who makes art out of pain.[9] Pnin tries to avoid such moral jeopardy by acting discourteously toward an artist-narrator who considers *all* reality—from emotional abuse to the Holocaust—to be fit material for fiction. The disquiet produced by both novels hinges on their successful transformation of horror into art. Unlike other novels about abuse or the Holocaust, *Lolita* and *Pnin* tame the violence they describe. We might say that they act as courteous hosts to guests who ought to find no shelter. No such host himself, Pnin tries to obliterate the memories that connect him to the Holocaust for fear that they might lead him to assimilate a reality that "no conscience, and hence no consciousness" could endorse (*Pnin* 394).

As articulations of the limits of art and courtesy, *Lolita* and *Pnin* are Nabokov's darkest novels. This darkness is underscored by comparing *Pnin* and *Lolita* to the body of work that Nabokov produced before and after them. It also becomes conspicuous when *Lolita* and *Pnin* are held up against the work of a major writer for whom, as for Vasily Botkin, the universality of beauty served as a first principle of his aesthetics. According to Jean-Yves Tadié, Proust's faith that beauty and poetry can be found everywhere is a distillation of ideas he imbibed from Carlyle and Emerson.[10] For Tadié, Proust's approving quotation of Emerson in an article from 1907 animates the entirety of *À la recherche du temps perdu*: "O Poet, true master of water, earth and air, shouldst thou travel the entire universe, you would never manage to find something that is without poetry and without beauty."[11] In *Pnin* and *Lolita*, however, the search for beauty and the memory-work that would preserve that beauty are no moral projects, but—to quote Will Norman—"structures of Holocaust complicity."[12]

As Yannicke Chupin reminds us, Nabokov prepared his lectures on Proust at the same time he was engaged in composing the novel that would become *Lolita*.[13] These lectures show that he was intimately familiar with Proust's hunger to find beauty in everything, from the paths that he walked as a child at Combray to the aerial bombardments that he saw as an adult walking through the streets of a darkened Paris. For Proust, the discovery of such beauty was not only an artistic imperative, but also a matter of teleology: the disparate elements of life, painful and unintelligible when experienced in isolation, become part of a coherent and enchanting reality when perceived as a whole. But whereas the *Search* yearns for a teleological vision in which all paths meet and all realities merge, *Pnin* and *Lolita* express Nabokov's terror that they should.

As is often the case in Nabokov, the world's darkness is less an existential predicament than a failure of the moral will to do what is right. Nabokov's polemics with the *Search* seek to refute Proust's faith in a beneficent teleology and make the world's darkness a matter of personal responsibility. In *Lolita* and *Pnin*, however, moral responsibility demands actions that are starkly opposed to the principles Nabokov cherished before he learned about children burnt in ovens. Pnin's moral conscience demands the expulsion of Mira Belochkin from the corridors of his memory. Readers of *Lolita* are made to undergo an analogous experience when they discover that their appreciation of Humbert's wit and eloquence is an affront to moral conscience. And just as Pnin's efforts to forget Mira end in failure, the moral inclination to avoid reading books whose narrators use art for evil ends brings us to a terminus from which there is no retreat or recovery. If books such as *Lolita* might be as harmful to one's moral conscience as Pnin's recollections of Mira, their existence is analogous to Mira's memory in another way: Pnin's life would be safer in the absence of the suffering caused by remembering Mira, but it would also be diminished. *Lolita*'s admirers are like Pnin insofar as they recognize the moral jeopardy of reading such a novel but are nonetheless unable to put it down or forget it.

MEMORY AND THE WILL

Nabokov's familiarity with Proust can be traced back to the mid-1920s. In a letter dated June 2, 1926, he informs Véra that he has finished reading *Albertine disparue* (*LV* 51). Later that same month, he praises Proust's "perfect artistry, depth, divine tongue-tiedness" (*LV* 96). Brian Boyd reports that Nabokov confided to Nikolay Raevsky in 1930 that he "simply adored" Proust and that he had already read through all twelve volumes twice (*VNRY* 354). This confession squares with an interview with Andrey Sedykh published in *Poslednie novosti* on November 3, 1932, where Nabokov is quoted as saying "I love Flaubert and Proust."[14] In an interview with Robert Hughes from 1965, Nabokov identified the "greatest masterpieces of twentieth-century prose" in the following order: "Joyce's *Ulysses*; Kafka's *Transformation*; Biely's *Petersburg*; and the first half of Proust's fairy tale *In Search of Lost Time*" (*SO* 57). According to J. E. Rivers, Nabokov singled out for praise only the first half of the *Search* because Proust did not live to revise and oversee the publication of his novel's second half.[15]

The scholars who have analyzed Nabokov's relationship to Proust tend to agree that no other twentieth-century writer is more intimately connected with Nabokov's aims and sensibility.[16] Their kinship is usually grounded in a shared effort to recover the past even as the mechanism of this recovery is conceptualized in opposing ways. As Robert Alter, John Burt Foster Jr., and Rivers have argued, what divides the two writers concerns their understanding of the relationship between memory and personal agency: Nabokov rejects Proust's central claim that only *involuntary* memory can provide an authentic recovery of the past in favor of a *volitional* view of memory.[17] Nabokov's characteristic stance is to cast his memoir as a series of "bright mental image[s] . . . conjured up by a wing-stroke of the will" (*SM* 380) even as he admits that some sections of *Speak, Memory* are the fruit of involuntary memory.

The claim that Nabokov differed most significantly from Proust in his volitional understanding of memory makes it possible to see Humbert as a parody, perhaps even a lampoon, of Nabokov's obsessive efforts to place the past under the will's authority. The fact that Nabokov was working concurrently on *Lolita* and *Speak, Memory* supports these claims. In this special sense, *Lolita*'s relationship to *Speak, Memory* is analogous to *Pale Fire*'s relationship to Nabokov's work on *Eugene Onegin*. Just as *Pale Fire* caricatures Nabokov's unconventional approach to Pushkin's text, *Lolita* turns on its head the temporal reconstructions that make up *Speak, Memory*'s central project. "I confess I do not believe in time," Nabokov asserts in *Speak, Memory* and goes on to describe time as a "magic carpet" that he can fold "in such a way as to superimpose one part of the pattern upon another" (479). *Speak,*

Memory is thus a testament to the artist's total authority over the temporal domain, just as Nabokov's monumental *Eugene Onegin* is a testament to his total authority over Pushkin's greatest work. And just as Kinbote is a stand-in for the insanity that lurks in the desire to master a literary text, Humbert's desire to master time is exposed as a crime and derangement.

UNTIMELINESS AND THE WILL

The celebrated first line of Proust's magnum opus begins with a recollection of childhood rituals: "*Longtemps, je me suis couché de bonne heure.*" "*Bonne heure*"—"good" or "right" time in literal translation, but "early" to a francophone reader—serves as shorthand for the careful calibrations between age and time necessitated by time-dwelling creatures. Marcel must return to his childhood ritual of going to bed early because the work he must write is hopelessly belated.

Ill health, self-doubt, social distractions, and laziness are some of the obstacles that cause Marcel to delay writing the work that we are now reading. But the most powerful obstacle that he must overcome is his lack of will. In the last pages of the novel, he traces this moral weakness to the withheld nightly kiss that constitutes the crux of the *drame du coucher* described in "Combray" (*SLT* 6.526; *RTP* 4.621; NRF 8.2.258). Not wanting to fall asleep without his mother's ceremonial nightly kiss, the young Marcel waits for his mother until she retires for bed. Though he expects to be punished, he is rewarded when his father takes pity on him and suggests to his wife that she sleep in their son's bedroom. But Marcel feels no joy at this boon because he realizes that his victory is a Pyrrhic one. This evening becomes a tragic milestone because his mother is forced to acknowledge that no amount of severity will make her son strong-willed. During this night at Combray, she "had to confess herself beaten" (*SLT* 1.50–51; *RTP* 1.38; NRF 1.1.40) and recognize that her son's nervous condition was "an involuntary ailment [*un mal involontaire*]" and not "a punishable offence [*un état nerveux dont je n'étais pas responsable*]" (*SLT* 1.50–51; *RTP* 1.37; NRF 1.1.40).

This night spent in his mother's company takes on the symbolic significance of an expulsion from Eden. Examining his life through the rearview mirror of advanced age, Marcel traces his subsequent failures and miseries to this fateful moment, which he regards as having inaugurated "the decline of my will" (*SLT* 6.526; *RTP* 4.621; NRF 8.2.258). The much older Marcel, whose mind returns to this scene of lost plenitude, imagines the strength of his will as having been "intact" before his life-changing decision to refuse to go to bed "*de bonne heure*" (*SLT* 6.526; *RTP* 4.621; NRF 8.2.258).

Temporal maladjustment also plays a key role in *Lolita*. Humbert's childhood and adolescence on the French Riviera is dominated, like Marcel's idyllic vacations at Combray, by a harmonious integration of life into the rhythms of time. The young Humbert and the young Annabel Leigh dwell in an Edenic world where time appears to be preternaturally synchronized with human experience: "Long before we met we had had the same dreams. We compared notes. We found strange affinities. The same June of the same year (1919) a stray canary had fluttered into her house and mine, in two widely separated countries" (*L* 11). But separation and Annabel's subsequent death cast out Humbert from the temporal harmonies he knew as a child. In the wake of these violent dislocations, Humbert can only love too early or, like Pushkin's Onegin, too late. His erotic attraction to the twelve-year-old Dolly Haze is tragically premature; his falling in love with the seventeen-year-old Dolly Schiller is tragically belated.

But if both Humbert and Marcel are made to suffer and cause suffering to others because of their failure to find the right "fit" in time, these failures occur for opposing reasons. Whereas Marcel blames his chronic procrastination on his lack of willpower, Humbert believes that he can control time. Marcel's abject humility in the face of time explains why the ethical vision that emerges in his work is at once quietly optimistic and morally quietist; personal guilt does not become a matter of significant moral concern because time rewards and punishes according to its own inscrutable purposes. He absolves himself of personal guilt by interpreting his actions through the lens of his mother's diagnosis of his dependence on her: his actions are involuntary and therefore do not count as punishable offenses.

Humbert, by contrast, aggrandizes the moral significance of his actions. Time, as conceived by Humbert, is neither vast enough nor inhuman enough to erode the significance of his personal transgressions. Two years before seeing Dolly at Coalmont, Humbert turns for help to a Catholic priest. His great hope, he explains, was "to deduce from my sense of sin the existence of a Supreme Being" (*L* 266). But the priest's efforts bear no fruit because the universe and Dolly herself strike Humbert as being every bit as memorious as he is:

> Alas, I was unable to transcend the simple human fact that whatever spiritual solace I might find, whatever lithophanic eternities might be provided for me, nothing could make my Lolita forget the foul lust I had inflicted upon her. Unless it can be proven to me—to me as I am now, today, with my heart and my beard, and my putrefaction—that in the infinite run it does not matter a jot that a North American girl-child named Dolores Haze had been deprived of her childhood by a maniac, unless this can be proven (and if it can, then life is a joke), I see nothing for the treatment of my misery but the melancholy and very local palliative of articulate art. (*L* 266)

Humbert concludes that time cannot extend him the courtesy of forgetting his crimes against Dolly, but his denial of the possibility that his crimes might lose their meaning within the vast expanse of time is not as straightforward as it might first appear. In order to convince himself that Dolly's story will not lose its significance over time, Humbert must disguise moral aspiration as metaphysical reality. For the "simple human fact" that "nothing could make my Lolita forget the foul lust I had inflicted upon her" is not a *fact* but a moral hope that is at once a vestige of Humbert's narcissistic grandstanding and a nascent reorientation toward the moral. Humbert's ostentatious self-condemnation is made not only in Dolly's name, but in the name of an "infinite run" of time that withholds the courteous forgetting that Humbert yearns for but fails to find.

Ironically, Humbert's insistence that time cannot forget the theft of a girl's childhood is a morally inflected version of the very attitude that led him to rob Dolly of her childhood in the first place. Both the theft and the hope resist time's authority by seeking to make time do what it cannot do—namely, stand still. Humbert's attempt to imprison Dolly within the walls of her "nymphetcy" is coextensive with his attempt to freeze time into a state of permanent recall. Still, there is something morally satisfying in Humbert's conception of time as an enduring testament to personal guilt. This image conjures into being a Kantian moral vision in which time and its consequences are removed from moral judgment and the whole of moral responsibility falls upon the individual will. Whereas consequentialist moral decisions depend upon a temporal progression that yields predictable outcomes, the Kantian perspective erects a barrier between ethical deliberation and time's progress. Humbert is thus following Kant in his insistence that genuinely *moral* acts are those that are immune from the passage of time.

WILLFUL FORGETTING: *PNIN*

Having labored meticulously over the course of two years to please himself at the cost of Dolly's suffering, Humbert cannot countenance the possibility of living in a universe where Dolly's suffering might be forgotten. In an intriguing asymmetry, Pnin—a character who began to haunt Nabokov's imagination while *Lolita* was still in progress—cannot live in a world where such things as his former love's death are remembered. When a chance encounter forces Pnin to recall Mira Belochkin, we learn why he has trained himself to forget her:

> In order to exist rationally, Pnin had taught himself, during the last ten years, never to remember Mira Belochkin—not because, in itself, the evocation of

> a youthful love affair, banal and brief, threatened his peace of mind . . . , but because, if one were quite sincere with oneself, no conscience, and hence no consciousness, could be expected to subsist in a world where such things as Mira's death were possible. One had to forget—because one could not live with the thought that this graceful, fragile, tender young woman with those eyes, that smile, those gardens and snows in the background, had been brought in a cattle car to an extermination camp and killed by an injection of phenol into the heart, into the gentle heart one had heard beating under one's lips in the dusk of the past. (*Pnin* 394)

The tone and imagery of this passage recall Humbert's epiphany during a walk in the company of Dolly and her school friend Eva Rosen. Dolly's stray remark to Eva about the solitude of dying flashes upon Humbert's consciousness as a revelation:

> It struck me, as my automaton knees went up and down, that I simply did not know a thing about my darling's mind and that quite possibly, behind the awful juvenile clichés, there was in her a garden and a twilight, and a palace gate—dim and adorable regions which happened to be lucidly and absolutely forbidden to me, in my polluted rags and miserable convulsions. (*L* 267)

The linguistic echoes linking these two passages—gardens and snows serving as a backdrop for the portrait of Mira; the garden and twilight that Dolly guards so resolutely against Humbert's intrusions—hint at the reasons why these two novels preoccupied Nabokov at the same time.

What they have in common is the Holocaust. Like Mira, Eva Rosen is Jewish. She is "a displaced little person from France" whose "glossy copper hair" allies her with "the great clan of intra-racial redheads" (*L* 177–78), which includes Swann's daughter Gilberte. Eva is part of what Susan Mizruchi calls *Lolita*'s "holocaust subtext" even though she escapes Mira's grisly fate.[18] The most visible marker of this subtext comes at the end of a nightmare that torments Humbert repeatedly in the wake of Dolly's disappearance. The nightmare sublimates Humbert's guilt toward Dolly, but Dolly becomes a composite ghost that encompasses all suffering women, including the Holocaust's female victims:

> She did haunt my sleep but she appeared there in strange and ludicrous disguises as Valeria or Charlotte, or a cross between them. That complex ghost would come to me, shedding shift after shift, in an atmosphere of great melancholy and disgust, and would recline in dull invitation on some narrow board or hard settee, with flesh ajar like the rubber valve of a soccer ball's bladder. I would find myself, dentures fractured or hopelessly mislaid, in hor-

> rible *chambres garnies* where I would be entertained at tedious vivisecting parties that generally ended with Charlotte or Valeria weeping in my bleeding arms and being tenderly kissed by my brotherly lips in a dream disorder of auctioneered Viennese bric-à-brac, pity, impotence and the brown wigs of tragic old women who had just been gassed. (*L* 238–39)

The terror of this recurring nightmare gestures toward the most important ethical distinction that separates *Lolita* from Proust's novel. Here Dolly is figured as a metonymic source of suffering that radiates backward in time as a kind of reverse teleology that will encompass not only Humbert's female victims but Hitler's too. The gallery of women whose ranks swell as the dream unfolds and time flows backwards seems to partake of the same ambition that bedevils Marcel's literary efforts—namely, the desire to extract a general law or an abstract truth from painful and bewildering experience.

It is hardly arbitrary that this dream is linked to Humbert's self-identification with Marcel. The dream is described in the immediate aftermath of Humbert's decision not to plagiarize Proust by calling this section of his memoir "*Dolorès disparue*." Still, he does lay claim to kinship with Marcel when he refers to him as "another internal combustion martyr" (*L* 238).[19] This kinship is inscribed in the composite dream that torments Humbert after Dolly's departure. By linking Humbert's crimes against Dolly to the Holocaust, *Lolita* is tracing the most significant distinction between the moral geographies of Proust and those of its own creator.

COURTESY AND PROUST'S ONE WORLD

As Nabokov observed in his lectures on Proust, it is Marcel's encounter with Mlle de Saint-Loup that moves him to embark upon his literary project after so much delay. Mlle de Saint-Loup's introduction to Marcel is presented as both the stimulus and culmination of an artistic project committed to the idea that—to quote Nabokov quoting Derrick Leon—all of its varied and seemingly separate worlds "are essentially the same world" (*LL* 212). As the granddaughter of Swann and Odette, and as the daughter of Gilberte and Robert, Mlle de Saint-Loup is an emblem of the all-encompassing unity that Marcel discovers at the end of his journey in time. By linking these people together, she collapses into one node the novel's artistic, erotic, and historical plots.

Though Nabokov objects to critical approaches that prioritize "the literature of ideas" over "the literature of the senses" (*LL* 237), he agrees with Leon's conclusion that Proust's philosophical ambition involves translating separateness into unity. Nabokov's quotation of Leon is instructive:

> Marcel does not realize until he sees the two walks of his childhood united in Swann's granddaughter (Gilberte's child) that the segments into which we splice life are purely arbitrary, and correspond not to any aspect of life itself, but only to the deficient vision through which we perceive it. The separate worlds of Madame Verdurin, Madame Swann, and Madame de Guermantes are essentially the same world, and it is only snobbery or some accident of social custom that has ever separated them. (*LL* 212)[20]

Nabokov follows Leon and most interpreters of Proust's novel when he devotes an extended amount of time to analyzing the motif of the two paths—the so-called Swann's way and the Guermantes way.

The vision of unity that concludes Proust's novel can be thought of as a grand gesture of courtesy by which Marcel fulfills Hamlet's injunction to Polonius to treat the players better than they deserve (*Hamlet* 2.2.524–28). Snobbery and other accidents of social custom that alienate the commoner from the aristocrat, the rich from the poor, the queer from the heteronormative, are overcome by an all-inclusiveness that finds its most powerful expression in Marcel's surprising discovery that the two walks of his childhood are, in fact, one: "the two 'ways' were not as irreconcilable as I had supposed" (*SLT* 6.3–4; *RTP* 4.268; NRF 7.2.206).

By contrast, Pnin's willed forgetfulness of Mira and Humbert's implacable memoriousness are testaments to Nabokov's misgivings about such harmonic integrations. As such, they can be interpreted as open acts of discourtesy. The world brought into being by the Holocaust turns courtesy into an anachronistic luxury that is incompatible with human decency. The niceties of courtesy have no place in a world that allowed the Holocaust to happen. No poetry, and certainly not the poetry of courtesy, could prettify such historical facts as the one Nabokov alludes to in his letter to his sister when he invokes the image of children burnt in ovens. The implacable memoriousness of time's "infinite run" shares this sense that Humbert does not deserve the courtesy of oblivion.

Swann's consummate courtesy makes it possible to see why Nabokov would have seen courtesy as complicit in unspeakable crimes like the Holocaust. As Marcel notes on more than one occasion, a key attribute of Swann's courtesy is his avoidance of "serious topics [*les sujets sérieux*]" (*SLT* 1.20; *RTP* 1.16; NRF 1.1.29). When solicited to give his opinion on a painting, for instance, "he would remain almost disobligingly silent" and compensate for such silence by volunteering some tangential details related to the painting, such as the museum in which it was hung or its date of composition (*SLT* 1.20; *RTP* 1.17; NRF 1.1.29). Later, Marcel explains this frustrating feature of Swann's conduct as belonging to his urbane courtesy: "this horror of having to give a serious opinion was something Parisian and refined, in contrast to the provincial dogmatism of my grandmother's sisters" (*SLT* 1.135; *RTP* 1.97; NRF 1.1.136). Still, Marcel feels that the cost of such courteous self-effacement is too high and yearns for Swann to be more forthright in expressing his true views on matters of importance: "What other life did he set apart for saying in all seriousness what he thought about things, for formulating judgments which he would not put between inverted commas, and for no longer indulging with punctilious politeness [*une politesse pointilleuse*] in occupations which at the same time he professed to find absurd?" (*SLT* 1.136; *RTP* 1.97; NRF 1.1.137).

Like Swann, who avoids serious topics for fear of interrupting the flow of polite conversation, Humbert tries to convince his readers that he suffers from an arcane pathology that ought to be met with a sophisticate's urbanity instead of provincial indignation. *Lolita*'s first readers complied, treating Humbert with the same courtesy that Swann extends to his interlocutors. (Alive to this predicament, Lionel Trilling confesses that he was "plainly not able to muster up the note of moral outrage.")[21] Subsequent generations of readers have tended to be less compliant even as they felt alarmed by their own readiness to draw aesthetic pleasure from reading about child abuse.

Like Swann, Pnin takes the codes associated with civil behavior very seriously, but unlike him, he refuses to act courteously toward those who do not deserve it. As a young man living in European exile, "prim Pnin would cover his front stud with a chaste hand" even for "decayed Mme. Roux" because he considered it unthinkable to "sho[w] himself to ladies minus collar and tie" (*Pnin* 301). During the American period of his exile, he is much less fastidious about his dress—he displays his scarlet-wool "sloppy socks" with jaunty unconcern (301)—but he continues to greet American ladies with a Russian gentleman's hand kiss (408). On the way to Cremona, he represses his frustration at having missed his bus to ask the bus-station attendant about his wife's labor (314). Yet in spite of his own adherence to the rituals of courtesy, Pnin refuses to extend his courtesy to Vladimir Vladimirovich, the man who stitches the story of Mira Belochkin into the work of art that bears Pnin's name.

DISCOURTESY AND LIZA BOGOLEPOV

Pnin is caught more than once in an act of discourtesy toward the narrator of the work that bears his name. On two separate occasions, Pnin rudely throws into doubt everything reported by Vladimir Vladimirovich by calling him a liar. Recalling a social encounter in Paris, Vladimir Vladimirovich reports how an innocuous conversation about an acquaintance led to an unexpectedly hostile outburst from Pnin: "Now, don't believe a word he says, Georgy

Aramovich," interrupted Pnin. "He makes up everything. He once invented that we were schoolmates in Russia and cribbed at examinations. He is a dreadful inventor [*on uzhasnïy vïdumshchik*]." Vladimir Vladimirovich reports that he and his interlocutors "were so astounded by this outburst that we just sat and looked at each other in silence" (*Pnin* 430–31).

Pnin's attack on the narrator's honor and integrity is an act of discourtesy difficult to square with Pnin's characteristic kindness and courtesy. It ceases to be puzzling, however, if we understand it as an accusation of being a scoundrel, or, to use the ritual formula employed by duelists to provoke a challenge, a "giving the lie" (i.e., calling the other a liar; *mentita* in Italian, *démenti* in French). As an accusation of lying, giving the lie was tantamount to an accusation of being dishonorable.[22] The narrator goes to great lengths to note that the community of Russian émigrés to which he and Pnin belong embrace a code of ethics that is unintelligible to nonmembers. These "firm-principled exiles" represent "a kind of special knighthood" that had nothing in common with less culturally refined Russian émigrés (*Pnin* 387, 430). *Pnin* is a novel that gains new meaning when read through the prism of the discursive structures of gentlemanly courtesy; indeed, its secret plot is incomprehensible outside them.

Pnin's animosity toward Vladimir Vladimirovich runs deep. In conversation with Konstantin Chateau, Pnin throws doubt upon his scientific expertise: "I have always had the impression that his entomology was merely a pose" (*Pnin* 389). He also asserts that he will "never work under him" even as he concedes to Hagen that he and Vladimir Vladimirovich are "friends" (420).[23] When Vladimir Vladimirovich offers him "in the most cordial terms I could muster to assist me in any way and to any extent he desired," Pnin responds curtly that he is through with teaching and will be departing from Waindell before Vladimir Vladimirovich's scheduled arrival (431–32).

Why does Pnin accuse the narrator of being dishonorable and why is he consistently hostile toward him? The first reason is easy to reconstruct. Pnin knows the details of Vladimir Vladimirovich's ignoble conduct toward Liza Bogolepov, the woman whom the narrator mistreated before her marriage to Pnin. Indeed, Liza accepted Pnin's proposal of marriage precisely because she was spurned by Vladimir Vladimirovich. The second reason is more difficult to reconstruct, for it involves a story that even a scoundrel like Vladimir Vladimirovich seems too ashamed to tell. This second reason involves Mira Belochkin, the young woman whose murder at Buchenwald serves as a terminus that no narrative can travel beyond.

Like Humbert, Vladimir Vladimirovich has the skill of recounting actions that reflect discredit on him with a legerdemain designed to insulate him from moral opprobium. Still, the story in question is conventionally sordid and easy to decode. Vladimir Vladimirovich, a rising poet in the Russian émigré community, complies with Liza Bogolepov's request that he appraise a batch of her poems. Unimpressed by her efforts, he writes her "that her poems were bad and she ought to stop composing." But upon meeting her again—sitting "abloom and ablaze among a dozen young Russian poets"—he suggests that she let him "see those poems again in some quieter place" (*Pnin* 428). The affair that follows ends with Liza's botched attempt to commit suicide. Vladimir Vladimirovich refers to her failure to kill herself as a "contretemps" and proceeds to quote verbatim a letter that Liza gives him two weeks later in a bid to reignite their affair. The quoted letter is a proposal of marriage written to Liza by Pnin (428–29).

Vladimir Vladimirovich finds no reason to blame himself for these events and reports them with detachment. Pnin's accusation that he is a scoundrel, however, focuses the reader's attention on what is occluded by the narrator's urbane reportage. What is more, the reader sees—firsthand as it were—that the narrator's lack of moral integrity goes beyond his ungentlemanly conduct in his affair with Liza. Vladimir Vladimirovich feels no reservations, for example, about quoting for the reader's pleasure Pnin's poignant proposal of marriage to Liza.

COURTESY AND MIRA BELOCHKIN

Pnin's second reason for impugning Vladimir Vladimirovich's honor is likely related to Mira and the memories that Pnin has taught himself to suppress. Though these are memories that might belong as much to Vladimir Vladimirovich as to Pnin, Vladimir Vladimirovich cannot or will not openly lay claim to them because they are not fit material for fiction-making. In spite of his willingness to describe his callous conduct toward Liza Bogolepov, Vladimir Vladimirovich seems unable to admit that he was responsible for breaking Mira and Pnin's engagement. The following reading, claiming as it does that Vladimir Vladimirovich had an affair with Mira Belochkin, is another example of the kind of indeterminacy one learns to cope with in Nabokov. According to this reading, it is not only Pnin, but also Vladimir Vladimirovich who submits to a willed amnesia in order to teach himself "never to remember Mira Belochkin." The memory of Mira's "gentle heart . . . heard beating under one's lips in the dusk of the past" belongs as much to Vladimir Vladimirovich as to Pnin (*Pnin* 394). Moral decency, however, dictates that Vladimir Vladimirovich assign this memory to Pnin alone.

Most scholars agree with Boyd's assertion that Mira is the silent moral center of *Pnin* (*VNAY* 279). Quoting from Nabokov's letter to Katharine White, Leonid Livak argues that Mira provides the "second (main) story" behind the "superficial, semitransparent" story of Pnin's American adventures. She is also, Livak argues further, at the center of the "poetics of absence" that informs most of Nabokov's treatment of Jewishness in his fiction.[24] As a barely audible whisper within a larger silence, Mira's role in *Pnin* is a radicalization of Dolly's marginal presence in the pages of *Lolita*, Hazel's in *Pale Fire*, and Lucette's in *Ada*. Mira's story, known to both Pnin and Vladimir Vladimirovich, is a story that they must both repress and that the novel itself *almost* represses.

The secret thread that connects Mira to Vladimir Vladimirovich and Pnin becomes visible when we notice that Pnin's hostility toward Vladimir Vladimirovich might predate the latter's caddish behavior toward Liza. Pnin's first public denial of Vladimir Vladimirovich's "dreadful inventions" occurs in the early 1920s at an émigré gathering in Paris. In an attempt "to amuse him and other people around us with the unusual lucidity and strength of my memory," the narrator gives a summary of all the former meetings between him and Pnin. Pnin's response is surprising:

> He denied everything. He said he vaguely recalled my grandaunt but had never met me. He said that his marks in algebra had always been poor and that, anyway, his father never displayed him to patients; he said that in *Zabava* (*Liebelei*) he had only acted the part of Christine's father. He repeated that we had never seen each other before. Our little discussion was nothing more than good-natured banter, and everybody laughed; and noticing how reluctant he was to recognize his own past, I switched to another, less personal, topic. (*Pnin* 427)

This awkward exchange takes place the same evening that Vladimir Vladimirovich meets Liza for the first time. What remains uncertain is whether this is also the first meeting between Pnin and Liza. If Pnin knew Liza prior to this evening, it is possible to interpret Pnin's hostility toward Vladimir Vladimirovich as a response to the fact that Liza becomes Vladimir Vladimirovich's "chief listener" while he describes his and Pnin's former encounters in Russia (427). If Pnin is *already* in love with Liza at this time, he would naturally feel animosity toward a man who has captured Liza's attention.

However, a significantly richer interpretive payoff comes to light if we see Pnin's hostile response to Vladimir Vladimirovich as having been triggered by events that involve Mira rather than Liza and which have taken place in their shared Russian past. One of these events is Pnin and Mira's participation in the staging of Arthur Schnitzler's play *Liebelei* (*Zabava* in Russian; *Flirtation* or *Playing with Love* in English). Initially reluctant to attend the performance, the sixteen-year-old narrator clearly enjoyed seeing it, for decades later he is able to describe it in loving detail (425–26). More to the point, the relevance of this extended description can only be justified if it has something to do with Pnin's story.

Schnitzler's *Liebelei* deepens the links between Vladimir Vladimirovich and his namesake, for Nabokov participated in a staging of *Liebelei* during his short sojourn in the Crimea (*VNRY* 148). He played the role of *Liebelei*'s central character, Fritz Lobheimer, a rich and dissolute young man who, as Vladimir Vladimirovich recalls, "toys with the heart of Christine" while at the same time conducting a "mysterious affair backstage with the Lady in Black Velvet, the Gentleman's wife" (*Pnin* 426). He remembers with particular vividness how "the betrayed husband produced a packet of love letters written to his wife by Fritz Lobheimer" and "flung them into Fritz's face." He recalls further that "this irate Gentleman" was played by Pnin, a recollection that Pnin denies (426, 427). Vladimir Vladimirovich's detailed account of the performance ends with a tender description of Mira in the role of Mizi, a secondary character who serves as a foil to the pure and naive Christine: "The role of the little milliner, Theodor's amoretta, Mizi Schlager," he recounts, "was charmingly acted by a pretty, slender-necked, velvet-eyed girl, Belochkin's sister, who got the greatest ovation of the night" (426).

Belochkin's sister is Mira, Pnin's "dead sweetheart" who makes her first appearance in the novel while Pnin waits to be summoned to the lectern in Cremona (315–16). Mira and Pnin's romance began the same summer that they amused themselves with amateur theatricals on the outskirts of the estate belonging to Vladimir Vladimirovich's aunt. Vladimir Vladimirovich reconstructs Pnin's memories of this enchanted summer with images Nabokov had used to describe Fyodor's meetings with Zina in *The Gift*, and his own meetings with Tamara in *Speak, Memory* (*Pnin* 393). The fragrant nocturnal meetings between Mira and Pnin must have led to an engagement, for Vladimir Vladimirovich ends these recollections with the following terse conclusion: "The Civil War of 1918–22 separated them: history broke their engagement" (393). And, indeed, this seems to have been the case, for "Timofey wandered southward, to join briefly the ranks of Denikin's army, while Mira's family escaped from the Bolsheviks to Sweden and then settled down in Germany, where eventually she married a fur dealer of Russian extraction" (393–94).

It is possible to see another drama lurking in this laconic account of Pnin's abortive romance with Mira. This secondary drama is alluded to—in code—in the description of the theatrical performance that brings together Pnin, Mira, and the young man who will become the chronicler of their brief romance several decades later. *Liebelei*, a play whose plot turns on a tragic love triangle, could be read as a *drame à clef* for *Pnin*. Why does Vladimir Vladimirovich describe the performance in such suspiciously unnecessary detail if not to signal that it was during this performance that he fell in love with Mira and determined, as Demon did in almost identical circumstances with Marina, to seduce her?[25] Such an affair would replicate the love triangle that powers *Liebelei*: Pnin *is* the "irate Gentleman" who challenges his wife's lover to a duel (in *Liebelei*) and the betrayed lover who reminds Vladimir Vladimirovich that he is a scoundrel (in *Pnin*).

Pnin denies everything that Vladimir Vladimirovich says at the émigré gathering in Paris not because he considers the latter's memory to be unreliable, but rather because he is protecting his self-esteem. The fact that he denies having played the role of the "betrayed husband" is instructive: by insisting instead that he played Christine's father, Pnin is likely refusing to acknowledge that Vladimir Vladimirovich placed him in the role of betrayed lover (*Pnin* 426, 427). In calling Vladimir Vladimirovich a liar, Pnin might be leveling against him a double accusation—both at the level of moral accountability within the novel's world, and at the level of literary accountability within the fictional world that he has created and named *Pnin*. Within the novel's world, Pnin could be calling Vladimir Vladimirovich a liar because he is a serial seducer who cannot meet "a pretty, slender-necked, velvet-eyed girl" without having an affair with her (426). Pnin and Mira's last meeting in Russia on the Neva embankment is said to have been a tearful one (393), and we are made to wonder, given Vladimir Vladimirovich's opportunistic reportage, if their engagement was broken not only by "history" as he claims (393), but also by a liaison between Mira and the sixteen-year-old dandy who rapturously admired her performance in *Liebelei* a few short months earlier.

If *Liebelei* is a coded account of a love triangle between Pnin, Mira, and the narrator, why does Pnin not challenge Vladimir Vladimirovich to a duel as the "irate Gentleman" played by Pnin does in *Liebelei*? And why, by the same logic, does not Vladimir Vladimirovich lord it over Pnin—as one happy rival over an unhappy one—in a more direct manner? The first answer has to do with the institution of dueling itself. Pnin cannot challenge Vladimir Vladimirovich to a duel because the modern European duel of honor is an institution that is as antiquated as Pnin's "*antikvarnïy liberalizm* [antiquarian liberalism]" (348) or the five-year-out-of-date schedule he consults before boarding the wrong train for Cremona (302).

But there are at least two other reasons, both of which have to do with Mira. Pnin cannot challenge the narrator to a duel without running the risk of ruining Mira's reputation. These are considerations that Nabokov knew well: Andrey Bolkonsky, for instance, seeks a reason to challenge Anatole Kuragin *other than* Anatole's seduction of Natasha because he knows that without a different reason, Natasha would be compromised (*WP* 2.743; *PSS* 11:33). Similarly, Vladimir Vladimirovich would be unable to denigrate Pnin without indirectly exposing his reasons for doing so. If there was an affair between them, the narrator would be bound to keep it a secret for the sake of protecting Mira's and his own reputations. This is the hard boundary which even Vladimir Vladimirovich seems unwilling to cross.

Whatever survives of Mira in *Pnin* is a cinematic still rather than a moving image. Only shadowy traces of that richer, more vibrant girl cremated at Buchenwald survive in Vladimir Vladimirovich's account of her: her "bashful slyness" (*Pnin* 394); her ovation-worthy impersonation of Mizi Schlager—a milliner full of irreverent vitality who clowns, flirts, and refuses to fret over her lovers (426); her capacity to inspire love not only in Pnin, Vladimir Vladimirovich, and the fur dealer whom she eventually marries, but also—as Roza Shpoliansky informs Pnin—in Misha Shpoliansky, Roza's brother (392). The story of Mira cannot be fully told because Mira anchors the novel's struggle with its own complicated relationship with history and with its own legitimacy as a literary text. Just as Pnin worries that he might not be entitled *to live* in a world where deaths such as Mira's are possible, *Pnin*'s narrator betrays his anxiety that he might not be entitled *to write* about the woman whose tragic end has repealed such entitlements.

MIRA BELOCHKIN AND THE LARIVIÈRE COUPLE

If Vladimir Vladimirovich had an affair with Mira, the most important reason for suppressing it might have to do with his artistic vocation. The story would have to remain untold because the circumstances surrounding Mira's death make it a story that lies beyond the reach of artistic redemption. As Merrill might say, it is also beyond the reach of the courtesy implicit in the act of narrative commemoration. Had Mira lived, as Liza does, she might have served as rich material for the transformative powers of fiction. But having been killed at Buchenwald, Mira becomes history of a particular kind. Her posthumous identity as a victim of the Holocaust encircles her with the same halo of historical inviolability that threatens to derail Proust's fictional project. Like the story of the Larivières in the *Search*, Mira's story is not a *story*, but the boundary at which stories must end.

In *Le Temps retrouvé*, Marcel interrupts the flow of his narrative to make a very peculiar confession about his work's relationship to history. It is a confession that comes upon the heels of a reference to two minor characters that remain offstage. But even though these characters are incidental to the development of Marcel's story, they disturb the flow of his narrative in an alarming way. The Larivière couple belongs to a different ontological dispensation than everyone else in Proust's novel. Millionaire cousins of Marcel's housekeeper, they are said to have come out of retirement in order to work fifteen hours a day, without wages and without a day's respite, in the small café owned by the widow of their nephew who was killed in action in the trenches at Berry-au-Bac (*SLT* 6.224–25; *RTP* 4.424–25; NRF 8.1.206–7). Their quietly heroic self-sacrifice moves Marcel to violate the rules of his project:

> In this book in which there is not a single incident which is not fictitious, not a single character who is a real person in disguise, in which everything has been invented by me in accordance with the requirements of my theme [*selon les besoins de ma démonstration*], I owe it to the credit of my country to say that only the millionaire cousins of Françoise who came out of retirement to help their niece when she was left without support, only they are real people [*des gens réels*] who exist. (*SLT* 6.225; *RTP* 4.424; NRF 8.1.207)

Marcel allows plain, undisguised reality to burst into his invented narrative because he feels the need to pay homage to the greatness of France in its time of crisis. This is the only moment in which historical reality is allowed to destabilize his vast fictional edifice. Former concessions to a reality that fell short of his romantic expectations—the unbecoming pimple at the corner of the Duchess of Guermantes's nose, the prosaic setting of the church at Balbec in the middle of a town square—are exposed here as reality-enhancing fictions.

Merrill might have said that this breaking of the fictional frame in favor of historical reportage is yet another inflection of Proust's "extreme courtesy": Marcel implies that writers of fiction owe history a special courtesy. The inviolability of history at such unique moments in the life of a nation demands a kind of courtesy that stands at the antipodes of the *deceptive* courtesies celebrated in *Pale Fire*. Theorists of medieval and Renaissance courtesy might say that this is part of courtesy's "fitness": whereas sometimes courtesy demands comforting lies, at other times it demands the unadorned truth. But the moral imperative to keep the Larivières outside the precincts of fiction also gestures toward art's complicated relationship with history. Marcel's reverential approach to history in his description of the Larivières implies the same mistrust of art that Vladimir Vladimirovich acknowledges in the final pages of his narrative when he intimates that his own art is nothing more than a refined version of Jack Cockerell's distasteful impersonations of Pnin.

In the final pages of his narrative, Vladimir Vladimirovich acknowledges a disturbing link between art and opportunism. His first evening at Waindell is spent in the company of Jack Cockerell, an academic celebrated for his impersonations of Pnin. He concludes that the evening "somehow left me with the mental counterpart of a bad taste in the mouth" in spite of declaring that Cockerell's impersonations of Pnin were "magnificent" (*Pnin* 433, 434). He is repelled by Cockerell's brilliant performance because it is a degraded version of his own literary achievements. (Since the narrator is Russian and Cockerell turns Pnin's Russian mannerisms to comic profit, it is also a spoof of his Russian heritage.) The novel that Vladimir Vladimirovich will begin writing (presumably shortly after the long evening spent watching Cockerell imitating Pnin) is a more refined version of Cockerell's performance.

Both *Lolita* and *Pnin* serve as allegories of the most disturbing aspects of writing fiction. Nabokov's complaint that *Don Quixote* is gratuitously cruel is extended here to all art and all artists, including the artist standing behind Humbert Humbert and *Pnin*'s narrator, the writer-entomologist Vladimir Vladimirovich Nabokov. For the accusation Nabokov levels at Cervantes also applies to *Pnin*'s narrator and, disquietingly, to Nabokov's own work: "come, ungentle reader, with me and consider into what ingenious and cruel hands I shall place my ridiculously vulnerable hero. And I hope you will be amused at what I have to offer."[26]

NABOKOV'S TWO WORLDS

If Vladimir Vladimirovich did, indeed, have an affair with Mira, his suppression of the story of their affair would underscore the most significant difference between Nabokov's and Proust's respective moral visions. Whereas Marcel interrupts his narrative to pay tribute to history, I argue that Vladimir Vladimirovich suppresses certain events in his personal history for the sake of saving face and, by extension, for the sake of preserving the last remnants of a discredited code of conduct and civility. This delicate asymmetry hinges on the distinction between Proust's and Nabokov's views of guilt and personal agency.

Vladimir Vladimirovich would have to sublimate any personal guilt regarding Mira because, as a creature belonging to Nabokov's fictional universe, he holds himself responsible for his actions. This places him at the antipodes of Proust's fictional universe, where characters are divested of such responsibility. The "one world" structure that Marcel discovers at the end of his journey provides what Malcolm Bowie sees as the novel's "distinctive moral design" (*PAS* 177). According to Bowie, the *Search* ends on a note of all-encompassing pity that makes no distinctions between good and evil, vice and virtue (*PAS* 201). Bowie is not entirely comfortable with Proust's "vast gesture of inclusion": he sees Marcel's "infinite pity" as moving "into the register of excess" that is at once an "audacity" and a "folly" (*PAS* 200, 201, 203). He nonetheless defends it on aesthetic grounds: "During artistic creation, the self has the higher duty to become indefinitely porous to what lies outside it; to press no individual claim other than that of its own power of sympathy; to welcome all comers, the whole raggle-taggle procession of them, into its now hugely extended interior world" (*PAS* 204).

But even this aesthetic justification does not fully appease Bowie. He has a second go at defending Proust when he tries to overcome his anxiety that such a moral inclusiveness is characteristic of the wistfulness of melodrama rather than of the severity of art (*PAS* 205). He sees Marcel looking "with a new clarity of vision at the ship of fools whose company he has sought, but to behold their foibles, lies and cruelties with a forgiving rather than an accusing eye. By way of a singular, again almost magical, process of self-transformation, the narrator accedes to the All, to the continuum" (*PAS* 207). "By the end of the book," he concludes, "pain, humiliation and cruelty have been so completely internalized by the narrator that there is in a real sense nothing left in the social world, no foible or vice, for him to forgive" (*PAS* 208).

The disquiet that Bowie acknowledges while he describes Marcel's accession "to the All" is most convincingly explained by the Holocaust. Proust was writing before it; Bowie—like Nabokov—was writing after it. Unlike Marcel, who discovers at the end of his journey that all paths meet in the "same world," Pnin experiences his world as having been split down the middle. The first of these worlds contains graceful, smiling women among gardens and snows; the second contains cattle cars delivering adults and children to extermination camps. Pnin must forget Mira because he cannot make the necessary mental adjustment to assimilate her death into a world in which he can consent to live. Vladimir Vladimirovich would similarly reject Marcel's accession "to the All" if he has suppressed an affair with Mira for the sake of being able to live with himself.

Another tacit invocation of this two-world model is Dr. Hagen's response to the Holocaust. A scholar and a German, Hagen is struck by the incongruity between Germany's rich cultural past and the death camps that blight its landscape. Buchenwald's proximity—a mere "hour's stroll from Weimar, where walked Goethe, Herder, Schiller, Wieland, the inimitable Kotzebue and others"—causes Hagen pain and indignation: "'*Aber warum*—but why—' Dr. Hagen, the gentlest of souls alive, would wail, 'why had one to put that horrid camp so near!'" (*Pnin* 395). Like Pnin but unlike Marcel, Hagen can find no synthesis to account for the incongruity between the Germany of poets and philosophers, and the Germany of the engineers of genocide. Whereas the Germany of poets and philosophers is the world that Hagen can comprehend, the Germany of Buchenwald leaves him crushed and confused. Though these two national entities are one and the same, for Hagen they are—whatever Proust might say—mutually exclusive.

Hagen's bewilderment plays a crucial part in what Boyd identifies as *Pnin*'s dominant moral concern: namely, to expose the cruelty and inhumanity that turns misfortune into a subject for amusement (*VNAY* 271–72, 278). As Boyd notes further, the story that Hagen tries to tell at Pnin's "house-heating" party is mildly antisemitic, which explains why Laurence Clements and Pnin refuse to listen to it, discourteous as such a refusal might be (*VNAY* 279). Hagen's willingness to trade in such stories and his bewilderment at the fact of the Holocaust sketch a continuum that Nabokov hoped readers would notice.

Pnin's effort to forget Mira is an implicit protest against social norms that make it possible to tolerate the entire spectrum of cruelty and inhumanity, from "amusing" antisemitic stories to Nazi death camps. And as such, it doubles as a protest against Marcel's all-encompassing authorial courtesy. Like his refusal to be amused by Hagen's antisemitic story or other "scabrous anecdote[s]" (*Pnin* 412), Pnin tries to expel Mira's memory from his mind in order to protect himself from the "porousness" that Marcel considers essential for becoming an artist. Being no artist himself, Pnin is not bedeviled by the fear, articulated in Adorno's famous statement that has now become a cliché: "To write poetry after Auschwitz is barbaric."[27] More modestly, but more devastatingly, Pnin tries to protect himself from the question Adorno will ask later—namely, "whether after Auschwitz you can go on living."[28] Pnin answers Adorno's second question in the affirmative, but only on the condition that one seals the borders of one's mind from realities such as Auschwitz.

LOLITA AND VIOLENCE AGAINST CHILDREN

It is important to note that Nabokov's rejection in *Pnin* and *Lolita* of Proust's grand synthesis is not produced by a mere discomfort with the unconventional. Nabokov's choice of statutory rape as the central crime of *Lolita* is no accident. It is to Nabokov's credit that, in spite of being made uncomfortable by homosexuality, he does not make homosexuality the moral horror of *Lolita*. Whatever other sexual identities might apply to Humbert, Quilty, and Gaston Godin, they only stand accused of hurting children. This decision bespeaks a moral imagination more expansive than Nabokov's detractors have supposed. Like Pnin, Nabokov shows himself capable of assimilating realities that made him uncomfortable. *Pnin* contains, for instance, a moving portrait of the homosexual Professor Lake, a beloved and revered teacher of art who is not, as Kinbote so often is, a source of fun and ridicule (*Pnin* 365). At the same time, Nabokov's decision to make violence against children the quintessential crime that no passage of time can pardon or obliterate identifies him with Pnin in another way: when composing *Pnin* and *Lolita*, Nabokov seems to have lost the capacity or the willingness to look evil in the face.

At an earlier time of his life before he learned about children burnt in ovens, Nabokov rose to this particular challenge. In *Bend Sinister*, he confronts evil directly by conflating violence against children with ideologically driven murder. David Krug's death by mutilation in a state-sanctioned experiment brings together what Nabokov will later treat separately in the stories of Dolly and Mira. Mira's story is a historical reenactment of David Krug's death at the hands of a murderous ideology. Dolly's story directs that violence toward children, but—in contrast to the story of David—it describes that violence while at the same time looking away. This unnerving blend of telling but not showing (or at least not showing *too* much) animates what Leona Toker sums up as "the rhetoric of reader entrapment" and what Norman identifies as Humbert's "second attempt at seduction, not of Dolores, but of the reader."[29]

The style that Humbert employs to distract attention from his crimes, but not to conceal them completely, has something important in common with Proust's style. Different readers have given different names to this key component of Proust's poetics. Walter Benjamin invokes it when he refers to Proust's "impassioned cult of similarity," while Christian Moraru calls it Proust's "epic associationism."[30] Leo Bersani invokes it, too, when he refers to Proust's "elaborately metaphorical imagination."[31] Like Bersani, Nabokov identifies this overriding attribute of Proust's style as a complex system of accumulating metaphors (*LL* 220, 233, 241) and, like most commentators on the *Search*, Nabokov sees this metaphorical style as the engine of a philosophical project (*LL* 248–49).

In his own version of Proust's compulsive metaphorical associationism, Humbert lists congeneric elements that suggest a unity in diversity, a fundamental sameness masquerading as difference: the "various pretty articles" he considers purchasing for Dolly include "sport shoes, sneakers, pumps of crushed kid for crushed kids" (*L* 101); Dolly herself is described as "brown and pink, flushed and fouled" (118). Buried in the long list of places they visit during their first trip across the continent is "Crystal Chamber in the longest cave in the world, children under 12 free, Lo a young captive" (146). Wedged into a list of texts that Humbert consults in order to find a legal means for keeping Dolly is "an impressive volume on the legal side of marriage" that "completely ignored stepfathers with motherless girls on their hands and knees" (161). The hypothetical mural Humbert imagines himself painting over the existing mural at The Enchanted Hunters is especially relevant here: "There would have been a lake. . . . There would have been a fire opal dissolving within a ripple-ringed pool, a last throb, a last dab of color, stinging red, smarting pink, a sigh, a wincing child" (126). As Toker sums up this rhetorical strategy, Humbert's "chains of homogeneous parts" function like "a conjuror's patter, making one crucial detail inconspicuous."[32]

These alarming details, nestled as they are in Humbert's mellifluous prose, remind us that reading fiction is governed by the conventions of courtesy. As Tom Whalen observes, *Lolita* is a very unpleasant book, and Nabokov knew this.[33] But Nabokov also knew that he could count on the courtesy of readers to continue reading in spite of its unpleasantness. The story recounted by Hannah Arendt in which Adolf Eichmann refuses to read

Lolita on account of its being an "unwholesome book" is notorious not because it is incomprehensible why an individual might refuse to read it, but rather because it is surprising that the man who orchestrated a genocide would not take Humbert's crimes in stride.[34]

The courtesy that most readers extend to fiction in general and to *Lolita* in particular plays into Humbert's hands by abetting his project of normalizing the unthinkable. By contrast, a reader like Pnin might feel aesthetically and morally repelled by Humbert's tendency to lump together "beer cans" and "stillborn babies" (*L* 136). The morally fastidious and chaste-eared Pnin would certainly have recoiled from Humbert's lurid epithets (*Pnin* 412–13)—"gonadal glow" (*L* 126), "glans mauve" (*L* 100), or "orchideous masculinity" (*L* 160)—but this turning away would also align him—however preposterous that alignment might be—with Eichmann.

After his visit to the Catholic priest in Quebec and the epiphany which follows that visit, Humbert rejects Proust's ideal of unity. Humbert concludes that the magnitude of his crimes against Dolly is so great as to make it impossible to envision a universe in which such crimes do not ultimately matter. But just as Descartes conceives—if only for the sake of rejecting—the possibility that God could be a deceiver, Humbert never claims that it is *inconceivable* to imagine a universe that might forget crimes such as his. Rather, Humbert is saying that although it *is* possible to imagine a world in which Dolly's stolen childhood is meaningless, such a vision comes at a cost that (to borrow the language of *Pnin*) "no conscience, and hence no consciousness" can accept. To pay such a price is to allow the world to collapse into nullity—"and if it can, then life is a joke" (*L* 266). Humbert is at once *capable of imagining* and *unwilling to imagine* a world in which Dolly's stolen childhood means nothing.

A similar predicament drives Pnin's decision to erase all traces of Mira from his memory. Although this decision is the antithesis of Humbert's refusal to forget Dolly's stolen childhood, Pnin's reasons for forgetting Mira are identical to Humbert's: Pnin feels that to remember Mira is to breathe life into a world that is self-canceling. Pnin's redemptive forgetting is a version of the *damnatio memoriae* of the ancient Romans (edicts condemning traitors whose actions have discredited the state to be permanently struck from the historical record) or the "acts of oblivion" of the sixteenth and seventeenth centuries that granted amnesty to the vanquished in Europe's wars of religion. Recent versions of such intentional, state-sanctioned forgetting range from the distortions of history by the Soviet regime to the grants of amnesty extended by South Africa's Truth and Reconciliation Commission.[35] Pnin feels that he must forget Mira because the conditions of her death threaten to undo the very principles that made her life and person worth remembering in the first place. Paradoxically, Pnin must master an "art of forgetting" that Kierkegaard describes as being carried out "under the supreme direction of memory." Such memory-induced forgetting is, to quote Kierkegaard again, "the Archimedean point from which one lifts the whole world."[36]

Humbert calls the world that Pnin refuses to assimilate "a world of total evil" (*L* 267). Though he is referring not to the Holocaust but to his "bestial cohabitation" with Dolly (*L* 270), he confesses that from the very beginning of this relationship, "I firmly decided to ignore what I could not help perceiving" (*L* 266). His many "smothered memories, now unfolding themselves into limbless monsters of pain" include not only Dolly's confession to Eva Rosen about her fear of death, but also her constant misery, helplessness, and despair (*L* 266–67). Unlike Pnin, however, Humbert is an artist imbued with an artist's utility-driven conviction that something of value can be distilled from pain.

In trying to rationalize his memoir from the vantage point of the present, Humbert intimates why his project cannot yield a Proustian synthesis:

> I am trying to describe these things not to relive them in my present boundless misery, but to sort out the portion of hell and the portion of heaven in that strange, awful, maddening world—nymphet love. The beastly and beautiful merged at one point, and it is that borderline I would like to fix, and I feel I fail to do so utterly. Why? (*L* 126–27)

Humbert's question remains unanswered because any answer would have to affirm the claim from which he departs: namely, that "the portion of hell and the portion of heaven," "the beastly and beautiful," can be made to merge in a single world that even Humbert cannot fully bring himself to imagine.

In his memoir's concluding words, Humbert assures "his" Lolita that the only immortality they may share is an artistic one. I take this to mean that in the world of human activity—the world whose moral principles Humbert acknowledges having violated with impunity—the kind of courteous synthesis articulated in Proust's novel is morally impermissible. Those "dim and adorable regions" that make up Dolly's psychic landscape must be kept separate from Humbert's world for the same reasons that Mira's death at Buchenwald must not be allowed to intrude upon those gardens and snows that served as the background of her Russian youth.

Yet Humbert's unanswered question also hints at another reason why his vision must remain riven by duality. "I am trying to describe these things not to relive them in my present boundless misery," Humbert assures his readers before proceeding to describe his failed attempt to arrive at a Proustian all-encompassing gesture of courteous inclusion. This caveat acts as an important confession that applies not only to *Lolita* but also to *Pnin*. Humbert's intention in writing his chronicle may, indeed, be an act of courtesy akin to Proust's accession "to the All," but the act of writing is a replication of the recorded crime. Humbert may not want to relive "these things" in the act of describing them, but he tacitly acknowledges that his project of commemoration gives him pleasure. As Norman notes, Humbert "is giving us not only an example of narration-as-performance, . . . but also a visceral sense of his own pleasure at doing so." This pleasure, Norman reminds us, extends to and is produced by even "the most tearfully tragic episodes in the novel."[37]

LETTERS TO THE DEAD

To build on Mizruchi's insight about *Lolita*, *Pnin* cannot be properly understood outside of its "holocaust subtext." Pnin's effort to forget Mira Belochkin is a version of the moral and artistic predicament that Vladimir Vladimirovich must confront when he writes *Pnin*. For Vladimir Vladimirovich, like Humbert Humbert, must acknowledge his own complicity in the crimes of "history" without making his readers recoil in disgust from his narrative of that acknowledgment.

The squirrels that punctuate *Pnin*'s narrative might be read as products of Vladimir Vladimirovich's guilt-wracked, Holocaust-haunted imagination. Charles Nicol and Gennady Barabtarlo were among the first to note the ubiquity of squirrels in *Pnin*.[38] Most recently, Stanislav Shvabrin has located the source of what Barabtarlo calls "the Squirrel Theme" in Nekrasov's consciousness-raising poem about a young serf woman who freezes to death in winter. Titled "Red-Nosed Frost," the poem is a call to arms against what Shvabrin identifies as the general complacency that allows such events to retain their "sheen of normality."[39] According to Shvabrin, Nabokov inverts the meaning of Nekrasov's squirrel: whereas the squirrel in "Red-Nosed Frost" announces nature's indifference to human suffering, *Pnin*'s squirrels are guardians of metaphysical hope. As reminders of Mira Belochkin ("*belochka*" is "squirrel" in Russian), the squirrels in Shvabrin's reading of the novel mark the "compassionate design" that underwrites Pnin's world.[40]

Shvabrin's compelling reading of the squirrel theme harmonizes with other Nabokovian narratives that contain comforting messages from the beyond. Yet in the case of *Pnin*'s squirrels, the range of allusion bends toward darkness. The first cluster of references to squirrels takes place during Pnin's complicated journey to Cremona, a town whose name recalls the fact that Mira was "cremated" at Buchenwald (*Pnin* 395). The squirrel whose thirst Pnin helps quench by "politely pressing the contraption" of a drinking fountain eyes him "with contempt" and departs "without the least sign of gratitude" (338). Such a response seems merited given that courtesy has become a hollow virtue in *Pnin*'s post-Holocaust world. But it is also merited given humanity's predatory relationship with the animal world: as Pnin reminds his interlocutors, Cinderella's slippers were made of squirrel fur, and, as the narrator reminds us, Mira ended up marrying "a fur dealer" (411, 394). Cinderella's fur-covered slippers and Mira's husband's professional occupation haunt the imaginative landscape of *Pnin* as balefully as "the brown wigs of tragic old women who had just been gassed" haunt Humbert's nightmares (*L* 239). As traces of human smugness and cruelty, they are also related to the bat that Kinbote imagines "writing a legible tale of torture in the bruised and branded sky" (*PF* 649).

It is tempting to see some kind of consoling message from Mira spelled out by the proliferation of squirrels that cross Pnin's path and haunt his memory, but it makes more sense to see the communication flowing the other way. The squirrels are not letters *from* the dead as they are in so many other Nabokovian texts, but letters *to* the dead. They are fruitless but necessary efforts at atonement directed at the audience of ghosts—Mira foremost among them—that visit Pnin in the hallucinatory vision he experiences before starting his lecture at Cremona (*Pnin* 316). Just as Humbert's confession morphs into a letter to Dolly in his memoir's concluding lines, Vladimir Vladimirovich's story can double as a letter to Mira. Both Humbert and Vladimir Vladimirovich can be seen as seeking to atone for actions against women who are beyond the reach of whatever words they might wish to address to them.

Unlike Hazel, Lucette, the Vane sisters, or Sineusov's dead wife in "Ultima Thule," these ghosts cannot speak from the beyond because their lives brought into being a world that no conscience and no consciousness can certify as real. Their *afterlives* must remain mute because no words can consecrate the *lives* that they come *after*. They are also useless as material for fiction because, unlike the aged friends and acquaintances at the *bal de têtes* at the conclusion of Proust's novel, they reside outside time and therefore have no stories to tell. In a letter to Mark Aldanov from December 8, 1945, Nabokov refers to his friends and acquaintances who perished in the Holocaust as having become "somehow celestially pure."[41] Still, though they exist beyond the imaginative reach of the living, the living can still send them messages like the one Vladimir Vladimirovich might be trying to send to Mira by writing *Pnin*. It is a matter of moral and artistic significance, as well as a matter of courtesy, that this message—the novel itself—restores to Pnin what the narrator might have stolen from him: namely, Mira's and Pnin's memories of their shared love. In a gesture of editorial courtesy, the narrator silently deletes himself from the account of his shared past with Mira and Pnin. It seems fitting, too, that "history"—the hook upon which Vladimir Vladimirovich hangs the blame for Pnin and Mira's broken engagement (*Pnin* 393)—becomes a bête noire in the world of *Pnin* for a different reason than he would have us believe. Though history *is*, at least in part, responsible for the end of Pnin and Mira's engagement, Vladimir Vladimirovich may have served as its accomplice. The reminder of such complicity would make memory unendurable and art suspect.

PLATO AND THE END OF ART

Marcel's interruption of his fictional narrative to speak in nonfictional terms about the quiet heroism of the Larivière couple is also a protest against the Platonic regime that organizes his literary ambitions. Martha Nussbaum assumes that Proust's philosophical project is implicitly Platonic when she selects Proust as Plato's most formidable *literary* rival in the philosophical search for the highest truths.[42] Bersani anticipates Nussbaum's pairing together of Proust and Plato when he argues that Marcel's

> way of thinking about his experience often seems Platonic: he feels that there must be eternal truths of nature, art, and love, truths more important than his experience of any particular countryside, painting, or woman. . . . Each person and each place carry with them the secret of a way of life—Albertine and the essence of the sea, Madame de Guermantes and the glamorous past of France, Madame de Stermaria and the soul of Brittany.[43]

In the case of the Larivières, however, this Platonic search for the highest truths is suspended because their conduct *is* philosophy. Their conduct cannot be translated into anything other than itself because it is a supreme act of moral virtue from which no higher truth can be extracted. Proust's elaborately metaphorical imagination becomes redundant in the face of conduct that speaks in the pure locutions of philosophy. Suspending his *démonstration* for the sake of talking about the Larivière couple, Marcel also implies that the virtuous—like Arcadians untroubled by the threat of death or happy families in the opening sentence of *Anna Karenina*—make poor material for fiction. Nussbaum might tell us that the Larivière couple gives us "a perspective from which there are no narratives or stories to tell."[44]

The crack created by the Larivière couple in the foundation of Marcel's fictional edifice has something important in common with Mira's presence in *Pnin* for it, too, demands a different treatment than what the narrative protocols of Nabokov's fiction could be expected to accommodate. First, *Pnin* stands out from among Nabokov's English-language achievements insofar as its protagonist does not fancy himself an artist and *his* story is not a first-person narrative. This seems to emerge from Nabokov's desire to inoculate Pnin from art's collusion with evil in a world in which the Holocaust has cast all art under suspicion. Unlike Humbert, Van, Vladimir Vladimirovich, and

Marcel—all of whom consider themselves artists and are therefore to some extent responsible for the worlds they portray—Pnin can view the ethical predicaments that interest Nabokov from the vantage point of one who is in no way responsible for the suffering that he contemplates. He had no hand in the Holocaust and, more to the point, he does not write a novel in which the Holocaust is put to artistic use.

Yet in a world in which free will is no illusion, the innocence of one character must be counterbalanced by the guilt of another. This explains why Vladimir Vladimirovich must discredit—in advance—his own moral integrity before providing the reader with his poignant description of Mira's death. As he confesses in the novel's first chapter,

> Some people—and I am one of them—hate happy ends. We feel cheated. Harm is the norm. Doom should not jam. The avalanche stopping in its tracks a few feet above the cowering village behaves not only unnaturally but unethically. Had I been reading about this mild old man, instead of writing about him, I would have preferred him to discover, upon his arrival to Cremona, that his lecture was not this Friday but the next. (*Pnin* 314)

Though Vladimir Vladimirovich seems to be confessing to a rare kind of malevolence, he is merely laying claim to an occupational hazard shared by all artists. Still, even the most consummate artists—those who know it in their bones that there can be no story without the threat of doom—might find it difficult to turn events such as Mira's death into art.

As stumbling blocks in the production of art, Mira and the Larivière couple express something important about the ways in which Proust and Nabokov experienced the world and understood their own relation to what they themselves created. While the nature of Proust's ethics has generated debate—Samuel Beckett, for instance, insists that "Proust is completely detached from all moral considerations," whereas Edmund Wilson refers to him as a "merciless moralist"[45]—the example of the Larivière couple portrays him as an optimist who thought that nothing needs to be done to history because history is good in itself. Even at his most pessimistic, there is a sense in Proust that suffering is a necessary part of existence, as we see in Marcel's approving quotation of Victor Hugo's verse (from "À Villequier"), "Grass must grow and children must die" (*SLT* 6.516; *RTP* 4.615; NRF 8.2.247).

Nabokov would have interpreted the Larivières' self-sacrifice as an example of moral agency, but this is not what Proust emphasizes. He draws attention instead to the ubiquity of such conduct among the French during World War I:

> These cousins had given an example of that beautiful conduct which was very frequent at this period throughout the country and which would bear witness,

> if there were a historian to perpetuate its memory, to the greatness of France, her greatness of soul, . . . a kind of conduct displayed as much by thousands of civilians living in safety far from the front as by the soldiers who fell at the Marne. (*SLT* 6.224; *RTP* 4.424; NRF 8.1.206)

Proust's moral prioritization of the historical over the fictional is clear here. The *real* Larivières, like thousands of their compatriots, can be counted on to do the right thing in wartime while the *invented* Charlus will use the new freedoms made possible by the war to satisfy his increasingly brutal desires. What is more, even the fictional Charlus lives in a world that is shot through with moral optimism. As Wilson wryly notes, Charlus's efforts to degrade himself are stymied by the fact that his paid torturers care nothing about being vicious; they would prefer to earn an honest buck and are repelled by Charlus's sadomasochistic demands (*SLT* 6.189; *RTP* 4.399; NRF 8.1.173).[46]

But in spite of living in a world that is, relative to *Pnin* and *Lolita*, an optimistic one, Marcel suffers from the same torments that haunt Humbert and Vladimir Vladimirovich. We see an example of this in the final sections of *Sodome et Gommorrhe* when Marcel, having determined to break up with Albertine, discovers that she is friends with Mlle Vinteuil. This discovery, made on a train ride from La Raspelière to Balbec, sets in motion his obsessive jealousy over Albertine that will become the main subject of *La Prisonnière* and *Albertine disparue*. More important, however, it shows Marcel experiencing guilt for an act that might be considered essential for the writing of fiction. He describes his overwrought reaction to Albertine's revelation as a fitting punishment for his childhood act of spying on Mlle Vinteuil at Montjouvain:

> At the sound of these words, uttered as we were entering the station of Parville, so far from Combray and Montjouvain, so long after the death of Vinteuil, an image stirred in my heart, an image which I had kept in reserve for so many years that even if I had been able to guess, when I stored it up long ago, that it had a noxious power, I should have supposed that in the course of time it had entirely lost it; preserved alive in the depths of my being . . . to make dazzlingly clear to my eyes the fatal consequences which evil actions eternally engender, not only for those who had committed them but for those who have done no more, or thought that they were doing no more, than look on at a curious and entertaining spectacle, as I, alas, had done on that afternoon long ago at Montjouvain, concealed behind a bush where . . . I had perilously allowed to open up within me the fatal and inevitably painful road of Knowledge. (*SLT* 4.702; *RTP* 3.499–500; NRF 5.3.215–16)

The guilt that Marcel describes here is a version of Vladimir Vladimirovich's guilt in the wake of Jack Cockerell's gifted impersonations of Pnin, and

Humbert's guilt when he tries to track down a photo of himself commemorating the night he spent with Dolly at The Enchanted Hunters:

> Passionately I hoped to find preserved the portrait of the artist as a younger brute. An innocent camera catching me on my dark way to Lolita's bed—what a magnet for Mnemosyne! I cannot well explain the true nature of that urge of mine. It was allied, I suppose, to that swooning curiosity which impels one to examine with a magnifying glass bleak little figures—still life practically, and everybody about to throw up—at an early morning execution, and the patient's expression impossible to make out in the print. (*L* 246)

This is the guilt of the artist who turns to good account the world's fallen nature and the guilt of the reader who derives pleasure from the art such opportunism engenders. Maxim Shrayer's conclusion that Pnin's recollection of Mira's death "belongs to the finest pages of literature about the Holocaust"[47] attests to the moral peril faced by artists who write about events that decent people like Pnin make every effort to forget.

Pnin resists the comforting conclusion that Vladimir Vladimirovich's identity as a scoundrel can be disentangled from his identity as an artist. It is even tempting to speculate that Nabokov created his name-bearing alter ego in *Pnin* as a concession to Plato's claim that art is a poor guide for moral conduct. When Pnin accuses Vladimir Vladimirovich of being a liar and a scoundrel, he is given the opportunity to do what Luzhin, Cincinnatus, Krug, Dolly, Hazel, Lucette, and Nabokov's other "galley slaves" (*SO* 95) were denied—that is, accuse their maker of spinning art from the frayed threads of human suffering. Pnin's accusation can be understood in the same terms that frame the challenge that Milton's Adam levels against his maker:

> Did I request thee, Maker, from my clay
> To mould me Man? did I solicit thee
> From darkness to promote me . . . ?[48]

Mary Shelley will use these lines for her epigraph to *Frankenstein*, another story that contests the hallowed idea that the good is advanced by suffering and, more important still, that the creative acts of art and science are intrinsically valuable.

Adam's famous challenge to his Maker has additional relevance to *Pnin* insofar as it identifies the status quo with an all-pervasive darkness that is, counterintuitively, preferable to the brightness of consciousness. *Pnin* is in some important ways the *darkest* of Nabokov's novels in spite of also being, as Galya Diment's luminous *Pniniad* attests, his most tender and compassionate work. For the "holocaust subtext" that Mizruchi detects as the unspoken force that unsettles *Lolita* is the same charged ground upon which *Pnin* rests.

As a harrowing acknowledgment of art's lack of innocence, *Pnin* is a heady mix of tenderness and intolerable pain. We see this most explicitly in the narrator's moving description of Pnin's agony when he remembers Mira. As in similar passages in *Lolita*, the description of Mira's death at Buchenwald is simultaneously a heartbreaking narrative of loss *and* a virtuoso exhibition of the master artist's craft. To borrow the words Nabokov applies to a passage in Proust, "There is an intense vibration of poetry about the whole passage" (*LL* 227). But to strive to disentangle the historical fact from the literary artifact, the sorrow from the showmanship, would be to misunderstand the dilemma staged by *Pnin*. Like the allusion to Joyce's *Portrait of the Artist as a Young Man* in Humbert's analysis of his urge to see a younger version of himself in a newspaper photograph, *Pnin* reminds us that art is born not of the innocence of *young men* but of the experience of *brutes*.

In the passage describing the guilt that visits him in consequence of his spying on Mlle Vinteuil at Montjouvain, Marcel also confesses to having felt the stirrings of a satanic exhilaration in the very midst of his suffering. Even the unflappable Vladimir Vladimirovich may have balked at making this particular confession:

> And at the same time, from my bitterest grief I derived a feeling almost of pride, almost of joy, that of a man whom the shock he has just received has carried at a bound to a point to which no voluntary effort could have brought him. . . . . It was a terrible *terra incognita* on which I had just landed, a new phase of undreamed-of sufferings that was opening before me. (*SLT* 4.702–3; *RTP* 3.500; NRF 5.3.216)

Marcel observes further that this strange feeling of pride and elation is generated by his discovery of a reality that is significantly more terrible, more painful, but also richer in artistic potential than his own imagination could have conceived.

The "one world" synthesis that marks the end of Marcel's journey in time presumably includes this "terrible *terra incognita*" glimpsed in the immediate aftermath of Albertine's revelation of her friendship with Mlle Vinteuil. For all of his debonair self-assurance, Vladimir Vladimirovich expresses his doubt about the artist's right to tread upon such morally murky territory. Still, he recognizes that he cannot reject Proust's one-world model without gesturing toward what it is that he is rejecting. He makes this gesture by describing what Pnin has trained himself to forget. The overwrought passage describing Mira's death testifies to the artistic necessity of gazing upon "evil actions" even when, as Marcel discovers on the train ride from La Raspelière to Balbec, such gazing makes the viewer complicit with "those who have committed them." But in a world such as *Pnin*'s, where personal guilt flows from a sense of personal responsibility, the guilty party feels culpable for more than vicarious observation or silent non-interference. Vladimir Vladimirovich seems to want his shameful contribution to be acknowledged in spite of going to great lengths to hide his active role in the tragic history that he recounts.

Vladimir Vladimirovich, inheritor of his creator's given name, patronymic, literary achievements, and scientific interests, has little in common with the monster that Nabokov brought to life in *Lolita*. Still, Vladimir Vladimirovich shares Humbert's artistic temperament, implacable memoriousness, and the degrading pleasures that attach to them. In addition to being an asset for his literary career, his memoriousness serves—as in Humbert's case—as a storehouse for shame and guilt. Mira's flickering presence in his narrative brings together the two most guilt-ridden and shame-generating episodes of Nabokov's life: his relationship with his brother Sergey and his affair with Irina Guadanini.

Like Mira, Sergey perished in a Nazi concentration camp and, as Nabokov's autobiography and letters attest, Nabokov had not treated him courteously or kindly.[49] The passages devoted to Sergey in *Speak, Memory* are strikingly unlike Vladimir Vladimirovich's virtuoso description of Mira's death. Speaking in his own voice, Nabokov uses a style that is deliberately and uncharacteristically restrained. Additionally, he begins and ends with a confession of helplessness: "For various reasons I find it inordinately hard to speak about my other brother. . . . It is one of those lives that hopelessly claim a belated something—compassion, understanding, no matter what—which the mere recognition of such a want can neither replace nor redeem" (*SM* 580, 581). The guilt and shame Nabokov experienced as a result of his affair with Irina Guadanini might also lie buried in the untold story of Mira. In a letter he wrote to Guadanini, he castigates himself by invoking the same vocabulary that Pnin uses against Vladimir Vladimirovich: "The inevitable vulgarity of deceit," he writes Guadanini in a letter quoted by Boyd. "And suddenly your conscience puts its foot down and you see yourself a scoundrel" (*VNRY* 438–39).

HUMBERT'S TWO WAYS

Pnin rejects the ultimate harmony that unifies Proust's world through volitional acts of forgetting that can be understood as betrayals of courtesy. If Vladimir Vladimirovich had an affair with Mira Belochkin, his suppression of the affair would serve as an implicit acknowledgment that some actions are beyond the pale of acceptance and forgiveness. In a similar way, Humbert refuses to countenance the possibility that an "infinite run" of time might extend him the courtesy of forgetting about his crimes against Dolly. This unwillingness to relegate the theft of Dolly's childhood to oblivion is a direct consequence of the same insistence on personal agency and responsibility we see in *Pnin*. And as in *Pnin*, too, the will's freedom is represented by an inversion of Proust's "two ways" motif.

During the most suspenseful moments in his narrative, Humbert laments his failure to take the "other path" that would have prevented him from becoming a child abuser. Preparing to have intercourse for the first time with Dolly at The Enchanted Hunters, he ponders the fork in the road that lies before him:

> In a few minutes . . . I would let myself into that "342" and find my nymphet, my beauty and bride, emprisoned in her crystal sleep. Jurors! If my happiness could have talked, it would have filled that genteel hotel with a deafening roar. And my only regret today is that I did not quietly deposit key "342" at the office, and leave the town, the country, the continent, the hemisphere,—indeed, the globe—that very same night. (*L* 116)

Earlier that same day, Humbert found himself at a similar crossroads when he saw Dolly for the first time at Camp Q:

> She was thinner and taller, and for a second it seemed to me her face was less pretty than the mental imprint I had cherished for more than a month: her cheeks looked hollowed and too much lentigo camouflaged her rosy rustic features; and that first impression . . . carried the clear implication that all widower Humbert had to do, wanted to do, or would do, was to give this wan-looking though sun-colored little orphan *aux yeux battus* . . . a sound education, a healthy and happy girlhood, a clean home, nice girl-friends of her age among whom (if the fates deigned to repay me) I might find, perhaps, a pretty little *mägdlein* for Herr Doktor Humbert alone. But "in a wink," as the Germans say, the angelic line of conduct was erased, and I overtook my prey . . . , and she was my Lolita again—in fact, more of my Lolita than ever. (*L* 104)

Lust diverts Humbert's thoughts from the "angelic" path of conduct, but not before he articulates both the possibility and moral imperative to have taken it. In Marcel's universe, this second path would have ultimately led to the same place as the first. In Humbert's world, however, the implication is that the path not taken would have led, for Dolly at least if not for the "pretty little *mägdlein*," to a decidedly different destiny.

Lolita encourages readers to view Humbert's two paths through the lens of Proust's dominant metaphor of the "two ways." The links between Dolly and Albertine (as prisoners and fugitives) have attracted the bulk of scholars' attention.[50] But there are also links between Dolly and Odette that similarly gesture toward Proust's and Nabokov's antithetical understanding of free will and personal responsibility.

Dolly and Odette are most closely bound up in Humbert's description of Dolly at Camp Q cited above:[51] her diminished prettiness, her hollow cheeks, her *yeux battus*, her wan-looking complexion recall the concluding lines of "Un amour de Swann." At a musical evening hosted by Mme de Saint-Euverte, Swann recalls a dream in which Odette appeared before him: like Humbert with Dolly at Camp Q, Swann is struck by "Odette's pallid complexion, her too thin cheeks, her drawn features, her tired eyes [*le teint pâle d'Odette, les joues trop maigres, les traits tirés, les yeux battus*]" (*SLT* 1.543; *RTP* 1.375; NRF 1.2.234). The recollection of the dream is part of Swann's famous *prise de conscience* during which he meditates upon his curious fate as a man of culture and social position who has sacrificed everything for a commonplace woman whom he did not even find initially attractive. The events that seem to have congealed into fateful irrevocability strike him, from the vantage point of the present, as containing possibilities for other paths that he might have taken: "Who indeed can say whether, in the event of his having gone elsewhere that evening, other happinesses, other griefs might not have come to him, which later would have appeared to him to have been inevitable?" (*SLT* 1.542; *RTP* 1.375; NRF 1.2.234). But this speculative openness is flattened out under the pressure of a more powerful—even providential—inevitability:

> But what did seem to him to have been inevitable was what had indeed taken place, and he was not far short of seeing something providential in the fact that he had decided to go to Mme de Saint-Euverte's that evening, because his mind, anxious to admire the richness of invention that life shows, and incapable of facing a difficult problem for any length of time, such as deciding what was most to be wished for, came to the conclusion that the sufferings through which he had passed that evening, and the pleasures, as yet unsuspected, which were already germinating there—the exact balance between which was too difficult to establish—were linked by a sort of concatenation of necessity [*une sorte d'enchaînement nécessaire*]. (*SLT* 1.542–43; *RTP* 1.375; NRF 1.2.234)

Swann's interpretation of his fate in terms of an enchained inevitability makes sense in a novel where the will is presented as a delusion and conflicts are dissolved in a final unity that is aesthetically and teleologically satisfying.

Humbert also feels chained to an overdetermined destiny and is haunted by phantom possibilities that accompany the suspicion that "life's course constantly branched" (*L* 152). Even though at the time he pens his memoir these labyrinths of possibility seem to have been struck into fixity, he insists upon noting the many moments when the links in the chain lay open. For instance, even as he steps into the room where Dolly sleeps at The Enchanted Hunters, he records an abortive hesitation which, if not ignored, might have taken him down a different path: "One could still—but the key was already in the lock, and then I was in the room" (120). Both Swann and Humbert feel simultaneously free and enchained, but the accent in Swann's case falls on enchainment whereas in Humbert's case it falls on freedom.

Humbert's crimes against Dolly belong to the same order of crime that placed Mira beyond the pale of Pnin's memory. Nabokov, like Pnin, wants there to be no convergence of ways between the world where fates such as Mira's and Dolly's are possible and the world that we might call home. His rejection of Proust's unifying vision is born of a moral necessity to banish both art and courtesy from a world where gardens and death camps are part of the same continuum. Dolly's exile from time's courteous forgetfulness and Mira's exile from the devotional rites of memory make *Lolita* and *Pnin* Nabokov's darkest novels. For here, as nowhere else in Nabokov's fiction, art and courtesy are not radiant signifiers of human freedom, but have shown themselves to be complicit in the placing of freedom into the service of evil ends.

Epilogue

Van, Gawain, and Kant's Green Iris

Cortesia es en guarnir
e en gent accuilir;
cortesia es d'onrar
e es en gen parlar.

Courtesy is to take care
of people and receive them.
Courtesy is to honor
and talk to people.
—Garin le Brun

PNIN AND *LOLITA* fork from the main stem of Nabokov's corpus because they were written in the wake of the Holocaust. During this darkest time of his literary career, Nabokov lost faith in art, memory, and courtesy. Pnin's moral conscience demands that he forget Mira Belochkin, while Humbert's lack of one enables him to convince his readers to extend their readerly courtesy to descriptions of statutory rape and child abuse. Attributes of courtesy—such as giving the other welcome or holding the other in memory—appear in *Lolita* and *Pnin* as perverted versions of themselves: Humbert's captivating eloquence is a moral trap, and Pnin's recollections of Mira are a moral liability. Yet as the memory of children burned in ovens receded from Nabokov's imagination, courtesy returned to its former place of supreme ethical and aesthetic importance.

In the two novels written after *Lolita* and *Pnin*, the deaths of Hazel and Lucette are connected to failures in courtesy. But unlike the scenario imagined in *Pale Fire*, where Pete Dean's rejection of Hazel is a glaring violation of courtesy, Van's rejection of Lucette's sexual advances before she commits suicide is more difficult to assess. For how does "a gentleman and an artist"—as Van styles himself (A 393–94)—reject a beautiful woman's sexual advances without offending her? This question is the central moral problematic of *Sir Gawain and the Green Knight*, the anonymous Arthurian romance written in the dialect of northwestern England in the late fourteenth century.

Though this particular question lies at the heart of *Sir Gawain*, most French romances that Nabokov studied at Cambridge were preoccupied with questions related to it. As Ad Putter notes, almost all of Chrétien's romances portray "a knight whose penchant for acting the lover is simply part and parcel of social gracefulness" (*FAR* 136). We might say further that this particular social grace is a key feature in the moral makeup of the *chevalier courtois*; Putter calls it an "ethic of conscientious worldliness" (*FAR* 3). To see its significance in Nabokov's moral and aesthetic philosophy, we might recall that his first novel begins with an act of discourtesy fueled by Ganin's not knowing how to break up with Lyudmila. There is a pleasing symmetry in Nabokov's return to the subject in *Ada*, his longest and most ambitious novel, written four decades later.

Yet the Arthurian romance that makes this question its central moral preoccupation does not appear on Nabokov's reading list at Cambridge. As a work of the English Middle Ages, *Sir Gawain and the Green Knight* would have no place on a French medieval tripos. Still, it is likely that during his studies at Cambridge Nabokov would have become familiar with its celebrated status as a masterpiece of the Middle Ages. While reading for his tripos, it is likely that he would have consulted Gaston Paris's long essay titled "Les romans en vers du cycle de la Table ronde," published in the thirtieth volume of *L'histoire littéraire de la France*. In this work from 1887, Paris hypothesizes that *Sir Gawain and the Green Knight* is an English version of a lost French poem and refers to it as "*le joyau de la littérature anglaise au moyen âge* [the gem of English literature of the Middle Ages]."[1]

While it is most likely that Nabokov learned about *Gawain* as an undergraduate at Cambridge, he probably read it much later because of the notorious difficulty of the West Midlands' dialect in which it was written. It is therefore unlikely that Nabokov read Sir Frederic Madden's original publication from 1839 or even the Oxford University Press edition produced by J. R. R. Tolkien and E. V. Gordon in 1925. The most likely scenario is that he read it in its various modern translations. For instance, he may have read the first modern French translation, *Sire Gauvain et le chevalier vert*, published in 1946 by Émile Pons. Like Paris, Pons describes the *Gawain*-poet's achievement in superlative terms: "*Sir Gawain and the Green Knight* is not only the most beautiful Arthurian poem in the English language, but one of the most vibrant examples of Arthurian literature in all countries and all times."[2] Alternatively, he might have read the poem's renderings into modern English by Theodore H. Banks (New York, 1929), Kenneth Hare (London, 1946, 1948), M. R. Ridley (Leicester, 1944; London, 1950, 1955) or Gwyn Jones (London, 1952).

Ada's composition in the 1960s coincided with a "surge of scholarly and critical work" on *Gawain*.[3] Writing in 1961, Morton W. Bloomfield could report that a fairly complete bibliography of *Gawain* contained 250 titles.[4] Given his lifelong interest in Arthurian literature, Nabokov might have read, for instance, *Arthurian Literature in the Middle Ages: A Collaborative History*, edited by Roger Loomis and published in 1959 by the Clarendon Press. *Gawain* is prominently discussed in this work.

As an Arthurian romance in the French literary tradition pioneered by Chrétien,[5] *Gawain* articulates the tensions produced by a long-standing fascination with *courtoisie* in the Middle Ages. This leads Pons to note that the poem is organized by the logic of a *"culte de 'Courtoisie'"* and Aldo Scaglione to observe that it "clearly marks a high point in the history of the civilizing process."[6] In like manner, *Ada*—the last great work of Nabokov's writing career—recapitulates its author's enduring interest in courtesy as a social virtue that he believed to transcend the logic of material determinism and ethical utilitarianism. The themes and motifs shared by *Gawain* and *Ada* are meaningful because they provide a summing up of the promises and limitations of an ethics that sees the civilities of life, to quote James Merrill, "as having ultimate importance."[7] To read *Ada* alongside *Gawain* is to make visible the medieval legacies that anchor Nabokov's thinking about ethics and to understand the reasons why he connected these legacies to the moral and aesthetic philosophy of Kant.

THE GREEN KNIGHT AND *ADA*'S GREEN WORLD

Lucette's predicament as a third wheel to Van and Ada's incestuous affair leads Van and Ada to adopt a number of schemes to snatch a few moments of lovemaking away from her. Tellingly, one such scheme plunges us into the world of medieval romance while another is retroactively linked to Kant. Curiously, too, most of these schemes contain references to the color green. In the first of these, Van and Ada tie Lucette to a willow tree so that Van, in the guise of a knight, might save her from Ada, a *green*-scaled dragon. Faithful to the world of medieval romance that inspires the scene, "dragon and knight" run off "'prancing' to feign swift escape and pursuit" (*A* 116). A second scheme involves convincing Lucette to have a bath while Van and Ada have intercourse in a nook hidden from "the sea-*green* eye of the bathroom looking-glass" (117; emphasis added). Another green eye—this time both Kant's and Lucette's—is invoked by Van when Lucette complains that he and Ada used to lock her up in a closet "at least ten times." Van's response is instructive: *"Nu uzh i desiat'* (exaggeration). Once—and *never* more. It had a keyless hole as big as Kant's eye. Kant was famous for his cucumicolor iris" (298). This recollection refers back to an earlier scene during which Van and Ada "could no longer restrain their amorous excitement, and under the absurd pretext of a hide-and-seek game they locked up Lucette in a closet . . . , and frantically made love, while the child knocked and called and kicked until the key fell out and the keyhole turned an angry *green*" (170; emphasis added).

These references to the color green go beyond the scenes that recall Van and Ada's stratagems for containing Lucette's movements. Indeed, the entire novel is steeped in the color green as if eager to advertise its kinship with the Green Knight, who earns his moniker because everything about him is green (he is "*overal enker-grene* [completely emerald green]") (*SGGK* line 150). On the morning of Van's first arrival at Ardis, he leaves the mansion to enter "into the green reality of the garden" (*A* 44); during his second sojourn at Ardis, he and Ada quell their hunger after a night of lovemaking as "the dark-green shadows drew in their claws" (153); in old age, they remember Ardis as "the green moving backdrop" of their childhood romance (463). From entomology to *terrology*, green is the dominant color of *Ada*'s world: Van imagines that the eggs of the mate-consuming fly *Serromyia amorata* Poupart are green (109, 110) and that Antiterra's purported sibling planet, Terra, is "a green world rotating in space and spiraling in time" (146).

Ada's most complex reference to the color green is an alliteration whose specificity further highlights its kinship with *Gawain*, a poem written in alliterative verse whose dramatic situation is coded green. Van's phrase "green lamps greening green growths" (*A* 361) echoes not only the Green Knight's astonishing verdancy, but also the holly branch that he carries, described by the *Gawain*-poet as "*grattest in grene when grevez ar bare* [brilliantly green when forests are bare]" (*SGGK* line 207). As in *Gawain*, alliteration is one of the hallmarks of *Ada*'s style: Ada is recalled as "adored and abhorred, heartless and heartbroken" (*A* 247), and Van's recollection of an oversized erection is dismissed as "senescent nonsense, says science!" (282). The end of their first summer of love is described in terms that signal Van's self-consciousness about his alliterative style: the summer is said to hint at "possible failings and fadings, at the fatigue of its fugue—the last resort of nature, felicitous alliterations (when flowers and flies mime one another)" (113). Van's decision to focus his academic studies on "the Idea of Dimension & Dementia" moves his mentor to predict, "You will 'sturb,' Van, with an alliteration on your lips" (291).

Yet in spite of *Ada*'s alliterative fecundity, the phrase "green lamps greening green growths" deserves closer scrutiny. Van invokes it as an image of adultery. Reflecting upon his decision not to attend his mother's funeral, Van wonders if his presence might have made Ada's husband a cuckold sooner: "the later antlers might have been set right then, with green lamps greening green growths" (361). It is tempting to think that this tongue-twisting alliteration serves as shorthand for *Ada*'s use of the color green to gesture toward its relationship with *Gawain*, a work whose plot turns on the risks of adultery.

VAN AND GAWAIN, LUCETTE AND THE GREEN KNIGHT

Though Van and Ada fall hopelessly in love with each other, they meet with countless impediments to exercise that love: they are prevented from being together by social custom, legal and parental prohibition, protracted terminal illness, and—most tangibly during their first summer at Ardis—the ubiquitous presence of their half-sister Lucette. But as the story of Lucette intimates, *Ada*'s central moral problematic is concerned neither with the laws of nature nor with the precepts of culture, but with universally binding moral laws that transcend both. Significantly, these moral laws do not deny freedom but authenticate it in a specifically Kantian way: they are laws that bind only those whose free will is capable of overcoming passion.

Ada is awash in the color green, but it is Lucette who is most conspicuously identified with the color. She is the "green imp" with "green eyes" who is always threatening to intrude upon Van and Ada's lovemaking (*A* 168, 169); she wears "willow-green shorts" or "green pajamas" (158, 182); her "darkening green eyes" match her "well-filled green shorts" (223, 224). When she visits Van at Kingston University, Van discovers that "her green eyes had grown" (292). A few days later, she dines with Van and Ada in "a lustrous cantharid green" gown and goes to sleep in a "pale green nightdress" (328, 332). The next morning, Ada plucks off this same "willow green nightie" when she initiates their *débauche à trois*, and a short time later Lucette scrawls her farewell note in "Arlen Eyelid Green" (335, 337). In his note of apology for the *débauche*, Van puts the blame on the allure of Lucette's "green eyes" (338).

The events that immediately precede Lucette's suicide seem deliberately attuned to *Gawain*'s Arthurian world and its Green Knight. Her final words are spoken to the bartender Toby, who used to serve on another transatlantic liner, the aptly named "*Queen Guinevere*" (*A* 380, 395). The Russified version of Hawaii and the Hawaiian Islands—"Gavaille" and "the Gavailles" (384)—are associated throughout Lucette's final day with the risk of drowning and seem to be a cognate of Gawain. Though Van's name is a contraction of the Russian *Ivan*, Van is both typographically and phonetically akin to Gawain (variously spelled as Gauvain, Gavain, or Wawan). Lucette's swimming suit is described in terms that recall the Green Knight's green armor: "her green breast-cups," "green pubic mask," and "green helmet" evoke chivalric combat more readily than a poolside frolic on a luxurious transatlantic liner (382, 383). Her cigarette case—"the emerald-studded cigarette case," "the little green-gemmed case" (383, 386)—that Van feels he must destroy (398) calls to mind the Green Knight's ornate green accoutrements such as "*his athel skyrtes, / That ever glemered and glent al of grene stones* [his splendid skirts / That constantly glittered and shone, all of green gems]" (*SGGK* lines 171–72).

Additionally, Lucette's links to the Green Knight go beyond specific attire and general appearance. Deeper layers of kinship connect them: Lucette disrupts Van and Ada's idyllic summer of love in a way that replicates the Green Knight's disruption of the revelries at Arthur's court. The Green Knight bursts in upon the Christmas festivities at Camelot to issue a terrifying challenge that attains a dual objective. First, the disruption unsettles the self-satisfied tenor of the protagonists' lives. Second, it serves as a reminder that certain moral principles are categorical and that no circumstances may justify their violation.

Three deceptively separate challenges teach Gawain this proto-Kantian lesson. The first challenge is issued by the Green Knight when he arrives at Camelot. Who will play his game in which each player must take a turn at striking and then suffering a blow without defending himself? To prevent Arthur from submitting to the test, Gawain insists on taking his place. He further agrees to the Green Knight's condition that after dealing the blow, he will visit him a year hence at his home to sustain a return blow. Gawain's blow smites off the head of the Green Knight with one clean stroke, but the Green Knight picks up his head and remounts his horse. The severed head informs Gawain that it belongs to the Knight of the Green Chapel and Gawain must present himself at the Green Chapel in a year's time to receive his blow.

True to his word, Gawain sets out for the Green Chapel a few days before the advent of the new year. After a long and arduous journey, he arrives on Christmas night at a castle where he is welcomed with courtesy and joy by its lord, Sir Bertilak of Hautdesert. His wife, the Lady of Hautdesert, is said to be even more beautiful than Guinevere. After he learns from Bertilak that the Green Chapel is only two miles distant, Gawain consents to become Bertilak's guest until New Year's morning. He also consents to participate in a merry game that constitutes the second challenge: for the next three days, Gawain is to remain indoors in the chatelaine's company while Bertilak goes hunting. When they meet in the evening, he and Bertilak are to exchange what each has won during the day.

This exchange-of-winnings game contains a third (and secret) challenge that Gawain must overcome: on each morning of the three days that follow, the Lady of Hautdesert visits Gawain in his chamber and offers him her love. As the preeminent knight of courtesy, Gawain deploys his social skills and successfully withstands the Lady's temptations. This enables him to remain faithful to the rules of the game he plays with Bertilak. On the third morning, however, the Lady offers to give him her green girdle, which she claims will protect him from harm. Worried about his imminent encounter with the Green Knight, Gawain accepts the girdle, does not relinquish it to Bertilak that evening, and thus violates the rules of the exchange-of-winnings game.

The next morning, a court retainer serves as Gawain's guide to the Green Chapel. The Green Knight's greeting—"*Now, sir swete, / Of steven mon may the trowe* [Good sir, / A man may trust your vow]" (*SGGK* lines 2237–38)—underscores that Gawain's three challenges all turn on the ideal of "*trawthe*"—that is, fidelity to one's pledged word. The Green Knight strikes two blows without touching Gawain and the third blow merely nicks Gawain's skin. The challenge over, the Green Knight reveals that he is Bertilak and that it was he who prompted his wife to tempt Gawain in order to test him. Bertilak rebukes Gawain for betraying his pledged word by withholding the green girdle, but also acknowledges that Gawain has proven himself to be "one of the most perfect men who ever walked on the earth" (line 2363). He explains further that Gawain's overall commitment to *trawthe* has saved his life. When Gawain kept the girdle he fell short—"*lakked a lyttel*" (line 2366)—from the knightly ideal, but since his betrayal was a consequence of his hunger for self-preservation, Bertilak blames him less (line 2368). Bertilak also reveals that it was Morgan le Fay who instructed him to visit Camelot a year ago in order to terrorize Arthur's court and frighten Guinevere to death. Gawain recounts these events in their entirety upon his return to Camelot in spite of being acutely ashamed of breaking his word. Arthur and his retainers enjoy the story and determine henceforward that all knights of the Round Table will wear a green girdle like Gawain's.

For Putter, the composite figure of Bertilak and the Green Knight serves as a stand-in for moral conscience: he is the inner spectator who always sits in judgment. "The idea of being judged, even when nobody appears to be watching," Putter observes, "is precisely what the spectacular climax at the Green Chapel has in store for us" (*FAR* 184). What is more, this imaginary onlooker holds Gawain to a Kantian standard: one ought to honor absolute standards of moral right even when such standards appear to be gratuitous, inconvenient, or even suicidal. Lucette's sublime act of courtesy to the Robinsons—her moral *high desert*, as we might call it—connects her to the scenes at Castle *Hautdesert*. This act of courtesy is gratuitous, inconvenient, and—as a result of an unpredictable concatenation of events—ends in suicide. It is also as *deceptively* trivial as the exchange-of-winnings game set in place by Bertilak (*FAR* 181).

The revelation that *Gawain*'s entire plot was orchestrated by Morgan le

Fay as an act of vengeance against Guinevere also seems relevant. Nabokov would have known from having read *Yvain* for his tripos that Gawain's search for Guinevere prevented him from coming to the aid of his niece and nephews, and this is why the task of helping them falls to Yvain (*Yvain* 3908–35). Van's fatal encounter with Lucette takes place on the *Tobakoff*, even though he observes, more than once, that his preferred transatlantic liner is the *Queen Guinevere* (*A* 273, 369, 380). *Ada*'s repeated allusions to the ocean liner that bears Guinevere's name seem keyed into the fact that Van's love of Ada, like the fealty of Arthur's knights to Guinevere, is complicit in Lucette's fate. For it is Ada's unexpected appearance in the film that is being screened on the *Tobakoff* that derails Lucette's efforts to seduce Van and ends in her suicide. Like Gawain, who cannot come to the aid of his relatives because he is preoccupied with Guinevere, Van is not available to come to the aid of Lucette because he is preoccupied with Ada, his personal Guinevere.

The most revealing parallel between the trials of Van and Gawain has to do with Gawain's temptation at Hautdesert. The chatelaine tempts Gawain in a way that anticipates Lucette's sexual temptation of Van. To evaluate Van's conduct toward Lucette through the lens of his medieval namesake's triumphs and failures is to see why courtesy resurfaced as a supreme moral aspiration in Nabokov's fiction after the Holocaust ceased to torment his imagination. It is also to see why courtesy plays a key role in Nabokov's moral philosophy and why Nabokov invoked Kant as its presiding spirit.

LUCETTE'S GREEN EYE AND KANT'S CUCUMICOLOR IRIS

Like the verdant alliteration that Van uses to describe adultery ("green lamps greening green growths"), Van's invocation of Kant's cucumber-colored (cucumicolor) iris is a morally charged remark that masquerades as a throwaway stylistic flourish. Van's baroque style both masks and exposes a moral blindness that is as opportunistic as it is damning. Kant's curious presence in this scene as a figure of moral judgment gestures toward a contradiction in Van's response to Lucette's protest against his and Ada's cruelties toward her: while he hopes to distract attention from the truth of her charge by playful banter, he must also realize—as someone who can invoke Kant's name with casual familiarity—that it is precisely the wittiness of his conversation that makes his moral blindness so suspicious. Within the Kantian framework to which he subjects himself in his remark about Lucette's accusing green eye, he conveniently pretends not to see that his capacity to turn to the resources of art also serves as proof of his capacity to act as a moral agent.

Van's later observations about the implacable authority of pain tell us that he is familiar with this Kantian insight even as he tries to deny it: "Rather humiliating that physical pain makes one supremely indifferent to such moral issues as Lucette's fate, and rather amusing, if that is the right word, to constate that one bothers about problems of style even at those atrocious moments" (*A* 466). As Kant might note, Van's attunement to the aesthetic—the fact that he "bothers" about stylistic matters even in the midst of physical agony—makes his "supreme indifference" to moral issues such as Lucette's fate a matter of choice rather than a matter of necessity. Van's claim that moral agency is obliterated in the face of pain is as self-serving as his companion claim that his aesthetic agency is stronger than his moral agency. Lucette's sublime act of courtesy to the Robinsons in the very midst of total psychic disarray refutes the first claim. Van's failure to treat Lucette as "a gentleman and an artist" would have done refutes his second claim that no amount of pain can prevent him from "bother[ing] about problems of style."

But how might "a gentleman and an artist" conduct himself in a situation like the one in which Van finds himself on the night of Lucette's suicide? How does a man show courtesy and esteem toward a woman whose sexual advances are unwelcome, imprudent, and likely to lead to disaster? This is the challenge put to Gawain when he agrees to participate in the exchange-of-winnings game at Bertilak's castle.

Gawain is the preeminent knight at Arthur's court because of his reputation as a paragon of courtesy: the *Gawain*-poet describes him as a "man most true of speech / And fairest-spoken knight" (*SGGK* lines 638–39). In a monograph that Nabokov may have read during his student days, Myrrha Borodine describes Gawain's reputation in French medieval romances in the following way: "Gawain is represented in all the romances as the model of knightly virtue and prowess. He is never vanquished or overcome by another, and it is a claim to fame for any knight to have faced him in single combat. But most of all, this ideal champion of the Round Table is courteous and wise [*courtois et sage*]."[8] It is no surprise that Gawain's arrival at Hautdesert is greeted by Bertilak's retinue as a rare opportunity to learn the art of courtesy from its supreme master:

> Each knight whispered to his companion,
> "Now we shall enjoy seeing displays of good manners,
> And the irreproachable terms of noble speech;
> The art of conversation we can learn unasked,
> Since we have taken in the source of good breeding." (*SGGK* lines 915–19)

The challenge that Gawain will have to confront at Hautdesert will strain to the utmost his legendary courtesy. It is—significantly—a challenge that Gawain meets with both triumph and failure.

LOVE AND COURTESY

The second time that the chatelaine visits Gawain in his bedroom, she tries to exploit his reputation for courtesy and chivalry in her effort to seduce him:

> "I would learn from you, sir," said that gentle lady,
> "If the question was not irksome, what the reason was
> That someone as young and valiant as yourself,
> So courteous and chivalrous as you are known far and wide—
> And of all the aspects of chivalry, the thing most praised
> Is the true practice of love, knighthood's very lore;
> For to speak of the endeavors of true knights,
> The written heading and text of their deeds is that:
> How knights have ventured their lives for true love,
> Suffered for their love-longings dismal times,
> And later taken revenge on their misery through valor,
> Bringing joy to their ladies through their personal merits.
> And you are the outstanding knight of your time,
> Your fame and your honor are known everywhere,
> And I have sat by you here on two separate occasions
> Yet never heard from your mouth a solitary word
> Referring to love, of any kind at all." (*SGGK* lines 1508–24)

As Putter notes, the chatelaine invokes here a familiar "chivalry topos" used by Chrétien, Geoffrey of Monmouth, and other medieval writers to argue that love is the most reliable spur for morally excellent deeds (*FAR* 104–5).

Yet what transpires in these extended seduction scenes has little to do with what the Lady calls "*lele luf* [true love]" or "*lel layk of luf* [the true practice of love]" (*SGGK* lines 1516, 1513). There is no suggestion of love gained or lost between Gawain and the Lady; rather, the dramatic urgency is generated by a battle of words in which the weapons of choice are witty banter and clever repartee. Instead of teaching her "*sum tokenes of trweluf craftes* [some elements of skill in true love]" (line 1527) as the Lady requests, Gawain demonstrates his *cortaysye* by a "show of sinuous politeness" deployed for the sake of "evading the action that the Lady would force upon him."[9]

As Laura Hibbard Loomis notes, the conversations between Gawain and the Lady remind us that "talk is an art."[10] Putter observes that these protracted temptation scenes "bring home the force which words exert on lives" (*FAR* 104). In his introduction to the French translation of *Gawain*, Pons argues that Gawain lives up to his reputation as an ideal knight "by his handling of the language of 'courtoisie,' the ingenuity that he deploys in his lively and delicate rejoinders, his precise yet never hurtful refusals, his skillful and irreproachable evasions."[11] The parade of words that Gawain directs at the chatelaine serves as a master class in the art of courteous rejection. Gawain's remarkable patience, self-restraint, and conversational dexterity demonstrate that his reputation as a paragon of courtesy is richly deserved. Ganin, Sebastian, and Van would have benefited by learning a thing or two from him.

During his first (and, as it will turn out, also *last*) dinner with Lucette, Van imagines his predicament in terms that recall Gawain's three-day seduction at the hands of the chatelaine:

> As he gloomily looked at her thin bare shoulders . . . , he reflected abjectly that he would have to endure, if conforming to his innermost code of honor, five such days of ruttish ache—not only because she was lovely and special but because he could never go without girl pleasure for more than forty-eight hours. He feared precisely that which she wanted to happen: that once he had tasted her wound and its grip, she would keep him insatiably captive for weeks, maybe months, maybe more, but that a harsh separation would inevitably come, with a new hope and the old despair never able to strike a balance. But worst of all, while aware, and ashamed, of lusting after a sick child, he felt, in an obscure twist of ancient emotions, his lust sharpened by the shame. (*A* 388)

Even though Van expects "his innermost code of honor" to prevail over his "ruttish ache" for the five days of the transatlantic crossing, his moral undoing takes a fraction of the time that the chatelaine requires to get Gawain to betray his pledged word by accepting her green girdle. For Van abandons himself to Lucette's seduction on the very *first* day of their journey:

> She brushed his cheek with her lips in the dark, she took his hand, she kissed his knuckles, and he suddenly thought: after all, why not? Tonight? Tonight.
>
> He enjoyed her impatience, the fool permitted himself to be stirred by it, the cretin whispered, prolonging the free, new, apricot fire of anticipation:
>
> "If you're a good girl we'll have drinks in my sitting room at midnight." (*A* 390)

This promise of a midnight assignation is made while they are watching the opening scenes of a movie in which Ada plays a minor role. Ada's unexpected appearance in the film unmoors Van and, "being upset beyond measure," he utters his "humorous bad-sailor excuse" to the Robinsons and "leave[s] the cinema hall to its dark lurching" (392).

Van describes the events that follow in a misleading and self-serving light. Upon returning to his cabin, he masturbates twice "for the sake of safety" (393) and begins to regain his composure: "He prided himself on his *willpower*. He welcomed the dull pain in his drained root" (393; emphasis added). When Lucette calls him on the telephone to take him up on his promise of drinks at midnight, he considers the lie that he utters—"*Ya ne odin* (I'm not alone)"—to be "morally right" even as he blames himself, "as a gentleman and an artist," for not finding a lie that might have been less "trite and cruel" (393–94).

Van fails to acknowledge here what Gawain is honest enough to admit about his own moral failure when he rebukes himself for "*the faut and the fayntyse of the flesche crabbed* [the corruption and frailty of the perverse flesh]" (*SGGK* line 2435) that led him to accept the girdle. For the "willpower" that Van invokes as a measure of his hard-won self-mastery is a red herring, a distraction from the fact that his actions are—as Kant would say—heteronomously determined. For Van's rejection of Lucette's offer of sexual intercourse when she telephones him is no assertion of agency, but its most abject denial. He refers to his second act of masturbation as a "disgusting but necessary act" that he must perform for "the sake of safety" (*A* 393). Yet this precaution can only be dubbed a *necessity* if Van cannot trust himself to exercise self-restraint in the presence of temptation. He masturbates precisely because he cannot trust himself to do what is right.

Moreover, Van's rejection of Lucette on the telephone qualifies as being "morally right" only in a hopelessly incidental way. His success in keeping Lucette "away from his bed" (393) betrays all the values that Putter lists as convening under the medieval conception of *courtoisie*: an etiquette of hospitality (he withdraws an invitation that he extended earlier), good manners (he utters a lie that he himself considers to be "trite and cruel"), a respect for contracts (he breaks his promise to spend the evening with her), self-restraint (he masturbates twice), and self-awareness (he refuses to acknowledge that his conduct is not "morally right" but morally abject) (*FAR* 8). Lucette's interruption of her own plans for the sake of extending courtesy to the Robinsons is the antithesis of Van's refusal to interrupt his sleep for the sake of showing her courtesy. To have shown her courtesy, Van would have needed to talk to her, and such talk would have taken a long time and been inconvenient given his somnolent state. It certainly could not have been accomplished by the three short Russian words "*Ya ne odin*."

Van's most poignant betrayal of Lucette during this fateful telephone conversation has to do with *trawthe*. Van fails to honor his pledged word; in doing this, he is like Gawain, who also violates the moral ideal of *trawthe* when he hides the green girdle that, according to the rules of the exchange-of-winnings game, belongs to Bertilak. The particularity of the lie that Van tells Lucette acts as a double betrayal of *trawthe*. First, he lies to her that he has company at a time when he is, in fact, alone. Second, the lie leads her to believe that he has lied to her earlier that afternoon and thus profaned the day that she had begged him to preserve as "sacred" (*A* 386).

When Lucette accuses Van earlier that day of lying about the so-called Miss Condor ("You deceived me, Van. It is, it *is* one of your gruesome girls!"), Van gives his pledged word (his *trawthe*) that he is not deceiving her: "I swear," he says, "that she's a perfect stranger. I wouldn't deceive you" (386). Lucette mistrusts Van even though he is telling the truth about Miss Condor: "You deceived me many, many times when I was a little girl. If you're doing it now *tu sais que j'en vais mourir*" (386). To Van's reminder that only recently she had promised him a harem, Lucette replies: "Not today, not today! Today is sacred" (386). Van's lie that he is "not alone" naturally convinces Lucette that he was lying that afternoon and that he cannot invite her to his cabin, as he promised, because he is busy entertaining Miss Condor. This sequence of reported events must also give Van significant pain because his deception cannot be abstracted from the fulfillment of Lucette's threat, however figuratively that threat is articulated, to die (*"j'en vais mourir"*) should Van deceive her again.

Van cannot ignore the tragic irony of his deception: the fabricated betrayal in which he implicates himself during the telephone call renders suspect all his other statements to Lucette, including his promise that he would not conceal from her his involvement with other lovers on board. But for Lucette, this is another example of the countless deceptions that Van and Ada inflicted upon her when she was a little girl. The betrayals that Lucette recalls so vividly and which Van guiltily associates with Kant lead her to interpret a fictitious betrayal as genuine.

Van's violation of the values comprised by the moral ideal of *trawthe* is the first of his two moral failures that concern Lucette. The second has less to do with moral principles than with words. Like the chatelaine who tells Gawain that "true love" is the most reliable spur to morally excellent deeds, Van and Ada see their lack of love for Lucette to be the determining factor in their own moral failures toward her. In his letter to Ada and her husband in the aftermath of the tragedy, Van insists that only "true love" could have prevented Lucette's suicide:

> As a psychologist, I know the unsoundness of speculations as to whether Ophelia would not have drowned herself after all, without the help of a treacherous sliver, even if she had married her Voltemand. Impersonally I believe she would have died in her bed, gray and serene, had V. loved her; but since he did not really love the wretched little virgin, and since no amount of carnal tenderness could or can pass for true love, and since, above all, the fatal Andalusian wench who had come, I repeat, into the picture, was unforgettable, I am bound to arrive, dear Ada and dear Andrey, at the conclusion

> that whatever the miserable man could have thought up, she would have *pokonchila s soboy* ("put an end to herself") all the same. (*A* 398)

Ada, too, makes love the missing ingredient in their relationship with Lucette:

> Oh, Van, oh Van, we did not love her enough. *That's* whom you should have married, the one sitting feet up, in ballerina black, on the stone balustrade, and then everything would have been all right—I would have stayed with you both in Ardis Hall, and instead of that happiness, handed out gratis, instead of all that we *teased* her to death! (*A* 466; emphasis in original)

By referring to their conduct as "teasing," Ada both miniaturizes their cruelty *and* touches upon the real measure of their moral failures in relation to Lucette.

Van's and Ada's separate claims that a lack of love was ultimately responsible for Lucette's fate make her survival dependent upon an emotion beyond the self's authority. As such, it exonerates them of culpability in the eyes of those who believe that responsibility is inseparable from agency. They also deflect attention from the moral transgression for which they can rightfully be held accountable and which Kant placed at the center of his practical ethics: respect. Unlike love (a heteronomous feeling which "no amount of carnal tenderness" can replicate), respect can be bestowed freely and placed under the will's command.

As in the case of Gawain's temptations at the hands of the chatelaine, the moral predicament showcased in Nabokov's fiction is frequently not about love or sex, but about words. Gawain is the rightful representative of the moral ideals that convene under the medieval conception of courtesy because his words fit the occasion. But as Thomas L. Wright reminds us, this poem about words is also, by extension, about "words that go unspoken."[12] The same can be said about Nabokov's most disquieting works: they are less about love or sex than about the words that get deployed to describe love or sex, or the silences that take their place. Sebastian's moral failure is his silent treatment of Clare at a time when he owes her a wordy explanation. Humbert employs a surfeit of fancy words to turn a story of rape and child abuse into a beguiling romance. John and Sibyl Shade fail to find the right words to make their daughter feel at home in the world, and Van and Ada do not find the right words to make Lucette find a home in theirs.

Unlike Gawain, who summons a multitude of words to extricate himself honorably from the chatelaine's temptations, Van utters a mere three words to Lucette when she calls him on the telephone. He immediately realizes that these three short words are incompatible with his self-image of a "gentleman" and "artist." Lucette, of course, had hoped for *love* instead of *words*, but, in the absence of love, she might have settled for the kinds of words that make the Lady of Hautdesert return to Gawain's chamber night after night until his departure. Van assures us that Lucette had already made up her mind on the very first night of their journey together to kill herself if her seduction were to fail, but his "trite and cruel" words make it impossible to know whether she would have done so. Gawain's patient and sensitive words to the chatelaine remind us that Van had the option of giving Lucette welcome. Though courtesy is too fragile and inconsequential to give someone a reason to live, it nonetheless holds out the promise of delaying—perhaps even indefinitely—someone's decision to die.

MASCODAGAMA AND THE GREEN KNIGHT

Van's guilt regarding Lucette conjures up the image of Kant's green eye because Van agrees with Kant that free will can rise above the laws of nature and the conventions of culture. His work as the variety artist "Mascodagama" derives its magical thrill "from overcoming gravity" and from "performing organically what his figures of speech were to perform later in life—acrobatic wonders that had never been expected from them and which frightened children" (*A* 148). Yet on the night of Lucette's suicide, his words fail to perform acrobatic wonders; indeed, he worries that their triteness and cruelty may have played a role in his half-sister's death.

The *Gawain*-poet is likely to have agreed with Van's identification of the literary arts with music-hall entertainments. Defined as behavior proper to court life, courtesy found its natural expression in jousting, dancing, and singing. This is how Arthur's courtiers amuse themselves before the Green Knight rudely interrupts their Christmas revels (*SGGK* lines 40–49). The spectacle that follows is both horror and entertainment: Gawain severs the Green Knight's head, the head flies off, and the Green Knight picks up his head by its hair as the head utters its parting instructions to Gawain.

Mascodagama's variety act bears an uncanny resemblance to this particular scene. Like the Green Knight (*SGGK* line 137), Mascodagama is alarmingly tall: Van describes him as an "unpleasant colossus" who measured "fully eight feet." Also like the Green Knight, he sports a "heavily bearded face." The performance itself bears a remarkable resemblance to the Green Knight's marvelous decapitation. As soon as Mascodagama "turned over in the air and stood on his head," "he jumped up and down, pogo-stick fashion—and suddenly came apart." When "his real feet kicked off and away the false head with its crumpled cap and bearded mask," the audience gasped before breaking into applause (*A* 147). Mascodagama's "false head" is an echo of the *trick head* that Gawain reminds the Green Knight of sporting when he arrived at Camelot and allowed Gawain to decapitate him ("*Bot thagh my hede falle on the stones, / I con not hit restore* [Though if my head should fall / I cannot put it back]"; *SGGK* lines 2282–83).

Van feels nothing but nostalgia for this thrilling period of his youth. At the same time, however, he feels ashamed for having offended his dancing partner Rita by asking her "for an assignation." Bearing "an odd resemblance to Lucette as she was to look ten years later," Rita "indignantly refused, saying she adored her husband (the make-up fellow) and loathed England" (*A* 149). Like the moral philosophy of Kant and the *romans courtois* Nabokov studied at Cambridge, Nabokov's fictional worlds construct a sense of what is done and what is not done. A variety act—even if predicated on a freak decapitation and even if it "frightened children" (*A* 148)—is morally acceptable because it is artistic make-believe and, like the ritual Christmas festivities at Camelot, is part of civilized life. But asking a married woman for an assignation tears at the fabric of civilization as readily as a trite and cruel rejection of a young woman's offer of love.

Perhaps Rita reminds Van of the grown-up Lucette because he offends both of them with his inappropriate words. When he writes his family chronicle, he recalls that "ugly dark words" used to scare young Lucette (*A* 170); when he records the night of her suicide, he recalls the "trite and cruel" words that are so hopelessly entangled in her death. As Putter observes, commentators on the *roman courtois* have long noted a correlation between courtesy's ritual ceremonies and the rhetorical extravagances used by medieval romancers to tell their stories. Chrétien's and the *Gawain*-poet's descriptions of sumptuous meals and rich attire were understood to be analogous to the lavishly performed ceremonies of hospitality that fictional hosts performed for their guests (*FAR* 54–55). By contrast, descriptions of inferior meals or dress were deemed unworthy of the time spent to describe them. This identifies the medieval artist's vocation with courtesy itself. Merrill applied this insight to Proust, but it also applies to Nabokov. Van's recognition that "a gentleman and an artist" must do better than offer a "lump of words" to a young woman in love expresses the same insight.

It seems appropriate that a literary craftsman as consummate as Nabokov should consider courtesy as a synthesis and distillation of the moral and the aesthetic, for as Van astutely observes, "figures of speech" are capable of performing "acrobatic wonders" (*A* 148). But on the night of Lucette's suicide, Van's speech is fatally inert. It fails to perform any wonders because Van allows himself to be engulfed by memories of Ada and the lassitude that follows the two acts of masturbation that help him resist Lucette's efforts to seduce him. Van's failure as "gentleman" and "artist" in this scene suggests that incest and masturbation serve as metaphors for a life turned inward. Van and Ada's incestuous love stands in for the desire to be left alone and undisturbed by others. The man who invented Van and Ada understood this desire all too well: as he says in an interview from 1962, "My pleasures are the most intense known to man: writing and butterfly hunting" (*SO* 3). But he also knew, as *Speak, Memory* attests, that such private pleasures could interfere with social obligations. He confesses with distressed lucidity that his butterfly-hunting expeditions often involved complicated stratagems to "shake[] off all pursuers" (*SM* 471). The itch to go butterfly hunting, for instance, led his younger self to violate his duties as host to a bereaved and impoverished friend, a memory that still caused him shame at the time he wrote *Speak, Memory* (*SM* 467). But even when less egregious, his butterfly collecting elicited acid remarks from the unsympathetic: he was often chastised, he recalls, for "spoiling everybody's pleasure" (*SM* 470). Kant's judgmental eye hovers over Van's family chronicle because Nabokov subscribed to Kant's insight that *what is* and *what ought to be* are morally distinct matters and that the latter ought to trump the former.

Just as the Green Knight's disruption of the Christmas revels at Camelot sets in motion *Gawain*'s plot, Lucette's disruption of Van and Ada's incestuous idyll spurs *Ada*'s plotline. In the case of Gawain, the Green Knight serves as a reminder that the moral life must be ventured outside the walls of an uncle's comfortable court. In the case of Van and Ada, the lesson is a version of the same: life is not an incestuous affair, but a relational one. Van and Ada yearn for solitude and seclusion, but they discover that living with others is an ineluctable existential condition. Reading *Ada* through the lens of *Sir Gawain* helps us see why Nabokov portrays incest as a species of inhospitality. The analogy is an apt one: as Julian Pitt-Rivers reminds us, hospitality is a universal law on a par with other laws that draw their universality from social necessity.[13] Incest is the supreme example of such a universal prohibition.

The correlation between incest and inhospitality established in *Ada* serves as an intriguing commentary to Nabokov's early masterpiece *Invitation to a Beheading*. Whereas the earlier work accentuates the right of Cincinnatus to live among "beings akin to him" (*IB* 223), *Ada* places the moral accent on living with those who do not share our gifts, interests, and values. These *others* are—significantly—figured not as *kin* (as they are in *Invitation* and in Van and Ada's incestuous relationship) but as *half*-kin (as Lucette is to Van and Ada) and as mere acquaintances (as Rita is to Van or the Robinsons are to Van and Lucette). Van, Ada, and Lucette's complicated triangular relationship suggests that it is natural and effortless to love those who resemble us (as Van and Ada preternaturally resemble each other) and to feel the presence of those who do not (such as Lucette) as a moral burden. But as Nabokov knew from the medieval literature he studied at Cambridge, it is a *moral duty* to be courteous to those one does not love and an *art* to pretend delight in its performance.

Notes

INTRODUCTION

Epigraph: Immanuel Kant, *Groundwork of The Metaphysics of Morals*, 4:401.

1. Pascal, *Pensées*, 472.

2. Nabokov, *The Original of Laura*, 155.

3. Panofsky, *Meaning in the Visual Arts*, 1. The original story appears in Wasianski, *Immanuel Kant in seinen letzten Lebensjahren*, 298. It is repeated in Stuckenberg, *The Life of Immanuel Kant*, 443, and (in abridged form) in Kuehn, *Kant: A Biography*, 422.

4. A number of readers and scholars have noted, in passing, the "Kantian" dimension of Nabokov's ethics. In her landmark review of *Pale Fire*, Mary McCarthy notes that Nabokov's "practical morality, like Kant's, seeks to reconcile the Enlightenment with universal maxims of conduct held as axioms" ("A Bolt from the Blue," 136). Zoran Kuzmanovich links Kant and Nabokov when he argues that the connection between ethics and aesthetics in Nabokov's personal philosophy emerges from a Kantian imaginative empathetic response ("'Splendid Insincerity,'" 40). Leland de la Durantaye arrives at a similar conclusion by way of Hannah Arendt's famous account in *Eichmann in Jerusalem* of the Nazi war criminal's outraged response to *Lolita*. Turning to Kant's *Critique of the Power of Judgment* (to which Arendt turned herself in an effort to formulate a new moral philosophy on the eve of her death), de la Durantaye highlights Nabokov's insistence that a moral response involves thinking "from the standpoint of somebody else" (*Style Is Matter*, 5, 9–10). Without naming Kant as an influence, Leona Toker deploys Bakhtin's conception of the carnivalesque to align Nabokov with a Kantian privileging of deontological criteria of moral duty over calculations of utilitarian goods (Toker, "'The Dead Are Good Mixers,'" 92–93). Chapter 3 of my *Vladimir Nabokov and the Poetics of Liberalism* offers a Kantian reading of Van and Ada's relations with Lucette. More recently still, Roy Groen dedicates a chapter of his dissertation on Nabokov to Kant, and Tatyana Gershkovich's forthcoming monograph reads Tolstoy's and Nabokov's aesthetics through the lens of Kant's aesthetic philosophy.

5. Smith, *The Theory of Moral Sentiments*, I.iii.1.13–14.

6. Taylor, *Hegel*, 31.

7. Alexandrov, *Nabokov's Otherworld*, 5.

8. Wood, *Kant*, 160.

9. Kuzmanovich anticipates my argument when he notes: "By situating the ethical impulse in our innate abilities to imagine a situation other than the one we find ourselves in, Nabokov is thoroughly Kantian, for in his own ethical theory Kant also uses imagination as the mental eye on the effect that our actions have on others" ("'Splendid Insincerity,'" 40).

10. Scruton, *Kant*, 104.

11. Nabokov identifies himself as "a product" of the Russian Silver Age in a letter to Edmund Wilson dated January 4, 1949 (*DBDV*, 246n11).

12. Poole, "Editor's Introduction," 73.

13. Vladimir Dmitrievich (Vladimir, son of Dmitri) Nabokov will be referred to as "V. D. Nabokov." His son, the writer Vladimir Vladimirovich (Vladimir, son of Vladimir) Nabokov, will be referred to as "Nabokov."

14. Struve, Preface, 9.

15. These words appear in Novgorodtsev's essay "Ethical Idealism in the Philosophy of Law," 305. The essay is collected in *Problemy idealizma* (1902; *Problems of Idealism*), translated into English by Randall A. Poole. *Problemy idealizma* appears in the catalogue of V. D. Nabokov's St. Petersburg library. See cat. no. 2161 in *Sistematicheskii katalog biblioteki Vladimira Dmitrievicha Nabokova* (1904).

16. *Sistematicheskii katalog biblioteki Vladimira Dmitrievicha Nabokova*.

17. For a discussion of Van's allusion to Kant's "cucumicolor iris" during a conversation with Lucette, see this book's epilogue and my *Vladimir Nabokov and the Poetics of Liberalism*, 143–55.

18. Solovyov, "Beauty in Nature," 33–34. Though Solovyov does not mention Kant, he admits that his definition of beauty is closely indebted to "the last great representatives of German philosophy." I am grateful to Randall Poole for bringing Solovyov's writings on aesthetics to my attention. Solovyov's essay was published for the first time in the journal of the Moscow Psychological Society, *Voprosy filosofii i psikhologii*—a major venue for the publication of idealist thought in late imperial Russia.

19. Dragunoiu, *Vladimir Nabokov and the Poetics of Liberalism*, 98–110, 142–85.

20. Rampton, *Vladimir Nabokov*, 43.

21. Rivers, "Proust, Nabokov, and *Ada*," 135.

22. Alter, *Partial Magic*, 180.

23. Foster, "*Bend Sinister*," 35.

24. Rodgers and Sweeney, *Nabokov and the Question of Morality*, 1.

25. Naiman, *Nabokov, Perversely*, 11.

26. Pifer, *Nabokov and the Novel*, iii–iv.

27. Rampton, *Vladimir Nabokov*, 3–30.

28. De la Durantaye, *Style Is Matter*, 21–31.

29. These responses, and others like them, are cited in de la Durantaye, *Style Is Matter*, 22.

30. Stegner, *Escape into Aesthetics*, 134.

31. Wilde, *The Complete Letters of Oscar Wilde*, 505 (my translation).

32. Ovid, *Metamorphoses*, 246.

33. Nietzsche, *Daybreak*, 3.

34. Bloomfield, "*Sir Gawain and the Green Knight*," 140.

35. Bellamy, "*The Faerie Queene* (1596)," 286.

36. Sweeney, "Whether Judgments, Sentences, and Executions Satisfy the Moral Sense in Nabokov," 175.

37. Merrill, *Recitative*, 33.

CHAPTER ONE

An earlier version of this chapter was published as "On Pity and Courtesy in Nabokov's Ethics," in *Nabokov Upside Down*, edited by Brian Boyd and Marijeta Bozovic.

Epigraph: W. B. Yeats, "A Prayer for My Daughter," written in 1919 and published in the collection *Michael Robartes and the Dancer* (Cuala Press, 1921).

1. Deontology (from the Greek *deon*, "duty") is a rule-based ethical theory that judges the morality of an action according to principles of right and wrong rather than by the consideration of consequences.

2. Stegner, *Escape into Aesthetics*, 98.

3. Ibid., 134.

4. Bell, "Introduction," 14; Tadié, *Marcel Proust*, 35.

5. Lewis, *The Allegory of Love*, 351–52.

6. Toker, "'The Dead Are Good Mixers,'" 93.

7. Pete Dean is Jane Dean's cousin. According to Kinbote, "Jane Dean" is the pseudonym that Shade selects for Jane Provost, his former secretary (*PF* 556, 579). It is Jane who makes the arrangements for the blind date between Hazel and Pete.

8. Austen, *Mansfield Park*, 93.

9. Wood, *The Magician's Doubts*, 195.

10. Ibid., 193.

11. Mayhew, *Prodicus the Sophist*, 66–67. The fragment makes its first appearance in Joannes Stobaeus's *Anthologium* (4.20.65) in a section dedicated to Aphrodite and Eros (Mayhew, *Prodicus*, 235–36). It was reprinted as Fragment B7 in H. Diels and W. Kranz's edition of *Die Fragmente der Vorsokratiker*.

12. Erasmus, *Ciceronianus*, 21.
13. Woolf, *Mrs. Dalloway*, 110.

CHAPTER TWO

Epigraph: Nabokov, *SM*, 590.

1. Nabokov, "Youth," 80; *Iunost'*, 55. Marina Minskaya found the poem among Nabokov's papers at the Berg Collection. It has been published both in the Russian original and in an English translation by Polina Liss and Marina Minskaya.

2. Johnson, "Vladimir Nabokov and Rupert Brooke," 191.

3. For a more detailed account of the eulogies that described V. D. Nabokov's chivalric personality, see my *Vladimir Nabokov and the Poetics of Liberalism*, 178–79.

4. The list of works that Nabokov would have read for his Modern and Medieval Languages tripos can be found in the University of Cambridge's *Student's Handbook to the University and Colleges of Cambridge*, 18th edition, 460–61. As Boyd notes, Nabokov elected for the French and Russian sections of the tripos (*VNRY* 170).

5. Ruck, *An Index of Themes and Motifs*, 119n1.

6. For a concordance of such ritual actions in French Arthurian literature, see Ruck, *An Index of Themes and Motifs*, 114–16.

7. *Le Morte d'Arthur* is one of the books that V. finds on Sebastian's shelves when he visits his apartment after his death (*RLSK* 31). It is also one of the two texts (the other is Vasco de Lobeira's *Amadis of Gaul*) from which Nabokov selected passages to distribute to his students in his course on *Don Quixote* (Nabokov, "Appendix," in *Lectures on Don Quixote*, 213–16). Johnson and Gerard de Vries have argued, separately, that Malory's *Le Morte d'Arthur* is an important intertext for Nabokov's fiction (Johnson, "Vladimir Nabokov and Rupert Brooke," 191; de Vries, *Silent Love*, 94–95). In his description of his *débauche à trois* with Ada and Lucette, Van alludes to Acrasia, the witch of Intemperance in the Bower of Bliss of Spenser's *The Faerie Queene* (*A* 335). He makes a second reference to Acrasia when he describes a rock-climbing trip through the Balkans "with crazy little Acrazia" (*A* 442). As Alexey Sklyarenko pointed out to me, Nabokov also mentions Spenser in the commentary to *Eugene Onegin* 2.25.

8. This is Spenser's intention for *The Faerie Queene* as articulated in his famous "Letter to Raleigh." See Spenser, *The Faerie Queene*, 714.

9. Nabokov, "Youth," 81; *Iunost'*, 57.

10. Ibid.

11. Frappier, *Chrétien de Troyes*, 89.

12. Ibid., 90.

13. Bezzola, *Le Sens de l'aventure et de l'amour*, 230; Kay, "Commemoration, Memory, and the Role of the Past," 37.

14. Auerbach, "The Knight Sets Forth," 133.

15. Ibid., 134.

16. Frappier, *Chrétien de Troyes*, 89.

17. Scaglione, *Knights at Court*, 125.

18. Kay, "Commemoration, Memory, and the Role of the Past," 40.

19. Shippey, "The Uses of Chivalry," 245.

20. Ibid., 250.

21. Ibid., 245.

22. Sweeney, "Whether Judgments, Sentences, and Executions," 164.

23. Kuzmanovich, "Suffer the Little Children," 49–57.

24. Rampton, "The Aesthetics of Moral Contradiction," 118.

25. In addition to his dramatic change of heart toward his father after his father's duel, there are other markers that align Sebastian with knighthood. The novel's allusion to "La Belle Dame Sans Merci"—finely discussed by de Vries and Stanislav Shvabrin—reminds us that Sebastian's undoing is a version of the plot described in Keats's ballad. Here, a "knight-at-arms" loses his way in life after a deadly romance with a mysterious faery woman whose business is the seduction and destruction of powerful men. Kings, princes, and warriors lose their sense of purpose in the wake of their encounters with the lady without pity. See de Vries, *Silent Love*, 18–20 ; and Shvabrin, "Vladimir Nabokov's 'La Belle Dame Sans Merci.'"

26. These installments of *Podvig* appeared under the nom de plume that Nabokov used throughout his career as a Russian writer in Europe: Vladimir Sirin. "Sirin" is the name of a fabled bird of paradise in Russian folklore; for an account of Nabokov's arrival at this pen name, see *VNRY* 180.

27. The first scholars to insist that Nabokov's fiction was deeply concerned with moral questions—Boyd, Pifer, Rampton, Toker—were making a tacit argument that Nabokov belonged in the same camp as Dickens and Austen rather than the camp of Beckett and Pynchon. More recently, Nabokov's work has struck scholars by its conspicuous anti-modernity. Wood notes that Nabokov's frequently asserted suspicion of "modern mimesis" is not powered by the vertiginous skepticism that characterizes so much "modern writing," but by "a belief that what lies behind all the obliquity is not more obliquity, but something as irrefutable as distress" ("Modern Mimesis," 216). Samuel Schuman has shown that Nabokov's work from the 1920s is permeated with themes and topoi borrowed from the Christian tradition. As Schuman further notes, these are invoked piously rather than ironically ("Nabokov's God; God's Nabokov," 83). Maxim Shrayer has investigated Nabokov's interest in Jewish religious questions in *The Gift* and *Pnin* ("Jewish Questions in Nabokov's Art and Life," 73–91).

28. Barabtarlo, "By Trial and Terror," 97, 101.

29. Ibid., 93–94.

30. Ibid., 94.

31. Scaglione, *Knights at Court*, 112.

32. Ibid., 117, 120.

33. *Aucassin et Nicolete*, trans. Roger Pensom, 37; *Aucassin et Nicolette: Chantefable du XIIIe siècle*, 10.9–12.

34. Morrison, *The Bluest Eye*, 206.

35. Beckett, *Molloy*, 76.

36. Morrison, *The Bluest Eye*, 206.

37. Tolstoy, *Anna Karenina*, 125.

38. Borodine, *La Femme et l'amour au XIIe siècle*, 14.

39. Dupin, *La Courtoisie au moyen âge*, 93.

40. Ibid., 110, 111.

41. Barabtarlo, *Aerial View*, 215–16.

42. Dupin, *La Courtoisie au moyen âge*, 41.

43. Ruck, *An Index of Themes and Motifs*, 120.

44. Dupin, *La Courtoisie au moyen âge*, 49–51.

45. Ibid., 51.

46. Wood, *The Magician's Doubts*, 163.

47. Hankins, *Source and Meaning in Spenser's Allegory*, 177.

48. Chamberlain, *Radical Spenser*, 106.

49. Elias, *The Civilizing Process*, 62.

50. Dupin dedicates the second chapter of *La Courtoisie au moyen âge* to the antithesis of *courtois* and *vilain*, 14–17.

51. Scaglione, *Knights at Court*, 129.

52. *Aucassin et Nicolete*, trans. Roger Pensom, 61; *Aucassin et Nicolette: Chantefable du XIIIe siècle* 15.1–2.

53. Austen, *Emma*, 174.

54. Rorty, *Contingency, Irony, and Solidarity*, xiv.

55. Shippey, "The Uses of Chivalry," 245.

56. Chamberlain, *Radical Spenser*, 106–9.

57. Woolf, *To the Lighthouse*, 76.

58. Davis, "Contemporary Deontology," 208–9; Taylor, *Sources of the Self*, 83–84.

59. Nagel, *The View from Nowhere*, 176.

60. Morgan, "Spenser's Conception of Courtesy," 20.

61. Lewis, *The Allegory of Love*, 351–52. Lewis borrows the phrase from Edmund Burke's *Reflections on the Revolution in France*.

62. Foucault, "On the Genealogy of Ethics," 264. Foucault's quotation is a loose paraphrase of sections 36–38 of *Nicocles or the Cyprians* (Isocrates, 98–99). This relationship between royal status and virtue is emphasized throughout *Nicocles or the Cyprians* and *To Nicocles*. As Isocrates writes in *To Nicocles*, "In all your actions remember that you are a king, and take care never to do anything which is beneath the dignity of your station" (section 37; Isocrates, 61).

63. Elias, *The Civilizing Process*, 53, 70, 102–3.

64. Baldwin, "A Question of Identity," 94.

65. Ibid.

66. Shapin, *A Social History of Truth*, 109–10.

67. Shippey, "The Uses of Chivalry," 247.

68. Woolf, *To the Lighthouse*, 80.

69. Lewis, *The Allegory of Love*, 351.

70. Morgan, "Spenser's Conception of Courtesy," 24.

71. Naiman, *Nabokov, Perversely*, 9.

72. Wood, "Modern Mimesis," 221.

73. Nabokov, *Zashchita Luzhina*, 463.

74. Proust uses this expression in his dedicatory preface, "À mon ami Willie Heath," to *Les Plaisirs et les jours*. He makes use of it again in a conversation between the Narrator and Elstir in Elstir's studio in *À l'ombre des jeunes filles en fleurs* (*RTP* 2.219; NRF 2.3.137). In the Moncrieff-Kilmartin translation, *élégance morale* is rendered as "moral refinement" (*SLT* 2.605).

75. Nabokov, *Despair*, xiii.

76. Nabokov, *Look at the Harlequins!* 724.

77. Nabokov, interview by Mati Laansoo, 41.

78. Dupin, *La Courtoisie au moyen âge*, 81.

79. Pitt-Rivers, *The Fate of Shechem*, 102.

80. Shapin, *A Social History of Truth*, 110.

81. Ibid.

82. Peltonen, *The Duel in Early Modern England*, 12.

83. Shapin, *A Social History of Truth*, 107–14; Bryson, *From Courtesy to Civility*, 274–75.

84. Shapin, *A Social History of Truth*, 114–19.

85. Nabokov, "Abram Gannibal," 158.

86. Ibid., 154.

87. As noted by de Vries and Priscilla Meyer, Percival's name can be traced to more than one source. De Vries notes that in addition to the allusion to Chrétien's work, Sir Percival Glyde is the protagonist of Wilkie Collins's *The Woman in White* (*Silent Love*, 42). This title is referenced (in the guise of a film) in *Success* (*RLSK* 76). Meyer associates Sebastian's Percival Q with his role in Malory's *Le Morte d'Arthur*, a book that V. finds on Sebastian's bookshelf (*Nabokov and Indeterminacy*, 30). Though all of these allusions are relevant, Nabokov's reading for his tripos would have made him aware that it was Chrétien who made Perceval famous.

CHAPTER THREE

Epigraph: R[obson], *The Court of Civill Courtesie*, fol. C3 (verso).

1. I have cited J. Thomas Shaw's translation of the letter in *The Letters of*

Alexander Pushkin, 820. The first volume of Ishimova's *History of Russia in Tales for Children* appeared in December 1836. For an hour-by-hour account of Pushkin's activities before his fatal duel, see Abramovich, *Predystoriia poslednei dueli Pushkina* [*The Prehistory of Pushkin's Last Duel*], 287–88.

2. Abramovich, *Predystoriia*, 288.

3. Nabokov, "Pushkin, or the Real and the Plausible," 39.

4. Named after the coal miner Aleksey Grigorievich Stakhanov (1906–1977), Stakhanovites were Soviet workers honored by the state for their assiduous efforts to increase production.

5. Nabokov, interview by Mati Laansoo, 41.

6. For the fullest account of these events (including the published correspondence relating to the anticipated duel), see Yuri Leving's "Antipatiia s predystoriei: Nabokovy i Suvoriny v zhizni i v proze" ["An Antipathy with a Prehistory: The Nabokovs and the Suvorins in Life and in Prose"].

7. For a history of the word "honor," see Stewart, *Honor*, 34–47. For a history of the word in the Russian context, see Reyfman, *Ritualized Violence*, 35–40.

8. V. D. Spasovich (1829–1907) was a distinguished criminal lawyer who played a very important role in the development of the "classical" school of Russian criminal law. On Spasovich's formative influence on V. D. Nabokov's professional development, see Dragunoiu, *Vladimir Nabokov and the Poetics of Liberalism*, 104–5. For an account of Utin's duel with Zhokhov, see Reyfman, *Ritualized Violence*, 88–91.

9. Ruck, *An Index of Themes and Motifs*, 119n1.

10. On the collapse of honor, see Stewart, *Honor*, 47–53; and Peter Berger's "On the Obsolescence of the Concept of Honor."

11. Greenberg, *Honor and Slavery*, 74.

12. Ibid.

13. Feldman, "Kantian Ethics," 295; Korsgaard, *Creating the Kingdom of Ends*, 152.

14. In an obituary printed in *Russkaia mysl'* on the occasion of V. D. Nabokov's death, Peter Struve suggested that V. D. Nabokov believed in fate: "Calm, almost cold, and in any case always reserved and frequently skeptical, Nabokov carried in his soul this kind of profound feeling. This was the feeling of fate [*oshchushchenie roka*]" (Struve, "Pamiati Vladimira Dmitrievicha Nabokova," 192–93). In his memoir *V dvukh vekakh* (*Two Centuries*), Joseph Hessen tells a story that bears out Struve's reminiscences. Upon his release from the Smolnyi Institute, where he had been detained by the Bolsheviks, V. D. Nabokov hurried to the Mariinsky Theater to attend a benefit performance for the Literary Fund (he was the president of the organization). In response to his friends' worries about his safety, he replied: "the bullet meant for me has not yet been poured [*Eshche ne otlita pulia, kotoraia dlia menia prednaznachena*]" (Hessen, *V dvukh vekakh*, 381–82). In the narrative arc he lends to his father's life in *Speak, Mem-*

ory, Nabokov pays tribute to the uncanny fact that his father was, in the end, killed by a bullet.

15. LaVaque-Manty, "Dueling for Equality," 722.

16. Nabokov begins his hypothetical reconstruction of these events with a well-known episode in young Pushkin's biography. Rumors that he had been whipped in the tsar's secret chancellery had incensed Pushkin so violently that he issued a challenge to Fyodor Tolstoy, whom he suspected of spreading these rumors. Nicknamed "the American" (*Amerikanets*), Tolstoy was Russia's most notorious *bretteur*, sporting the reputation of having killed eleven men in duels and for approaching his duels with an extreme brutality (Reyfman, *Ritualized Violence*, 76–77; Binyon, *Pushkin*, 94–95). As a result of serendipitous circumstances and judicious interventions by friends, the duel was avoided. But according to Nabokov, the degrading rumors sparked a second challenge, this time by Pushkin to Ryleev who, "in his antigovernmental fervor, repeated the rumor as a fact (e.g. 'The government is now flogging our best poets!')" (Pushkin, *Eugene Onegin*, 2.433). Batovo, Nabokov's paternal grandparents' country estate, belonged at the time to Ryleev's mother. Scholars have found Nabokov's hypothesis that Pushkin fought a duel with Ryleev at Batovo plausible even if not entirely convincing. Lotman refers to it, in a footnote, as a "poetical conjecture" (Binyon, *Pushkin*, 96; Lotman, *Besedy*, 167).

17. The double bind that V. D. Nabokov invokes here by quoting Bazarov is repeated in Thomas Mann's *The Magic Mountain* when Settembrini explains his decision to accept Naphta's challenge to fight in a duel: "Theoretically I disapprove of the duel, I am of a law-abiding temper. In practice, however, it is another matter. There are situations where—quarrels that—in short, I am at this man's service" (698).

18. My English translation borrows heavily from Nabokov's translation of these lines in his annotations to *Eugene Onegin* (3.51).

19. Lermontov, *Polnoe sobranie stikhotvorenii*, 2:7.

20. Both Reyfman and Lotman tell the story of a duel orchestrated by the leaders of the Decembrist conspiracy that turned out to be fatal for both principals: Vladimir Novosil'tsev (an aide-de-camp of Alexander I) and the Decembrist Konstantin Chernov (a respectable nobleman but no social match for his high-placed opponent). The Decembrists turned Chernov's funeral into Russia's first political street protest (Lotman, *Besedy* 167). The poem written by Pushkin's friend Wilhelm Küchelbecker in memory of Chernov became a Decembrist revolutionary manifesto (Reyfman, *Ritualized Violence*, 82–83).

21. Montesquieu, *The Political Theory of Montesquieu*, 194.

22. Herzen, "Neskol'ko zamechanii ob istoricheskom razvitii chesti" ["Some Observations about the Historical Development of Honor"], 163; emphasis in original.

23. Like most of the extant correspondence surrounding the duel, Dan-

zas's letter refers to d'Anthès as "Heeckeren." The name was bequeathed to d'Anthès by his adoptive father, the Dutch ambassador at the Russian court, Baron Heeckeren. After Baron Heeckeren announced that his petition to the king of the Netherlands to adopt d'Anthès had been successful, Georges-Charles d'Anthès took the name of Georges-Charles de Heeckeren d'Anthès. Contemporary accounts also sometimes refer to d'Anthès as "Dantes."

24. Nabokov, "Pushkin, or the Real and the Plausible," 40.

25. By 1937 when Nabokov gave his Paris lecture on Pushkin, he may also have encountered a version of Grossman's claim that Pushkin aimed for a long time in Shcherbinin's account quoted in V. V. Veresaev's 1936 compilation of Pushkin-related documents. Here, Pushkin is said to have aimed for two minutes before firing (Veresaev, *Pushkin v zhizni*, 392).

26. Danzas, "Poslednie dni zhizni i konchina Aleksandra Sergeevicha Pushkina" ["The Last Days in the Life and the Death of Alexander Sergeevich Pushkin"], 404.

27. Zhukovsky, "Pis'mo V. A. Zhukovskogo k S. L. Pushkinu" ["V. A. Zhukovsky's letter to S. L. Pushkin"], 155; Viazemsky, "Pis'mo Kniazia P. A. Viazemskogo k Velikomu Kniaziu Mikhailu Pavlovichu" ["Prince P. A. Viazemsky's letter to Grand Duke Michael Pavlovich"], 226.

28. Simmons, *Pushkin*, 416–17; Vitale, *Pushkin's Button*, 242; Binyon, *Pushkin*, 599. I am deeply grateful to the late Gennady Barabtarlo for his expert guidance in my efforts to separate fact from fiction in these records of Pushkin's last duel.

29. Unlike Pierre, Settembrini does adopt the conventional defensive posture while awaiting Naphta's shot at the end of *The Magic Mountain*: "Herr Settembrini, lifting his face toward the sky, had turned himself somewhat sidewise to his opponent. It was touching to realize that he had heard one should not offer one's breast full face to an opponent's fire; and that he was acting according to the regulations" (Mann, 705). Although Nabokov was no fan of Mann and there is no evidence that he had read *The Magic Mountain* (*Der Zauberberg*, 1924) before he gave his lecture on Pushkin, it is impossible to believe that he would make the same error as Naphta, who—untutored in "the regulations" of dueling—calls Settembrini a "coward" for adopting the conventional defensive stance (705).

30. These descriptors are Nabokov's. The Russian version of Boyd's biography gives us the actual modifiers used by Nabokov: "*volosatyi, obez'ianopodobnyi* [hirsute, ape-like]" (Boyd, *Vladimir Nabokov: Russkie gody*, 319).

31. Hessen, *Gody izgnaniia* [*The Years of Exile*], 134–35.

32. Nabokov, *Poems and Problems*, 66–67. The verse omitted in the English translation of the poem ("*chto ne sluzhu ia nikomu* [because I serve no one]") underscores the incompatibility of honor and servitude.

33. Nabokov, "Youth," 66; *Iunost'*, 27. I depart here slightly from Polina Liss

and Marina Minskaya's translation in order to capture Nabokov's archaic locutions.

34. "Delia," one of several monikers for a poetic, often abstract woman, figures in three poems ("Bezverie," "K Delii," "Delia") written by Pushkin while he was a student at the Imperial Lyceum at Tsarskoe Selo (Pushkin, *Polnoe sobranie sochinenii*, volume 1, 250–53, 275, 276). "Boldino's sacred leaf fall" alludes to the famous "Boldino autumn"—that is, the three months of extraordinary productivity Pushkin spent in 1830 at his country estate owing to a sanitary cordon set in place to prevent the spread of cholera. During this period of enforced seclusion, Pushkin completed *Eugene Onegin* and a number of other masterpieces.

CHAPTER FOUR

Epigraph: Marie-Luce Chênerie, *Le Chevalier errant dans les romans arthuriens en vers des XIIe et XIIIe siècles*.

1. Binyon, *Pushkin*, 4–6.
2. Ibid., 6.
3. In 1827, Pushkin completed six chapters and began a seventh on the subject of Gannibal. This historical romance was published posthumously as *Arap Petra Velikhogo* (1837; *The Blackamoor of Peter the Great*).
4. See I. Levidova, "Ira Aldridge's Performances in Russia as Reviewed in the Russian Press," 582–89.
5. Quoted in Lindfors, *Ira Aldridge,* 111; Zotov, "Petersburg Chronicle," 1478.
6. Quoted in Smith, "Ira Aldridge (1860)," 46n3.
7. Quoted in Lindfors, *Ira Aldridge,* 106; Panaev, "Petersburg Life," 257.
8. Pitt-Rivers, *The Fate of Shechem*, 107.
9. Dupin, *La Courtoisie au moyen âge*, 26.
10. Pitt-Rivers, *The Fate of Shechem*, 101–2; Putter, *French Arthurian Romance,* 84; Chênerie, *Le Chevalier errant*, 505–6.
11. Chênerie, *Le Chevalier errant*, 506.
12. Naiman, *Nabokov, Perversely*, 51.
13. Blackwell, "Nabokov's Fugitive Sense," 20.
14. Ibid., 21.
15. Ibid., 16; Nabokov, *Nabokov's Butterflies,* 302.
16. Nabokov, "Notes on Neotropical Plebejinae," 3.
17. Blackwell, "Nabokov's Fugitive Sense," 21.
18. Strandberg, "Nabokov and the 'Prism of Art,'" 189.
19. Meyer, "Nabokov's Short Fiction," 131.
20. Shakespeare makes no mention of the color of Cassio's hair, but the color of d'Anthès's hair played an important role in the story of Pushkin's last duel. Nabokov's fascination with Pushkin's obsession with fate would have made

him appreciate the uncanny correspondence between the circumstances surrounding Pushkin's death and an early prophetic warning that was a well-known detail in Pushkin's biography. As reported by several of Pushkin's close friends and acquaintances, a German fortuneteller predicted that Pushkin would enjoy a long life and great fame if only he did not die in his thirty-seventh year as a result of "a white horse, or a white head, or a white man" (qtd. in Sobolevsky, "Mysterious Omens in the Life of Pushkin," 117). Sobolevsky observes that Pushkin frequently talked about this prophecy and even altered his movements in order to avoid its fulfillment (ibid., 114–19). As Serena Vitale notes, Pushkin must have lingered over this prophecy with particular anxiety as he prepared to fight a duel with a blond-haired man (*belokuryi*, or "white-haired" in Russian) who often sported the white-dress uniform of the Chevalier Guards (Vitale, *Pushkin's Button*, 232–33). In making his Cassio blond-haired, Nabokov invokes this widely circulated omen in Pushkin's biography.

21. Rampton, "Jealously Guarded Secrets," 80.

22. Maddox, *Nabokov's Novels*, 8; Barabtarlo, *Aerial View*, 87.

23. Nabokov, "On a Book Entitled Lolita," 295.

24. McCarthy, "A Bolt from the Blue," 135.

25. Dolinin, "*The Gift*," 155.

26. Diment, "Nabokov's Biographical Impulse," 171.

27. Baldwin, "A Question of Identity," 94.

28. Nussbaum, "Kant and Cosmopolitanism," 31.

29. Pushkin continued to admire Mickiewicz long after they parted in May 1829, but he fiercely opposed Mickiewicz's advocacy of Polish independence. For an account of Pushkin's response to Mickiewicz's nationalist writings, see Binyon, *Pushkin*, 420–21.

30. Emerson, *The Cambridge Introduction to Russian Literature*, 1.

31. Trousdale, "'International Fraternity,'" 99, 100.

32. Ibid., 99–100.

33. Rivers, "Proust, Nabokov, and *Ada*," 135.

34. Auerbach, "The Philology of World Literature," 265. Auerbach's English translation is taken from *The Didascalicon of Hugh of St. Victor*, 101. The Latin original reads as follows: "*Delicatus ille est adhuc cui patria dulcis est. Fortis autem jam cui omne solum patria est, perfectus vero cui mundus totus exsilium est*" (Hugonis, *Opera Omnia* 3.20.778B). A more literal translation of Hugh's final clause is especially relevant to Nabokov's particular case: "he is perfect to whom the entire world is a place of exile."

35. Boyd, *Vladimir Nabokov: The Russian Years,* 271–72; Boyd, *Vladimir Nabokov: Russkie gody*, 319.

36. Strandberg, "Nabokov and the 'Prism of Art,'" 197.

37. This conception of race as a *fugitive* taxonomic category harmonizes with Leonid Livak's claims about Nabokov's efforts to avoid clichés when represent-

ing Jewish characters in his fiction. Livak contends that like other contemporary Russian writers, Nabokov searched for ways "to normalise Jewish personages" in order to eschew not only repellent Judeophobe methods of representation, but also their "patronizing, saccharine" Judeophile opposites (Livak, "Jewishness as Literary Device," 228).

38. Cavell's debt to Kant's formulation of reason's paradox is most comprehensively elaborated in *The Claim of Reason*.

39. Nabokov, interview by George Feifer, 22.

40. Markell, *Bound by Recognition*, 34.

41. Macarthur, "Living Our Skepticism of Others through Film," 123.

42. Blackwell, "Nabokov's Fugitive Sense," 22.

43. Brontë, *Wuthering Heights*, 122.

44. Waldron, "What Is Cosmopolitan?" 166.

CHAPTER FIVE

Epigraphs: Vasily Botkin to Ivan Turgenev, July 10, 1855, in *V. P. Botkin i I. S. Turgenev; Neizdannaia perepiska*, 62; and Austen, *Emma*.

1. Genereux, "The Crisis in Russian Literary Criticism," 127–28, 132.

2. Ibid., 126.

3. This is the connection stressed by de Vries in his "Nabokov's *Pale Fire*, Pushkin, Belkin, Botkin and Kinbote." De Vries cites George Genereux's detailed account of Botkin's influence as a critic on *The Contemporary* after Belinsky's death in 1848. This influence began to wane after 1854 when Chernyshevsky joined the staff of the criticism department, and came to an end after 1856 when Chernyshevsky became the acting editor of *The Contemporary* (Genereux, "The Crisis in Russian Literary Criticism," 124, 138). Shvabrin speculates that Fet was "Tiutchev's close rival for third place in Nabokov's pantheon of Russia's greatest lyric poets" (Shvabrin, *Between Rhyme and Reason*, 255).

4. Botkin, "A. A. Fet," trans. Genereux, 39–41, 43.

5. Ibid., 33.

6. Ibid., 50–51; Botkin, "A. A. Fet," in vol. 2 of *Sochineniia Vasiliia Petrovicha Botkina*, 388.

7. De Vries, "Nabokov's *Pale Fire*, Pushkin, Belkin, Botkin and Kinbote," 110–11.

8. Boyd speculates that Nabokov returned to work on Fyodor's biography of Chernyshevsky between the first draft and the first revision of *Invitation* (*Vladimir Nabokov: Russian Years*, 408).

9. Boyd, *Vladimir Nabokov: The Russian Years*, 416; Dolinin, "*The Gift*," 136–37.

10. Paperno, "How Nabokov's *The Gift* Is Made," 310.

11. Ibid., 311.

12. Tolstoy's "Sevastopol in May" was first published in significantly abridged form under the title "Noch' vesnoiu 1855 goda v Sevastopole" in the September issue of *The Contemporary*.

13. Tolstoy, *Sevastopol*, 122; *PSS* 4:59.

14. Among the first readers of *Pale Fire* to argue that the novel is an exercise in self-parody were Clarence Brown, "Nabokov's Pushkin and Nabokov's Nabokov," 203–8; Anthony Burgess, "Pushkin and Kinbote," review of *Eugene Onegin*; and John O. Lyons, "*Pale Fire* and the Fine Art of Annotation."

15. Alladaye, *Darker Shades*, 25.

16. Alter, *Partial Magic*, 215.

17. Haegert, "The Author as Reader as Nabokov," 422.

18. Couturier, "Nabokov's *Pale Fire*," 68.

19. Mary McCarthy called it "a Jack-in-the box, a Fabergé gem, a clockwork toy, a chess problem, an infernal machine, a trap to catch reviewers, a cat-and-mouse game, a do-it-yourself novel" ("A Bolt from the Blue," 124). Alladaye calls it "a critical hall of mirrors" (*Darker Shades*, 42), and James Ramey refers to it as "a funhouse full of mirrors, full of deceptions, just like nature" ("Parasitism and *Pale Fire*'s Camouflage," 192).

20. Boyd, *Stalking Nabokov*, 230, 231.

21. Alter, *Partial Magic*, 193, 212.

22. Tolstoy, *Tolstoy's Letters*, 1.142.

23. I am grateful to Tatyana Gershkovich for bringing to my attention Tolstoy's unfinished essay.

24. Locke, *Essay*, 3.10.34.

25. Kant, "On a Supposed Right to Lie," 8:427.

26. Ibsen, *The Wild Duck*, 121–22.

27. Wilde, *The Works*, 834.

28. Thomas L. Carson argues that Kant's views on the morality of lying became less permissive and more absolute between 1784–85 (the time he delivered his lectures on ethics) and 1797 (the year he published *The Metaphysics of Morals* and "On a Supposed Right to Lie for Philanthropic Reasons" (Carson, *Lying and Deception*, 77–79). Carson aims to refute the influential penultimate chapter of Allen Wood's *Kantian Ethics*, in which Wood argues that Kant's scandalous example of the "murderer at the door" in "On a Supposed Right to Lie" misrepresents his own views. According to Wood, Kant's unconditional prohibition against lying is limited to the kind of lie that involves a "declaration (*Aussage, Deklaration*)." In Wood's definition of this Kantian notion, a declaration is only relevant in the context of Kant's *doctrine of right* and, as a result, is limited to lies that violate the juridical duty to tell the truth to those authorized to know it (*Kantian Ethics*, 241). By contrast, an untruthful statement that does not qualify as a "declaration" is merely a "falsification (*falsiloquium*)" and is not prohibited in all cases (240).

29. Naiman, "When Nabokov Writes Badly," 566.

30. Given the prominence of the "Boy Who Cried Wolf" fable in Tolstoy's definition of art, Naiman speculates that Nabokov may have been deliberately engaging Tolstoy in his own invocation of it (ibid.).

31. Rosemary Edmonds translates "*diablement laide*" as "devilishly plain" (*War and Peace,* 1:260).

32. Rampton, *Vladimir Nabokov*, 151.

33. Knapp, "Hazel Ablaze," 106; Petrie, "Moonrise over the Moor," 3.

34. Wood, *The Magician's Doubts*, 194, 195.

35. Ibid., 193.

36. Korsgaard, *Creating the Kingdom of Ends*, 388n1; emphasis in original.

37. Woolf, *Mrs. Dalloway*, 86.

38. Orwin, *Tolstoy's Art and Thought*, 99.

39. I have opted here for Pevear and Volokhonsky's translation because it is significantly closer to the original than Edmonds' "Handsome is, as handsome does." Though Edmonds's variant is more idiomatic and more in line with Rostov's earthy, direct personality, it loses both the chiastic structure of the original and its key insight that people's sympathies affect their perceptions. The meaning of the epigram invoked by Rostov could be summed up as follows: "People love not the person who is truly good/pretty, but they find someone good/pretty because they love the person." In *What Is Art?* Tolstoy dwells at length on the semantic correlation in several European languages between the adjective "good [*khorosh*]" (as an ethical category) and the adjective "beautiful [*krasivyi*]" (as an aesthetic category that is inflected with a moral dimension) (*PSS* 30:38–40).

40. Tolstoy, *Anna Karenina*, 95.

41. See Shoshana Knapp, "Hazel Ablaze: Literary License in Nabokov's *Pale Fire*"; Matthew Roth, "A Small Mad Hope: *Pale Fire*, Hazel Shade, and the Oedipal Disaster"; Eric S. Petrie, "Moonrise over the Moor: Hazel's Death in Nabokov's *Pale Fire*"; and de Vries, "Hazel Shade's 'Pale Spectres' and 'Purple Fires.'"

42. Levine, "The Design of *A Tale of a Tub*," 217.

43. Zunshine, "Alexander Pope's *The Rape of the Lock* and Vladimir Nabokov's *Pale Fire*," 162.

44. Levine, "The Design of *A Tale of a Tub*," 218.

45. Zunshine, "Alexander Pope's *The Rape of the Lock* and Vladimir Nabokov's *Pale Fire*," 165.

46. Ibid., 176; Macdonald, "Eighteenth-Century Optimism as Metafiction in *Pale Fire*," 29.

47. Pope, *An Essay on Man*, 2.154.

48. De Vries, "Nabokov's *Pale Fire*," 110.

49. Ibid., 111–12; Knapp, "Hazel Ablaze," 107; Petrie, "Moonrise over the Moor," 6; Wood, *The Magician's Doubts*, 195.

50. I am referring here to Boyd's reading in *Nabokov's "Pale Fire": The*

Magic of Artistic Discovery in which he overturns the interpretation he had first published in his biography of Nabokov. According to this more recent reading by Boyd, Zembla is a gift bestowed upon Kinbote by Hazel from the otherworld, and Shade influences Kinbote's commentary after his own death.

51. Alladaye, *Darker Shades*, 153–55.

52. Ibid., 153, 155. Having cast Hazel as the author of *Pale Fire*, Alladaye goes on to argue that she is not the only author. Sybil collaborates with her daughter and—together—they create a double-voiced text that comes to resemble "The Vane Sisters" (*Darker Shades*, 171–76).

53. It is puzzling that Shade should have been tormented by such an assumption in the first place since he invites his readers to marvel at the fact that a young woman as beautiful as Sybil found it possible to fall in love with *him*: a young man "uncouth, hysterical," "lame and fat" (*Pale Fire,* lines 271–74, line 129). Shade's lack of faith in a similar good fortune for Hazel is never explained.

54. Tolstoy, *Anna Karenina*, 434.

55. Wood, "Crabby, Prickly, Bitter, Harsh."

56. Woolf, *Diary*, 248.

57. Alter, *Partial Magic*, 199.

58. Wyllie, *Vladimir Nabokov*, 153.

59. Austen, *Emma*, 148.

60. Rivers, "Proust, Nabokov, and *Ada*," 138.

61. Ibid., 140.

62. De la Durantaye, *Style Is Matter*, 162–63.

63. Borodine, *La Femme et l'amour*, 25n2.

64. McCarthy, "A Bolt from the Blue," 126.

65. Johnson, *Worlds in Regression*, 72.

66. Wood, *The Magician's Doubts*, 178.

67. Offord, *Portraits of Early Russian Liberals*, 96–97, 103–5.

68. Ibid., 104–5.

69. Orwin, *Tolstoy's Art and Thought*, 60.

70. Sreznevsky, *Perepiska L. N. Tolstogo s V. P. Botkinym* [*L. N. Tolstoy's Correspondence with V. P. Botkin*], 3–4.

71. As de Vries notes, Nabokov praises Carlyle in his lecture "Pushkin, or the Real and the Plausible" and mentions Carlyle in *Glory*, *Lectures on Literature*, *Eugene Onegin* ("Nabokov's *Pale Fire*, Pushkin, Belkin, Botkin and Kinbote" 111). Given that Jane Carlyle's letters became available to the public as early as 1883, it is possible that Nabokov read them.

72. Carlyle, *Letters and Memorials*, 109–10.

73. Alter, *Partial Magic*, 196.

74. Toker, *Nabokov*, 31; Alter, *Partial Magic*, 197.

CHAPTER SIX

Epigraph: Proust, *SLT* 6.3–4; *RTP* 4.268; NRF 7.2.206.

1. Because Proust's narrator refers to himself as "Marcel" only once in a hypothetical clause, this term of self-reference has been viewed with suspicion. Nonetheless some scholars continue to refer to him as either "the Narrator" or "Marcel" even though most scholars refer to him exclusively as the Narrator. In keeping with Nabokov in his lectures on Proust, I refer to Proust's narrator as "Marcel" throughout this chapter.

2. There is a substantial body of scholarship on Nabokov's relationship to Proust. J. E. Rivers's "Proust, Nabokov, and *Ada*" from 1977 is especially useful: it recounts his interview with Nabokov on the subject of Proust, provides an overview of Nabokov's allusions to Proust from his earliest work, and offers a close analysis of *Ada*'s engagement with Proust's work. David Jones and William Anderson were the first to draw attention to *Lolita*'s many allusions to the *Search*, and Robert Alter and John Burt Foster Jr. agree that Nabokov's aims and sensibility are intimately aligned with those of Proust. In an essay on *Despair*, Timothy L. Parrish claims that Nabokov uses Proust as a medium to assert his mastery over Dostoevsky. Christian Moraru argues that *Speak, Memory* stages a dialogue with Proust's novel by paying homage to the Proustian project of seeking an aesthetic condition that resides outside of time's medium. Roy Groen argues that Nabokov's reading of Proust played a foundational role in influencing the key principles of Nabokov's aesthetics as these are articulated in his fiction and his lectures ("Nabokov in Conversation," 173–217).

3. Swann's chief attribute is his courtesy, but he is also known to deviate from it. In "Un amour de Swann," the reader is informed that there was "an element of caddishness [*une certaine muflerie*]" in Swann's nature that was nonetheless "redeemed by many rare refinements [*rachetée par de rares délicatesses*]" (*SLT* 1:272; *RTP* 1:190; NRF 1.1.261). The most conspicuous example of this caddishness is his solicitation of letters of introduction from friends in order to get invited to places where he could meet the women who catch his amorous interest.

4. Merrill, *Recitative*, 33.

5. I quote here Toker's translation of the passage in her *Nabokov: The Mystery of Literary Structures*, 177–78. The original appears in Nabokov, *Perepiska s sestroi* [*Correspondence with Sister*], 41.

6. Several scholars have argued that *Lolita* is a novel born of the Holocaust. For Susan Mizruchi, *Lolita* is a product of Nabokov's interest in the Nuremberg trials: Humbert's "fascination with scientific experiments, his obsession with recording his actions, and his ongoing effort to transform the transgressive into the conventional" align him with the Nazis tried at Nuremberg (Mizruchi, "*Lolita* in History," 640). Douglas Anderson identifies a complex web of images that implicates Humbert's narrative in "the spectacle of Europe's recently liberated exter-

mination camps" ("Nabokov's Genocidal and Nuclear Holocausts in *Lolita*," 82). In *Nabokov, History, and the Texture of Time*, Will Norman argues that *Lolita* and *Pnin* are products of Nabokov's pained attempts to think through the Holocaust. Norman's understanding of complicity is aligned with Toker's claim that *Lolita* relies upon a "rhetoric of reader entrapment" (Toker, *Nabokov*, 199). Both insights inform my reading of *Lolita* and *Pnin* as novels in which courtesy traps us into becoming complicit with truths and realities that ought to be resisted.

7. I am grateful to Stephen Blackwell for bringing to my attention the link between Cremona and crematoria.

8. We find out at the beginning of the novel that Pnin's lecture in Cremona had been sponsored by the "Cremona Women's Club" (*Pnin* 302).

9. In the introduction to his *Style Is Matter*, de la Durantaye provides a detailed account of *Lolita*'s reception history as a novel that continues to generate both rapture and alarm. On the subject of *Lolita*'s controversial nature as a work that pits ethics against aesthetics, see also Nomi Tamir-Ghez, "The Art of Persuasion in Nabokov's *Lolita*"; and Jacqueline Hamrit, "The Ordeal of Undecidability in *Lolita*."

10. Tadié, *Marcel Proust*, 345.

11. I have quoted here the English version as it appears in Tadié's *Marcel Proust*, 345. The French translation, as quoted by Proust, appears in Proust's review "*Les Éblouissements* par la Comtesse de Noailles," 540.

12. Norman, *Nabokov, History, and the Texture of Time*, 125.

13. Chupin, "Nabokov's Reflections on 'Proust's Prismatic People,'" 30.

14. Nabokov, interview by Andrey Sedykh, 4243.

15. Rivers, "Proust, Nabokov, and *Ada*," 137. As Jane Grayson notes, Nabokov's *Camera Obscura* (1933) contained an extended parody of a second-rate imitator of Proust that Nabokov deleted when he translated the novel into English as *Laughter in the Dark* (Grayson, *Nabokov Translated*, 42). For a detailed account of Nabokov's contradictory claims about his reading of Proust and his attitude toward Proust, see Groen's "Of Words and Worlds," 185–86.

16. Harold Bloom, for instance, claims that Proust is Nabokov's "most daunting precursor" ("Introduction," 2). For Parrish, Nabokov's aesthetic stance is significantly closer to Proust's than to the other three writers whom he identified as masters of twentieth-century literature: Joyce, Kafka, and Biely ("Nabokov, Dostoevsky, Proust," 454).

17. Alter, "Nabokov and Memory," 620; Foster, "Nabokov and Proust," 478. Rivers notes that, unlike Proust, Nabokov sets voluntary and involuntary memory "on equal footing and draws upon them simultaneously in his attempts to recapture the past in art" ("Proust, Nabokov, and *Ada*," 148).

18. Mizruchi, "*Lolita* in History," 631.

19. As Dolinin has noted, *Albertine disparue* remains "one of the most important (and least studied) subtexts of *Lolita* which deserves special discussion"

("Nabokov's Time Doubling," 39n78). Dolinin also points out that Nabokov preserved *Lolita*'s allusions to Proust in his Russian translation of the novel (ibid., 31, 39).

20. Leon, *An Introduction to Marcel Proust*, 219. Nabokov has changed somewhat the quotation he culls from Leon.

21. Trilling, review of *Lolita* in *Encounter*, 94.

22. Shapin, *A Social History of Truth*, 109; Peltonen, *The Duel in Early Modern England*, 4, 5.

23. Pnin's full response to Hagen reads as follows: "Yes, I know him thirty years or more. We are friends, but there is one thing perfectly certain. I will never work under him" (*Pnin* 420). Pnin's assertion loses its contradictory nature if viewed through the lens of the duel. Pnin is saying that though he and Vladimir Vladimirovich are peers ("friends"), he cannot accept a subordinate position from a man who has violated the code of honor that binds them as social equals.

24. Livak, "Jewishness as Literary Device in Nabokov's Fiction," 239.

25. This reconstruction of events anticipates Demon's speedy seduction of Marina after falling in love with her during an Antiterran production of *Eugene Onegin*. Like Vladimir Vladimirovich, Demon is "not *quite* a gentleman in amorous matters" and feels no qualms about making a wager with his orchestra-seat neighbor that he will successfully "possess her between two scenes" (*Ada* 13).

26. Nabokov, *Lectures on Don Quixote*, 51–52.

27. Adorno, "Cultural Criticism and Society," 34.

28. Adorno, *Negative Dialectics*, 362–63.

29. Toker, *Nabokov*, 199; Norman, *Nabokov*, 116.

30. Benjamin, "The Image of Proust," 204; Moraru, "Time, Writing, and Ecstasy," 176.

31. Bersani, *Marcel Proust*, 9.

32. Toker, *Mystery*, 187.

33. Whalen, "'And So the Password Is—?'" 22.

34. Arendt, *Eichmann in Jerusalem*, 49. De la Durantaye begins *Style Is Matter* with a discussion of Arendt's story about Eichmann's response to *Lolita* (1–2, 4–6).

35. For an extended account of such forms of "judicial forgetting," see Lewis Hyde, *A Primer for Forgetting: Getting Past the Past*. Hyde distinguishes between two types of amnesty: "amnesic" and "memorable." The *damnatio memoriae* of the ancient Romans and the distortions of the historical record by the Soviets belong to the former category. South Africa's Truth and Reconciliation Commission belongs to the second category because its grants of amnesty depended upon a full disclosure of the crime. As Hyde elaborates, the mandate for "a public search for truth" makes such amnesties dependent upon memory work (235).

36. Kierkegaard, *A Kierkegaard Anthology*, 27–28.

37. Norman, *Nabokov*, 115.

38. Nicol, "Pnin's History," 199–202; Barabtarlo, *A Phantom of Fact*, 21–23.

39. Shvabrin, *Between Rhyme and Reason*, 261.

40. Ibid., 263.

41. Quoted in Livak, "Jewishness as Literary Device in Nabokov's Fiction," 233.

42. Nussbaum, *Love's Knowledge*, 246–59.

43. Bersani, *Marcel Proust*, 22.

44. Nussbaum, *Love's Knowledge*, 250.

45. Beckett, *Proust*, 66; Wilson, *Axel's Castle*, 162.

46. Wilson, *Axel's Castle*, 156.

47. Shrayer, "Jewish Questions," 85.

48. Milton, *Paradise Lost*, 10.743–45.

49. In *Speak, Memory*, Nabokov admits to having been "something of a bully" towards the "quiet and listless" Sergey. He describes his habit of creeping up behind him and prodding him in the ribs ("a miserable memory" he calls it). He also recalls his reading of Sergey's diary and showing it to his tutor, who in turn showed it to their father (*Speak, Memory*, 580). In *Letters to Véra*, we see that Sergey's private correspondence was violated by his family as a matter of course, no doubt on the grounds of anxiety on his behalf (*Letters to Vera*, 77). By the time Nabokov wrote *Pnin* and determined to have Vladimir Vladimirovich reproduce Pnin's love letter to Liza, Sergey was dead and the feelings of guilt described in *Speak, Memory* had time to ripen. For a definitive account of Sergey's death at the Neuengamme concentration camp, see Dieter Zimmer, "What Happened to Sergey Nabokov."

50. See, for instance, Alladaye, "Geôle, enjôler, enjoliver: Surveiller et (p)unir dans *Lolita*"; Jones, "Dolorès Disparue"; and Ragussis, *Acts of Naming: The Family Plot in Fiction*, 204–14.

51. Just as Odette is repeatedly compared by Swann to Botticelli's Zipporah (from the *Scenes from the Life of Moses* in the Sistine Chapel), Humbert tells us that Dolly resembles "Botticelli's russet Venus—the same soft nose, the same blurred beauty" (*Lolita*, 254). As Olga Voronina has noted, there is a close resemblance between Botticelli's Zipporah and Venus because they share the same type of beauty ("The Tale of Enchanted Hunters," 158). Humbert underscores the resemblance further when he makes reference to Dolly's "Florentine hands" (*Lolita*, 188–89) and "Florentine breasts" (*Lolita*, 258). Given Nabokov's injunction to his students to attend to Swann's habit of seeing "the physical appearance of this or that character in terms of paintings by famous old masters, many of them of the Florentine School" (*Lectures on Literature*, 228), Dolly's Florentine features must have been linked in his own mind to Odette.

EPILOGUE

Epigraph: Garin le Brun, "L'Enseignement."

1. Paris, "Les romans en vers du cycle de la Table ronde," 71, 73.
2. Pons, Introduction, 15.
3. Howard and Zacher, Preface, xii.
4. Bloomfield, "*Sir Gawain and the Green Knight*," 132.
5. Ibid., 142–43; Putter, *French Arthurian Romance*, 4–7.
6. Pons, Introduction, 16; Scaglione, *Knights at Court*, 137.
7. Merrill, *Recitative*, 33.
8. Borodine, *La Femme et l'amour*, 23n2.
9. Spearing, "Gawain's Speeches and the Poetry of 'Cortaysye,'" 179.
10. Loomis, "*Gawain and the Green Knight*," 20.
11. Pons, Introduction, 21.
12. Wright, "*Luf-Talkyng* in *Sir Gawain and the Green Knight*," 85.
13. Pitt-Rivers, *The Fate of Shechem*, 109, 113.

Bibliography

Abramovich, Stella. *Predystoriia poslednei dueli Pushkina* [*The Prehistory of Pushkin's Last Duel*]. St. Petersburg: Rossiiskaia akademiia nauk, 1994.

Adorno, Theodor W. "Cultural Criticism and Society." 1955. In *Prisms*, translated by Samuel and Shierry Weber, 17–34. London: Neville Spearman, 1967.

———. *Negative Dialectics*. 1966. Translated by E. B. Ashton. London: Routledge, 1973.

Alexandrov, Vladimir E. *Nabokov's Otherworld*. Princeton, NJ: Princeton University Press, 1991.

———, ed. *The Garland Companion to Vladimir Nabokov*. New York: Garland, 1995.

Alladaye, René. *The Darker Shades of "Pale Fire": An Investigation into a Literary Mystery*. Paris: Michel Houdiard, 2013.

———. "Geôle, enjôler, enjoliver: Surveiller et (p)unir dans *Lolita*." *Sillages Critiques* 11 (2010). http://journals.openedition.org/sillagescritiques/1682.

Alter, Robert. "Nabokov and Memory." *Partisan Review* 58, no. 4 (1991): 620–29.

———. *Partial Magic: The Novel as a Self-Conscious Genre*. Berkeley: University of California Press, 1975.

Anderson, Douglas. "Nabokov's Genocidal and Nuclear Holocausts in *Lolita*." *Mosaic* 29, no. 2 (1996): 73–90.

Anderson, William. "Time and Memory in Nabokov's *Lolita*." *The Centennial Review* 24 (1980): 360–83.

Appiah, Kwame Anthony. *Cosmopolitanism: Ethics in a World of Strangers*. New York: Norton, 2006.

———. *The Honor Code: How Moral Revolutions Happen*. New York: Norton, 2010.

Arendt, Hannah. *Eichmann in Jerusalem: A Report on the Banality of Evil*. Revised and enlarged edition. New York: Penguin, 1964.

Aucassin et Nicolette: Chantefable du XIIIe siècle. Edited by Mario Roques. 2nd ed. Paris: Honoré Champion, 1962.

Auerbach, Erich. "The Knight Sets Forth." 1946. In *Mimesis: The Representa-*

tion of Reality in Western Literature, translated by Willard R. Trask, 123–42. Princeton, NJ: Princeton University Press, 1991.

———. "The Philology of World Literature." In *Time, History, and Literature: Selected Essays of Erich Auerbach*, edited with an introduction by James I. Porter, translated by Jane O. Newman, 253–65. Princeton, NJ: Princeton University Press, 2014.

Austen, Jane. *Emma*. Edited by James Kinsley, introduction by David Lodge. Oxford: Oxford University Press, 1971.

———. *Mansfield Park*. Introduction by Peter Conrad. New York: Alfred A. Knopf, 1992.

Baldwin, James. "A Question of Identity." 1954. In *Collected Essays*, 91–100. New York: Library of America, 1998.

Barabtarlo, Gennady. *Aerial View: Essays on Nabokov's Art and Metaphysics*. New York: Peter Lang, 1993.

———. "By Trial and Terror." In Rodgers and Sweeney, *Nabokov and the Question of Morality*, 87–108.

———. *Phantom of Fact: A Guide to Nabokov's "Pnin."* Ann Arbor, MI: Ardis, 1989.

Battles, Paul. Introduction to *Sir Gawain and the Green Knight*, edited by Paul Battles, 11–26. Peterborough, ON: Broadview, 2012.

Beckett, Samuel. *Molloy*. Translated by Patrick Bowles in collaboration with the author. New York: Grove, 1955.

———. *Proust, and Three Dialogues with Georges Duthuit*. London: John Calder, 1965.

Bell, William S. Introduction to *Un Amour de Swann*, by Marcel Proust, 1–30. New York: Macmillan, 1965.

Bellamy, Elizabeth Jane. "*The Faerie Queene* (1596)." In *The Oxford Handbook of Edmund Spenser*, edited by Richard A. McCabe, 271–92. Oxford: Oxford University Press, 2010.

Benjamin, Walter. "The Image of Proust." In *Illuminations*, edited by Hannah Arendt, translated by Harry Zohn, 201–16. New York: Schocken, 1969.

Berger, Peter. "On the Obsolescence of the Concept of Honor." In *Revisions: Changing Perspective in Moral Philosophy*, edited by Stanley Hauerwas and Alasdair MacIntyre, 172–81. Notre Dame, IN: University of Notre Dame Press, 1983.

Bersani, Leo. *Marcel Proust: The Fictions of Life and of Art*. 2nd edition. Oxford: Oxford University Press, 2013.

Bezzola, Reto R. *Le Sens de l'aventure et de l'amour: Chrétien de Troyes*. Paris: La Jeune Parque, 1956.

Billacois, François. *Le Duel dans la société française des XVIe–XVIIe siècles*. Paris: École des Hautes Études en Sciences Sociales, 1986.

———. *The Duel: Its Rise and Fall in Early Modern France*. Edited and translated by Trista Selous. New Haven, CT: Yale University Press, 1990. Translation of *Le Duel*, 1986.

Binyon, T. J. *Pushkin: A Biography*. New York: Knopf, 2003.

Blackwell, Stephen. "Nabokov's Fugitive Sense." In Norman and White, *Transitional Nabokov*, 15–29.

Bloom, Harold. Introduction to *Vladimir Nabokov*, edited by Harold Bloom, 1–4. New York: Chelsea House, 1987.

Bloomfield, Morton W. "*Sir Gawain and the Green Knight*: An Appraisal." In *Essays and Explorations: Studies in Ideas, Language, and Literature*, 130–57. Cambridge, MA: Harvard University Press, 1970.

Borodine, Myrrha. *La Femme et l'amour au XIIe siècle d'après les poèmes de Chrétien de Troyes*. 1909. Geneva: Slatkine Reprints, 1967.

Botkin, Vasily. "A. A. Fet." In *Stat'i po literature i iskusstvam*, vol. 2 of *Sochineniia Vasiliia Petrovicha Botkina*, 352–94. St. Petersburg: N.A. Lebedev, 1891. Originally published in *Sovremennik*, January 1857.

———. "A. A. Fet." Translated by George Genereux. *Russian Literature Triquarterly* 17 (1982): 23–60.

Botkin, Vasily, and I. S. Turgenev. *V.P. Botkin i I. S. Turgenev; Neizdannaia perepiska, 1851–1869* [*V. P. Botkin and I. S. Turgenev: Unpublished Correspondence*]. Edited by N. L. Brodskii. Moscow-Leningrad: Academia, 1930.

Bowie, Malcolm. *Proust Among the Stars*. New York: Columbia University Press, 2000.

Boyd, Brian. *Nabokov's "Pale Fire": The Magic of Artistic Discovery*. Princeton, NJ: Princeton University Press, 1999.

———. *Stalking Nabokov: Selected Essays*. New York: Columbia University Press, 2011.

———. *Vladimir Nabokov: The American Years*. Princeton, NJ: Princeton University Press, 1991.

———. *Vladimir Nabokov: The Russian Years*. Princeton, NJ: Princeton University Press, 1990.

———. *Vladimir Nabokov: Russkie gody* [*Vladimir Nabokov: The Russian Years*]. Translated by Galina Lapina. St. Petersburg: Nezavisimaia gazeta/Symposium, 2001.

Brontë, Emily. *Wuthering Heights*. 1847. Edited by David Daiches. London: Penguin, 1985.

Brown, Clarence. "Nabokov's Pushkin and Nabokov's Nabokov." In *Nabokov: The Man and His Work*, edited by L. S. Dembo, 195–208. Madison: University of Wisconsin Press, 1967.

Bryson, Anna. *From Courtesy to Civility: Changing Codes of Conduct in Early Modern England*. Oxford: Oxford University Press, 1998.

Burgess, Anthony. "Pushkin and Kinbote," review of *Eugene Onegin*. *Encounter* 24 (May 1965): 74–78.

Carlyle, Jane Welsh. *Letters and Memorials of Jane Welsh Carlyle*. Vol. 2, prepared for publication by Thomas Carlyle, edited by James Anthony Froude. New York: Scribner, 1883.

Carson, Thomas L. *Lying and Deception: Theory and Practice*. Oxford: Oxford University Press, 2010.

Castiglione, Baldassare. *The Book of the Courtier*. Translated by Thomas Hoby. 1561. Edited by Virginia Cox. London, 1994.

Cavell, Stanley. *Must We Mean What We Say?* Updated edition. Cambridge: Cambridge University Press, 2002.

Chamberlain, Richard. *Radical Spenser: Pastoral, Politics and the New Aestheticism*. Edinburgh: Edinburgh University Press, 2005.

La Chanson de Roland. Translated and edited by Léon Gautier. 5th edition. Tours: Alfred Mame, 1875.

Chênerie, Marie-Luce. *Le Chevalier errant dans les romans arthuriens en vers des XIIe et XIIIe siècles*. Geneva: Librarie Droz, 1986.

Chrétien de Troyes. *Erec et Enide*. In *Romans suivis des "Chansons," avec en appendice, "Philomena,"* edited by Michel Zink, 55–283. Paris: Librairie Générale Française, 1994.

———. *Lancelot, ou Le Chevalier de la charrette*. In *Romans suivis des "Chansons," avec en appendice, "Philomena,"* edited by Michel Zink, 495–704. Paris: Librairie Générale Française, 1994.

———. *Perceval, ou Le conte du Graal*. In *Romans suivis des "Chansons," avec en appendice, "Philomena,"* edited by Michel Zink, 937–1211. Paris: Librairie Générale Française, 1994.

———. *The Story of the Grail (Li Contes del Graal), or Perceval*. Translated by William W. Kibler, edited by Rupert T. Pickens. New York: Garland, 1990.

———. *Yvain, ou Le Chevalier au lion*. In *Romans suivis des "Chansons," avec en appendice, "Philomena,"* edited by Michel Zink, 705–936. Paris: Librairie Générale Française, 1994.

Chupin, Yannicke. "Nabokov's Reflections on 'Proust's Prismatic People.'" In *Vladimir Nabokov's Lectures on Literature: Portraits of the Artist as Reader and Teacher*, edited by Ben Dhooge and Jürgen Pieters, 19–34. Leiden: Brill Rodopi, 2018.

Connolly, Julian W. *Nabokov's Early Fiction: Patterns of Self and Other*. Cambridge: Cambridge University Press, 1992.

Connolly, Julian W., ed. *The Cambridge Companion to Nabokov*. Cambridge: Cambridge University Press, 2005.

———, ed. *Nabokov and His Fiction: New Perspectives*. Cambridge: Cambridge University Press, 1999.

Couturier, Maurice. "Nabokov's *Pale Fire*, or The Purloined Poem." *Revue Française d'Études Américaines* 1 (1976): 55–69.

Danzas, Konstantin K. "Poslednie dni zhizni i konchina Aleksandra Sergeevicha

Pushkina v zapisi A. Ammosova" ["The Last Days in the Life and the Death of Alexander Sergeevich Pushkin as Recorded by A. Ammosov"]. In vol. 2 of *Pushkin v vospominaniakh sovremennikov* [*Pushkin in the Recollections of His Contemporaries*], 395–410. St. Petersburg: Akademicheskii proekt, 1998.

Davis, Nancy. "Contemporary Deontology." In *A Companion to Ethics*, edited by Peter Singer. Oxford: Blackwell, 1993.

de la Durantaye, Leland. *Style Is Matter: The Moral Art of Vladimir Nabokov*. Ithaca, NY: Cornell University Press, 2010.

de Vries, Gerard. "Hazel Shade's 'Pale Spectres' and 'Purple Fires.'" *Nabokov Online Journal* (*NOJ*) 12 (2018). http://www.nabokovonline.com/uploads/2/3/7/7/23779748/6_gerard_de_vries.pdf.

———. "Nabokov's *Pale Fire* and Alexander Pope." In *The Goalkeeper: The Nabokov Almanac*, edited by Yuri Leving, 102–23. Boston: Academic Studies, 2010.

———. "Nabokov's *Pale Fire*, Pushkin, Belkin, Botkin and Kinbote." Edited by B. V. Averin. *Nabokovskii Sbornik* 1 (2011): 104–15.

———. *Silent Love: The Annotation and Interpretation of Nabokov's "The Real Life of Sebastian Knight."* Boston: Academic Studies, 2016.

Diment, Galya. "Nabokov's Biographical Impulse: Art of Writing Lives." In Connolly, *The Cambridge Companion to Nabokov*, 170–84.

———. *Pniniad: Vladimir Nabokov and Marc Szeftel*. Seattle: University of Washington Press, 1997.

Dolinin, Alexander. "*The Gift*." In Alexandrov, *The Garland Companion to Vladimir Nabokov*, 135–69.

———. "Nabokov's Time Doubling: From *The Gift* to *Lolita*." *Nabokov Studies* 2 (1995): 3–40.

Dragunoiu, Dana. *Vladimir Nabokov and the Poetics of Liberalism*. Evanston, IL: Northwestern University Press, 2011.

Duel' Pushkina s Dantesom-Gekkernom: Podlinnoe voenno-sudnoe delo 1837 goda [*Pushkin's Duel with d'Anthès-Heeckeren: The True Account of a Military-Legal Event 1837*]. Moscow: Belyi gorod, 2012.

Dupin, Henri. *La Courtoisie au moyen âge (d'après les textes du XIIe et du XIIIe siècle)*. Paris: A. Picard, 1931.

Elias, Norbert. *The Civilizing Process: The History of Manners*. 1939. Vol. 1, translated by Edmund Jephcott. New York: Urizen Books, 1978.

Emerson, Caryl. *The Cambridge Introduction to Russian Literature*. Cambridge: Cambridge University Press, 2008.

Erasmus, Desiderius. *Ciceronianus; or, A Dialogue on the Best Style of Speaking*. Translated by Izora Scott. New York: Columbia University Press, 1908.

Feldman, Fred. "Kantian Ethics." In *Ethical Theory: Classical and Contemporary Readings*, edited by Louis P. Pojman, 288–301. 2nd edition. Belmont, CA: Wadsworth, 1995.

Foster, John Burt, Jr. "*Bend Sinister.*" In Alexandrov, *The Garland Companion to Vladimir Nabokov*, 25–36.

———. "Nabokov and Proust." In Alexandrov, *The Garland Companion to Vladimir Nabokov*, 472–81.

———. "Nabokov before Proust: The Paradox of Anticipatory Memory." *Slavic and East European Journal* 33, no. 1 (1989): 78–95.

Foucault, Michel. "On the Genealogy of Ethics: An Overview of Work in Progress." In *Ethics: Subjectivity and Truth*, edited by Paul Rabinow, vol. 1 of *Essential Works of Foucault: 1954–1984*, 253–80. New York: New Press, 1997.

Frank, Siggy. *Nabokov's Theatrical Imagination*. Cambridge: Cambridge University Press, 2012.

Frappier, Jean. *Chrétien de Troyes*. Nouvelle édition revue et augmentée, illustrée. Paris: Hatier, 1968.

Garin le Brun. "L'Enseignement." Edited by Carl Appel. *Revue des Langues Romanes* 33 (1889): 403–22.

Genereux, George. "The Crisis in Russian Literary Criticism: 1856—the Decisive Year." *Russian Literature Triquarterly* 17 (1982): 117–40.

Glynn, Michael. *Vladimir Nabokov: Bergsonian and Russian Formalist Influences in His Novels*. New York: Palgrave Macmillan, 2007.

Grayson, Jane. *Nabokov Translated: A Comparison of Nabokov's Russian and English Prose*. Oxford: Oxford University Press, 1977.

Greenberg, Kenneth S. *Honor and Slavery*. Princeton, NJ: Princeton University Press, 1996.

Groen, Roy. "Nabokov in Conversation: A Philosophico-Critical Exploration of the Moral Dimension of His American Works." PhD diss., Radboud University, 2016.

———. "Of Words and Worlds: The Role of Proust's Aesthetics in Nabokov's *Lectures on Literature*." In *Vladimir Nabokov's Lectures on Literature: Portraits of the Artist as Reader and Teacher*, edited by Ben Dhooge and Jürgen Pieters, 185–98. Leiden: Brill Rodopi, 2018.

Grossman, Leonid. *Zapiski d'Arshiaka* [*The Memoirs of d'Archiac*]. 1931. Moscow: Khudozhestvennaia literatura, 1990.

Haegert, John. "The Author as Reader as Nabokov: Text and Pretext in *Pale Fire*." *Texas Studies in Literature and Language* 26, no. 4 (1984): 405–24.

Hamrit, Jacqueline. "The Ordeal of Undecidability in *Lolita*." In *Kaleidoscopic Nabokov: Perspectives françaises*, edited by Lara Delage-Toriel and Monica Manolescu, 85–92. Paris: Michel Houdiard, 2009.

Hankins, John Erskine. *Source and Meaning in Spenser's Allegory: A Study of "The Faerie Queene."* Oxford: Clarendon, 1971.

Herzen, Aleksandr I. "Neskol'ko zamechanii ob istoricheskom razvitii chesti" ["Some Observations about the Historical Development of Honor"]. In vol. 2 of *Sobranie sochinenii v tridtsati tomakh*, 151–76. Moscow: Izdatel'stvo akademii nauk SSSR, 1954.

Hessen [Gessen], Iosif [Joseph] V. *Gody izgnaniia: Zhiznennyi otchet* [*The Years of Exile: An Autobiographical Account*]. Paris: YMCA, 1979.

———. *V dvukh vekakh: Zhiznennyi otchet* [*Two Centuries: An Autobiographical Account*]. Berlin: Speer & Schmidt, 1937.

Hessen [Gessen], Sergey I. "Bor'ba utopii i avtonomii dobra v mirovozzrenii F. M. Dostoevskogo i Vl. Solov'eva" ["The Struggle between Utopia and the Autonomy of the Good in the Worldview of F. M. Dostoevskii and Vl. Soloviev"]. *Sovremennye zapiski* 45–46 (1931): 271–305, 321–51. Reprinted in Sergey Hessen, *Izbrannye sochineniia*, 609–77.

———. *Izbrannye sochineniia*. Edited by Andrzej Walicki and N. Chistiakova. Moscow: ROSSPEN, 1999.

Howard, Donald R., and Christian Zacher. Preface to *Critical Studies of "Sir Gawain and the Green Knight,"* ix–xii. Notre Dame, IN: University of Notre Dame Press, 1968.

Hugh of Saint Victor. *The Didascalicon of Hugh of St. Victor: A Medieval Guide to the Arts*. Translated by Jeremy Taylor. New York: Columbia University Press, 1961.

Hugonis de S. Victore. *Opera Omnia*: *Operum pars tertia, Opuscula mystica*. In vol. 176 of *Patrologia: Cursus Completus*. Paris: J. P. Migne, 1834.

Hyde, Lewis. *A Primer for Forgetting: Getting Past the Past*. New York: Farrar, Straus and Giroux, 2019.

Ibsen, Henrik. *The Wild Duck*. Translated by Eleanor Marx Aveling. Boston: Walter H. Baker, 1890.

Isocrates. *To Demonicus. To Nicocles. Nicocles or the Cyprians. Panegyricus. To Philip. Archidamus*. Translated by George Norlin. Loeb Classical Library 209. Cambridge, MA: Harvard University Press, 1928.

James, Henry. *The Portrait of a Lady*. 1881. Edited with an introduction by Philip Horne. Penguin: London, 2011.

Johnson, D. Barton. "Vladimir Nabokov and Rupert Brooke." In Connolly, *Nabokov and His Fiction: New Perspectives*, 177–96.

———. *Worlds in Regression: Some Novels of Vladimir Nabokov*. Ann Arbor, MI: Ardis, 1985.

Jones, David L. "Dolorès Disparue." *Symposium* 20 (1966): 135–40.

Joyce, James. *A Portrait of the Artist as a Young Man*. Edited with an introduction by Jeri Johnson. Oxford: Oxford University Press, 2000.

———. *Ulysses: The 1922 Text*. Edited with an introduction and notes by Jeri Johnson. Oxford: Oxford University Press, 1993.

Kant, Immanuel. *Anthropology from a Pragmatic Point of View*. Translated by Victor Lyle Dowdell, revised and edited by Hans H. Rudnick. Carbondale: Southern Illinois University Press, 1978.

———. *Critique of the Power of Judgment*. Translated by Paul Guyer and Eric Matthews, edited by Paul Guyer. Cambridge: Cambridge University Press, 2000.

———. *Kant's Gesammelte Schriften*. Edited by the Royal Prussian (later German) Academy of Sciences. Berlin: Georg Reimer, later Walter deGruyter & Co., 1900–.

———. *Groundwork of The Metaphysics of Morals*. 1785. In *Practical Philosophy*, edited and translated by Mary J. Gregor, 37–108. Cambridge: Cambridge University Press, 1996.

———. *Lectures on Ethics*. Edited by Peter Heath and J. B. Schneewind, translated by Peter Heath. Cambridge: Cambridge University Press, 1997.

———. *The Metaphysics of Morals*. 1797. In *Practical Philosophy*, edited and translated by Mary J. Gregor, 363–603. Cambridge: Cambridge University Press, 1996.

———. "On a Supposed Right to Lie from Philanthropy." 1797. In *Practical Philosophy*, edited and translated by Mary J. Gregor, 605–15. Cambridge: Cambridge University Press, 1996.

Karshan, Thomas. *Vladimir Nabokov and the Art of Play*. Oxford: Oxford University Press, 2011.

Kay, Sarah. "Commemoration, Memory, and the Role of the Past in Chrétien de Troyes: Retrospection and Meaning in *Erec et Enide*, *Yvain* and *Perceval*." *Reading Medieval Studies* 17 (1991): 31–50.

Kierkegaard, Søren. *A Kierkegaard Anthology*. Edited by Robert Bretall. Princeton, NJ: Princeton University Press, 1946.

Knapp, Shoshana. "Hazel Ablaze: Literary License in Nabokov's *Pale Fire*." *Essays in Literature* 14, no. 1 (1987): 105–15.

Korsgaard, Christine M. *Creating the Kingdom of Ends*. Cambridge: Cambridge University Press, 1996.

Kuehn, Manfred. *Kant: A Biography*. Cambridge: Cambridge University Press, 2001.

Kuzmanovich, Zoran. "'Splendid Insincerity' as 'Utmost Truthfulness': Nabokov and the Claims of the Real." In *Nabokov's World, Volume 1: The Shape of Nabokov's World*, edited by Jane Grayson, Arnold McMillin, and Priscilla Meyer, 26–46. Basingstoke, UK: Palgrave Macmillan, 2002.

———. "Suffer the Little Children." In *Nabokov at Cornell*, edited by Gavriel Shapiro, 49–57. Ithaca, NY: Cornell University Press, 2003.

LaVaque-Manty, Mika. "Dueling for Equality: Masculine Honor and the Modern Politics of Dignity." *Political Theory* 34, no. 6 (2006): 715–40.

Leon, Derrick. *An Introduction to Marcel Proust: His Life, His Circle and His Work*. London: Routledge and Kegan, 1951.

Lermontov, M. Iu. *Polnoe sobranie stikhotvorenii v dvukh tomakh*. Vol. 2. Leningrad: Sovetskii pisatel', 1989.

Levidova, I. "Ira Aldridge's Performances in Russia as Reviewed in the Russian Press." (In Russian). *Shekspir* (*Shakespeare: A Bibliography*) (1964): 582–89.

Levine, Jay Arnold. "The Design of *A Tale of a Tub* (with a Digression on a Mad Modern Critic)." *ELH* 33, no. 2 (1966): 198–227.

Leving, Yuri. "Antipatiia s predystoriei: Nabokovy i Suvoriny v zhizni i v proze" ["An Antipathy with a Prehistory: The Nabokovs and the Suvorins in Life and Prose"]. *Novoe literaturnoe obozrenie* 96 (2009): 154–90.

Lewis, C. S. *The Allegory of Love: A Study in Medieval Tradition.* Oxford: Oxford University Press, 1936.

Lindfors, Bernth. *Ira Aldridge: The Last Years, 1855–1867.* Rochester, NY: University of Rochester Press, 2015.

Livak, Leonid. "Jewishness as Literary Device in Nabokov's Fiction." In *Vladimir Nabokov in Context*, edited by David M. Bethea and Siggy Frank, 228–39. Cambridge: Cambridge University Press, 2018.

Locke, John. *An Essay Concerning Human Understanding.* Vol. 2, edited with an introduction by John W. Yolton. London: Dent, 1974.

Loomis, Laura Hibbard. "*Gawain and the Green Knight.*" In *Critical Studies of "Sir Gawain and the Green Knight,"* edited by Donald R. Howard and Christian Zacher, 3–23. Notre Dame, IN: University of Notre Dame Press, 1968.

Lotman, Yury M. *Besedy o russkoi kul'ture* [*Conversations about Russian Culture*]. St. Petersburg: Iskusstvo, 1994.

Lyons, John O. "*Pale Fire* and the Fine Art of Annotation." In *Nabokov: The Man and His Work*, edited by L. S. Dembo, 157–64. Madison: University of Wisconsin Press, 1967.

Macarthur, David. "Living Our Skepticism of Others through Film: Remarks in Light of Cavell." *SubStance* 45, no. 3 (2016): 120–36.

Macdonald, D. L. "Eighteenth-Century Optimism as Metafiction in *Pale Fire*." *The Nabokovian* 14 (1985): 26–32.

Maddox, Lucy. *Nabokov's Novels in English.* Athens: University of Georgia Press, 1983.

Mann, Thomas. *The Magic Mountain.* Translated by H. T. Lowe-Porter. New York: Vintage International, 1992.

Manolescu, Monica. *Jeux de mondes: L'Ailleurs chez Vladimir Nabokov.* Bordeaux: Presses Universitaires de Bordeaux, 2010.

Markell, Patchen. *Bound by Recognition.* Princeton, NJ: Princeton University Press, 2003.

Mayhew, Robert. *Prodicus the Sophist: Texts, Translations, and Commentary.* Oxford: Oxford University Press, 2011.

McCarthy, Mary. "A Bolt from the Blue." *New Republic*, June 4, 1962: 21–27. Reprinted in *Nabokov: The Critical Heritage*, edited by Norman Page, 124–36. London: Routledge and Kegan Paul, 1982.

Merrill, James. *Recitative.* Edited with an introduction by J. D. McClatchy. San Francisco: North Point, 1986.

Meyer, Priscilla. *Nabokov and Indeterminacy: The Case of "The Real Life of Sebastian Knight."* Evanston, IL: Northwestern University Press, 2018.

———. "Nabokov's Short Fiction." In Connolly, *The Cambridge Companion to Nabokov*, 119–34.

Milton, John. *Paradise Lost*. Edited by A. W. Verity. Cambridge: Cambridge University Press, 1910.

Mizruchi, Susan. "*Lolita* in History." *American Literature* 75, no. 3 (2003): 629–52.

Montesquieu, Charles Louis de Secondat, Baron de La Brède et de. *The Political Theory of Montesquieu*. Edited by Melvin Richter. Cambridge: Cambridge University Press, 1977.

Moraru, Christian. "Time, Writing, and Ecstasy in *Speak, Memory*: Dramatizing the Proustian Project." *Nabokov Studies* 2 (1995): 173–90.

Morgan, Gerald. "Spenser's Conception of Courtesy and the Design of *The Faerie Queene*." *The Review of English Studies* 32, no. 125 (1981): 17–36.

Morris, Paul D. *Vladimir Nabokov: Poetry and the Lyric Voice*. Toronto: University of Toronto Press, 2010.

Morrison, Toni. *The Bluest Eye*. New York: Penguin, 1994.

Nabokov, V. D. [Vladimir Dmitrievich]. "Duel' i ugolovnyi zakon" ["The Duel and Criminal Law"]. *Pravo* 50 (December 13, 1909): 2729–44; 51 (December 20, 1909): 2833–47.

Nabokov, Vladimir. "Abram Gannibal." In *Notes on Prosody and Abram Gannibal: From the Commentary to the Author's Translation of Pushkin's "Eugene Onegin,"* 107–68. Bollingen Series 72. Princeton, NJ: Princeton University Press, 1964.

———. *Ada, or Ardor: A Family Chronicle*. 1969. In Nabokov, *Vladimir Nabokov: Novels 1969–1974*, 1–485.

———. *Bend Sinister*. 1947. In Nabokov, *Vladimir Nabokov: Novels and Memoirs 1941–1951*, 161–358.

———. *The Defense*. 1930. Translated by Michael Scammell in collaboration with the author. New York: Vintage, 1990.

———. *Despair*. 1936; revised 1965. New York: Vintage, 1989.

———. *The Gift*. 1963. Translated by Michael Scammell with Vladimir Nabokov. New York: Vintage, 1991.

———. *Glory*. Translated by Dmitri Nabokov with Vladimir Nabokov. New York: McGraw-Hill, 1971.

———. Interview by George Feifer. *Saturday Review*, November 27, 1976: 20–26.

———. Interview by Mati Laansoo. *The Nabokov Research Newsletter* 10 (1983): 39–48.

———. Interview by Andrey Sedykh. *Poslednie novosti*, November 3, 1932: 42–43. Reprinted in *Think, Write, Speak: Uncollected Essays, Reviews, Interviews, and Letters to the Editor* by Vladimir Nabokov. 113–14. Edited by Brian Boyd and Anastasia Tolstoy. New York, NY: Knopf, 2019.

———. *Invitation to a Beheading*. 1959. Translated by Dmitri Nabokov with Vladimir Nabokov. New York: Vintage, 1989.

———. *Iunost'*. Edited by Marina Minskaya. St. Petersburg: Renomé, 2016.

———. *King, Queen, Knave*. Translated by Dmitri Nabokov in collaboration with the author. Greenwich, CT: Fawcett, 1968.

———. *Lectures on Don Quixote*. Edited by Fredson Bowers, foreword by Guy Davenport. San Diego, CA: Harvest, Harcourt, Bruccoli Clark, 1983.

———. *Lectures on Literature*. Edited by Fredson Bowers. San Diego, CA: Harvest, Harcourt, Bruccoli Clark, 1980.

———. *Lectures on Russian Literature*. Edited by Fredson Bowers. San Diego, CA: Harvest, Harcourt, Bruccoli Clark, 1981.

———. *Letters to Véra*. Edited and translated by Olga Voronina and Brian Boyd. New York: Alfred A. Knopf, 2015.

———. *Lolita*. 1955. In Nabokov, *Vladimir Nabokov: Novels 1955–1962*, 1–298.

———. *Lolita*. In vol. 2 of *Vladimir Nabokov: Sobranie sochinenii amerikanskogo perioda v piati tomakh* [*Vladimir Nabokov: Collected American Period Works in Five Volumes*], translated by the author, edited by S. B. Iliina and A. K. Kononova, 11–390. St. Petersburg: Symposium, 2000.

———. *Mary*. 1970. Translated by Michael Glenny with Vladimir Nabokov. New York: Vintage, 1989.

———. *Mashen'ka*. In vol. 2 of *Vladimir Nabokov (V. Sirin): Sobranie sochinenii russkogo perioda v piati tomakh: 1926–1930* [*Vladimir Nabokov (V. Sirin): Collected Russian Language Works in Five Volumes, 1926–1930*], edited by M. V. Kozikova, 43–127. St. Petersburg: Symposium, 1999.

———. *Nabokov's Butterflies: Unpublished and Uncollected Writings*. Edited by Brian Boyd and Michael Pyle. Boston: Beacon, 2000.

———. *Nikolai Gogol*. 1944. New York: New Directions, 1961.

———. "Notes on Neotropical Plebejinae (Lycaenidae, Lepidoptera)." *Psyche* 52 (1945): 1–61.

———. "On a Book Entitled *Lolita*." In Nabokov, *Vladimir Nabokov: Novels 1955–1962*, 293–98.

———. *The Original of Laura (Dying Is Fun)*. Edited by Dmitri Nabokov. New York: Alfred A. Knopf, 2008.

———. *Pale Fire*. 1962. In Nabokov, *Vladimir Nabokov: Novels 1955–1962*, 437–667.

———. *Perepiska s sestroi* [*Correspondence with Sister*]. Ann Arbor, MI: Ardis, 1985.

———. *Pnin*. 1957. In Nabokov, *Vladimir Nabokov: Novels 1955–1962*, 299–435.

———. *Poems and Problems*. New York: McGraw-Hill, 1970.

———. "Pushkin, or the Real and the Plausible." Translated by Dmitri Nabokov. *New York Review of Books*, March 31, 1988: 38–42. https://www.nybooks.com/articles/1988/03/31/pushkin-or-the-real-and-the-plausible/. Translation of "Pouchkine ou le vrai et le vraisemblable," *Nouvelle Revue Française*, March 1, 1937: 362–78.

———. *The Real Life of Sebastian Knight*. 1941. In Nabokov, *Vladimir Nabokov: Novels and Memoirs 1941–1951*, 1–160.

———. *Selected Letters, 1940–1977*. Edited by Dmitri Nabokov and Matthew J. Bruccoli. San Diego, CA: Harcourt Brace Jovanovich, 1989.

———. *Speak, Memory: An Autobiography Revisited*. 1967. In Nabokov, *Vladimir Nabokov: Novels and Memoirs, 1941–1951*, 359–635.

———. *The Stories of Vladimir Nabokov*. New York: Vintage International, 1997.

———. *Strong Opinions*. 1973. London: Weidenfeld and Nicolson, 1974.

———. *Vladimir Nabokov: Novels and Memoirs 1941–1951: The Real Life of Sebastian Knight, Bend Sinister, Speak Memory: An Autobiography Revisited*. Edited by Brian Boyd. New York: Library of America, 1996.

———. *Vladimir Nabokov: Novels 1955–1962: Lolita, Pnin, Pale Fire, Lolita: A Screenplay*. Edited by Brian Boyd. New York: Library of America, 1996.

———. *Vladimir Nabokov: Novels 1969–1974: Ada, Transparent Things, Look at the Harlequins!* Edited by Brian Boyd. New York: Library of America, 1996.

———. "Youth." In Nabokov, *Iunost'*. Translated by Polina Liss and Marina Minskaya, 63–81. St. Petersburg: Renomé, 2016.

———. *Zashchita Luzhina*. In vol. 2 of *Vladimir Nabokov (V. Sirin): Sobranie sochinenii russkogo perioda v piati tomakh: 1926–1930* [*Vladimir Nabokov (V. Sirin): Collected Russian-Language Works in Five Volumes, 1926–1930*], edited by M. V. Kozikova, 306–465. St. Petersburg: Symposium, 1999.

Nabokov, Vladimir, and Edmund Wilson. *Dear Bunny, Dear Volodya: The Nabokov-Wilson Letters, 1940–1971*. Revised edition, edited by Simon Karlinsky. Berkeley: University of California Press, 2001.

Nagel, Thomas. *The View from Nowhere*. New York: Oxford University Press, 1986.

Naiman, Eric. *Nabokov, Perversely*. Ithaca, NY: Cornell University Press, 2010.

———. "When Nabokov Writes Badly: Aesthetics and Morality in *Laughter in the Dark*." *The Russian Review* 73 (2014): 550–70.

Nicol, Charles. "Pnin's History." *Novel: A Forum on Fiction* 4, no. 3 (1971): 197–208.

Nietzsche, Friedrich. *Daybreak: Thoughts on the Prejudices of Morality*. Edited by Maudemarie Clair and Brian Leiter, translated by R. J. Hollingdale. Cambridge: Cambridge University Press, 1997.

Norman, Will. *Nabokov, History, and the Texture of Time*. New York: Routledge, 2012.

Norman, Will, and Duncan White, eds. *Transitional Nabokov*. Bern: Peter Lang, 2009.

Novgorodtsev, Paul [Pavel]. "Ethical Idealism in the Philosophy of Law." In *Problems of Idealism: Essays in Russian Social Philosophy*, edited and translated by Randall Poole, foreword by Caryl Emerson, 274–324. New Haven, CT: Yale University Press, 2003.

Nussbaum, Martha. "Kant and Cosmopolitanism." In *The Cosmopolitanism Reader*, edited by Garrett Wallace Brown and David Held, 27–44. Cambridge: Polity, 2010.

———. *Love's Knowledge: Essays on Philosophy and Literature*. New York: Oxford University Press, 1990.

Offord, Derek. *Portraits of Early Russian Liberals*. Cambridge: Cambridge University Press, 1985.

Orwin, Donna Tussing. *Tolstoy's Art and Thought: 1847–1880*. Princeton, NJ: Princeton University Press, 1993.

Ovid. *The Metamorphoses of Publius Ovidius Naso in English Blank Verse*. Vol. 1, translated by J. J. Howard. London, 1807.

Page, Norman, ed. *Nabokov: The Critical Heritage*. London: Routledge and Kegan Paul, 1982.

Panaev, I. I. "Petersburg Life: Notes of a New Poet." *Sovremennik* 72, nos. 11–12 (1858): 257–84.

Panofsky, Erwin. *Meaning in the Visual Arts*. Chicago: University of Chicago Press, 1955.

Paperno, Irina. "How Nabokov's *The Gift* Is Made." In part 2 of *Literature, Culture, and Society in the Modern Age: In Honor of Joseph Frank*, edited by Edward J. Brown et al., 295–322. Stanford, CA: Stanford Slavic Studies, 1992.

Paris, Gaston. "Les romans en vers du cycle de la Table ronde." In vol. 30 of *L'histoire littéraire de la France*, 1–270. Paris, 1888. Nendeln, Liechtenstein: Kraus Reprint, 1971.

Parrish, Timothy L. "Nabokov, Dostoevsky, Proust: *Despair*." *Studies in 20th & 21st Century Literature* 28, no. 2, article 8 (2004). https://doi.org/10.4148/2334-4415.1586

Pascal, Blaise. *Pensées*. Texte établi, annoté et présenté par Philippe Sellier. Paris: Bordas, 1991.

Peltonen, Markku. *The Duel in Early Modern England: Civility, Politeness and Honor*. Cambridge: Cambridge University Press, 2003.

Pensom, Roger. *Aucassin et Nicolete: The Poetry of Gender and Growing Up in the French Middle Ages*. Bern: Peter Lang, 1999.

Petrie, Eric S. "Moonrise over the Moor: Hazel's Death in Nabokov's *Pale Fire*." *Nabokov Online Journal* 7 (2013): 1–24.

Pifer, Ellen. *Nabokov and the Novel*. Cambridge, MA: Harvard University Press, 1980.

Pitt-Rivers, Julian. *The Fate of Shechem or The Politics of Sex: Essays in the Anthropology of the Mediterranean*. Cambridge: Cambridge University Press, 1977.

Pons, Émile. Introduction to *Sire Gauvain et le chevalier vert*. Poème anglais du XIVe siècle. Traduction avec le texte en regard, une introduction et des notes par Émile Pons. Paris: Aubier, 1946.

Poole, Randall A. "Editor's Introduction: Philosophy and Politics in the Russian Liberation Movement." In *Problems of Idealism: Essays in Russian Social Philosophy*, edited and translated by Randall Poole, foreword by Caryl Emerson, 1–83. New Haven, CT: Yale University Press, 2003.

Pope, Alexander. *An Essay on Man*. In *The Poems of Alexander Pope*, edited by John Butt, 501–47. New Haven, CT: Yale University Press, 1963.

———. *The Rape of the Lock*. In *The Poems of Alexander Pope*, edited by John Butt, 217–42. New Haven, CT: Yale University Press, 1963.

Prodicus. Fr. B7. In *Die Fragmente der Vorsokratiker*, edited by H. Diels and W. Kranz. 6th edition. Berlin: Weidmann, 1952.

Proust, Marcel. *À la recherche du temps perdu*. Bibliothèque de la Pléiade. 4 vols. Edited by Jean-Yves Tadié. Paris: Gallimard, 1987–89.

———. *À la recherche du temps perdu*. Éditions de la Nouvelle Revue Française. 8 vols. Paris: Gallimard, 1919–27.

———. "*Les Éblouissements* par la Comtesse de Noailles." In *"Contre Sainte-Beuve" précédé de "Pastiches et mélanges" et suivi de "Essais et articles."* Bibliothèque de la Pléiade, édition établie par Pierre Clarac avec la collaboration d'Yves Sandre, 533–45. Paris: Gallimard, 1971.

———. *In Search of Lost Time*. Translated by C. K. S. Moncrieff, T. Kilmartin, A. Mayor, and revised by D. J. Enright. 6 vols. New York: Modern Library, 2003.

Pushkin, Aleksandr S. *Eugene Onegin: A Novel in Verse*. Translated by Vladimir Nabokov. 4 vols. Bollingen Series 72. New York: Bollingen, 1964.

———. *The Letters of Alexander Pushkin*. Vol. 3, translated by J. Thomas Shaw. Bloomington, IN: Indiana University Press, 1963.

———. *Stikhotvoreniia: 1813–1820,* vol. 1 of *Polnoe sobranie sochinenii v desiati tomakh*. Moscow: Akademiia nauk SSSR, 1956.

Putter, Ad. *"Sir Gawain and the Green Knight" and French Arthurian Romance*. Oxford: Clarendon, 1995.

Ragussis, Michael. *Acts of Naming: The Family Plot in Fiction*. New York: Oxford University Press, 1986.

Ramey, James. "Parasitism and *Pale Fire*'s Camouflage: The King-Bot, the Crown Jewels, and the Man in the Brown Macintosh." *Comparative Literature Studies* 41, no. 2 (2004): 185–213.

Rampton, David. "The Aesthetics of Moral Contradiction in Some Early Nabokov Novels." In Rodgers and Sweeney, *Nabokov and the Question of Morality*, 109–25.

———. "Jealously Guarded Secrets: Nabokov's Women and the Vicissitudes of Desire." In *Nabokov's Women: The Silent Sisterhood of Textual Nomads*, edited by Elena Rakhimova-Sommers, 77–91. Lanham, MD: Lexington, 2017.

———. *Vladimir Nabokov: A Critical Study of the Novels*. Cambridge: Cambridge University Press, 1984.

Reyfman, Irina. *Ritualized Violence Russian Style: The Duel in Russian Culture and Literature*. Stanford, CA: Stanford University Press, 1999.

Rivers, J. E. "Proust, Nabokov, and *Ada*." In *Critical Essays on Vladimir Nabokov*, edited by Phyllis A. Roth, 134–57. Boston: G. K. Hall, 1984. Reprinted from the *French-American Review* 1 (1977): 173–97.

R[obson], S[imon]. *The Court of Civill Courtesie*. London: Richard Ihones, 1591.

Rodgers, Michael, and Susan Elizabeth Sweeney, eds. *Nabokov and the Question of Morality: Aesthetics, Metaphysics, and the Ethics of Fiction*. New York: Palgrave, 2016.

Rorty, Richard. *Contingency, Irony, and Solidarity*. 1989. Cambridge: Cambridge University Press, 2005.

Roth, Matthew. "A Small Mad Hope: *Pale Fire*, Hazel Shade, and the Oedipal Disaster." In *Nabokov's Women: The Silent Sisterhood of Textual Nomads*, edited by Elena Rakhimova-Sommers, 37–56. Lanham, MD: Lexington, 2017.

Ruck, E. H. *An Index of Themes and Motifs in Twelfth-Century French Arthurian Poetry*. Cambridge: D. S. Brewer, 1991.

Scaglione, Aldo. *Knights at Court: Courtliness, Chivalry, and Courtesy from Ottonian Germany to the Italian Renaissance*. Berkeley: University of California Press, 1991.

Schuman, Samuel. "Nabokov's God; God's Nabokov." In Rodgers and Sweeney, *Nabokov and the Question of Morality*, 73–86.

Scruton, Roger. *Kant: A Very Short Introduction*. Revised edition. Oxford: Oxford University Press, 2001.

Shakespeare, William. *Hamlet*. Edited by Harold Jenkins. London: Routledge, 1994.

———. *King Lear*. Edited by William Aldis Wright. Oxford: Clarendon, 1879.

———. *Othello*. Edited by Edward Pechter. New York: W. W. Norton, 2017.

Shapin, Steven. *A Social History of Truth: Civility and Science in Seventeenth-Century England*. Chicago: University of Chicago Press, 1994.

Shchegolev, P. E. *Duel' i smert' Pushkina* [*Pushkin's Duel and Death*]. Moscow: Kniga, 1987.

Shippey, T. A. "The Uses of Chivalry: 'Erec' and 'Gawain.'" *Modern Language Review* 66, no. 2 (1971): 241–50.

Shklovsky, Viktor. *Material i stil' v romane L'va Tolstogo "Voina i mir"* [*Substance and Style in Lev Tolstoy's "War and Peace"*]. Moscow: Federatsiia, 1928.

Shrayer, Maxim D. "Jewish Questions in Nabokov's Art and Life." In Connolly, *Nabokov and His Fiction*, 73–91.

Shvabrin, Stanislav. *Between Rhyme and Reason: Vladimir Nabokov, Translation, and Dialogue*. Toronto: University of Toronto Press, 2019.

———. "Vladimir Nabokov's 'La Belle Dame Sans Merci': A Study in the Ethics and Effects of Literary Adaptation." *Comparative Literature* 65, no. 1 (2013): 101–22.

Simmons, Ernest J. *Pushkin*. New York: Vintage, 1964.

Sir Gawain and the Green Knight. Edited by Paul Battles. Peterborough, ON: Broadview, 2012.

———. Edited and translated by James Winny. Peterborough, ON: Broadview, 1992.

Sistematicheskii katalog biblioteki Vladimira Dmitrievicha Nabokova. St. Petersburg: Tovarishchestvo khudozhestvennoi pechati, 1904.

Smith, Adam. *The Theory of Moral Sentiments*. 1759. Edited by D. D. Raphael and A. L. Macfie. Oxford: Clarendon, 1976.

Smith, James McCune. "Ira Aldridge (1860)." In *Ira Aldridge, The African Roscius*, edited by Bernth Lindfors, 39–47. Rochester, NY: University of Rochester Press, 2007.

Sobolevsky, S. A. [Sergei Alexandrovich]. "Mysterious Omens in the Life of Pushkin." Translation and introduction by Donald B. Pruitt. *Ulbandus Review* 5 (1987): 109–20.

Solovyov, V. S. "Beauty in Nature." In *The Heart of Reality: Essays on Beauty, Love, and Ethics*, edited and translated by Vladimir Wozniuk, 29–66. Notre Dame, IN: University of Notre Dame Press, 2003.

The Song of Roland: The Oxford Text. Translated by D. D. R. Owen. London: Allen and Unwin, 1972.

Spearing, A. C. "Gawain's Speeches and the Poetry of 'Cortaysye.'" In *Critical Studies of "Sir Gawain and the Green Knight,"* edited by Donald R. Howard and Christian Zacher, 174–81. Notre Dame, IN: University of Notre Dame Press, 1968.

Spenser, Edmund. *The Faerie Queene*. Edited by A. C. Hamilton, Hiroshi Yamashita, and Toshiyuki Suzuki. Harlow, UK: Longman, 2001.

Sreznevsky, V. I. "Perepiska L. N. Tolstogo s V. P. Botkinym: Vvodnaia zametka" ["L. N. Tolstoy's Correspondence with V. P. Botkin: Introductory Note"]. In *Tolstoi: Pamiatniki tvorchestva i zhizni*, vol. 4, 3–8. Moscow: Kooperativnoe t-vo, 1923. http://az.lib.ru/t/tolstoj_lew_nikolaewich/text_1862_perepiska_s_botkinym_oldorfo.shtml.

Stegner, Page. *Escape into Aesthetics: The Art of Vladimir Nabokov*. New York: Dial, 1966.

Stewart, Frank Henderson. *Honor*. Chicago: University of Chicago Press, 1994.

Stobaeus, Joannes. *Ioannis Stobaei Anthologium*. Vol. 4, edited by C. Wachsmuth and O. Hense. Berlin: Weidmann, 1909. Reprinted 1958.

Strandberg, Victor. "Nabokov and the 'Prism of Art.'" In *Torpid Smoke: The Stories of Vladimir Nabokov*, edited by Stephen G. Kellman and Irving Malin, 189–202. Amsterdam: Rodopi, 2000.

Stuckenberg, J. H. W. *The Life of Immanuel Kant*. 1882. Bristol: Thoemmes, 1990.

Struve, Peter [Pyotr]. "Pamiati Vladimira Dmitrievicha Nabokova" ["Recollections of Vladimir Dmitrievich Nabokov"]. *Russkaia Mysl'* 4 (1922): 192–93.

———. Preface to *Sub'ektivizm i individualizm v obshchestvennoi filosofii*, by Nicholas A. Berdiaev, 5–78. Moscow: Kanon, 1999. Originally published in 1901.

Sweeney, Susan Elizabeth. "Thinking about Impossible Things in Nabokov." In Norman and White, *Transitional Nabokov*, 67–78.

———. "Whether Judgments, Sentences, and Executions Satisfy the Moral Sense in Nabokov." In Rodgers and Sweeney, *Nabokov and the Question of Morality*, 161–81.

Tadié, Jean-Yves. *Marcel Proust: A Life*. Translated by Euan Cameron. New York: Penguin, 2000.

Tamir-Ghez, Nomi. "The Art of Persuasion in Nabokov's *Lolita*." In *Vladimir Nabokov's "Lolita": A Casebook*, edited by Ellen Pifer, 17–37. Oxford: Oxford University Press, 2003.

Taylor, Charles. *Hegel*. 1975. Cambridge: Cambridge University Press, 2005.

———. *Sources of the Self: The Making of the Modern Identity*. 1989. Cambridge: Cambridge University Press, 1992.

Teskey, Gordon. "'And Therefore as a Stranger Give It Welcome': Courtesy and Thinking." *Spenser Studies* 18 (2003): 343–59.

Toker, Leona. "'The Dead Are Good Mixers': Nabokov's Versions of Individualism." In Connolly, *Nabokov and His Fiction*, 92–108.

———. *Nabokov: The Mystery of Literary Structures*. Ithaca, NY: Cornell University Press, 1989.

Tolstoy, Leo [Lev]. *Anna Karenina*. The Maude translation, revised by George Gibian. 2nd edition. New York: Norton, 1995.

———. "O tom, chto nazyvaiut iskusstvom" ["About What Is Called Art"]. In vol. 30 of *Polnoe sobranie sochinenii*, 243–70.

———. "Perepiska L. N. Tolstogo s V. P. Botkinym," in vol. 4 of *Tolstoi: Pamiatniki tvorchestva i zhizni*, edited by V. I. Sreznevskii, 9–87. Moscow: Kooperativnoe t-vo, 1923. http://az.lib.ru/t/tolstoj_lew_nikolaewich/text_1862_perepiska_s_botkinym_oldorfo.shtml.

———. *Polnoe sobranie sochinenii*. 90 vols. Moscow: Gosudarstvennoe izdatel'stvo "Khudozhestvennaia literatura," 1928–58.

———. *Sevastopol*. Translated by Isabel F. Hapgood. New York: Thomas Y. Crowell, 1888.

———. *Tolstoy's Letters*. Selected, edited, and translated by R. F. Christian. 2 vols. London: University of London, Athlone Press, 1978.

———. *War and Peace*. Translated by Rosemary Edmonds. 2 vols. Harmondsworth, UK: Penguin, 1978.

———. *What Is Art?* Edited by W. Gareth Jones, translated by A. Maude. London: Bloomsbury, 1994.

Trilling, Lionel. Review of *Lolita. Encounter*, October 1958. In Page, *Nabokov: The Critical Heritage*, 92–102.

Trousdale, Rachel. "'International Fraternity': Nabokov, Chabon, and the Model Transnational." In Norman and White, *Transitional Nabokov*, 99–113.

University of Cambridge. *The Student's Handbook to the University and Colleges of Cambridge*. 18th edition, revised to May 31, 1919. Cambridge: Cambridge University Press, 1919.

Veresaev, V. *Pushkin v zhizni*, vol. 2. 6th edition. Moscow: Sovetskii pisatel', 1936. Reprinted by Slavistics Printings and Reprintings, edited by C. H. Van Schooneveld. The Hague: Mouton, 1969.

Viazemsky, P. A. "Pis'mo Kniazia P. A. Viazemskogo k Velikomu Kniaziu Mikhailu Pavlovichu ot 14 fevralia 1837 goda" ["Prince P. A. Viazemsky's Letter to Grand Duke Michael Pavlovich from February 14, 1837"]. In Shchegolev, *Duel' i smert' Pushkina*, 221–31.

Vitale, Serena. *Pushkin's Button*. Translated by Ann Goldstein and Jon Rothschild. Chicago: University of Chicago Press, 1999.

Voronina, Olga. "The Tale of Enchanted Hunters: *Lolita* in Victorian Context." *Nabokov Studies* 10 (2006): 147–74.

Waldron, Jeremy. "What Is Cosmopolitan?" In *The Cosmopolitanism Reader*, edited by Garrett Wallace Brown and David Held, 163–75. Cambridge: Polity, 2010.

Wasianski, E. A. C. *Immanuel Kant in seinen letzten Lebensjahren*. 1804. In *Immanuel Kant, Sein Leben in Darstellungen von Zeitgenossen*, edited by Felix Gross, 215–306. Darmstadt: Wissenschaftliche Buchgesellschaft, 1968.

Whalen, Tom. "'And So the Password Is—?': Nabokov and the Ethics of Rereading." In Rodgers and Sweeney, *Nabokov and the Question of Morality*, 21–32.

Wilde, Oscar. *The Complete Letters of Oscar Wilde*. Edited by Merlin Holland and Rupert Hart-Davis. New York: Henry Holt, 2000.

———. *The Works*. London: Spring Books, 1963.

Wilson, Edmund. *Axel's Castle: A Study of the Imaginative Literature of 1870–1930*. New York: Charles Scribner, 1931.

Wood, Allen W. *Kant*. Oxford: Wiley Blackwell, 2004.

———. *Kantian Ethics*. New York: Cambridge University Press, 2008.

Wood, Michael. "Crabby, Prickly, Bitter, Harsh." *London Review of Books* 30, no. 10 (May 22, 2008): 11–13. https://www.lrb.co.uk/the-paper/v30/n10/michael-wood/crabby-prickly-bitter-harsh.

———. *The Magician's Doubts: Nabokov and the Risks of Fiction*. London: Pimlico, 1994.

———. "Modern Mimesis." In Rodgers and Sweeney, *Nabokov and the Question of Morality*, 213–24.

Woolf, Virginia. *The Diary of Virginia Woolf, Volume Two: 1920–1924*. Edited by Anne Olivier Bell. New York: Harcourt, 1978.

———. *Mrs. Dalloway*. Edited by Stella McNichol, introduction and notes by Elaine Showalter. London: Penguin, 1992.

———. *To the Lighthouse*. Edited by David Bradshaw. Oxford: Oxford University Press, 2008.

Wright, Thomas L. "*Luf-Talkyng* in *Sir Gawain and the Green Knight*." In *Approaches to Teaching "Sir Gawain and the Green Knight,"* edited by Miriam Youngerman Miller and Jane Chance, 79–86. New York: Modern Language Association of America, 1986.

Wyllie, Barbara. *Vladimir Nabokov*. London: Reaktion Books, 2010.

Yeats, W. B. *The Collected Poems of W. B. Yeats: A New Edition*, edited by Richard J. Finneran. New York: Macmillan, 1989.

Zhukovsky, V. A. "Pis'mo V. A. Zhukovskogo k S. L. Pushkinu o smerti Pushkina." ["V. A. Zhukovsky's letter to S. L. Pushkin on Pushkin's death"]. In Shchegolev, *Duel' i smert' Pushkina*, 138–72.

Zimmer, Dieter. "What Happened to Sergey Nabokov." 2015. http://dezimmer.net/PDF/SergeyN.pdf

Zotov, R. "Petersburg Chronicle: The African Tragedian Aldridge in Shakespeare's *Othello*." *St. Petersburg vedomosti*, November 28/December 10, 1858.

Zumthor, Paul. *Essai de poétique médiévale*. Paris: Seuil, 1972.

Zunshine, Lisa. "Alexander Pope's *The Rape of the Lock* and Vladimir Nabokov's *Pale Fire*." In *Nabokov at the Limits: Redrawing Critical Boundaries*, edited by Lisa Zunshine, 161–82. New York: Garland, 1999.

Index